Success Secrets of University Students

Lilly J. Schubert Walker

Memorial University of Newfoundland

Dieter Jürgen Schönwetter

The University of Manitoba

Toronto

National Library of Canada Cataloguing in Publication Data

Walker, Lilly J. Schubert (Lilly Julia Schubert), 1945–
    Success secrets of university students / Lilly J. Schubert Walker,
Dieter Jürgen Schönwetter

Includes bibliographical references and index.
ISBN 0-13-092647-7

    1. College student orientation.   2. Study skills.   3. Success.
I. Schönwetter, Dieter J.   II. Title.

LB2343.3.W335 2002   378.1'98   C2002-903126-5

ISBN 0-13-092647-7

Vice President, Editorial Director: Michael J. Young
Marketing Manager: Toivo Pajo
Signing Representative: Duncan MacKinnon
Executive Developmental Editor: Marta Tomins
Production Editor: Tammy Scherer
Copy Editor: Maria Gacesa
Proofreaders: Ron Jacques/Karen Bennett
Production Manager: Wendy Moran
Page Layout: Janette Thompson
Art Director: Julia Hall
Cover Design: Michelle Bellemare
Front Cover Image: Luc Hautecoeur, Stone (Getty Images)

1 2 3 4 5   07 06 05 04 03

Printed and bound in Canada.

Contents

Student Success Portraits

It's More Than Common Sense Boxes

Preface

Shaped by the times in which they live, students bring unique combinations of experience, expertise, and expectation to the classroom. In spite of differences in language, culture, religion, age, socio-economic background, and educational preparation, they share a common dream: to be successful. This involves discovering and developing the attitudes and actions of achievement. This also requires actively exploring possibilities, overcoming challenges, attempting new ways of doing things, persisting in spite of setbacks, believing in oneself, and acquiring self-regulating habits. Our goal is to strive to equip students with the tools they need to achieve success in university. By providing them with a textbook that increases their self-awareness, enhances their self-confidence, adds to their self-discipline, and develops their capabilities, students can achieve that dream of success.

Becoming successful is a personal journey of self-awareness and self-mastery. We want our student readers to experience the excitement of discovery, the satisfaction of achievement, and the rewards of expanding their personal capabilities. We want students to learn about themselves as they develop strategies, become more confident, refine skills, acquire self-control, and attain success. To achieve this, the textbook utilizes a self-development model to provide students with a unique approach for understanding and developing the competencies of the successful student scholar. This model stimulates students to develop their "success identity" by adding attitudinal factors that build confidence and actions that build self-reliance to their current core capabilities. It provides students with options for developing competencies associated with academic achievement and for expanding social resources so that they are supported in their learning.

The self-development/self-identity model invites students to learn about themselves, to assess the demands of the learning environment, to connect to resources, and to master new competencies so that they can learn, perform, and confidently put their knowledge into practise. The organization of the text reinforces achievement by integrating research findings with practical strategies to support the development of students' core competencies. Each chapter features strategies for expanding self-awareness, enhancing self-mastery, and building self-confidence so that students become independent, self-directed learners.

The text presents seven core themes that are essential for success as a university student. These include searching for connection, uncovering self-mastery strategies, communicating effectively, creating community, evaluating learning strategies, solving problems, and seeking personal and professional success. Significant to this text are a number of important features that are intended to enrich its value for readers. These include:

- An educational approach that integrates practical strategies for enhancing learning with the developmental needs of first-year students.

- A presentation of relevant research findings so that students become knowledgeable of the evidence that supports the value of various learning strategies.

- An approach to learning that recognizes differences in learning styles and provides exercises that involve students in observing, reflecting, experimenting, exploring, doing, and applying.

- A student's perspective, in which students share their personal experiences and recommendations for making the most of university.

- Canadian experts discussing the relevance and applicability of their research for first-year students.

- Questions and objectives at the beginning of each chapter to focus students' consideration of the relevance of the chapter content for their own personal development.

- Exercises to promote self-awareness and self-development such as self-assessment reviews, success strategy exercises, and assignments that provoke students to put into practise their learning and apply their knowledge.

- Group discussion topics and group assignments to reinforce the importance of peer learning and social support.

- Integrative Reflect–Act assignments to engage students in the self-reflection and personal action that are the basis for self-development. These assignments challenge students to reflect on their experience, view that experience within the context of their learning, and develop specific action plans for adding to their capabilities as a student.

An accompanying Instructor's Manual will provide teaching strategies, exercises, tests, and helpful PowerPoint slides for each chapter.

We have designed this book to expose students to key concepts related to becoming a successful university student, and to provide activities that will encourage them to develop abilities and attitudes associated with success. Since each student's search for success builds on their uniqueness, each will discover, within the chapters, different combinations of core concepts and self-reflective exercises that focus their development. However, in order to achieve success, all students will need to engage actively with the material, practise these new skills, and help their fellow students practise them as well. Learning to be successful will not always be easy. However, it becomes easier with peer support. Sharing with peers is a powerful learning tool. This book—with its integrated self-development focus, research-based skills, and practical exercises—provides students with a guided process for becoming a successful student.

To achieve the promise of creating a successful future, students need guidance, support, skills, and information. We believe this book provides the developmental framework for achieving that success.

Lilly J. Schubert Walker
Dieter Jürgen Schönwetter

Acknowledgments

The process of writing a textbook is similar to the journey of becoming a successful student—achieving the goal depends upon the contributions of many. Some contributors are known, others are unknown. Each adds an imprint on the ultimate outcome. We especially appreciate the encouragement and talents of family, friends, colleagues, students, and mentors who supported us as we collaborated in the complex task of creating this book.

We both thank the collaborators on this project: K. Lynn Taylor and Michael Doyle for their writing talents and expert knowledge; Shelly Birnie-Lefcovitch, Rodney Clifton, Peter Cornish, Adam Driedzic, John Garland, Paul Grayson, Clarry Lay, Trina O'Brien Leggott, Rob Renaud, Gerard Seijts, Don Stewart, and Richard Young for their research features; Christine Adams, Rob Cegielski, Myrna Cook, Heather Francis, Ray Foui, Joelle Kobylak, Heather Lehmann, Krista McKay, Steve Quigley, Brandy Usick, Adam Warren, and Holly White for their student perspectives; the Pearson team of editors—Marta Tomins, Tammy Scherer, Maria Gacesa, Ron Jacques, and Karen Bennett—for checking the details; and to Duncan MacKinnon for believing in the uniqueness of our vision.

We are also grateful for the encouragement and suggestions offered by our teaching team of 099.111 instructors; to all the Introduction to University students who have reviewed and provided valuable feedback during the initial writing of the chapters; to Heather Francis for all her editing, researching, and highlighting of valuable student resources; to the University Teaching Services and University 1 at the University of Manitoba for their resources, and above all, to K. Lynn Taylor and Beverly Cameron who supported our writing endeavours. We thank Michael Doyle of Memorial University, Michael Ridley of the University of Guelph, K. Lynn Taylor of the University of Manitoba, and Robert Zenaud of the University of Manitoba, all of whom provided us with valuable feedback during the preparation of this book.

A special thanks to Jim who sacrificed precious time together so that Lilly could spend days and nights writing, to T. J. who gives me hope, to Kristen Harris and Sean Ryan for their library research, and to Memorial University colleagues within Student Affairs and Services whose humorous perspective and professional expertise added perspective to this endeavour. To my students who asked difficult questions, made me laugh, searched for personal answers in unexpected places, and taught me lessons I needed to learn, I am especially grateful.

A heartful thanks goes to Dieter's family, who gave tremendous support in many ways. To Sandra, my soulmate and partner in life, I give thanks for your love, encouragement, and for believing in me. I thank my two beautiful children for emulating an eagerness to learn and inquisitiveness to discover. To the Schönwetters and the Heppners, I offer thanks for being family. To my students—thanks for teaching me what student success is all about. I am indebted to Lynn Taylor for her mentoring, understanding, and support throughout this project. Finally, a special thanks goes to the University of Manitoba Research Office for the Social Sciences and Humanities Research Council of Canada research grants, and all the research partners—Teresa Dawson at University of Toronto at Scarborough, Moira McPherson and William Montelpace at Lakehead University, and assistants who have contributed in making the first-year research project at the University of Manitoba a success.

Understanding Success Through Self-Theory

chapter 1

If it is to be, it is up to me!

Questions

What can I do to be successful in university?

How can I use models or guidelines to assist me in managing the academic and social requirements of university?

How can I develop greater confidence in my abilities?

Which strategies will help me develop as a student?

Objectives

- Discover the factors that influence university achievement.

- Learn about the stages of identity development.

- Recognize the strategies that successful students use.

Student Success Portrait

A Story of Hope

Raymond Foui
The University of Manitoba

As an eleven-year-old growing up in Wales, I gave little thought to my weekend activities, let alone my education and future career. In the last year of elementary school all students were given the option of writing the "Eleven Plus Exam," the result of which would determine whether the student would go on to secondary school or grammar school. Grammar school was the only entrance to university.

In my school, like most, we had A, B, and C classes. Students in the A class were children whose fathers were primarily business and factory owners. These children lived in the same part of town; they frequently socialized together, played together at recess, and collectively represented the largest proportion of students who passed the exam. Those in the B class were students whose fathers made up the ranks of middle managers. These people managed the day-to-day affairs of local businesses. As a cohort, these students also did most things together. While the majority of them wrote the exam, typically close to half of them would not succeed.

Then we had my cohort, the C class. We were all members of working-class families. My father worked in a coal mine, as did many others in my family, and my mother was a homemaker. Like each of the other cohorts, working-class children shared similar living conditions, fun activities, and prospects for the future. It was unheard of for C class students to write the exam. Our fate meant four years of secondary school, at which point, as fifteen-year-olds, we would find work—work that was very similar to that of our parents.

My parents had no intention of allowing fate to take its course. They insisted that I write the exam. My teacher and headmaster tried repeatedly to convince my parents that while I was a sweet boy I did not have the wherewithal to succeed and that the experience would be humiliating. I, in the company of these other students, wrote the exam. My teacher and headmaster were right; I failed miserably.

By this point my parents had decided to immigrate to Canada. My junior high school years were tough. I was terribly homesick and, to make matters worse, the only things I knew about Canada were that it was cold, that it had the Rocky Mountains and endless prairies, and no one played cricket. Despite my shaky start, I managed to finish high school on time.

In 1997, I completed my Ph.D in sociology at the University of Manitoba. Needless to say, this was a very exciting day for my entire family. For me, it was the culmination of hard work, dedication, and the belief that I had the ability to attain the goals I set for myself. I currently teach Introduction to University and sociology courses at the University of Manitoba.

The "Eleven Plus Exam" has since then been abolished. After a number of inquiries I later found out that the questions on that exam were based on the curriculum taught each year to the A class, a curriculum that was substantially different from the one given to C-class students. This exam was but one mechanism designed to maintain social class distinction.

Many of us have been told at one time or another that we do not have what it takes to be or do something in particular. Subsequently we are often slotted or categorized into programs that reflect our beliefs in these assumptions. How badly do you want a career? Last, but not least, how hard are you willing to work for it? There is always hope, but it is you who must provide it.

The Test: The Hero's Journey

You've decided. Your application has been accepted. You've registered for your courses, paid your fees, bought your books, and found a new place to live. You feel ready. Ready to start a new academic adventure. Ready to learn. Ready to meet new people. Ready to meet the challenges that await you. Ready to hone the skills that will help you create your future. Ready to step outside the world you know well, expand your horizons and explore the unknown path that is before you.

To be a student is to be a learner, explorer, and discoverer. To be a student is to learn new information, develop new perspectives, discover new ideas, experiment, experience greater understanding, and find a new personal identity. To be a student is to take risks, find answers, make mistakes, deal with uncertainty, and to change. There are aspects of this experience that feel quite familiar. There is also much that is different. In the upcoming weeks and months, the newness and academic opportunities of university will challenge you. Through this experience, you will discover much about yourself.

In learning about yourself, you will discover how to define yourself. You will develop an awareness of your academic aptitudes, talents, and interests. You will uncover new roles and responsibilities. Importantly, you will learn to see yourself from the perspective of the web of relationships of which you are a part. Today, when someone asks you to talk about yourself, you speak of academic achievements, family and friendship connections, athletic or artistic accomplishments, and volunteer or work activities. Tomorrow, how will you speak of yourself? How do you see yourself changing as a result of your university experience? Who do you want to become?

Your journey of self-discovery parallels the journeys that have been identified in Greek myths, fables of First Nations people, Irish folktales, children's fairytales, and literary novels. You, like the heroes in the classic stories, are learning about personal enlightenment. You are exploring the hero's journey. As the mythological hero, you will be drawn to the threshold of adventure—a place of encounter. You will encounter a shadow presence that guards the passage. Like the hero, you will be threatened or tested. Along the way you will discover assistance and aid. Though at times it is difficult, you know that you must continue on your quest, finding answers that will give you wisdom and developing competencies as you overcome challenges. Finally, you will meet your greatest test, and if you triumph, you will gain your reward and be able to go forward with powers that others do not have. However, if you fail, you will remain behind.

Your academic journey, like the hero's journey, is a story of personal change, or transformation. You will leave the world that you know well, a world of certainty, to discover a new place. You will face hardships, experience defeat, be forced to take risks, and be required to develop new skills. You will need to solve problems that will require you to think and respond in new ways. You will understand for the first time the value of seeing things from a new perspective. You will be provoked to expand your awareness so that you are capable of seeing the world differently. As you experience the transformation that will define you as an educated person, you may at times feel lost, uncomfortable, confused, and uncertain. Although these feelings are an integral part of the process of self-discovery and academic growth, your challenge is to use your feelings productively. The information you will learn through this text can assist you to focus your reactions and your actions.

Your education is more than memorizing formulas and repeating information. Your education is more than expanding your knowledge and skill base. Your education is more than career preparation. Your education is the basis upon which you will develop a new sense of your personal identity, or sense of self. As you master the challenges that the university environment presents, your identity evolves. Through lessons within and outside of the classroom, education will transform you.

Who or what will guide you through the uncharted, challenging world of the unfamiliar? Who will help you define your sense of self? Who will help you become who you want to be? There are maps and mentors along the way. This textbook provides a map of strategies, suggestions, and solutions which, when appropriately used, can be the guide that will assist and enable you to master the demands and complexities of the university terrain. Also, you will find mentors—experienced students, student affairs professionals, and professors—who can help you uncover the answers you need.

Know Thyself...

The Socratic imperative "Know Thyself" is not only essential to the successful completion of your academic journey, but is also one of the major goals of your journey. Your awareness of your own capabilities and limitations, and your knowledge of your needs and aspirations, will help you anticipate and master the academic challenges that await. Self-reflection and personal assessment are valuable tools for developing greater personal self-awareness. Thus, exercises and questions are provided throughout the book to assist you in learning more about yourself. Begin with the questions in Chapter 2 that focus you to think productively about the unique components of your self-identity that are related to academic accomplishments. Use these questions as a starting point for assessing your own awareness of the abilities you possess and those you need to develop so that you are able to master the demands of university. Your answers will provide you with important self-knowledge to commence this voyage of personal discovery.

In addition to self-knowledge, you must also develop an awareness of environmental demands. The academic and social environment of the university contrasts with the familiar school environment to which you have become accustomed. Although initially there appear to be some familiar lampposts, you will soon discover that the university is a unique place with expectations, procedures, and pedagogical principles that are unfamiliar. You will find that if you are to master the life lessons that will unfold during your journey, you must know how to respond to the demands of the academic, physical, and social environment.

You have commenced this academic journey because you aspire to create a purposeful and successful life path for yourself. Your success in creating this path is related to your ability to develop the awareness, confidence, and competencies needed to navigate through the challenges you experience as a university student. Your ability to develop new aptitudes and attitudes will provide the basis for your developmental growth and transformation.

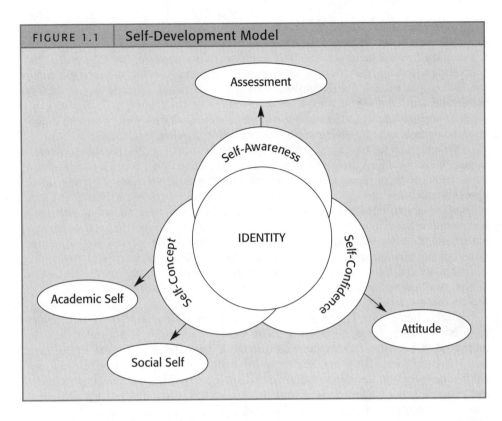

FIGURE 1.1 | Self-Development Model

Assessment

Self-Awareness

IDENTITY

Self-Concept

Self-Confidence

Academic Self

Social Self

Attitude

This process of growth has been described as the cycle of self-development. As seen in the Self-Development Model on this page, there are three phases of this cycle: **self-awareness**, **self-confidence**, and **self-concept**. Self-awareness involves the ability to reflect and exam oneself, to assess the situational demands, and to evaluate other individuals and social expectations. Through a process of effective self-analysis you will gain insight and self-understanding that will affect your self-confidence and provide the basis for developing an accurate self-concept. Self-confidence is an individual's attitude toward, and assessment of, adequacy and worth. It is influenced by the individual's capability to reliably meet various challenges in life, to set realistic goals, and to effectively use cognitive skills to motivate oneself. Self-concept is an individual's assessment of one's competencies in comparison with those of others (Pascarella & Terenzini, 1991). It is how you objectively describe yourself, usually based on your roles, traits, experiences, and abilities. In the university environment there are two important aspects of self-concept: academic self and social self. You will pass through the three phases of self-development frequently during your academic journey, as it is a continuous process of evaluation, adaptation, and acquisition. Each sequence adds to the others. Consequently, when you add to your skill levels you develop greater awareness, which fuels an examination process, which is then reflected in your self-confidence and in the evolving sense of your self-concept. Through this evolving process of development, you will reinvent your own self-identity.

Finding your way on your academic journey can be made easier by learning about the environment and the experiences of others who have travelled this path before you. Educational and psychological researchers who have analyzed students' experiences have discovered principles and have developed theories that can serve as guides for your journey.

These principles are as follows. As a student your success is related to your ability to successfully manage the stages of self-development: self-awareness, self-confidence, and self-concept. You will face some predictable phases of development (Belenky et al., 1986; Chickering & Reisser, 1993; Maslow, 1970; Perry, 1970), and you will be required to develop specific competencies (Kuh, 1993). Your approach to learning is affected by your gender, culture, personality, and your previous academic experiences (Baxter, 1992; Belenky et al., 1986). Your ability to integrate your "out-of-class" experiences with your classroom experiences will greatly enhance your learning and self-understanding (Astin, 1996).

One approach for steering your course is through understanding the developmental stages that you will pass through on your way to becoming fully educated (Chickering & Reisser, 1993). Chickering and Reisser have identified seven dimensions of identity development, which are the significant changes that students experience throughout their years of university education. These changes, termed vectors, describe both the direction and magnitude of your growth in self-identity. They are: developing competence, managing emotions, moving through autonomy toward interdependence, developing mature interpersonal relationships, establishing identity, developing purpose and developing integrity. As you master many of the tasks of these first years in university you will be able to note your progress through these vectors. The self-appraisal exercises throughout this text are one means of monitoring your progression.

Another perspective is to view your development and academic success through a process of satisfying needs. Maslow's (1970) model demonstrates that individuals are motivated to have their needs satisfied through a hierarchical fashion from the most basic needs of safety, food, and shelter to the higher-level needs of love, esteem, and belonging. Once you have comfortably established yourself in your new environment, feel at home, know the locations of your classes and the offices that provide assistance, and have enough financial resources for food, books, transportation, accommodation, and other basic needs, you can begin to concentrate on developing relationships with others, which will satisfy your emotional, social, intellectual, and personal development.

Because your success in this new environment demands that you enhance your intellectual abilities, knowing more about these competencies is critical for you. The process of understanding the developmental stages that you will experience commenced with the research of William Perry (1970) who observed that most students progressed through four phases of thinking. These phases have been extended and adapted by the research of others (Baxter, 1992; Belenky et al., 1986). Thinking, or ways of knowing and understanding, evolve from simple to complex methods, and from concrete, rigid, superficial thinking to more flexible, relativistic, and contextual thinking. Thinking evolves so that with experience and exposure to the advanced intellectual demands required in university subjects, you will learn to develop advanced critical thinking capabilities. You will also learn to integrate disparate informational sources, and understand diverse approaches to thinking.

Your ability to navigate your way successfully depends upon more than intellectual abilities. Kuh (1993) has discovered five factors that are essential for your success in university: personal competence, cognitive complexity, knowledge and academic skills, practical competence and altruism, and estheticism. Pascarella and Terenzini (1991) have observed that you will be challenged to develop social-affective abilities in addition to your cognitive abilities. University will challenge you to develop social competencies as well as abstract and practical thinking skills that will enable you to get along with others, accept differences, communicate effectively, and demonstrate empathic and altruistic actions. As the process of discovery that defines the university experience challenges you, you will be required to assess and articulate your own personal values clearly, and integrate these values into your actions and decisions. Even more importantly, you will need to develop the motivational skills to persevere in spite of disappointment, difficulty, and defeat.

In determining you own success path, you will soon discover that your ability to learn and achieve success may differ from the capabilities and approaches of your fellow students. Some of these differences are expressed in your comfort with particular course content, your preferences for the ways in which material is presented, or the ease with which you master some concepts but have difficulty with others. Researchers have helped us understand these differences and we now know how learning is affected by gender, culture, personality, and previous academic experiences (Baxter, 1992; Belenky et al., 1986).

Your ability to use the experiences of others to benefit you can provide you with an advantage as you chart your direction. Numerous students have plotted the academic road ahead, tried various routes, and many have arrived successfully. Of interest to various psychology and educational researchers are the affective, behavioural, and cognitive indicators of these successful students. These include emotions such as optimism (Noel et al., 1987; Peterson & Barrett, 1987), low test anxiety (Schönwetter, 1996), and course enjoyment (Pekrun, 1992). Behaviours that are associated with academic success are persistence when failing, seeking help, and finding additional resources. Two significant cognitive factors are a sense of control over one's learning environment (Perry, 1991; Schönwetter, 1996), and a sense of success (Schönwetter et al., 1993).

As you progress along your academic path, you may search for insights that can give you an edge in your pursuit of success and self-understanding. You'll discover this advantage through your involvement in extracurricular experiences such as student groups, leadership positions, attendance at campus cultural events, informal interactions with peers and professors, and participation in sports events. These out-of-class experiences are opportunities for you to enrich your learning, develop intellectual and practical skills, and build self-confidence. They facilitate critical thinking and promote an enhanced capacity for personal reflection, competence, and self-direction. The specific impact of these various extracurricular experiences on your learning and development will vary as a result of your gender, as women value interpersonal socialization experiences as a means of self-development, while men choose more practical activities as a source of personal growth (Kuh, 1993; Springer et al., 1995).

Developing Your Self-Identity

As you experience the hero's journey, you are seeking to discover an identity that serves you well. It is an identity that is based on greater awareness, heightened sensibilities, evolving competencies, and realistic self-confidence. The process of developing your self-identity is a process of evolution during which you will face intellectual and personal challenges, take risks, make choices, experience both success and failure, develop insights, and add to your capabilities. It follows the cycle of self-development and personal transformation.

Stage 1: Self-Awareness

Self-awareness involves a continuous process of assessment and action. Assessment involves the examination and exploration of one's self within the context, expectations and demands of a situation. Action includes the decisions and the activities that occur as a result of this process of personal observation and evaluation. The specific focus and direction of your actions and the amount of effort you invest are related to the feedback you receive and your analysis of this information.

Becoming more self-aware is a process of taking risks; observing yourself; testing your abilities; reflecting on your experiences, thoughts, and perceptions; and listening to and responding to feedback. Because each person's life experiences and personal psychological defences vary, the levels of self-awareness among individuals vary. Some university students are more self-aware than others, but in general all university students possess some degree of self-knowledge as well as some areas in which they lack insight. One of the significant outcomes of your academic journey is a heightened awareness of your true self. As seen in the Johari Window below, there are four areas of self-awareness. Some things you know about yourself (cells B and D), and other things you do not know about yourself (cells A and C). Some information you are not aware of, but others know it about you (cell C). There are aspects about you that are a mystery both to you and to others (cell A).

As a result of your academic and social engagement you can develop a greater sense of self-awareness and of others' perceptions of you, reducing the blind spots that can inhibit your ability to function effectively (cell C). Basic to a heightened sense of self-awareness is your ability to assess your own abilities, evaluate the situation, compare yourself with others, and receive feedback. The exercises provided throughout this textbook will assist you in this process.

You add to your self-awareness by clarifying your aspirations and taking action. Through the feedback that results from mistakes or mastery, you add to your self-knowledge. This feedback allows you to affirm your strengths, discover limitations, and set goals for improving your self-knowledge, self-confidence, and self-concept. Your actions produce insight. The resulting feedback from your analysis and action can add to, or detract from, your feelings of self-confidence.

FIGURE 1.2	Johari Window		
		Self	
		Unknown	**Known**
Others	Unknown	A BLIND SPOTS: to self and others	B BLIND SPOTS: To others Self hidden from others
	Known	C BLIND SPOTS: To self Seen by others	D Aware to all

Based on Luft, J. (1969). *Of Human Interaction.* Palo Alto, CA: National Press Books.

Stage 2: Self-Confidence

Your self-confidence, or sense of self-worth, evolves from your personal evaluation of your own abilities and adequacy. It is influenced by your belief in your capabilities to reliably perform specific tasks (i.e., self-efficacy), your sense of self-mastery or personal control (i.e., self-regulation), and your internal dialogue (i.e., self-talk). Your self-confidence is continually evolving and is particularly affected by your self-appraisal of events and experiences. How you evaluate experiences, in terms of whether or not they add to or detract from your feelings of competence and control, is a consistent influence in determining how confident you feel.

Your level of self-confidence is influenced by your past experiences and personal expectations (Mruk, 1995; Pascarella & Terenzini, 1991). You may have thought about specific aspects of your personal history and hypothesized about factors that you believe could have influenced the level of confidence you currently possess. What you probably observed is that your previous experience in school, and your involvement in sports, music, community, or work activities has influenced specific areas of personal confidence. You may also have recognized that your relationships with family and friends, as well as your birth order, are significant factors that have been influential determinants of the level of confidence you possess.

One important aspect of self-confidence is how you, as a university student, take control of your own levels of personal confidence. If you are like most people, your experiences at university will significantly affect your confidence in directing your life path. Whether or not you are successful in meeting the challenges facing you at this time, and whether or not you feel you have some influence over the situations that affect you academically, will affect your self-confidence. If you persevere and reach a goal that may be difficult for you, you will add significantly to your sense of self-confidence. When you feel valued and validated by others, you will also add to your sense of confidence.

Even your personality affects your self-confidence. If you are optimistic, independent, assertive, open to feedback, reliable, and able to problem-solve creatively, you tend to be more self-confident. Your self-confidence influences how you interpret feedback, respond to difficulties, and handle disappointment. If you are high in self-confidence, you take risks more easily, are more open to learn from the feedback you receive, and are more able to effectively handle the stress associated with university. If you have less self-confidence, you may easily doubt yourself and possibly feel discouraged, inadequate, and anxious. Your ability to manage your self-confidence level is related to the dynamics of your reactions to a situation. Analyzing your reactions, answering questions that are provided to stimulate your awareness, and anticipating alternative ways to react will provide you with strategies for enhancing and building your self-confidence levels as well as improving your chances of succeeding in university.

Everyone is different when it comes to self-confidence. While you may prefer frequent feedback, or require a high number of achievements in many areas in order to feel confident, others may not. Determining the unique combination of factors that produce a high level of self-confidence for you is critical for your academic and personal success. You can most effectively begin this process by becoming aware of the ways in which you take control of your own success, through your ability to master three success strategies for effective learning: **self-efficacy**, **self-regulation**, and **self-talk**.

Self-efficacy is your belief in your own capabilities to succeed. Bandura (1977, 1986, 1989) has studied students' views of their ability to succeed in university and has discovered that if your beliefs are unrealistically high or unrealistically low, your performance in university will be adversely affected. Your beliefs influence your motivations to perform and persist. When your self-efficacy beliefs match your actual ability levels you are best able to manage the academic demands facing you because you adjust both your effort and your approach to the task.

Self-regulation is your ability to control and direct your actions so that you can achieve a specific goal. It requires that you are actively involved in establishing your learning priorities and are able to effectively monitor your progress toward achieving these learning goals. Self-regulated learning requires that you possess a high level of awareness of yourself and your learning tasks, coupled with an ability to utilize a varied repertoire of learning approaches (Garner, 1987). As you develop the self-regulation skills of a successful student, you increase your proficiencies as an active, analytical, and self-directed learner.

Self-talk is your interpretation of your experiences and your inner dialogue as they affect both your self-confidence and self-efficacy. Psychologists (Ellis, 1995; Meichenbaum, 1977) have discovered that individuals often engage in a silent inner dialogue of which they may or may not be aware. If your self-talk is positively focused and action-oriented, you are better able to manage your university workload than students who have not developed this thinking habit. If you tend to worry or often feel hopeless and helpless, then your self-talk may be interfering with your ability to succeed in your courses. Educators and psychologists (Foersterling, 1985; Perry & Penner, 1990; Weiner, 1986) have developed teaching strategies, known as attribution retraining or cognitive reframing, to foster the development of adaptive thinking strategies that, when used appropriately, improve the academic performance levels of those students whose self-talk has been defeating them.

Knowing yourself is a continuous process of increasing your awareness of your own self-efficacy beliefs, self-regulation behaviours, and self-talk. The information and exercises provided throughout this textbook will assist you in becoming a more astute observer of the impact of your beliefs, actions, and inner dialogue on your ability to confidently and reliably meet the academic demands and personal challenges of your university experience. They will also provide information you can use to enhance your self-concept so that you are able to achieve the success you desire.

Stage 3: Self-Concept

Your self-concept is your objective description of yourself, particularly your roles, attributes, and abilities (Pascarella & Terenzini, 1991). It refers specifically to your judgment of yourself relative to your perception of other students' competencies. Your self-concept is formed through your experiences with your environment and is especially affected by your relationships with others. Two aspects of your self-concept appear to be particularly important to your identity development in your university years: your **academic self** and your **social self.**

Your academic self is related to your achievement, your orientation, your abilities to handle the cognitive complexity and informational demands of your courses, and your competencies in developing the new cognitive and intellectual skills that university demands. Your perception of your academic abilities within the context of your performance in the university environment is the basis of your academic self. Whether or not your academic self stagnates or evolves depends upon your attitudes, appraisal, and actions. If you are able to overcome disappointment, withstand threat, attempt more difficult material, challenge yourself, strive to improve your performance, and discover academic areas that interest and engage you, you will develop a stronger, more highly differentiated sense of your academic self. Your academic self is continuously changing as a result of your academic performance. It is quite common during your first year of university when you are figuring out new study strategies and striving to develop new cognitive and intellectual abilities for you to feel threatened and question your academic abilities. Although this questioning is a normal part of the self-assessment process of identity development, how you respond to this process will affect whether or not you are able to develop a more highly differentiated sense of academic self-worth.

Your social self refers to your assessment of your ability to establish and maintain relationships. It includes your social confidence in different situations, your ability to understand and get along with others, your popularity, your leadership capabilities and your engagement with others. Just as university challenges you to develop new intellectual abilities, it also challenges you to develop socially. An important part of the transition to the university environment is establishing new friendships and social networks as you leave behind some familiar relationships. This demands developing improved communication skills, becoming more accepting of cultural, social and personal differences, and developing new perspectives and values. Your social confidence influences your choice of a peer group. Researchers have demonstrated that your involvement in your new peer group significantly affects every aspect of your development during your university years (Astin, 1993).

During the university years you will continue to develop an expanded view of your definition of self. Your self-identity develops as you successfully manage the challenges and changes that are a part of the university transition. The feedback you receive through experience, and your ability to use this information productively, provide the basis for adding to your self-confidence and self-concept. As you succeed in assuming responsibilities, managing risks, and developing new roles, you add to your competencies, your confidence, and your evolving sense of self.

Basic to the successful evolution of your self-identity is your ability to productively use the information you glean through your experience. Experience without analysis often means repeating the same mistakes again and again. Learning to use the assessment-action process productively to foster healthy self-growth is critical. Your ability to succeed increases as you develop your metacognitive competencies. **Metacognition** is your ability to think about your thinking and is demonstrated through your ability to describe and analyze your cognitive processing strategies. Like all the abilities you develop in university, your metacognitive abilities increase developmentally and become more refined with practice. In order to help you develop these cognitive skills, the authors have included, throughout this book, "Reflect–Act" assignments. These assignments provide the vehicle for you to develop the critical evaluation and assessment skills to improve your insight and enhance your effectiveness in learning.

Your identity is intimately connected to the interactions you have with others, the feedback you receive from the environment, and your analysis and utilization of this information. Your ability to use your experiences productively so that you develop a **success identity** (Bandura, 1986; Solberg et al., 1998) relates to your beliefs in your own abilities to adapt effectively to changing life circumstances and overcome threatening situations. In other words, self-efficacy and outcome expectations are critical components of a success identity.

Your capability to develop a success identity relates to your ability to use both personal and environmental resources in order to progress from where you are now to where you need to go. Your personal resources can include your attitude, expectations, thinking patterns, skills, and experience in overcoming difficulties. Your environmental resources may include support systems, knowledge of the environment, the structure of courses, and your relationships with faculty and fellow students. Your success identity grows as you develop community connections that support you. It also evolves as you add to your academic and social competencies and improve in your ability to effectively manage the learning tasks and personal demands associated with your transition to university. The more able you are to actively take charge of your learning, to assume new roles and to become a confident, capable member of the university community, the stronger your success identity will become.

The challenges that university presents to you are the basis upon which you will change your self-identity. Similar to university students who have gone before you, you are capable of significant and important changes. These changes will add to your ability and motivational levels, your view of yourself, and your understanding of the world. Importantly, both your successes and your failures will add to your evolving sense of an identity. Upon reflection, it will be easy to perceive how your successes in mastering new course content or using information to enhance your understanding of events from a different vantage point can add to your confidence regarding your ability to perform well in university. However, your failures also teach you. They teach by showing you the discrepancies between your current actions and the required environmental demands. Viewing failures as sources of feedback provides you with the opportunity to figure out how you will manage the discrepancy between your current actions and the activities and aptitudes that are necessary for success. As you successfully develop capabilities to manage these discrepancies, you add significantly to a new view of your own sense of self.

Just as you have expanded your definition of self by adding new competencies, so too will you add to your identity by solving the personal questions that define your life quest. The academic journey presents you with many existential questions. As you search for fulfillment, happiness, and purpose you will add to your definition of self. Finding a meaningful career path and relationships that enrich your life are discoveries that will give you some of the answers you seek.

Why University?

Why have you chosen university? Fill in the short survey provided on the next page and see how your results match those of first-year students across Canada (Affairs, 1999; Walker, 1998).

You, like many of your fellow students, as seen in the results graph on page 14, are choosing to pursue the academic avenue of university because you believe it will give you expertise and experience to create a better life for yourself. You are attending university for a variety of reasons, but primarily you want to ensure your future success. To do this you must expand your competencies so that you can effectively live in a technologically changing, culturally complex, global world. You know that you must possess broad-based competencies so that you can establish a career path, continuously maintain your competitive edge, and be prepared to cope with constant change.

If you are like most university students, you are attending university to develop the competence, creativity, confidence, critical thinking, and compassionate caring that are essential for success in the twenty-first century. You are committed to doing all you can do to succeed in your university career and learn what you need to know. You especially want to maximize the opportunities that will make this educational journey personally meaningful and professionally productive.

FIGURE 1.3	Survey of First-Year Students: Reasons for Attending University

Using the scale below, rate each statement according to how accurately it describes you. Strive to be as accurate as you can be in describing yourself as you are now. Assign each statement a number from zero to three.

I am going to university to ...	Not Important 0	1	Very Important 2	3
1. Meet expectations of present employer	0	1	2	3
2. Use time while unemployed	0	1	2	3
3. Meet parental expectations	0	1	2	3
4. Meet new friends	0	1	2	3
5. Become a more cultured person	0	1	2	3
6. Improve leadership skills	0	1	2	3
7. Obtain a degree for entrance to post-grad program	0	1	2	3
8. Prepare for graduate or professional school	0	1	2	3
9. Make more money	0	1	2	3
10. Discover career interests/plans	0	1	2	3
11. Develop base of flexible skills	0	1	2	3
12. Develop critical thinking and reasoning	0	1	2	3
13. Increase knowledge in academic field	0	1	2	3
14. Get a good general education	0	1	2	3
15. Obtain a degree for workforce	0	1	2	3
16. Prepare for job/career	0	1	2	3
17. Get a good job	0	1	2	3

Let us assume that to assist you in making this journey personally triumphant, your wisest, most trusted, most respected and experienced friend has shared with you a treasure map that reveals the secrets that will ensure your success. As you decipher the clues on this treasure map, you understand for the first time that though the map reveals significant secrets, it is in applying these secrets that the true treasure is uncovered. If the secrets are used wisely, you will create for yourself a personal success that breeds even greater success. Your challenge is to make these secrets work for you. In that process you will create your own map for managing your first year of university, discovering yourself and creating your future.

Seven Success Secrets

Wherever you find yourself, knowing your place of belonging is essential for a sense of safety and direction. Managing change and making a successful transition is based upon learning how to leave a familiar situation, venturing forward, and developing roots in an unfamiliar situation. The first secret of success, *Searching for Connection*, provides you with the skills and strategies for creating your sense of place and belonging in the unfamil-

Results: Reasons for Attending University

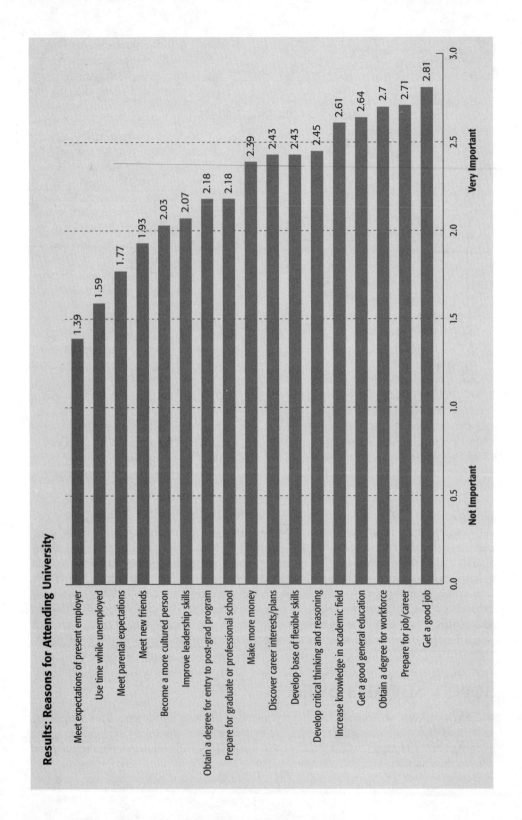

Reason	Rating
Meet expectations of present employer	1.39
Use time while unemployed	1.59
Meet parental expectations	1.77
Meet new friends	1.93
Become a more cultured person	2.03
Improve leadership skills	2.07
Obtain a degree for entry to post-grad program	2.18
Prepare for graduate or professional school	2.18
Make more money	2.39
Discover career interests/plans	2.43
Develop base of flexible skills	2.43
Develop critical thinking and reasoning	2.45
Increase knowledge in academic field	2.61
Get a good general education	2.64
Obtain a degree for workforce	2.7
Prepare for job/career	2.71
Get a good job	2.81

iar landscape of the university. Figuring out where to go and how to handle the academic workload, the anonymity, and the "angst" or fear associated with new social and personal opportunities, as well as finding ways to connect to the resources and support that can assist you are all included in the chapters on understanding yourself and the system.

Building on your increased awareness, you must now hone the skills to ensure that you will effectively manage the academic demands of this new environment. The university environment requires a different approach to learning than the study strategies you have previously used. You will be required to develop skills as a self-disciplined, self-reliant, independent learner. This means that you will not only be required to master the academic content of courses, but also to master the challenge of improving your own learning effectiveness and capabilities. The second secret, *Uncovering Self-Mastery Strategies*, will provide you with the personal management, thinking strategies, and learning tools that are necessary for enhancing your learning efficiency. These chapters will provide strategies for increasing your ability to motivate yourself, manage time, learn from lectures, read meaningfully, summarize notes, study effectively, and master tests.

How do you demonstrate that you are developing the competencies required for success? Your ability to articulate ideas, present your views, and prove the value of your perspective relies on your ability to communicate. The third secret, *Communicating Effectively*, provides you with information on ways to enhance your presentation skills, your assertive communication skills, and your writing abilities. If you are like most students, one of the challenges that appears to be most daunting is to write academically and professionally. These chapters will guide you to glean the proficiencies of paraphrasing, précis construction, patterns of development, paper composition, and proper citations.

With almost all of your academic tasks, even your academic writing, you will soon discover the value of peer assistance to help you with the undertaking. Your ability to establish relationships which nurture your academic and personal growth is crucial to your eventual success. *Creating Community*, the fourth secret, provides you with approaches for developing collaborative partnerships, building study and student work groups and bridging diversity differences.

As you are challenged to enhance your learning capabilities you will discover that you will need to adjust your learning methods to match the pedagogical approach of different classes. The fifth secret, *Evaluating Learning Strategies*, provides you with insight on ways to improve your learning efficiency. As you explore diverse learning style models you will be able to crystallize a personalized learning style that will help you manage a variety of learning environments.

Throughout your academic journey you will develop competencies that will add to your overall capabilities. A constant component that is necessary for your survival as well as your success is your ability to productively solve the problems that life presents. The sixth secret, *Solving Problems*, provides you with critical thinking and creative problem-solving systems that can enhance your functioning. This chapter will expand your logical reasoning, metacognitive capabilities, and critical evaluative skills, as well as assist you to more creatively manage life's issues and momentary problems.

You continue on your academic journey aiming to create a future for yourself that is personally meaningful and fulfilling. The seventh secret, *Seeking Personal and Professional Success*, helps you focus on creating career and personal life plans that give you a sense of stability in a world of change.

You are just launching your heroic academic journey. There are many secrets waiting for you to uncover. Begin now to commence a journey of a lifetime.

It's More Than Common Sense

Helping Rural Students Succeed at University

Shelly Birnie-Lefcovitch, Ph.D.
Memorial University of Newfoundland

A small, but consistent, body of empirical evidence shows that students who graduate from rural high schools have much more difficulty achieving success at university than do their urban counterparts. For example, in an early study of student retention conducted at the University of Colorado, Aylesworth and Bloom (1976) found that rural students leave university prematurely in larger numbers than do urban students. Also, in a study conducted at Oregon State University, Jackman (1994) found that students from rural communities are less satisfied with their university experiences than are urban students. In Canada, a study conducted at Memorial University of Newfoundland revealed that rural students take longer to adjust academically and as a result they have more difficulty gaining entry to highly selective majors and professional programs (Goudie, 1996). In a second, more recent study conducted at Memorial, Birnie-Lefcovitch (2000) found that first-semester, rural students not only achieve lower grades than do urban students, but that on a measure of self-reported university adjustment (Baker & Syrik, 1989), rural students seem to experience lower levels of both academic and personal-emotional adjustment.

What can rural students and universities do to help counter these trends? Tinto (1993) proposes a theory of student departure from university that may offer some useful guidance. He argues that students' pre-university characteristics and experiences—that is, family background, skills and abilities, and prior schooling—influence initial goals and commitments to higher education. Tinto believes that these initial goals and commitments affect the way students get involved in the academic and social systems of the university and thus help determine the extent to which students are integrated into campus life. Tinto argues further that this initial integration at university influences students' subsequent goals and commitments, and their eventual decision to leave or stay. In support of this conceptual model, empirical studies highlight the importance of academic and social integration, and student goals and commitments in the departure process (Stoecker, Pascarella, & Wolfle, 1988; Beil, Reisen, Zea & Caplan, 1999; Bray, Braxton & Sullivan, 1999).

Since it appears, in general, that students who are committed to their programs of study and who are integrated into the academic and social aspects of campus life are more likely to be satisfied with their university experiences and achieve the goal of graduation, it may be especially important for rural students to engage in activities which strengthen their connections to the university. Specifically, rural students may want to develop informal relationships with other students, become involved in extracurricular activities, maintain out-of-class contact with university faculty and staff, and actively participate in their academic course work (Pascarella & Terenzini, 1991). In addition, since it also appears that the majority of student departure occurs during the first year of undergraduate study (Levitz & Noel, 1989; Tinto, 1993), it may be especially important that rural students begin to engage in these activities as soon as possible in the first semester.

In order to address this objective, a number of universities offer Freshman Interest Groups (FIGS) to their first-year students. Initially developed at the University of Oregon (MacGregor, 1988), FIGS typically cluster together groups of 15 to 20 new undergraduates who are enrolled in the same degree program. Since these students take some of the same courses together, they share a common academic experience. In addition, because they are all new students entering university at the same time, they face many transitional challenges together. Led by a senior student who is also enrolled in the same degree program, these collaborative learning communities provide new students, immediately upon arrival on campus and throughout their first year, with a ready-made network of friends with whom to attend classes, work on course assignments, and discuss academic matters. In addition, FIGS provide a forum where students are able to talk about the anxieties and excitements of being new university students as well as to socialize and have fun.

Evaluation studies conducted by Tokuno and his colleagues (Tokuno & Campbell, 1992; Tokuno, 1993), report very positive results for students who participate in FIGS. Specifically, these students achieve higher grades, show greater persistence at university, and make speedier progress toward completing their degrees. However, while this evidence indicates that FIGS may be very effective in helping new students in general, it is not yet clear if FIGS will help rural students address the specific challenges they face at university. Thus, an important next step is to conduct further research to investigate the effectiveness of FIGS in helping rural students make a successful transition to higher education.

Success Strategies FOR SELF-AWARENESS

Self-awareness
The most personally useful ideas I learned in this chapter are…

Self-confidence
One experience that has added to my confidence as a student is…

Self-concept
Academic skills that I believe will help me succeed in university are…

Chapter Summary

Chapter 1 describes education as a personal journey of self-discovery. It presents a self-development model in which students increase three key aspects of their identity as they meet the challenges that university presents: self-awareness, self-confidence, and self-concept. Various models are presented that illustrate the stages of development students encounter as they develop the abilities and attitudes to succeed in the academic world and in their future endeavours. The chapter introduces seven success strategies that can facilitate personal growth and academic achievement. These will be further developed in later chapters.

Exercises

REFLECT–ACT

The following Reflect–Act exercises are designed to help you develop increased self-awareness and effectiveness through the process of reflective thinking, analysis, and productive action. These Reflect–Act exercises focus on the developmental issues you will encounter initially in your academic journey.

Reflect   Identify a list of 5 to 10 potential challenges that students may encounter during their first six weeks of university.
Act   Describe any university resources you have discovered that can help to manage these challenges.

Reflect   During the past years many experiences have affected you. Select one significant positive and one negative experience that you believe has had a major influence on you. Describe the impact of these experiences on you. Which one has had the greatest impact? Why?
Act   Provide an example of how you can use this experience now, as you commence university, to enhance your probability of success.

Reflect   Compare and contrast the similarities and differences between your previous school and university.
Act   Describe what you have done to feel more comfortable in the new educational environment. Describe what you have learned about the available resources that can help you succeed in university.

Reflect   Think about a situation in your past in which you felt confident and able. Describe the situation. Analyze the factors that produced these feelings of confidence. Describe your current reactions as a university student. Identify ways in which your past feelings of confidence and success relate to your current experience.
Act   Identify actions you can take to bolster your feelings of confidence as a university student and ensure your academic success.

Reflect   Review the feedback you have received in the past five years as a result of your educational, social, extracurricular, or work experience. Using the ideas presented in the Johari Window of the known and unknown self, describe one important insight you learned about yourself that could previously have been described as a personal blind spot.
Act   Share your plan for using this increased sense of personal awareness to help you succeed in university.

Reflect   Identify two positive events and two frustrating events you have experienced during your first two weeks at university. Evaluate these experiences by considering how Maslow's or Chickering's developmental theory increases your understanding of these situations.
Act   Identify what you can do to cope more effectively with situations that frustrate you.

GROUP DISCUSSION

1. Share perceptions regarding the five most important factors that you believe are most necessary to ensure university success.

2. Discover the differences in the educational experiences of individuals who have attended a small school versus those who have attended a large school. Discuss how the transition to university may be different for these two groups of students.

3. Identify which campus resources help students meet the five categories of needs as described by Maslow's hierarchy.

4. The courses in which you are involved teach you information as well as different approaches to thinking and learning. Consider three courses from different areas. Describe the differences in assignments, teaching approaches, and thinking skills that are required to master each one.

5. Identify as many reasons as possible why students choose to attend university. As a group, rank these reasons in order of importance. How does the group ranking vary from individual rankings?

APPLY TO LIFE

Now that you have developed an understanding of the many factors that influence success at university, distinguish the significant factors you believe are related to your own academic development and success. Use the following questions to focus your discovery.

1. What are the three most important factors that have influenced your successful development as a student?

2. In analyzing the information you have learned about yourself and student development theory, what have you learned that can help you succeed in university?

3. How can you continue to build on the insights you learn in this course so that you are well prepared for future challenges?

Searching for Connection

"Nobody but nobody can make it alone out here." Maya Angelou

The adventure begins. Adventure requires a point of departure. Just as the ship must leave the harbour in order to explore new horizons, education requires that you leave the familiar and reach out to the unknown. Education challenges you to venture forth, embrace new places, uncover new perspectives, and meet new people. Your adventure will provide you with possibilities, opportunities, and challenges. To prepare you to use the opportunities and overcome the challenges you will encounter, the first secret, *Searching for Connection,* provides you with an awareness of the personal resources you possess and the practical processes you can use in order to achieve the success you desire. Because your success depends upon connecting to others and to your own capabilities, learning to find the resources that can benefit you will ensure your success.

How prepared are you? Imagine that you are about to take a long journey to a distant destination. Knowing what to pack would depend upon what you need and where you are going. Just as certain types of clothing, survival gear, and travel guides may be appropriate in one place and not relevant in another, so too may specific abilities, learning approaches, and experience be useful in some educational environments and not in others. Equally important is knowing how to locate, consult with, and relate to the people who can assist you.

One way to prepare yourself is by evaluating what you possess currently and comparing it with what you may need. This self-appraisal connects you to your own capabilities and gives you an awareness that can fuel self-confidence in your own abilities to succeed in a new place. It also alerts you to competencies you may need to add in order to overcome any obstacles along the way, so that you are able to achieve all that you desire. An initial self-appraisal of attitudinal factors and actions that add to self-confidence, the academic competencies that are required, and the social skills that ensure achievement provide the basis for developing a personalized information guide for your educational journey.

Another way to prepare yourself is by developing greater clarity about the environment in which you find yourself, and connecting with the important resources that will ensure success. Just as various environments present special challenges, educational institutions present demands that require different approaches to learning. "Nobody but nobody can make it out here alone." Your success depends upon how well you connect with the people who can guide, assist, support, and advise you, so that you are better able to meet the unique demands of the new learning environment.

By connecting to resources, your own and others, you prepare yourself for your educational journey. By connecting to resources, you can develop a plan that can assist you in overcoming obstacles that may block your success. By connecting to resources, you are better able to confidently pursue the adventure that awaits.

How Prepared Are You?

chapter 2

"I am the maker of my own fortune." Tecumseh

Questions

What do I need to know to feel more prepared for university?

Objectives

- Discover how I fit into the university environment.
- Identify the competencies I possess.
- See myself within a developmental context.
- Develop strategies for managing the challenges I will face.

Student Success Portrait

Finding Your Place at University

Heather Lehmann
University of Manitoba

In my university career, I have learned that life is like a heart monitor. A life which is flat is lifeless, while a life with peaks and valleys is vibrantly alive, growing and changing. What I have discovered is that the peaks and valleys are the result of how I choose to spend my time, both inside and outside class. The truth is that post-secondary education is not just about school—it's about life experience. At the end of your time at university, it won't be the theorems and formulae that really stand out in your memory, but the life skills you have gained. Skills like critical thinking, problem-solving, decision-making, time management, cooking, doing laundry, making new friends, and succeeding in a job interview are learned through experience, volunteering, work, and leadership activities.

"Introduction to University" is a valuable course for any first-year university student, no matter how capable you may think you are. It helped me to improve my time-management skills, to prepare for essay writing and oral presentations, and to familiarize myself with various services and organizations on campus. This basic knowledge instilled in me much-needed confidence as a new university student, and reminded me of the importance of involving myself in the community.

When I came to university, I moved into residence on campus—an established community. My floor became my surrogate family, and the residence student staff provided us with many activities that encouraged a balanced lifestyle of fun and work. By October, I couldn't count the number of new people I had met. My residence experience also provided leadership opportunities. There is so much that I have taken away from that experience: lifelong friends, fun memories, valuable contacts and references, public-speaking skills, a sense of independence, and the knowledge that sometimes it is quicker to get a pizza delivered than to get an ambulance. What is my message to you? Get involved! Join a club, play a sport, participate in student politics, talk to your professors outside of class. Find some way to connect with the university that is not strictly academic. This helps to broaden your educational experience and makes you feel that you belong. When I look at the big picture of my life, I know that an A+ will make me happy for a couple of weeks, but my connections and involvements give me joy each and every day of my life. Learn from your mistakes, which are the valleys of your university experience, and participate actively. Involvement provides the peaks in your university life. Savour these.

You have commenced this educational journey because you want to be better able to direct your own future. Simply stated, you want to live a life that is uniquely your own. Doing that requires that you truly understand yourself, who you are now, what your options are, and whom you want to become. Living your own life involves becoming the autonomous, confident, self-determined person you desire to be.

Becoming your own person demands that you develop new competencies to meet the challenges presented, master your fears, and overcome your confusion or disillusionment. It requires channeling your hopes, focusing your desires, and building on convictions. You must release yourself from failures that have previously held you back. With directed and deliberate efforts you will move through the developmental stages (Chickering & Reisser, 1993; Maslow, 1970; Perry, 1970), that provide the basis for defining your sense of self. Discovering this core identity is essential for directing your pursuit of your own life path.

The lessons of the next few years will make a difference in the trajectory of your life. Whatever those lessons are, they will propel you forward. What you do with them and how you integrate them will determine whether or not you arrive at the place you aspire to be. Through classroom lectures, books you read, encounters with others, conversations, leadership opportunities, and extracurricular activities, you will evaluate your assumptions, perceptions, and beliefs. In this process you will gain a new perspective on the events that have shaped you and the environment in which you live. These insights will help you chart your course for the future.

This adventure requires a willingness to depart from the familiar in order to discover new ideas, inspirations, and involvements. It is fueled by your curiosity, fed by the challenges you meet, and determined by the choices you make.

What will you bring with you? What do you know about yourself and your abilities? You must begin by honestly appraising what you possess. Facing yourself honestly means evaluating who you are now. It means accurately reflecting on your strengths and weaknesses, and attempting to understand how they influence your experience and expectations. Do not be fooled into presenting yourself as you wish yourself to be. To create the life you desire, you must begin as you are now.

Who Are You?

Becoming self-aware is an ongoing process. Sometimes you become more self-aware through reflection and self-analysis. Other times, it's through the feedback you receive from others. The feedback can be direct or indirect, clear or unclear, helpful or hurtful. Feedback not only comes from others through comments, observations, and suggestions, but also through the subtle non-verbal reactions of approval, dislike, and irritation. One of the most important sources of feedback will be the information you receive regarding your performance. Grades are one form of performance feedback, but there are others such as your ability to manage the complexity of academic assignments, or your effectiveness in maximizing your time so that you are a healthy, involved student. Through continuous assessment and action you will add to the self-awareness that feeds your self-confidence and self-concept (Pascarelli & Terenzini, 1991).

To assist you in evaluating your readiness for your academic adventure the following questions have been provided. These questions will guide you in determining the competencies you already have and those you need to develop. These questions are intended to provide a frame of reference to assist you in systematically evaluating your self-confidence, academic self, and social self-concept. With this information you can more productively focus your skill development in order to move through the developmental stages (Belenky, Clinchy, Goldberger, & Tarule, 1986; Chickering & Reisser, 1993) that are essential to your evolution as a student.

Begin by answering each question as honestly as you can. This provides you with your own self-appraisal. Your self-appraisal is only one important source of information. You can add to the depth and accuracy of this analysis by discussing your responses with someone who knows you well. They can give you the supplemental information that may alert you to potential blind spots that could trip you up on your journey. With this combined information, you are able to use the scores as your own personal gauge for directing your efforts.

Self-Confidence

There are times when you feel confident and other times when you do not. How prepared you are to create success for yourself in this new environment is directly related to your self-confidence, self-talk, and self-efficacy. Take the opportunity to discover for yourself how prepared you are by completing the self-assessment exercises that follow.

Self-Confidence Assessment

Using the scale below, rate each statement according to how accurately it describes you. This is not a test; there are no right answers. Strive to be as accurate as you can be in describing yourself as you are right now. Assign each statement a number from one to five.

Not At All Descriptive	Somewhat Descriptive	Very Descriptive
1		5

Self-Talk Thoughts

___2___ 1. When I receive poor grades it is usually because the professor was an inadequate instructor.*

___3___ 2. I have changed the habits that were interfering with my success.

___1___ 3. I accept myself just as I am, even my faults and weaknesses.

___3___ 4. Strategies I use to help me cope are complaining, blaming and making excuses.*

___4___ 5. I write down important things so I won't forget them.

___1___ 6. Whether or not I am happy depends upon me.

___2___ 7. The quality of my life is largely the result of the choices I have made.

___2___ 8. I don't make the same mistake twice.

___3___ 9. I am self-disciplined.

___4___ 10. I have looked to others (i.e., family, coaches, friends, teachers) to motivate me.*

Self-Talk Thoughts Score   16   9

Total = (add items 2,3,5,6,7,8,9) − (add items 1,4,10).   7

Attitude

___4___ 1. My greatest personal accomplishments have come from hard work and persistence.

_____4_ 2. If something can go wrong for me, it will.*

_____4_ 3. I prefer to think that life is a matter of luck.*

_____4_ 4. I see myself as largely responsible for my performance throughout my university career.

_____5_ 5. It is important for me to figure out strategies for doing well in my university courses.

_____2_ 6. Things usually work out the way I want them to.

_____1_ 7. I'm a believer in the idea that "every cloud has a silver lining."

_____1_ 8. I believe that even in difficult times there are positive outcomes.

_____3_ 9. I know that with time and effort most problems can be solved.

_____3_ 10. Whether or not I am successful depends upon the power and actions of others.*

Attitude Score   20   11   9

Total = (add items 1,4,5,6,7,8,9) – (add items 2,3,10).

Test Anxiety

_____2_ 1. I do not understand why some people get so upset about tests or exams.

_____4_ 2. I dread courses where the professor has the habit of giving unannounced quizzes.*

_____1_ 3. On exams I think that if I do not know the material already, there is no point worrying about it.

_____4_ 4. The harder I work preparing an assignment or writing a test, the more confused I become.*

_____1_ 5. When writing an exam, my emotions do not interfere with my performance.

_____2_ 6. During an exam, I often get so nervous that I forget the facts I really know.*

_____2_ 7. I feel confident when I have to write a "surprise" quiz.

_____3_ 8. During exams, I scan the test and focus first on the questions I can confidently answer.

_____1_ 9. I seldom feel the need for "cramming" for a test or exam.

_____2_ 10. If I feel uneasy or upset before writing an exam, I use those feelings as signals to concentrate as well as I can.

Test Anxiety Score   12   10   2

Total = (add items 1,3,5,7,8,9,10) – (add items 2,4,6).

Goals (Purpose)

_____2_ 1. I live day to day, without much of a plan for the future.*

(continued)

_2_ 2. One of the ways in which I have been successful is by setting long- and short-term goals, and working to achieve them.

_2_ 3. I can be counted on to finish what I start.

_4_ 4. I am not sure what I want to accomplish this term.*

_1_ 5. I am excited about what I am doing right now.

_3_ 6. When I look at the important choices I've made in my life, I know why I made each one.

_1_ 7. I'm confident that I will accomplish my greatest goals and dreams.

_2_ 8. When I fail to reach a goal I try to figure out what went wrong.

_2_ 9. I overextend myself by making too many commitments.*

_2_ 10. I can picture what I will be doing with my life ten years from now.

Goals Score   15   9
Total = (add items 2,3,5,6,7,8,10) – (add items 1,4,9)   6

Time

_1_ 1. I usually feel in control of my time.

_2_ 2. I work best under pressure, so I believe that procrastination actually helps me to achieve.*

_3_ 3. When choosing between completing an academic assignment or having fun, I finish my work first, then have fun.

_2_ 4. I seldom waste time doing unimportant things.

_3_ 5. I find myself having too much to do and not enough time to do it.*

_3_ 6. I usually accomplish all the things I plan to do in a day.

_2_ 7. I am learning to understand the hidden motivations for my procrastination.

_3_ 8. I know when I am trying to do too much and have learned to prioritize my commitments so that my time is used efficiently.

_1_ 9. I find that my part-time job interferes with my studies.*

_2_ 10. I have a system for scheduling my time, and I use it on a regular basis.

Time Management Score   16   6
Total = (add items1,3,4,6,7,8,10) – (add items 2,5,9).   10

Self-Confidence Total	
Your self-confidence total score is derived from adding each of the above scales.	
Self-Talk Thoughts Score	7 /20
Attitude Score	9 /20
Test Anxiety Score	2 /20
Goals Score	6 /20
Time Score	10 /20
Total	34 /100

Summary

These self-confidence scores reveal important information about you. They provide insights into how your previous life experiences are influencing your actions and attitudes. Although you cannot change your past, you can change your future. The choices you make in how you will use this information are critical. You can change those behaviours and beliefs that interfere with your success by using the strategies that are presented in the subsequent chapters. By recognizing your typical responses you can then find alternative methods for handling the challenges of your university experience. For each of the above scales, identify the items that reflect your less-than-ideal thoughts and behaviours. These include high scores on the asterisk items* and low scores on the non-asterisk items. Focus on changing these this semester with the help of the strategies mentioned in each of the following chapters.

Academic Self-Concept

You have commenced this academic journey with a personal view of your ability as a student (i.e., your academic self-concept). Your academic self-concept has evolved as you have advanced in your educational career. Each year you have added to your knowledge, practical experience, and intellectual ability. Through trial and error, you have learned how to be a student. You have learned to adapt in order to face demands at different stages. There are many elements that compose your academic self-concept (Pascarella & Terenzini, 1991), that you may or may not be aware of. Indeed, it is quite possible that you now take for granted the capabilities necessary to your survival. However, knowing what makes you efficient, understanding the processes you use in figuring out problems, or recognizing your ability to master complex concepts are aspects of your academic self-concept that you will use to overcome the academic challenges of the university experience.

What do you know about your academic self? Can you tell others, in detail, why you are a successful student? Do you know how to change your approach to learning when you are unable to grasp the new ideas that are necessary to progress? When you find that you are simply working at too slow a pace to manage the workload, how do you adapt? Have you figured out why some subject areas are easy for you, while others seem overwhelmingly impossible? Your assessment of your academic self, and your analysis of how you approach various academic tasks, will provide you with an academic self-concept, as well as ways of using it to reinforce your success.

Academic Self-Concept Assessment

Using the scale below, rate each statement according to how accurately it describes you. This is not a test; there are no right answers. Strive to be as accurate as you can be in describing yourself as you are right now. Assign each statement a number from one to five.

Not At All Descriptive	Somewhat Descriptive	Very Descriptive
1		**5**

Learning from Lectures (Note-taking)

_____ 1. I know the difference between listening and hearing.

_____ 2. My mind often wanders in class.*

_____ 3. I usually sit in the front of the class in order to ask questions.

_____ 4. I have a well-developed system of taking notes that allows me to efficiently get all the important information I need.

_____ 5. I do not know how effective or ineffective my own system of note-taking is.*

_____ 6. Because some of my professors are difficult to understand, I make sure that I ask for clarification when I am confused.

_____ 7. To help me understand the lecture material, I usually prepare by reading the assigned reading before class.

_____ 8. I try to record everything the professor says.*

_____ 9. As soon as I can after class, I read my notes and add any missing information so that my notes are accurate and up-to-date.

_____ 10. I have developed a system of abbreviations and symbols that helps me record information more efficiently.

Note-Taking Skills Score

Total = (add items 1,3,4,6,7,9,10) – (add items 2,5,8).

Reading and Comprehension

_____ 1. I am an efficient reader and enjoy the challenge of adjusting my reading capabilities to best master the information I must learn.

_____ 2. I find that other things seem to get in the way of going to class and studying on a regular basis.*

_____ 3. I have developed a reading system such as SQ3R that allows me to read, synthesize, and remember information.

_____ 4. I am able to make connections between reading assignments and class lectures.

_____ 5. I have difficulty getting started on my assignments and reading.*

_____ 6. I think of questions as I read.

_____ 7. I think about how the information I am reading can be used and applied.

_____ 8. In planning my studying, I allocate more time to those subjects that I have more difficulty comprehending.

_____ 9. I underestimate the time I need to successfully complete my assignments.*

_____ 10. When studying different subjects, I use different approaches to learn the material.

Reading Skills Score

Total = (add items 1,3,4,6,7,8,10) – (add items 2,5,9).

Test-Taking

_____ 1. I know how to apportion my time on an exam in order to maximize my effectiveness.

_____ 2. I have to cram the night before most examinations because of poor study planning.*

_____ 3. I have developed specific approaches for improving my performance on multiple-choice exams.

_____ 4. I know the best strategies for ensuring success on problem-solving tests.

_____ 5. I have developed the writing skills to respond effectively to the requirements of different types of essay questions.

_____ 6. I have figured out how to avoid some of the mistakes that have resulted in lower grades on examinations.

_____ 7. I review returned examinations in order to learn what types of questions I have difficulty answering.

_____ 8. Because I worry about tests, I sometimes have difficulty concentrating and remembering.*

_____ 9. I have developed some adaptive strategies for reducing my anxiety.

_____ 10. I am usually disappointed in my test performance and have not figured out what it means to study effectively.*

Test-Taking Skills Score

Total = (add items 1,3,4,5,6,7,9) – (add items 2,8,10).

(continued)

Learning Strategies

_____ 1. I prefer working on projects alone.

_____ 2. I need the professor's guidance to understand significant aspects of particular problems.*

_____ 3. When I have a difficult course, I find a partner with whom I can study.

_____ 4. I dislike the pressure of having to work to obtain good grades.*

_____ 5. I keep track of my own progress to determine whether or not I am succeeding as I expect.

_____ 6. I prefer a concrete, hands-on, practical approach that lets me apply what I've learned.

_____ 7. I like courses in which I can analyze information and challenge others.

_____ 8. I am comforted by rules and like it better when my work is structured.*

_____ 9. To understand complicated concepts, I break them into smaller components.

_____ 10. I am able to recognize patterns and understand relationships.

Learning Strategies Score

Total = (add items 1,3,5,6,7,9,10) − (add items 2,4,8).

Problem-Solving & Critical Thinking

_____ 1. I make good decisions, even when I am upset.

_____ 2. I find value in the feedback I get.

_____ 3. I tend to repeat my mistakes.*

_____ 4. When I discover that I'm off course, I usually know why.

_____ 5. I have difficulty making important decisions.*

_____ 6. I expect professors to provide me with the truth.

_____ 7. I believe that there are multiple answers to the same problem.

_____ 8. I can identify central issues, make correct inferences from data, apply principles, and interpret conclusions accurately.

_____ 9. I am able to perceive the assumptions and fallacies in people's arguments.

_____ 10. I am uncomfortable learning information that conflicts with my beliefs. *

Thinking-Strategies Score

Total = (add items 1,2,4,6,7,8,9) − (add items 3,5,10).

Academic Self-Concept Total	
Your academic self-concept total score is derived from adding each of the above scales.	
Note-Taking Score	/20
Reading and Comprehension Score	/20
Test-Taking Score	/20
Learning Strategies Score	/20
Problem-Solving and Critical Thinking Score	/20
Total	/100

Summary

The diversity of scores that compose your academic self-concept demonstrates the complicated, interactive nature of the factors that determine your academic capabilities. And as you progress with your university education, you will soon discover that within these competencies there are levels of abilities. Once you master a lower level, you are better able to advance to the next level. Your ability to strengthen your academic self-concept scores will positively affect your ability to increase your grade-point average (Clifton, 1997). For each of the above scales, identify the items that reflect your less-than-ideal thoughts and behaviours. These include high scores on the asterisk items* and low scores on the non-asterisk items. Focus on changing these this semester with the help of the strategies mentioned in each of the following chapters.

Social Self-Concept

Like most university students, one of your main reasons for attending university is to develop a clearer understanding of yourself, your abilities, and your career path (Astin & Kent, 1983; Kuh, 1993; Pascarella, Ethington, & Smart, 1998). This search for increased insight and self-acceptance is influenced by your openness to new ideas and world-views, your maturing sense of autonomy, the quality and variety of your relationships and your involvement in your university community. As you successfully develop connections, enhance your communication capabilities, and foster collaborative partnerships, you will experience an increased sense of belonging and personal direction.

Social Self-Concept Assessment

Using the scale below, rate each statement according to how accurately it describes you. This is not a test; there are no right answers. Strive to be as accurate as you can be in describing yourself as you are right now. Assign each statement a number from one to five.

Not At All Descriptive	Somewhat Descriptive	Very Descriptive
1		**5**

Communication (Written and Oral)

_____ 1. I am a good listener.

_____ 2. I express my opinions and concerns directly and assertively.

_____ 3. I am uncomfortable presenting information formally to groups.*

_____ 4. I enjoy public speaking.

_____ 5. I consider myself to be a good writer.

_____ 6. I have difficulty with spelling and grammar.*

_____ 7. I understand the differences between informal writing and academic writing.

_____ 8. I am able to properly use the various documentation systems for bibliographic entries that my professors may require.

_____ 9. I have developed accurate paraphrasing and synthesizing abilities.

_____ 10. I am unsure of how to avoid plagiarism when I download information from the Internet for my papers.*

Communication Skills Score

Total = (add items 1,2,4,5,7,8,9) − (add items 3,6,10).

Connection to Others

_____ 1. I listen to others even when it takes a lot of effort to understand them.

_____ 2. When listening to others, my mind wanders.*

_____ 3. Others see me as accepting of and interested in them.

_____ 4. I listen primarily for facts, rather than ideas, when someone is speaking.

_____ 5. I am able to detect what a person may be feeling by looking at their face.

_____ 6. It is difficult for me to talk with individuals who may differ from me culturally or politically.*

_____ 7. I welcome and invite others to state their views.

_____ 8. There have been situations when I am so committed to my own ideas that I am unwilling to listen to an alternative viewpoint.*

_____ 9. When I am offended, I am willing to listen to the other person's side of the story without becoming defensive.

_____ 10. When somebody is talking to me, I listen carefully.

Connection to Others Score
Total = (add items 1,3,4,5,7,9,10) – (add items 2,6,8).

Connection to Community

_____ 1. I ask for help when I encounter a problem.

_____ 2. I am not familiar with the available campus resources that can help me succeed.*

_____ 3. I have a network of people in my life whom I can count on for assistance.

_____ 4. I know how to locate the career-planning office at my institution.

_____ 5. I am confused about how to effectively use the library resources on my campus.*

_____ 6. I have learned how to avoid some of the typical problems that first-year students experience by consulting with the available advisers.

_____ 7. Because I am commuting, I spend less than twenty hours a week on campus.*

_____ 8. I have introduced myself to all of my professors.

_____ 9. I know at least two other students in each of my classes.

_____ 10. I have joined a campus organization.

Connection to Community Score
Total = (add items 1,3,4,6,8,9,10) – (add items 2,5,7).

Collaborative Teamwork

_____ 1. I participate regularly in a study group.

_____ 2. I get impatient when group discussions bog down and we are unable to meet our goals successfully.*

_____ 3. I enjoy contributing ideas and encouraging others to share their views during group discussions.

_____ 4. Others often perceive me as an effective leader.

_____ 5. I have taken advantage of the opportunity to develop friendships with individuals from different cultures, geographic areas, and socioeconomic classes.

_____ 6. I believe that many of the communication problems between men and women can never be changed.*

(continued)

_____ 7. I strive to understand the views of individuals who differ from my own perspective.

_____ 8. I believe it is important to support legislation that ensures equal rights, access, and opportunity for all, particularly for those who have previously been discriminated against.

_____ 9. I know that many of the societal problems of today relate to society's efforts to embrace political correctness and the subsequent loss of definitive rules.*

_____ 10. I believe it is my responsibility to contribute to the welfare and care of others in the world who are less fortunate.

Teamwork Score

Total = (add items 1,3,4,5,7,8,10) – (add items 2,6,9).

Career (Purpose)

_____ 1. Developing a clear sense of who I am is important to me.

_____ 2. I currently have a clear career goal.

_____ 3. I have chosen my current career goal primarily because of pressure from other people in my life.*

_____ 4. I am developing an awareness of my core values and how they influence my choice of a career direction.

_____ 5. I am uncertain about whether I have the abilities to pursue the career I would like.*

_____ 6. I can clearly describe my characteristics and how they relate to my vocational choices.

_____ 7. I am able to articulate my interests and abilities, which helps me focus on career possibilities that suit me.

_____ 8. I see my career as a means of gaining status and respect.

_____ 9. I believe that all I need to make a good career decision is to have someone give me a few options from which I should choose.*

_____ 10. I believe that the salary I will earn is an important factor in selecting a career.

Career Score

Total = (add items 1,2,4,6,7,8,10) – (add items 3,5,9).

Social Self-Concept Total	
Your social self-concept total score is derived from adding each of the above scales	
Communication Score	/20
Connection to Others Score	/20
Connection to Community Score	/20
Collaborative Teamwork Score	/20
Career Score	/20
Total	/100

Summary

Whatever your personality, your social self-concept scores provide you with information regarding your comfort with yourself, relative to your life direction, and your satisfaction with your relationships with others. As you increase your integration into the university community, you are more likely to achieve higher grades (Bidwell, 1989; Pascarella & Terenzini, 1991). For each of the above scales, identify the items that reflect your less-than-ideal thoughts and behaviours. These include high scores on the asterisk items* and low scores on the non-asterisk items. Focus on changing these this semester with the help of the strategies mentioned in each of the following chapters.

Assessment–Action

You now have an initial appraisal of your self-confidence, academic self-concept, and social self-concept. This knowledge will help you identify the competencies that allow you to function effectively, and will provide a framework for the actions you must take to be successful. However, as you attempt to master specific areas, you will immediately discover new information about your abilities. This can provide you with additional information that will affect your assessment. For example, you may currently assess yourself with high capabilities as a writer because you have extensive experience in creative writing, are well-versed in basic grammar, know how to construct effective paragraphs, and can catch spelling errors. However, after writing your first essay in university, you could find that your well-developed skills are not quite adequate to perform successfully at the higher level of writing that is required. Thus, your choices become how to develop an intellectual, third-person approach to construction, how to perfect paraphrasing skills, and how to learn the basics of making citations and using preferred reference systems.

This self-appraisal is your initial step. With it complete, you have expanded your awareness of the competencies you possess and those you must develop as you prepare to meet the challenges that await. The experience and expertise you bring with you gives

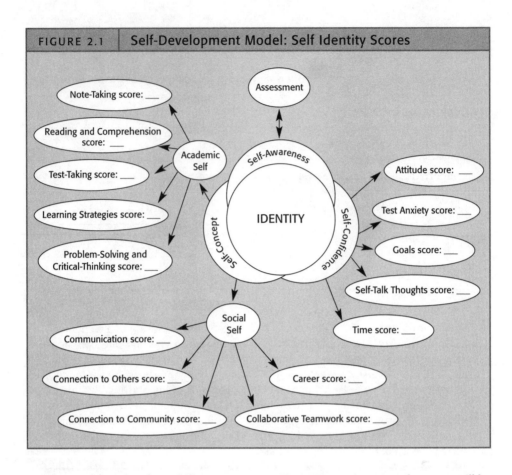

FIGURE 2.1 | Self-Development Model: Self Identity Scores

Note-Taking score: ___

Reading and Comprehension score: ___

Test-Taking score: ___

Learning Strategies score: ___

Problem-Solving and Critical-Thinking score: ___

Academic Self

Self-Awareness

IDENTITY

Self-Concept

Self-Confidence

Assessment

Attitude score: ___

Test Anxiety score: ___

Goals score: ___

Self-Talk Thoughts score: ___

Time score: ___

Social Self

Communication score: ___

Connection to Others score: ___

Connection to Community score: ___

Career score: ___

Collaborative Teamwork score: ___

you the confidence and capability to persevere. Your progression toward success will be enhanced as you develop the capability to meet the demands of the university experience. Your curiosity has provided the impetus to look honestly at yourself. Now it fuels your desire to seek answers, explore options, and develop competencies that will help you better manage the road before you.

Because you are curious, you are open to possibility, exhilarated by newness, delighted by surprise, and driven to define your own destiny. Curiosity provides the motivational energy needed to invest in developing the skills that are required in university. Curiosity is the ingredient you will use to seek alternative answers. Curiosity opens you to the paths that will define your future.

Each path will have crossroads, points at which you must choose one way and not another. Sometimes your choice will involve what you do, and other times it will involve what you do not do. Because choices are about action as well as avoidance, you need to become aware of the choices that you are making.

Your choices can be informed ones because many of the challenges that await you are known. Others are unknown. Though they arise unexpectedly, you can still be prepared. Like the mountain climber who surveys the landscape, or the kayaker who assesses the rapids, your anticipation and analysis of the challenges that await you can help to effectively manage the terrain. In combination with your self-appraisal, the information in the following chapters can prepare you for the challenges ahead.

It's More Than Common Sense

The Importance of "Soft Skills"

J. Paul Grayson, Ph.D.
York University

Employers in both Canada and the United States want to hire university graduates with more than good marks and knowledge of a particular field. They want people who can communicate effectively, work in teams, and critically analyze problems they are likely to encounter in their jobs.

This message has been clear for some time, although many students continue to feel that as long as they get good grades, and are enrolled in the right program, they will be okay. Several years ago, however, the Conference Board of Canada, which includes in its membership many high-powered employers like IBM and General Motors, listed "soft skills" like communication, critical thinking, commitment to life-long learning, positive attitudes and behaviours, responsibility, adaptability, and the ability to work with others as skills required of the Canadian workforce (CBC, 1997). As emphasized in an article in *University Affairs*, "There is a growing recognition among employers that much of the value of a university degree lies not in the vocational aspect of the training, but in teaching students how to think, to communicate those thoughts, to be open to lifelong learning, and to manage time commitments" (Frank, 1997:8). Quite frequently, taking a liberal arts program gives students better skills in these areas than taking technical subjects such as business or engineering. As a result, while it may be difficult for some liberal arts graduates to get through some corporate doors, once they are hired, they can move through corporate ranks as rapidly as anyone else.

Further confirmation of the importance of soft skills is evident in the results of a survey of 150 Canadian Chief Information Officers of companies with more than 100 employees. Overall, 37 percent said that the most important soft skills for job candidates were interpersonal skills. Twenty-four percent said that written and verbal communication skills were most important and 16 percent identified the ability to work under pressure. Only 2 percent mentioned technical skills and knowledge (CIO Canada, 1998:7).

The situation is the same south of the border. A study undertaken under the auspices of the National Center on Postsecondary Teaching, Learning, and Assessment found that American employers wanted many of the same soft skills as Canadian employers (Jones et al., 1994). More evidence of the importance of soft skills is found in the 1997 National Employer Survey conducted by the U.S. Bureau of the Census. In this study of 5,400 private companies with 20 or more employees, respondents were asked to rank on a five-point scale the type of things taken into consideration when making hiring decisions. The highest score, 4.6, was for the applicant's attitude. Communication skills ranked second with a score of 4.1. By contrast, academic performance scored only 2.5. The general belief is that while specific skills, like operating a computer, can be learned, it is much more difficult to teach employees generic skills, such as communication, and to promote the right attitudes.

Given the importance of soft skills that are in demand by employers, a study was undertaken at York University in Toronto to see if the university experience contributed to skill development. For the study, information was collected through surveys from students in four faculties: the Schulich School of Business, Arts, Fine Arts, and Pure and Applied Science.

The research indicates improvement in most soft skills between first year and graduation. For example, increases in analytic skills were 26, 22, 23, and 10 percentile points for graduates of Business, Arts, Fine Arts, and Science respectively. Communication skills increased 32 percentile points for students who had pursued a business program and 24, 22, and 20 percentile points for graduates of Arts, Fine Arts, and Science. While the personal skills of Fine Arts students did not increase over the course of their studies, the personal skills of Business students increased by 21 percentile points while those of Arts and Science students increased by 13 and 2 percentile points respectively. The organizing skills of Business graduates improved by 29 percentile points and those of Arts graduates increased 20 points. The gains in organizing skills of Fine Arts and Science students were 17 and 20 points respectively. The least improvement between first and graduating years was shown in comparative skills (i.e., the ability to compare Canada to other societies). Business graduates showed no increase in this area, the skill level of Fine Arts students actually declined by 3 points, and Science graduates increased only 1 percentile point. The greatest increase, 10 percentile points, was shown by Arts graduates. In the realm of basic numeracy skills, greatest improvements were shown by students in Fine Arts: 24 percentile points. Arts graduates improved 11 points, while Business and Science students each showed improvement of 4 percentile points. In computer skills, Business students showed an increase of 30 percentile points while the gains of Arts, Fine Arts, and Science students were 10, 15, and 25 percentile points respectively.

The findings show two things. First, over all faculties, there is an increase in soft skills between the first and graduating year. Second, increases in some skills are greater in some faculties than others (for more information see Grayson, 1999a and 1999b).

In order to see if the soft skills developed over the course of students' university careers had implications for future jobs, a second study was conducted focussing on job satisfaction, the degree to which students were able to get jobs related to their education, income, job security, and whether or not students had "healthy" jobs. Overall, it was shown that students with high organizing skills ended up with jobs they were satisfied with, thought that there was a close relationship between their education and their jobs, had relatively high incomes, and reported healthy jobs. Those with relatively high numeracy scores reported higher incomes than others, as did students with high computer scores (Grayson, 2001). Overall, the findings from the studies show two things. First, there is a general improvement in soft skills between first and graduating years. Second, consistent with our knowledge of what employers are looking for, certain soft skills had implications for various aspects of graduates' jobs. The message to students is clear. In addition to concentrating on the subject matter of your discipline, you should do whatever you can to improve your soft skills.

Success Strategies FOR SELF-DEVELOPMENT

Self-awareness
To build my current skills I have discovered that…

Self-confidence
One strategy I can use to increase my confidence so that I am able to overcome problems I may experience is . . .

Self-concept
To add to my current academic abilities I will…

Chapter Summary

Following up on the ideas presented in the previous chapter, Chapter 2 focuses on self-assessment exercises that will assist the student in identifying his/her competency levels in terms of self-confidence, academic self, and social self. The results of these tools provide a means for ability assessment, and indicate what needs to be done in order to prepare for future challenges.

Exercises

REFLECT–ACT

The following Reflect–Act exercises are designed to enhance your self-awareness and self-understanding through the process of reflective thinking, analysis, and productive action. These Reflect–Act exercises focus on the self-confidence and self-concept issues that are related to your success in your academic journey.

Reflect　University has been described as a place where students learn not so much about how to make a living, but how to make a life. How does this statement fit your educational goals?
Act　Describe the specific actions you will take this year to ensure that at the end of your first year you will be able to state that you are on target toward achieving your goals.

Reflect　If you could spend your life in your own way, how would you spend it?
Act　Describe three specific examples of actions you are currently taking that demonstrate your independence.

Reflect　The difference between what you are capable of becoming and what you have thus far become has been influenced by many factors. Identify two specific factors that have prevented you from developing to your potential. Identify three factors that have positively influenced you.
Act　Describe your plan for how you will use this information to support your achievement.

Reflect　An important part of becoming a successful student is being able to identify your strengths and your challenges.
Act　Go through each of the above scales and identify your strengths (high-scored

items without the asterisks) and your challenges (high-scored items with asterisks). Once you have identified these strengths and challenges, place them in an obvious spot and refer to them as you continue to read through the text. Your task now is to use the strategies in the following chapters to make the necessary changes for becoming a more successful student. To encourage change, ask your friends to keep you accountable on a weekly basis, to see whether you are still working at changing.

GROUP DISCUSSION

1. Each person in your group has their own definition of success in university. After each group member has provided their own definition of personal success as a university student, identify the common factors in these definitions.

2. One of the key ingredients that determine university success is the choices that students make. Identify some of the choices that students make that facilitate success and others that hinder success.

3. After group members have completed their self-assessment, each individual should identify five priorities for enhancing their self-confidence, academic self-concept, and social self-concept. Discuss and compare results. Determine any commonalities among the group members.

APPLY TO LIFE

Now that you have completed the questions included in the self-assessment, you can use this information to more clearly delineate your plans for making your university years personally successful. Use the following questions to guide your continued discovery and development of personal strategies that will make a difference for you now and in the future.

1. In which areas do I need to improve in order to feel more self-confident as a university student?

2. After analyzing the information about self-confidence, and academic and social self-concept, what can I do to improve my chances of success at university?

3. How will the actions I take now to improve my competencies affect my future?

Connections to the University Environment

chapter 3

The Truth shall set you free. John 8:32

Questions

How do I successfully journey through the academic culture of the university?

Are there important differences between university and high school?

Is there information available to help me expand my awareness of resources?

What are some important steps I can take to ensure my success in university?

Objectives

- To discover how a student fits into the university environment.
- To identify the cultural expectations of university.
- To recognize the resources available to students.
- To gain information on involvement.

Introduction of the University Culture

You've arrived. Standing at the edge of campus you notice that amidst the collection of old and new buildings are interesting places to eat, relax, study, buy supplies, and meet other students. A **university** is similar to a small town—with a variety of services to make your experience more enjoyable. After you walk around campus, find the location of your classes, and purchase your textbooks, you stop briefly for a coffee and the chance to catch your breath. As you glance around, you notice the differences between where you are and your old school. For the first time you realize that in many ways you are like a stranger in a new culture. Like any new visitor, you must learn to understand and appreciate this new academic culture. It is a culture of rich history, with unique and important traditions, and it is a culture that will place new demands on you.

As seen in the self-development model on page 45, being a successful student in a new academic environment requires self-awareness, self-confidence, and self-concept. The successful university student identity is created by knowing the academic culture, its values, and its expected behaviours. In your quest for success as a student, you begin with self-awareness by assessing your knowledge about the rich history of the university culture and the expectations required to be successful. Your responses to the "connection to others" and "connections to community" in Chapter 2 provide you with basic information about your ability to be a successful scholar. Self-confidence as a thinker is enhanced by attitudes of scholarship, and a desire to learn and be mentored. The development of your self-concept as a university student is influenced by both academic and social experiences. By investing time in understanding the history and the current cultural expectations of the university, you enhance your success as a student. By taking the initiative to access the various resources available to you, as well as to engage in networking, you further develop your social self and thereby strengthen your university student self-concept. As you progress through this chapter, become aware of how successful students respond to the new academic environment. By identifying and celebrating the skills you have that overlap with theirs, and adopting those that you have not fully developed, you can strengthen your capabilities as a new university student.

In order to fit into the university environment, you need to be aware that you are in a new culture. This culture presents you with a new set of demands that are similar to those placed on a foreigner entering a new culture, such as new ways of thinking, acting, and feeling. Most cultures have a rich history or a tradition that dictates how one thinks, acts, and feels. As you enter the new university culture, there are a variety of ways to respond.

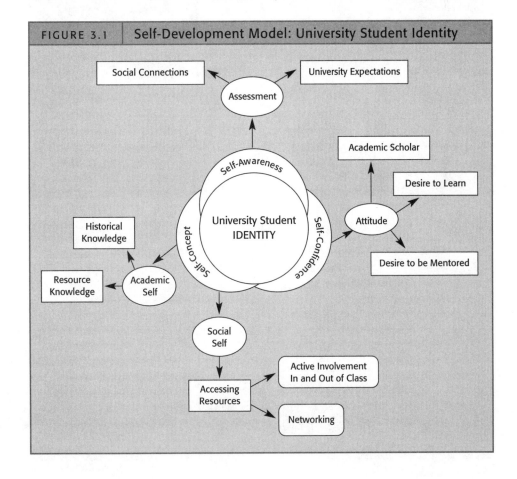

FIGURE 3.1 | Self-Development Model: University Student Identity

Either you are prepared and ready to accommodate these new expectancies, or you are unprepared, overwhelmed, and unwilling to attempt to adapt to this foreign culture. Most students are totally unaware of the nature of the culture they are about to enter, and have no previous experience with university. They assume that university is just like high school. This assumption causes problems for many students because the differences

TABLE 3.1	High School versus University	
Attribute	High School	University
Environment	high structure	low structure
Academic community	community-based	international
Atmosphere	interpersonal	competitive
Age	14–18	16–60+
Class size	20–40	100–600 (in first year)
Lessons	activity-based	lecture-based
Teacher role	authority	expert
Teacher profession	educator	authority in the field
Learner	child	adult/peer/junior colleague
Learner work-style	dependent	independent
Student body	intellectually heterogeneous	intellectually homogeneous
Academic year	10 months	8 months
Content	easier/smaller amount	complex/larger amount
Pacing	slower	faster
Workload	specified by teacher	unspecified by professor
Learning location	mostly in-class	mostly out-of-class
Course outline	not essential	essential
Discipline	teacher's responsibility	up to individual students
Autonomy	low	high
Grading policy	marks	curve
Feedback	high frequency	low frequency
Interaction	teacher initiates contact	student expected to initiate
Use of resources	minimal expectation	high expectation
Reward system	based on teaching	based on scholarship
Academics	limited subjects	wide variety
Cost	none	$3000+
Schedule	fixed	make your own
Responsibilities	dependent	independence
Class size	smaller	larger
Structure	more focused	more lecture time
Time	8:30a.m. – 3:30p.m.	15 hours, plus labs
Campus	small	larger
Atmosphere	more friendly; less friendly	less friendly; more friendly
Individual	name	number

between university and high school, as seen in Table 3.1, demand that students respond differently. Those who journey successfully through this new academic culture understand and make the best of these differences.

How can you learn about the expectations of the academic culture? One of the best ways to identify how you can be prepared is by developing an awareness of the culture, and talking with others who have successfully travelled this path, adjusted to the academic culture, and reached their destination of academic success. What follows is an overview of the academic culture, beginning with the origin of the university culture and ending with the current culture at many Canadian universities. Academic expectations of the university culture are then defined in terms of the six stages of cognitive development. Next follows an exploration of the resources available to the academic traveller that make the journey more enjoyable, more economical, and more secure. Finally, this chapter will uncover the importance of becoming immersed in the academic culture.

Origin of the Academic Culture

There are various claims to the first university, Nalanda university in India (c. 500; Britannica Encyclopaedia, 2001), Salerno in Italy—as the first medical school (c. 900), Bologna as the first school of canon and civil law and Paris as the first school of theology (c. 1200; Marsh, 2000). Historically, institutions of education have been the centres for nations attempting to realize their social and spiritual ideals (Duggan, 1948). As such, the university is seen as a community that devotes itself to the "unremitting pursuit of the highest knowledge" (Baillie, as cited in Seeley, 1948, p. 4). In other words, the university is a society or a community, and together, its members are in the pursuit of knowledge "in order that one may have a better understanding of life, and one's attitude toward it" (Seeley, 1948, p. 13). On many cornerstones of university buildings, and on many of the university seals or logos are Latin inscriptions that refer to the inquiry of Truth. An accompanying symbol to many of these inscriptions is that of an open book, often referring to one of the key passages in the Bible, "The Truth shall set you free" (John 8:32). This quest for Truth has been central in many institutions. Most university traditions find their origins in one of two ideals: by passing on traditional knowledge as seen in many Eastern institutions, or in the securing of new knowledge, as prevalent in many of the Western institutions (Duggan, 1948).

Common to both traditions, though, is the method by which students are educated—the mentoring process. In Greek mythology, mentoring refers back to a friend of Odysseus entrusted with the education of Odysseus' son Telemachus. Today it refers to a trusted counsellor, guide, tutor, or coach (Merriam-Webster, 1986). Various historical accounts illustrate this teacher-student relationship: Socrates mentored Plato and Xenophon; Plato mentored Aristotle; Jesus mentored 12 disciples; Mohammed mentored his followers; and Buddha mentored his supporters (Duggan, 1948). Some of your professors have also been mentored by well-known scholars such as Carl Rogers (psychology), Karl Marx (political science), Albert Einstein (physics and mathematics), David Suzuki (environment), Marshall McLuhan (technology and culture), and Northrop Frye (education). This tradition still continues today.

Based on the mentoring method, colleges and universities developed during the Middle Ages to educate men, and only recently women (1870), in theology, law, and medicine. Some of the most well-known universities include Oxford, Cambridge, and Paris (all founded in the 12th century), Salamanca (c.1230), Prague (1348), Vienna (1365), Uppsala (1477), Santo Domingo in the Dominican Republic (1538), Mexico (1551), San Marcos in

Lima (1551), Leiden (1575), and Moscow (1755). Most of these were established by religious or royal initiatives. Some universities, like Oxford, were founded by students (Marsh, 2000).

History of Canadian Academic Culture

The oldest university in Canada is the University of Dalhousie, founded 1818 by George Ramsay, the 9th Earl of Dalhousie (Dalhousie University, 2001). Based on a university in Scotland, he desired an accessible college that adhered to the principles of religious toleration (Dalhousie University, 2001). Religion has had a major influence in the development of most Canadian universities (Sheehan, 1985). For instance, the University of Manitoba, the oldest university in Western Canada, was founded by three religious institutions in 1877—St. Boniface College (Roman Catholic); St. John's College (Anglican); and Manitoba College (Presbyterian). Over the next few decades, various major universities were established across Canada. The trend still continues. Just recently, a new university found its beginning through the amalgamation of three religious colleges: Menno Simons College, Concord College, and the Canadian Mennonite Bible College have joined to form the Canadian Mennonite University (see www.cmu.ca). Today, there are over 167 institutions of higher education across Canada (see www.uwaterloo.ca/canu/ for a complete listing).

Current Canadian Academic Culture

Since 1911, a number of universities and colleges in Canada have united to create the Association of Universities and Colleges in Canada (AUCC: www.aucc.ca/dcu/). The membership ranges from small, undergraduate liberal arts institutions to large, multi-campus universities offering a broad selection of undergraduate, graduate, and professional programs. Although each institution has its unique community, most have similar academic cultures with similar expectations of their students. One of the best ways to understand the academic culture and its accompanying expectations at your college or university is to be familiar with the philosophy, mission statement, and goals of the institution. For most Canadian universities and colleges, these are fairly similar.

Philosophy Statements

These are important to universities. A philosophy statement clarifies what a university stands for, provides rationale for its existence, guides its operation, and organizes the evaluation of its teaching. Common among the major AUCC institutions' philosophy statements are the following ideals: to serve, to educate, to enlighten, and to advance knowledge. For instance, one Canadian university's philosophy statement is as follows. "The University of Calgary is a place of education and scholarly inquiry. Its mission is to seek Truth and disseminate knowledge. Our aim is to pursue this mission with integrity for the benefit of the people of Alberta, Canada, and the world" (2001).

Mission Statements

Mission statements are also significant to universities, as they define the specific tasks that are to be carried out. The mission statement of many AUCC institutions focuses on creating, preserving, and disseminating knowledge, first for those in the immediate surroundings of the university, and then to those farther away. For example, the Memorial University of Newfoundland's mission statement is "to develop in the province an institution of higher learning deserving of respect for the quality of its academic standards and of its research; to establish new programmes to meet the expanding needs of the province; and to provide the means whereby the University may reach out to all the people" (2001).

Goal Statements

Goals provide the institutions with direction. In-depth clues about a given academic culture can be extracted from an institution's goals. Here again there are various similarities among the AUCC institutions. These include providing excellence in teaching, enhancing intellectual and personal growth, conducting creative works (i.e., from research to music compositions), serving the community, ensuring academic freedom and intellectual independence, and promoting equity in access. For example, the University of Manitoba states the following goals: provide the highest possible quality of teaching; enhance student success by fostering an environment conducive to intellectual and personal growth; conduct original scholarship and basic and applied research, and produce creative works of highest quality as judged by international standards; serve the community directly by making its expertise available to individuals and institutions, and by providing as much access to the University's intellectual, cultural, artistic, and physical resources as its primary teaching and research responsibilities permit; preserve and protect academic freedom and intellectual independence, and provide a forum for critical inquiry and debate; and, promote equity in access and employment and in the conduct of the University's affairs (University of Manitoba, 2002, p. 5).

Students' Code of Responsibilities

Guided by a philosophy, a mission, and a set of goals, each institution has a set of expectations of their students, usually referred to as the Students' Code of Responsibilities. These codes include a commitment of all its members to the "advancement of learning, the dissemination of knowledge, and the well being of all its members" (University of Manitoba, 2002, p. 75). A set of equally important values defines how the commitments are to be carried out by all members, including students. For instance, University of Brock students "may think, speak, write, create, study, learn, pursue social, cultural, and other interests, and associate together for these purposes subject to the principles of mutual respect for the dignity, worth, and rights of others ..." (Office of the Registrar, 2001). Another includes the "affirmation of the dignity, worth, and equality of all citizens in the community; the importance of reasoned debate and inquiry in all academic pursuits; and the practice of ethical conduct and personal integrity in all aspects of academic life" (University of Manitoba, 2002, p. 75).

As members of the academic community, students and scholars alike need to be open and accepting of others' views, yet critical about what is accepted as Truth; to be motivated by the desire to know more while creating new works and giving credit where credit is due. Most institutions give further detail about each of the above in Student Handbooks. A good understanding of the handbook helps students understand the expectations that each institution has of them.

The academic culture of the university as defined by its philosophy, mission statement, goals, and students' code of responsibilities, is a culture of knowledge acquisition and the rendering of service. As potential academicians, students are mentored in the pursuit of knowledge and taught competencies that they are expected to use personally and professionally to benefit themselves. In turn, students are expected to use their knowledge in ways to further both the immediate and more global community. The following sections will focus on how universities strive to develop the aspiring academician and how students are expected to give back to the learning process.

Developing Academicians: Becoming a Student Scholar

One of the main goals of the university enterprise is to train **academicians**. Academicians, often referred to as scholars, are the members of an academy that promote the discovery and dissemination of Truth. This includes attempting to make sense of the universe that we live in, and identifying the laws that govern how the world and all that exists within it works. Medical academics search for new cures for diseases; botanists look for new strains of disease-resistant plants; engineers test new materials for supporting large structures; political scientists grapple with new ways to run a country; educators uncover effective strategies for learning and mastering new knowledge; and historians reveal the interactive factors that undermine civilizations. As a student you are also expected to develop the competencies of the scholar. One of the goals of the student scholar is to search for Truth by mastering a specific knowledge area, becoming a self-disciplined learner, and developing the skills of a critical thinker.

Development of the Academic

As seen in the Self-Development Model on page 45, your development as a university student requires your active participation in both in-class and out-of-class activities. As you actively involve yourself in the learning environment provided by lectures, discussion, seminars, field research, mentoring, apprenticeships, leadership activities, work placements, and extracurricular activities, you will add to your academic and social self-concept as well as your thinking capabilities. As you develop, you will add significantly to your cognitive capabilities.

According to Bloom (1956), cognitive development spans across a continuum, beginning with the acquisition of new information or knowledge and ending with the evaluation of complex thought. As seen in Table 3.2, for many students, this process involves six stages. Students tend to advance cognitively from the very first day of classes through to graduation, beginning with concrete thoughts and ending with abstract thoughts. For the transference of knowledge to occur between the master and the student, many mentors or professors follow Bloom's cognitive taxonomy (1956). They design their courses and even their assignments and test questions to reflect these developmental stages. You can enhance your own cognitive development by more clearly understanding **Bloom's taxonomy**.

Knowledge

Your cognitive journey begins as you enter your first-year courses. Mentors or professors view you at best as neophytes, as potential scholars or novices in the discipline. Your

TABLE 3.2	Bloom's Levels of Cognitive Development	
Level	Process	Type of Performance
	Abstract	
6. Evaluation		Capable of making a critical judgment based on internal and external criteria.
5. Synthesis		Capable of accomplishing a personal task after devising a plan of action.
4. Analysis		Capable of identifying the elements, relationships, and organizational principles of a situation.
3. Application		Capable of remembering knowledge or principles in order to solve a problem.
2. Comprehension		Capable of transposing, interpreting, and extrapolating from a certain body of knowledge.
1. Knowledge		Capable of recalling words, facts, dates, conventions, classifications, principles, theories, etc.
	Concrete	

Based on B.S. Bloom (1956). *Taxonomy of Educational Objectives.* New York, NY: David McKay.

knowledge base is limited and requires extensive factual information about a given area. It is like learning a new language. Becoming an expert in the area requires you to know how to speak and think in that language. First-year courses tend to reflect the learning of a new language, but in an intensive format. You will be exposed to many new words, including technical jargon representative of the discipline; historical development of the discipline; the important scholars in the field and their theories; and the discipline's current ways of thinking, reading, writing, and conducting research. You enter Bloom's first stage. As seen in the preceding table, you have entered the "knowledge" zone. At this level, you are expected to learn and know the basic facts about the discipline. Your first-year textbooks are filled with introductory information providing you with the background that you need in order to advance as a scholar in the field. You receive countless facts and details about the discipline in your lectures. Your assignments and exams test you to ensure that you are capable of recalling terminology, specific facts, dates, conventions, classifications, principles, generalizations, theories, trends, sequences, classifications, categories, structures, criteria, methodology, and names of VIPs representative of the discipline. Other testable items include how well you can distinguish between facts and opinions; how well you can recognize stereotypes, over-generalizations, bias, emotional factors, propaganda, value orientations and ideologies; and how well you can determine what information is relevant. What better way to test all this than a multiple-choice exam where you are asked to repeat information with few or no changes?

Comprehension

First- and second-year courses also engage you in an understanding of the basic discipline's knowledge—stage two of Bloom's taxonomy. As a student you are exposed to various significant theories with the expectation of being able to understand their basic premises. You are expected to be capable of transposing, translating, interpreting, and extrapolating from a certain body of knowledge. This would be similar to being able to translate from one language to another. You are taught how to identify or specify the problem and unstated assumptions. You are able to define and clarify a thesis or position statement, to identify central issues or problems, and to express claims clearly and concisely. Here your assignments and exams will be based on how well you understand ideas and are able to use rules and follow directions. Exams testing your comprehension level will tend to be multiple choice, as well as short answer and essay responses.

Application

Although this is a more common expectation among second- and third-year courses, some professors are keen to help students develop application abilities in their first year. Application involves using the content information from your textbooks and classes in order to solve a problem. You will be tested on your ability to use information in specific and concrete situations, to be able to identify reasonable alternatives, to infer reasonable conclusions from evidence and to formulate appropriate questions. Although less common, some multiple-choice tests challenge your ability to apply knowledge to a new situation. But for the most part, your ability to apply knowledge to novel situations will be tested through short answers or essay-type questions.

Analysis

Once you have mastered the ability to remember important information, have a good understanding of the material, and are able to apply it to solve problems, you can analyze how things work. You have entered the "analysis" zone. Here you will be trained to identify the elements, relationships, and organizational principles of a situation. You can recognize similarities and differences, test conclusions or hypotheses, distinguish between evidences or reasons for a conclusion, and the conclusions drawn from the evidence. A good test of this level of thinking would be in how well you are able to see relationships between ideas, how well you can break information into parts, and how well you analyze how things work.

Synthesis

The expectations now turn from basic knowledge, comprehension, application, and analysis of information in the discipline, to creating new ideas. As implied by the word "synthesis," you are expected to produce unique communication (whether written or oral), in the form of a plan, a proposed set of operations, a derivation of a set of abstract relations, or a prediction of probable consequences of a belief or course of action. You focus on solving problems and drawing conclusions. You will be putting ideas and information about your discipline together in a unique way. Here, your efforts will focus on your creative ability to take old ideas and synthesize them into new theories, solutions, and conclusions. A good test of your ability to synthesize material will come in writing major research papers, or through the potential of conducting new research. For many students, the ideas generated at this level are continued on into a graduate program. For instance, an interest in stress and coronary heart disease may become your thesis project in graduate school.

Evaluation

As seen in Table 3.2, evaluation is the final frontier of Bloom's taxonomy. It is the stage where you begin to assume many of the responsibilities as a master of the discipline. You have attained the expert level. You know the content area inside and out. You are able to see the weaknesses in ideas and theories. Your critical thinking skills are at a point where you can make judgments about the content material. You are capable of making critical judgments and assessing the value of information in your discipline based on internal and external criteria. You are able to judge information related to a thesis or position statement. You have the skill to evaluate advantages and disadvantages of alternatives, and to assess the relevance and adequacy of data, and all conclusions drawn. Here tasks will focus on how well you can make judgments. At this point, you will be able to train others and provide leadership in your discipline. This may take place in teaching, research, or laboratory assistantships.

Bloom's cognitive development stages will be repeated throughout your academic journey. As you increase in your knowledge of Truth, you will have opportunities to apply what you learned by helping others, both in class and outside of class. Mentorship might include becoming a student mentor, peer tutor/adviser, and involvement in undergraduate research. In doing so, you complete the cycle of the university's mandate: to promote the discovery and dissemination of Truth.

In addition to developing your skills as a scholar, you will also be developing your career competencies. Becoming an educated person is more than learning information and developing cognitive skills. Educated people also develop their interpersonal, social, creative, problem-solving, and aesthetic skills. As you learn about the opportunities and resources that are available on your campus, you will be better able to involve yourself in in-class and out-of-class activities that will add to your development as an educated person.

Resourcing the Aspiring Academic

In order to ensure the success of developing academicians, Canadian universities and colleges provide various resources for both personal and professional development. As a new scholar, gaining access to these resources can be the difference between succeeding and not succeeding in this new culture.

Personal Development

Your personal development is as critical to your success as a university student as is your cognitive development. In fact, for most students, their most significant learning occurred outside the classroom (Astin, 1997; Kuh, 1993). Thus institutions spend millions of dollars to ensure that resources supporting the various aspects of personal development are available and accessible to students. The activities and resources that can assist you in developing personally are often located in divisions named Student Affairs or Student Services. These services are organized differently on various campuses but tend to fall into the following domains: cognitive, physical, psychological, social, spiritual, and financial.

Cognitive Probably the most overlooked cognitive resources are the classroom, the teacher, and fellow students. The classroom is the place where cognitive stimulation of ideas is generated. Successful students tend to be the ones who have high attendance. Access to teachers and their assistants are two other key resources successful students rely on. Many teachers provide office hours to meet one-on-one with students. Teaching assistants, laboratory assistants, tutors, peer educators, advisers, and mentors are also resourceful people, especially given their recent completion of the course. Again, successful students make use of these individuals on a weekly basis, usually seeking answers to their questions and strategies on how to read, study, complete assignments, and prepare for exams. Finally, your peers in the classroom are also an invaluable resource. Successful students work with other students, sharing notes and solutions to assignments, and forming study groups. In times of illness or family difficulty, your peers become invaluable in keeping you informed about the classes and assignments missed.

Another valuable yet less-known resource is the Honour's Program. Students who have demonstrated high levels of academic performance in their first two years of studies can participate in an accelerated program with smaller classes and, often, better teachers. Mentoring is prevalent in these smaller classes and students have direct access to the experts in the discipline. Most Honour's students successfully enter graduate school because of the intense, mentored training program. Many professional connections are made with the teachers in the Honour's Program that allow for future referrals to well-known mentors or graduate supervisors in national and international graduate schools.

Given the various learning challenges that students face when entering higher education, universities have invested in Learning Assistance and English as Second Language Centres. These centres help students identify their learning strengths and weaknesses. Various resources are available to enhance the learning of most students. Disadvantaged due to past experiences, many students find a new freedom through these resources and successfully achieve their dreams of completing a degree in higher education.

One of the more visible resources on many university campuses is the library. Known to many only as a storehouse of information, the library also provides many other resources. These include workshops on conducting on-line research, developing research skills, and referencing material. Active participation in many of these resources yields varied, successful, and efficient research skills.

Physical   A healthy mind is often fueled by a healthy body and thus, your physical well-being should also be of importance. Various resources are available to help you sustain a healthy body. These include medical, dental, athletic therapy, fitness, recreational, and nutritional resources. Recreational and competitive sports, in both individual and team venues, are an excellent way to maintain physical well-being while nurturing relationships with others who participate in sports. Facilities are also available to encourage the physical well-being of students. These can include gymnasiums, swimming pools, indoor and outdoor tracks, weightlifting equipment, specialized courts, and ice arenas.

Psychological   Each person comes to the academic culture as a unique individual with various psychological needs. Counselling Services helps individuals discover their potentials and challenges, come to terms with past and current issues that may be adversely affecting their academic program, and modify ineffective behaviours, thoughts, and feelings to more effective ones (i.e., test anxiety, self-confidence, etc.). Student Development offices, Testing Centres, and Student Disability Services ensure that all students receive the best possible access to learning, regardless of their challenges.

Spiritual   Many successful students also find meaning in equipping their souls as well as their minds. As the centre of one's values and beliefs, the soul needs stimulation, and many campuses provide various resources for students to develop spiritually. Many of the larger campuses have representation from various religious groups, including different spiritual mentors or chaplains. Spiritual awareness is promoted through open, formal debates, in ecumenical activities, in representation from most major religious groups, through group and individual mentoring, and in places of individual and group meditation or worship.

Social   A vital part of university life is community, the interaction of academics on a social level. Various university resources support social interaction. Of significance are residences and residence life. Other resources are significant in ensuring the successful integration of different types of students into the community (i.e., international, first year, native, women, gay/lesbian/bisexual, etc.). Special interest groups focusing on women's issues, environmental issues, and peace issues are invaluable resources to students on many campuses. When difficulties arise between members of the community, the Student Advocacy Office can provide excellent mediation.

Financial   Many students are concerned about their financial resources. Here too, the university provides valuable information on financial assistance such as scholarships, bursaries, and student loans. Successful students have access to these resources in order to find means of support and/or sponsorship for their education.

Successful students are those who use many of the above resources to enhance their journey through the academic culture. As an aspiring academic, you also have various resources to choose from to help you develop personally in the cognitive, physical, psychological, social, spiritual, and financial domains. Each resource has the potential to strengthen your abilities to successfully achieve your goal of graduating with a degree. However, graduates are not true academics if they have not been professionally developed in the process of mentoring. Hence, many academic institutions also invest in the development of mentors.

Professional Development

Aspiring academics not only have access to resources for personal development but also to those for professional development. These include communication, career enhancement, computer technology, and administrative skills. All these skills are critical in the development of effective mentors. Student Affairs or Student Services provides many of these resources.

Communication   There are various resources on campus to help improve you communication skills. These include English as Second Language Centres, Toastmasters, and a variety of conferences where students are invited to speak. These resources focus on encouraging students to enhance their public speaking skills.

Career   An institution would not be complete without a Career Centre. Here you are able to meet with trained counsellors who can help guide your decisions for seasonal employment, employment related to your discipline, work-experience employment, as well as your future direction for a professional career. Some institutions also provide alumni mentors for students interested in specific professions. The alumni nurture and encourage students in academic development toward the acquisition of a professional position.

Computer technology   In a world of increasing computer technology, learning no longer occurs only in the classroom. Virtual learning environments are becoming more popular. Successful students strive to become computer literate. Here again, academic communities provide various resources. As a student, you have access to computer labs, training in various software applications (e.g., MS Word, WordPerfect, SYSTAT, etc.), and access to various online courses from professionals around the world. New technology promises to make communication and research more efficient. Academic institutions are challenged with keeping their members fully trained or qualified to meet the demands of this new technology.

Administration   Administrative skills are also an important component of an academic's life. Here, institutions provide various opportunities to help you acquire these skills. Students are invited to participate in various academic committees. These include search committees for new faculty, academic policy committees for making decisions on academic protocols, and a variety of positions in student government (e.g., student council, president, etc.). Many successful leaders in the community have actively participated at various levels in university committees.

Professional development in the areas of communication, career enhancement, computer technology, and administrative skills, is critical for aspiring academics. These professional development opportunities on campus provide valuable resources for your future as an academic. See how well you can identify these resources by doing the exercise "Discovering the University Resources." With these skills, you can more effectively mentor future students, whether in the traditional classroom, workplace environment, community, or home.

Exercise 3.1 DISCOVERING THE UNIVERSITY RESOURCES

Becoming a successful university student involves developing an awareness of the university community, people, policies, resources, and traditions. This assignment will help you develop an initial awareness of the roles, functions, and services of some of the university offices as well as some of the rules and regulations that are important for your success. A secondary goal of this exercise is to begin to develop a cooperative learning style with a fellow member of your class. In addition to discovering the answers to these problems, you are to work collaboratively with this individual and get to know more about each other in the process. Visit the offices that will most effectively solve the problems presented and gather additional information about how these resources help students succeed at university. The *General Calendar* and the *Student Handbook–Rulebook* will be useful resources. Also check your university's Web pages.

Student Problems

1. Raffi is a lonely first-year student who has been at the university for five months. He has decided that he wants to join a club related to his interests in ecology. Where can he find out about a relevant club?

2. In your textbooks you have read that one of the keys to becoming a successful university student is to get involved in the university community. Where can you discover what activities and organizations are available on campus?

3. Your friend is hearing impaired. He has been covering up and compensating for this problem, but is finding that it is no longer feasible to do so because his university courses are all lecture. He has only recently admitted to you that he has a problem and is requesting your help.

4. You began university thinking that your career goal was medicine. You are enrolled in the science courses and have received only average grades. You are now questioning whether it is the right goal for you, and are wondering about other possible career options that would be more appropriate for you. Where do you go for assistance?

5. As a first-year student you have experimented with relationships and different lifestyles. For the past six weeks you have been feeling sluggish, tired, unable to concentrate, and are reluctant to go to your family doctor. You have recently read that these symptoms may be related to a physical illness and are wondering how serious your problem may be. Where can you get the answers and help you need?

6. Jan is a first-year student who finds university to be quite overwhelming. She needs to talk to someone about her confusion and the adjustment to university. Jan is quite shy and feels uncomfortable about approaching older adults. She would prefer to talk to another student to get some advice about how to cope with school. Who can Jan approach for help?

7. Susan's instructor accuses her of plagiarism on a term paper, charging that she has taken ideas from a recognized authority without giving a proper acknowledgment. Susan has never read the reference; she tries in vain to convince the instructor, but the instructor is adamant and indicates that a suspension is forthcoming. Who can help Susan defend herself?

Cultural Immersion Involvement in the University World

Immersing a person in a new culture is not a new idea. Many programs have successfully graduated students in foreign languages through intense immersion programs. Students who fully immerse themselves in the academic culture and partake in a variety of the personal and professional development resources are also more likely to be successful at university. The testimonies of students who have gone before you vividly demonstrate that involvement in the university environment is a key component of university success.

Many studies of university undergraduates (Astin, 1997; Pascarella & Terenzini, 1991) have shown that the greater the student's involvement in the culture of the university, the greater the learning and personal development (Astin, 1997). As students participate more actively in the university experience, and increase the amount of time spent in out-of-class and in-class activities, they increase their cognitive and emotional growth (Astin, 1997). Those students who are more involved in the university community achieve higher grades, are more satisfied with their educational experience, and are more likely to graduate.

Two of the most potent forms of involvement (Astin, 1993; Astin, 1997) are faculty-student involvement and student-student (i.e., peer group) involvement. The more you talk to your professors, the greater your learning and development. In the lecture atmosphere of the university, it is important for you to take the effort to get to know your professors. Seek them out. Introduce yourself. Ask questions. Participate actively in your courses, enjoy oral presentations, critical reviews, field studies, and cooperative learning assignments, as they are critical in ensuring that you are academically integrated into the intellectual life of the university (Grayson, 1994). Too many students take their peers for granted. Surprisingly, the single strongest source of influence on cognitive and affective development is a student's peer group. Some peer activities are more personally productive than others. According to the research by Astin (1997), a number of peer group activities that most positively influence students' academic success are participation in residence-life programs, involvement in peer mentoring or advising programs, and participation in academically focused clubs (e.g., geography club, environmental society, Oxfam student group).

Through your participation in the classroom environment and interactions with professors outside of class, you learn more than the course content. You develop abilities to conceptualize, solve technical and analytical problems, organize your assignments and manage your time. They enhance your knowledge, refine literacy skills, develop critical thinking capabilities, increase your global awareness and help you gain an appreciation of various forms of inquiry. However, the primary source for students to develop self-confidence, risk-taking, stress management, responsibility, social skills, political and social awareness, leadership/influence (Astin, 1997), concern and caring for others, and creativity was through "out-of-class activities" (Evers & Gilbert, 1991). For 90 percent of students, half of the important information and abilities they gained as a result of their university education resulted from their participation in extracurricular activities. For 40 percent of students, extracurricular activities provided the opportunity for their most significant educational experiences (Moffat as cited in Kuh, 1993).

In reflecting on their university experience, graduating students have reported that their participation in extracurricular experiences impacted on their learning and personal development in several distinctive ways. Their view was that involvement in extracurricular activities added to their self-confidence, self-directedness, self-awareness, and sense of purpose in their lives. They described being better able to think critically and to appreciate disparate opinions and perspectives. Because they had increased their appreciation of cultural, racial, and ethnic backgrounds they reported feeling more sensitive to the needs of others and better able to work with people whose value systems or life views differ from their own. They believed that the practical experiences of their extracurricular activities prepared them to be better able to manage their personal affairs and be economically self-sufficient. Through these activities they developed the attitudes and aptitudes to become contributing members of their community (Kuh, 1993).

Both Astin (1993, 1997) and Tinto (1993) have provided significant research evidence demonstrating the relationship between involvement and persistence. Along with their colleagues, they have demonstrated a clear progression between students' increased involvement and connection to the university community with an improved quality of effort by students to learn and persist. Activities that negatively affected students' success and development were activities that removed them physically from the university environment, such as working off campus, employment, commuting, and athletic involvements (Astin, 1997).

Take the challenge and immerse yourself in the new academic culture. Take advantage of as many of the resources offered by the institution as possible. In doing so, you will gain more than an education.

As a beneficiary of all that an education has to offer, students are expected to recompense their experience by sharing it with others. In other words, what you gain needs to be shared with others. In sharing with others, the experience of journeying through the academic culture becomes most meaningful and enriching. It is here that the most important element of education is initiated—the mentoring of others. The heart of the mentor awakens and takes shape in various forms such as becoming a tutor for first-year students, leading others through student council, becoming a student ambassador, making the public aware of a social issue, sharing your athletic abilities with others, and mentoring through Big Brothers/Big Sisters. It is your opportunity to share with others what you have learned. It is a chance to apply your learning in practical ways to help the community, both locally and globally.

Above all, sharing with others strengthens the learning that occurs in the classroom. It solidifies the abstract thoughts of the classroom into concrete and applicable solutions for the many challenges of our world. Mentoring others not only helps others; it also reinforces what you have learned. As seen in Figure 3.2, teaching others provides the highest form of retention of information (Briggs, 1999).

Passive Bystander or Active Traveller

As you embark on your journey through the academic culture, you have the choice of being a passive bystander and watching the academic culture unfold in front of you, or you can actively participate in a culture filled with incredible resources. Be prepared by knowing what to expect. As a result, your journey will be much more meaningful, your interaction with the culture more insightful, and your travelling experience more life-changing as a result. It is your choice. You can take control of your learning environment or allow it to control you.

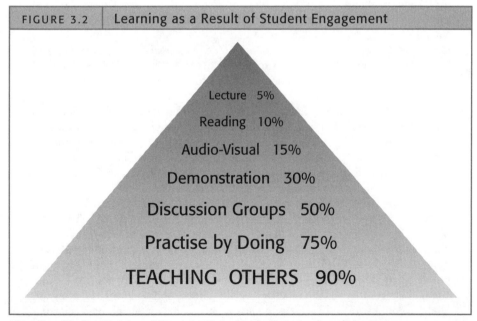

| FIGURE 3.2 | Learning as a Result of Student Engagement |

Lecture 5%

Reading 10%

Audio-Visual 15%

Demonstration 30%

Discussion Groups 50%

Practise by Doing 75%

TEACHING OTHERS 90%

Adapted from "The Best Way To Learn," Biggs, J. (1999). *Teaching for Quality Learning at University.*

It's More Than Common Sense

Canadian Research on the Academic Culture of the First-Year Student

Rodney A. Clifton, Ph.D.
University of Manitoba

I'm a sociologist and we are interested in how groups function and the way people progress, either effectively or ineffectively, from group to group. In your lives, no doubt you have realized that the groups you joined increased in complexity and size. Daycare centres are relatively small and simple but generally larger and more complex than families. In turn, early years schools (grades 1 to 4) are larger than daycare centres; middle years schools (grades 5 to 8) are even larger; and senior years schools (grades 9 to 12) are larger yet. As you discovered recently, universities, with thousands of students, are larger and more complex than schools. Because of this, we should ensure that the transition students make from school to university is relatively easy.

Even though it was a long time ago, I will never forget my experience in Introductory Sociology during my first year at the University of Alberta. During the first lecture in the course, my professor explained the course outline, as I expected. As I did not expect, she seemed to have little understanding of me and the other students in the class. She never asked about our lives, where we came from, or what we planned to do in our careers. In fact, our professor did not seem to care much about us! As far as we could see, she never applied this important sociological principle—a principle she taught in her course—to her own course; she never considered the transition we were making from high school to university.

With barely an acknowledgment of our existence, our professor began explaining the things that we were required to do in the course. One of the most troubling was to write a term paper, worth 50 percent of the final grade, on "The Nature of Humankind." At that time, I had no idea what a term paper was, few ideas about how to write one, and very little understanding of the nature of humankind. My professor did not explain any of these things and she did not put an example of a good term paper in the library for me to read. So much for making my transition to university easy!

Now, 35 years later, I have a much better understanding of students and universities. Specifically, if you think about term papers using Bloom's taxonomy (as presented starting on page 50), you realize that good term papers synthesize the literature within a discipline. In the example, the professor was asking her students to synthesize the literature on a very complicated topic before they had much understanding of the basic concepts in the discipline.

Over the years, my scholarly work has led me to believe that courses should be more closely designed on the basis of Bloom's taxonomy of educational objectives. As a consequence, I think that a major objective of first-year courses, particularly in Education, Humanities, and Social Sciences, should be to help students use the lower levels of understanding in Bloom's taxonomy: to know, comprehend, and apply the major concepts in the disciplines. Senior courses, in turn, should help students use the higher levels of understanding in the taxonomy: to analyze, synthesize, and evaluate the arguments and evidence in the disciplines.

Thus, term papers are appropriate in senior courses, and not in introductory courses before students have a good understanding of the basic concepts.

My work suggests that for professors to be effective teachers, particularly for first-year students, they need to have five distinctive qualities. First, good teachers need to be empathetic toward their students. Good professors consider where their students come from and where they plan to go. Second, good teachers need to design their courses to build on their students' strengths while recognizing their weaknesses. Third, good teachers need to be well organized. In first-year courses specifically, professors need to lead students into knowing, comprehending, and applying the basic concepts in logical and coherent ways. Fourth, good teachers need to demand good work from students. Specifically, they need to set their expectations just above their students' performances so that their minds are continually stretched to higher levels of understanding. Finally, good teachers need to be enthusiastic about their discipline and they need to speak clearly and concisely so that their students are drawn into a broad and deep understanding of the discipline.

My colleagues and I have characterized teachers with these qualities as warm-demanders; they are warm because they are empathetic toward their students and they are demanding because they hold high expectations for them. We have contrasted these teachers with sentimentalists (warm-nondemanders), traditionalists (cold-demanders), and sophisticates (cold-nondemanders) (see Clifton and Roberts, 1993, 78-102). Good examples of warm and demanding teachers are illustrated, albeit for schools and not for universities, in the movies *Dangerous Minds* (1995), *Mr. Holland's Opus* (1995), and *Stand and Deliver* (1987). As an enjoyable exercise, watch the videos to see truly exceptional teachers at work.

As the title of this essay says, surviving in university is more than common sense. My advice to you, particularly if you are in first year, is to study with warm, articulate, well-organized, and demanding professors. If you do, you will enjoy your courses much more, you will understand the basic concepts much better, and your transition to university will be much smoother.

Success Strategies FOR SELF-DEVELOPMENT

Self-awareness
As I leave the land of familiarity (e.g., high school, home community, friends, etc.) and enter the academic world, I am aware of …

Self-confidence
One strategy I can use to increase my confidence so that I am able to make new friends at university is …

Self-concept
To add to my current academic abilities, I will make myself aware of the following university resources available to students …

Chapter Summary

University is a culture with its own resources, philosophy, goals, and challenges. In this chapter, you were introduced to the university culture and how you can most effectively assimilate yourself by taking a proactive approach to your place in this new environment. In order to do so, you must be aware of and willing to expand upon your academic, social, physical, and spiritual development. Helpful tips have been provided to assist you in getting the most out of your academic learning experience. By meeting the demands that are placed on members of the university culture, you will greatly enhance your academic experience.

Exercises

REFLECT–ACT

The following Reflect–Act exercises are designed to enhance your self-awareness and self-understanding through the process of reflective thinking, analysis and productive action. These Reflect–Act exercises focus on the self-confidence and self-concept issues that are related to your success in your academic journey.

Reflect   University has been described as a foreign culture with expectations quite different than high school. How foreign is this new culture to you? Identify the differences and the new expectations by referring to Table 3.1.
Act   Based on these differences and expectations, describe the specific actions you will take to ensure that you will succeed in adapting to these differences and in meeting these expectations.

Reflect   Research shows that certain activities negatively affect your success and development. Identify the activities that remove you physically from the university environment.
Act   What actions do you think are necessary to reduce and potentially eliminate these activities? Which activities will you replace them with that are more conducive to becoming a successful student? Act on these as soon as you can.

Reflect   You are on a journey that will take you through the academic culture. As you journey, you will encounter each of the six levels of cognitive development as outlined by Bloom (1956) in Table 3.2. You can anticipate the type of questions on your assignment and exams for each of your courses if you have a thorough understanding of them.
Act   Go back through this chapter and create two exam questions that identify each of the six levels of Bloom's taxonomy based on the content of this chapter.

Reflect   Your university's philosophy, mission statements, and goals will determine the types of learning outcomes that you can expect. The Students' Responsibilities in your institutions are meant to guide your behaviour and thinking as well. Find and read these statements (either in the University Calendar or on the Web site).
Act   To what extent do you agree with these statements? To what extent are these similar to your goals as a student? Identify the behaviours that you may need to change in order to be successful according to these statements and act upon them.

Reflect   Years ago, when your university was first established, a group of individuals established the seal of your institution. These seals have symbols with significant meaning to your institution.

Act   Find a copy of your institution's seal and approach a historian or a librarian who may have information about the meaning behind the seal. Also, find the cornerstone of the first building on campus. What does it mean? What are the Latin words inscribed in this stone? What is the significance of each of these symbols to your institution?

GROUP DISCUSSION

1. Each person in your group comes from a varied cultural experience. Share the differences that each member has experienced and how, as a group, you can help each person make a successful transition into the university culture.

2. A key to being successful at university is fitting into the new academic culture. As a group, come up with a number of important strategies that will help you to succeed as you adapt to this new culture.

3. As a group, share your solutions to Exercise 3.1 (*Discovering the University Resources*). Find out where each of these resource centres is located on your campus.

APPLY TO LIFE

Use the following questions to guide your continued discovery and development of personal strategies that can make a difference for you now and in the future.

1. Effective learning in university is based on the mentoring system. Of all the professors you have come in contact with so far this year, who do you think would make your best mentor? Take time to make an appointment with that person and tell him or her about your interest in their area of expertise, and about your desire to begin a mentor-student relationship.

2. In order to improve your competencies at university, make at least one new friend in each of your large classes. Use this friendship for studying, assignments, and for keeping you informed about the classes that you might miss.

secret

Uncovering
Self-Mastery Strategies 2

"To master oneself is the greatest mystery."

Seneca

The treasure map that you use to guide you during the university sojourn takes you through unfamiliar territory. The terrain will at times test and challenge you. In your quest to arrive at a place where you have never been, and to experience vistas previously unknown, you will be required to possess a combination of capabilities to ensure your ability to continue the journey. In order to succeed, honing self-mastery strategies is essential.

One of the critical lessons that the university experience teaches is that success as a learner is a personal responsibility. In your early years of learning, many others nurtured development by structuring learning and promoting basic skill development. Now you are free and independent; you are no longer closely supervised or firmly directed by others. One of the exhilarating benefits of being a university student is the freedom you have to choose options and learn in your own way. With this freedom comes the insight that people are responsible for their own success. The wise student discovers the power of self-determination and self-responsibility. Acknowledging personal responsibility for one's own life provides the basis for *Uncovering Self-Mastery Strategies* that promote personal success.

Self-mastery provides you with the tools to persist in spite of confusion, distractions, or discouragement. Self-mastery gives you the capacity to trust your own abilities to read the environment and respond adaptively. If there are times when you doubt your own ability to succeed, you will benefit by understanding which strategies you can use to fuel your efforts and ignite your motivation. There is much to distract you as a university student; however, insights about personal goal-setting will keep you focused on your destination. Most importantly, focusing your time for your own personal advantage gives you a sense of self-mastery that is critical to your success. Especially important in successfully navigating the intellectual territory is the honing of study and learning strategies that complement those you already use.

Each of the next chapters provides you with critical information for surviving and thriving in the university environment. Each chapter provides you with practical approaches for enhancing your personal effectiveness. By applying the ideas you learn from each of these chapters, you will discover that you are better able to motivate yourself and to direct your energies as you gradually improve your learning efficiency. Seek the practical strategies that will ensure your ability to maximize your learning. With time you will find that you are able to combine the insights you have gained about sustaining effort, setting goals, and managing time, to develop the self-discipline that is essential for academic and personal achievement. You will learn how to improve your efficiency in mastering the academic challenges of university by experimenting with the study, reading, test-taking, and learning approaches that have been proven to be effective.

Discovering the factors and activities that facilitate your academic success can allow you to direct your own destiny. As you apply the strategies in the following chapters you are uncovering your own secrets that prepare you to become the master of your own success.

Developing
Success-Focused
Learning Strategies

chapter 4

"If you don't succeed at first, try, try again."
Success is a journey, not a destination.

Questions

What are the underlying principles or processes of successful students?

What learning strategies best predict success in learning?

What emotions (or affects), behaviours, and cognitions predict student success?

Objectives

- To understand the affects, behaviours, and cognitions (ABCs) of successful students.

- To realize that fundamental to the success of most students is effort.

- To discover how these principles can be applied to enhance success.

Student Success Portrait

Surviving and Succeeding in University

Joelle Kobylak
The University of Manitoba

Over the past several years as a student, I have acquired different strategies to succeed in university. Having been both a student and an instructor at the university, I would like to share a few tips that helped me survive and succeed in my academic endeavours.

Time Management and Organization

Perhaps the most critical strategy that I learned early in my academic career came from my Introductory Psychology professor. This particular professor spent two full classes discussing how to successfully manage and organize our time in order to prevent procrastination and subsequent anxiety or burnout. As a graduate student I can tell you that I never would have made it this far without learning to organize my time efficiently. As you will soon realize, free time will become very valuable to you throughout your university experience, so use it wisely! When you begin a new course, you'll receive a course outline that includes the dates of your tests and assignments. In the following day or two, buy the course text and a day planner. Spend a few hours planning out the course from the beginning to the final exam, allocating a few hours each day to spend on your courses. For example, if you have four weeks until your first test that covers the first four chapters in the text, you may decide to spend the first two weeks reading the chapters required for the test and the next two weeks reviewing and studying the chapters for the test. It is important (and much less stressful) to spend an hour each day per subject, rather than do nothing for the first three weeks and panick the week before a major assignment is due. By planning out each course at the start of the academic year, you'll know ahead of time exactly what you need to do each day for each course and how much free time you'll have in between. This strategy also allows you to plan around special social events (for instance, if you want to celebrate your birthday, you may plan for extra work the day before and after, so you can take a break and enjoy your day). A rule of thumb I followed as an undergraduate was never to do school work on Sundays, giving myself one full day a week away from academics. This required careful planning and hard work the rest of the week, but it was worth it knowing I could look forward to a full day to myself each week. Try not to spend too much time doing extra school work on days that you have classes. You may need to adjust your schedule to allow more study time for difficult courses. By planning to use your time wisely, you'll avoid studying when you're too tired or stressed out.

Test-Taking Tips

When preparing for a test, there are a few ways to make the experience as stress-free as possible. Again, plan out when to study to avoid last-minute cramming and unnecessary anxiety. The best defence against test anxiety is being prepared. *Know the material.* This takes effort and hard work. If the course offers a study guide, buy it! Prepare for your tests by first reading and reviewing the lecture notes and chapters. Then, make notes on definitions or on important concepts. Using flash cards may also be helpful. When you think you have studied enough, test yourself using the quizzes provided by your study guide. This will provide an accurate indicator of whether you are ready for the test or not. Study groups are most effective after you have already studied alone. These groups work best for quizzing each other and reviewing together. When arriving for a test, bring extra pencils and erasers and try not to arrive until about five minutes before the test, to avoid those "last minute" anxious classmates who failed to prepare sufficiently for the test. They can make you nervous and stressed out before the test even begins! If you follow your study schedule, you should not need to study the night before a test. Instead, relax, rent a movie, or have a nice dinner. Get a good night's sleep and walk into that test feeling confident that you are prepared for it.

Communication

Perhaps the biggest mistake I made as an undergraduate student was not asking enough questions. I was intimidated by the professors and scared of appearing stupid in front of my classmates. As a result, I was often confused about some of the professor's directions or comments. So talk to your professors! If you are too shy to ask a question during class, write it down so you remember it and approach your professor after class or during his or her office hours. If you are studying at home and have a question, call or e-mail your professor with your question. As an professor, I am always puzzled when students cannot find an answer or are confused regarding an assignment and simply choose to leave that question out rather than talking to me about it. As a result, their marks suffer, simply because they did not bother to talk to me. Do not feel like you are bothering your instructors; it is their job to teach you, and part of teaching is addressing your concerns or questions regarding the course.

The common theme in the above suggestions is *effort*. Succeeding in university depends on hard work, not on your natural ability. If you want to succeed, you need to put in the time and effort required. No one else can do it for you. There will be courses that you like less than others and assignments you would rather not think about, but there is no greater feeling than succeeding when you know you have worked really hard. That is what has kept me motivated throughout my academic career. I assure you, if you want them badly enough and if you work hard enough, you can reach all of your academic goals.

Your learning experience in high school may have been easy in comparison to the daunting tasks in university. University is much more challenging, and rightfully so. It is a place of higher education, a place where brilliant minds come together to learn more about Truth. But why is it that some students seem to excel at university, while many others struggle to achieve a good grade? What is the secret to success at university? In both university and the workforce, there are a number of characteristics that predict successful people, many of which overlap. Psychological research has identified these characteristics, especially in university students. Being aware of and adopting their strategies is an effective means to becoming successful. So what makes these students different from the rest? What is the secret to their success? What are the predictors of their academic achievement?

Let's revisit the student self-development model. As seen below, self-awareness, self-confidence, and self-concept form the identity of a successful student. First, self-awareness is strongly related to assessment, being aware of the strengths and weaknesses that students have in relation to becoming successful. The learning characteristics of successful students are used as ideals and adopted to strengthen one's own potential for success. Second, self-confidence is directly related to the attitude that students have toward learning process. Here again, successful student attitudes, such as optimism, are emulated in order to increase the potential for success. Third, the self-concept is derived from the social and the academic selves. Effective characteristics of the social self include relationship with others, whereas the academic self is characterized by the roles, attributes, and abilities in dealing with academic challenges.

Your success at university is a direct function of applying the student self-development model. As we continue, we will be identifying the affects, behaviours, and cognitions of successful students in relationship to the student self-development model in terms of your self-awareness, self-confidence, and self-concept. Characteristics of successful students will be identified, explanations of why these characteristics work will be given, and examples of how you can apply these to your life will be provided.

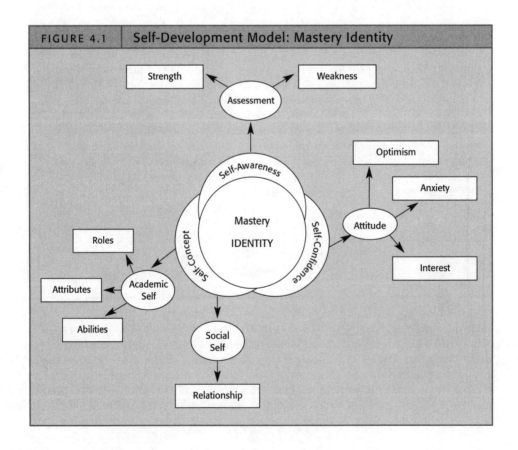

FIGURE 4.1 | Self-Development Model: Mastery Identity

Success Indicators: The ABCs of Successful Students

Successful university students are predicted through a variety of unique characteristics. Most of these characteristics can be grouped into one of three categories: affective, behavioural, and cognitive. They can be controlled by most students and can be adapted to fit almost any student. "Controllable" implies that you can actually adapt each of these characteristics to improve your learning. You can take **control** of them and apply them to become more successful. Let's explore each of these success indicators in relation to the student self-development model.

Self-Awareness: Taking a Critical Look at Yourself

Many successful students do not begin their educational journey with successful strategies. They often come totally unprepared to learn in a university environment. Their learning strategies are not conducive to studying and achievement. However, what sets these students apart so that they are able to become successful is their ability to observe others who have achieved, learn from them, and emulate them. They use information they learn about accomplishment and success to guide their development as student scholars.

Successful students also critically assess their own competencies and characteristics relative to expectations of their new learning environment. Awareness begins by identifying the affects, behaviours, and cognitions you have as a student that make you successful. It also involves an honest reflection of your strengths and your weaknesses as a student. In other words, it is an awareness of what you need to develop in order to be successful.

Throughout this chapter you will learn about the ABCs of successful students that are associated with confidence and competence. As you read each of the success predictors, identify the strength and/or weakness of the characteristic within yourself. Go back and reflect on your pre-test scores from the scales in Chapter 2: Learning from Lectures, Reading and Comprehension, Test-Taking, and Learning Strategies. Once aware, build on your strengths and take the necessary steps to eliminate any weaknesses.

Developing the Confidence of Successful Students

Affective States in Relation to Self-Confidence

Successful students quickly learn that there are a number of attitudes that enhance their learning. Three of the most important ones are optimism, curiosity or interest in course material, and anxiety.

Optimism

As a university student, you are bound to face many stressful situations, both in your academic and your private life. Optimism is an emotional predisposition, or a predictor of successful adaptation to these stressful encounters. As a belief that good prevails over evil, optimism is the tendency to take the most positive or hopeful view of circumstances in most situations (Pintrich et al., 1986). Take time to conduct an awareness check by completing the Optimism Awareness Scale above. Calculate your level of optimism and compare your score with that of a successful, optimistic student.

Optimistic students, in comparison to pessimistic students, perform better academically in final exams, course marks, and grade-point averages (Bandura, 1986). Why is this the case? Optimistic students are more problem-focused in their coping, more likely to seek social support, and to emphasize the more positive aspects of stressful situations (Scheier & Carver, 1987). Optimistic students are also less likely to repress their feelings and thoughts, and tend to be less anxious than their counterparts (Myers & Steed, 1999).

So what does that mean to you as a student seeking to be successful? When a stressful situation arises in your academic or private life, do what the optimists do. Focus your effort by looking at the stressor—the situation—as a problem that requires a solution, rather than ignoring the fact that a problem exists. View the problem as a challenge rather than as a threat. For example, the next time you do poorly on an important exam, use this situation as a challenge to increase your efficiency in studying for the next exam. Next, in your search for a solution, involve others. This is the social support that optimists seek during challenging times. Ask your friends and peers to help you, to encourage you, and most of all, to support you through these difficult situations. By working hand in hand with your colleagues, you will uncover efficient means by which to accomplish your goals, to master challenges, and to overcome difficulties. By sharing your struggles with others, you are also more likely to come across a solution that will make your challenge conquerable.

Above all, try to take on the mindset of an optimist, focusing on the positive aspects of all situations, including the difficult ones. In other words, seek out the positive in all circumstances, regardless of how painful or challenging. By applying the mindset of an optimist, you will be less likely to feel the overwhelming sense of anxiety that often accompanies pessimists (Myers & Steed, 1999). You will also spend less time focusing on stressful issues and more time on developing strategies for situational setbacks that could adversely affect your academic and personal life.

Curiosity and Interest

Curiosity and interest in a course are also emotional predictors of student success in university. Course content, interesting term projects or assignments, small classes, and professors' approaches are factors that will enhance your curiosity or excitement in a given course and thereby increase your learning (Pekrun, 1992).

Course Content   Let's begin with the course. If you were to rank your courses from your most favourite to your least favourite, don't be surprised to find a positive relationship between your ranking and your grades. It is very likely that you will have higher grades for your more favourite courses and lower grades for your other courses. Why? The time spent for each course is directly related to your interest in them, so a favourite course is likely to get more of your effort than a less favourite one.

Above all, your interest in a course will be instrumental to you in a number of ways. Students study more for a given topic because of their interest in the material. This has often been referred to as intrinsic motivation. You do it for the sheer sake of interest, personal pleasure, and not for some material reward. You are doing it for yourself and not for the professor or the course. Students who enjoy their classes and the content material are also more likely to put in more effort. You will be more attentive to the lectures, and thus increase your recall of the material later in exams. Your interest will also be displayed in your attitude—you will likely ask more questions. Course interest also increases based on its relevancy to a student's personal and career goals. This personal inquisitiveness in the content material becomes the intrinsic motivation that drives you to excel. When you are able to make direct personal connections to the content material, you increase the retention of that information for future assignments and tests. Your career goal is also a major factor in the interest you have in a course. Your commitment to courses with personal meaning and career relevancy increases your efforts in learning the material, and as a result the learning outcome is far greater than for courses with limited relevancy to you and your career aspirations.

Driven by an intrinsic need to know more, you put in more effort. More effort produces better recall of the content for future exams and, consequently, higher grades. All this translates into increased potential for success as a student. Successful students are aware of this phenomenon and, when registering for courses, choose the most desirable ones. They also choose research topics for their papers that are of personal interest.

Enrolling in the Smallest Classes   Smaller classes offer the opportunity to participate more actively in the class and to interact with the professor. Usually this translates into courses that are more interesting and more relevant, given that the professor can spend more time teaching to meet the personal needs of students. Research shows that smaller classes provide students with more contact time with the professor, which is often related to higher grades (Feldman, 1984; McKeachie, 1980). In most cases, the professor will have more time to cover the specific course content needs of the students in smaller classes.

Based on the above, you have the control to make significant choices to improve your chances of success at university. If you have a choice, choose the course of most interest. Further, when writing a research paper or conducting a research project, take the time to find a subject that most interests and excites you. If you are able, choose the smallest class. By taking any or all of these suggestions, your interest in the subject matter is expanded, and in turn your motivation to do well and your efforts are increased, providing you with the best potential for success.

What happens if you have to take a class prerequisite, or there is no choice in the class, or the term project is clearly defined with little or no choice for the student? Choose the role of an optimist. Look for the positive. Find something about this topic area that you might be interested in. If this does not work, find a way to make yourself interested in the topic area. A little interest in the subject material will go a long way in improving your grade.

Success as the Result of Decoding Professors Unfortunately, not all courses can be pre-selected. There are a number of courses that you will need to take as part of a program. These courses are referred to as required courses. However, successful students have another tip for improving their level of motivation in a less desirable course. They compensate the course content by choosing the best professor for that course. Studies show that students exposed to effective professors perform better in classes than students exposed to ineffective professors (Feldman & Paulsen, 1998; McKeachie, Pintrich, Lin, & Smith, 1986; Schönwetter, 1993). Specific effective teaching behaviours known to have direct impact on student learning include **professor organization** and **professor expressiveness** (Schönwetter, 1996).

Use the organization of your professors to increase your interest and involvement in the course material. As seen in Figure 4.2, "Behaviours to Seek in an Effective Professor," following the course syllabi and lecture outlines provided by professors can help you to increase your learning substantially (Schönwetter, 1993). Intact outlines provided at the beginning of the class serve to guide note-taking. The use of headings and intact outlines optimizes both immediate and delayed learning (Frank, Garlinger, & Kiewra, 1989). If confused about the organization that is provided by the professor, ask questions so that you are clearer about the structure that is being provided to help you learn.

Use the expressiveness of your professors to alert you to important ideas. As seen in the figure on page 75, both physical movement and voice intonation of the professor are the visual and/or audible changes of stimuli in your learning environment that attract your attention and provide you with learning cues as to what is considered important information (Schönwetter, 1993). Because eye contact creates an intense interest (Perry, 1991) and a sense of personal relationship between the student and the professor (Sherwood, 1987), looking at your professor during the lecture is helpful. Many professors use humour as it is instrumental in improving your comprehension, enhancing your retention (Johnson, 1990), and increasing your learning of substantive facts and awareness of attitudes (Safford, 1991). It is also known to lower students' anxiety (Ziv, 1988), to promote a positive and cohesive class environment (Civikly, 1986), and to maintain your interest and facilitate learning of new information (Gentilhomme, 1992). So look for qualities in your professor such as expressiveness and organization as important aids to assist you in your learning.

How do you discover information about the professors for each of your classes? Successful students have access to various sources. They consult their peers and/or family members who have experience taking courses with different professors and use this information in order to make an informed decision about the various teaching

FIGURE 4.2	Behaviours to Seek in an Effective Professor	
Effective Teaching Behaviours	**Identifiable Behaviours**	**Student Information-Processing Activity and Behaviours**
Organization	Lecture outline	Provides memory storage cues, knowledge of structure, schemata; chunking; predictability
	Links course material: headings, subheadings, topic transitions	Cognitive integration of content topics, meaningfulness, predictability
	Syllabus	Predictability
	Seriation of relevant points	Knowledge of what is considered important
Expressiveness	Eye contact	Creates intense interest or challenge, attraction, credibility; enhances recall
	Physical movement or body posture	Selective attention
	Voice inflection	Selective attention
	Humour	Selective attention, comprehension, retention, reduces anxiety, maintains interest

approaches. Many universities have records of course and professor evaluations that are accessible to students. These are usually found in the library reference section or housed in the Student Union office. Successful students use this information to identify the best professors—those who demonstrate high levels of organization and expressiveness.

Ideally, combining each of the above choices—course of interest, choice of major course project, a smaller class, or selecting the most effective professor—will provide you with the best advantage to being successful in the classroom. The initial investment of identifying your favourite courses, finding the smallest class and the best professors well in advance of registration pays the best dividends and makes learning most enjoyable. Who said learning has to be boring? It's your choice.

Anxiety

Anxiety can either motivate students or overwhelm them. For many successful students, anxiety provides them with the required motivation to persist at studying, at conducting more research about a given topic, and to do well in test situations. According to Domino (1975), these students use anxiety as an "**energizing source**" to facilitate and enhance learning. For instance, when exposed to anxiety-producing situations, successful students are more motivated to find solutions. They persist longer at difficult tasks and are more likely to find the difficult situation as a challenge. In other words, these students are more optimistic and become empowered to try harder in stressful situations.

Anxiety becomes problematic when it causes individuals to avoid situations perceived as threatening and dangerous (Plutchik, 1980). One of its most pronounced forms in the university setting is **test anxiety**, which results in feelings of apprehension and nervousness, worried thoughts and physical symptoms such as an upset stomach and headaches (Spielberger, Gonzalez, & Fletcher, 1979). In short, test anxiety is a pattern of intense and substantial reactions that result in one of the most pervasive problems of university students (Tobias, 1985). Conduct an awareness check. Refer back to the Anxiety Scale in Chapter 2, and calculate your level of test anxiety.

Test anxiety is an important affective contributor to student learning outcomes in college (Hembree, 1988; Tobias, 1986). Students who have high levels of anxiety often display less adaptive study habits, spend less time studying (Grimes, 1997), and procrastinate more (Rothblum, Solomon, & Murakami, 1986). They display higher levels of cognitive interference (Swanson & Howell, 1996), report more negative self-thoughts, and demonstrate diminished levels of personal control (Blankenstein, Flett, & Batten, 1989). Highly anxious students are less confident problem solvers (Blankenstein, Flett, & Batten, 1989) and experience poorer learning outcomes (Lyons, Young, Haas, Hojat, & Bross, 1997).

Test-anxious students are characterized by poorer learning outcomes. Their attention may be reduced, due to what researchers have labeled as the **interference model** (Darke, 1988). These students are known to excessively ruminate about their failure and vulnerability (Beck & Emery, 1985; McKeachie, Pollie, & Spiesman, 1985) and thus may be distracted from critical learning requirements such as attendance in lectures. Disadvantaged because of the cognitive interference associated with high test anxiety, their maladaptive learning orientations become a "crippling obstacle" to scholastic achievement (Domino, 1975). In other words, too much anxiety, especially if the task at hand is highly ego-involving (Schwarzer, 1981), substantially reduces and cripples effective learning and may lead to feelings of helplessness and depression (Schwarzer, Jerusalem, & Stiksrud, 1984).

There are a variety of ways to manage anxiety: changing one's attitude, turning the anxiety into an energy source, and seeking help from significant others.

Given that anxiety is directly related to how one perceives a given situation, a significant method of managing the ill effects of anxiety is to find ways of reducing or eliminating the situations that cause feelings of threat or feelings of being out of control. However, leaving the classroom to avoid anxiety is not effective for successful students. One of the most effective strategies is to adopt an optimistic attitude. As mentioned earlier, optimists view difficult situations as challenges, not as threats. This change in thinking is critical to dealing with anxiety. Threatening situations become challenging ones. Difficult circumstances are seen as opportunities to find something valuable and meaningful. The first step is to adopt the attitude of the optimist.

Another effective strategy in dealing with anxiety is to view it as an energizing source (Domino, 1975). As an energizing source, it provides the motivation to try harder. Students who perceive difficult tasks as challenging tend to increase their motivation for finding ways of solving the problem. They are more likely to persist at the task and ask for help. In other words, successful students productively use their anxieties to regulate their motivation and affect, focusing them toward learning.

There are situations where tasks begin to seem insurmountable, the feelings of being out of control are overwhelming, and the level of anxiety unmanageable. Here successful students seek advice from a professional. Most academic institutions provide various counselling services through Student Services that focus on mediating the ill effects of anxiety. Counselling services provide excellent workshops on how to deal with stressful situations, help students identify effective coping strategies, and provide them with excellent management skills to deal with future occurrences of stressful situations. It is advisable to seek counselling as soon as you perceive a sense of overwhelming anxiety. It is easier to conquer anxiety in its earliest stages rather than wait until the situation becomes unbearable.

Developing the Competence of Successful Students

The competence of successful students is directly related to the social and academic self. The social self is characterized by behaviours and cognitions that increase the success of relationships with others in the academic community. The academic self is characterized by behaviours and cognitions that reflect an achievement orientation, cognitive competencies and academic abilities such as note-taking, reading, and writing term papers. Each of these characteristics is important in the development of competence. Below, the social self and the academic self are highlighted in more detail.

Developing the Social Self

The specific characteristics of the social self have a number of essential components. These include engagement with others, the ability to establish and maintain relationships, social confidence, getting along with others, communication, teamwork, community, and leadership. Each of these components has a direct impact on the student's social self. You may be able to identify with a number of these. Successful students are characterized as having high levels of these characteristics. Let's explore some of these in turn, identifying the behaviours and cognitions that define these essential characteristics.

Engage with others

More than 70 percent of college students' learning comes from active out-of-class experiences (Astin, 1997; Terenzini, Pascarella, & Blimling, 1999). These experiences include structured and unstructured activities that are not part of the university's formal, course-related, instructional process, but rather include a host of social activities (Terenzini et al., 1999). Active participation in these social activities is fundamental in the development of a strong social self-image; they require that successful students become involved with others. Specifically, these include living in residence, participating in student organizations, being involved in intercollegiate athletics, employment, extracurricular activities, and faculty and peer interactions (Terenzini et al., 1999). Of greatest importance to learning are the interactions with peers and faculty (Terenzini et al., 1999).

Peers   The people who have the most impact on your learning at university, ironically, are not your professors. In fact, your best teachers are your fellow classmates, the teaching assistants for each course, the tutors, and students who have successfully completed the course before you (Terenzini et al., 1999). Successful students make connections with other potentially successful students in the classroom. They develop working relationships such as buddy systems and study groups that will enhance their learning productivity (see Chapters 7 and 10 for further information).

Administrators   Relationships with others begin before classes commence. Successful students make positive relationships with people who provide administrative support. These include people in the registration, financial aid, advisory, and computer support offices. A successful student knows that the key to success at university is having connections to important people.

Professors   Academic relationships with university professors are also important to successful academic outcomes (Terenzini et al., 1999). Unfortunately, many students have a faulty perception that the professor is not approachable. He/she might appear to be too busy, distant, or critical of students. Given that students also have busy lives, their activities often interfere with making connections to professors. One of the major differences that first-year students discover between their previous educational experience and university is the responsibility that they must assume in initiating contact with professors. Most professors are student-focused and are willing to spend time helping students, provided students meet the professors during office hours. The key here is to approach your professors early in the semester, to establish relationships with them so that when you have a concern, question, or comment to discuss, you will feel more confident in approaching them. Take time in the first class to introduce yourself to your professors, to tell them your interest in taking the course, and your desire to be able to approach them during times of need.

Attend all classes. This strengthens your connection with your professors. The more often they see you in class, the more you will be perceived as interested in the course. A student who frequently misses class will have less of an opportunity to have a good relationship with the professor than the student who attends classes.

Be respectful. Almost all people appreciate some form of respect. This is especially the case for many professors who have spent years building their careers to earn their degrees. So whenever possible address the professor by the appropriate title, such as Doctor or Professor. Learn about your professor. Professors do more than teach; they also conduct research and devote time to community service. You can learn about the professor through the examples they provide in class. Also, check their Web site or the home page for the department that they represent. Often, there will be short descriptions highlighting their interests, research publications, and professional activities. During class, be an attentive, respectful, and engaging student.

Resource staff   Establish relationships with support and/or resource staff, such as the resource librarians, writing specialists, and the staff in academic support services. Each of these individuals is available to help you with the learning tasks of university. Resource librarians will provide you with access to key literature for your research projects, both online and hard-copy resources. Academic support services and writing centres assist you in improving your skills in particular areas.

Expand Your Social Network

Key to your social self-concept is the ability to establish and maintain relationships. Entering the university culture can be threatening, given the many new faces. It is often easier to hide in the crowd than to engage with others. However, taking the first step forward by introducing yourself to the people mentioned above often opens up doors for continued dialogue and continued relations throughout the semester and throughout your academic career.

Get involved   Your social self-concept is also developed through your involvement in university activities. By introducing yourself, greeting others, and conversing about mutual interests with fellow classmates you develop friendships within the classroom. By joining extracurricular activities you develop social relationships that will sustain you throughout the term and your university career. Many successful students become involved in one or more of the extracurricular activities highlighted in Chapter 3.

Through these activities successful students develop greater connection to the university. Many become leaders and in doing so further develop their social self. Others provide leadership or participate in volunteer activities, thereby applying their theoretical knowledge. Choose activities that further enhance your learning experience and expand your educational process.

Participate actively as a team member You can become a member of various types of teams. These include athletic, fine arts, and research. Working in teams has its benefits as well. Here too, the social self becomes more transparent as you share responsibilities with others in a team. Working together for a common goal has the potential of enhancing the bond between members. As the team becomes more trusting and more intimate, it can provide some of the best support for encouraging your social strengths, and supporting and nurturing your social challenges. For instance, if you are somewhat shy, the team can provide the necessary support to help you gain the confidence in speaking, first to them and then to others.

Become a volunteer Of significance is the fact that many volunteer activities help successful students to elaborate on the content learned in class by applying it to the activity at hand. The course content then takes on new meaning. For instance, students taking courses in psychology or health who volunteer in hospitals very quickly adapt the theoretical material learned in class to the volunteer environment. The application of the course content, in turn, strengthens the memory of that material for the student, especially in terms of recall for exams.

Developing the Academic Self: Strategies for Motivating Learning

The academic self has three important characteristics: **achievement orientation**, cognitive competencies, and academic abilities. Each of these components is essential to the development of the student's academic self. You may be able to identify with a number of these. Let's explore each of these in turn, identifying the behaviours and cognitions that define these essential characteristics. As you are exposed to each one of these successful characteristics, make a note as to where you stand in comparison to the successful student. When the successful student characteristic and your present ability overlap, acknowledge this and be encouraged to continue. However, when you notice a lack of similarity between the successful student characteristic and your present characteristic, it is time to learn more about this characteristic and to adopt the more successful one.

Achievement Orientation

Achievement orientation is defined by the need for achievement, the expected value of a task, the student's sense of confidence or self-efficacy in completing the task, the hope, the attributional style chosen for similar tasks completed, and the goals set in order to achieve the task (McKeachie et al., 1986). Successful university students have developed the attitudes and attributional styles that promote achievement. Important factors that foster success include a need for achievement, a positive expectation about their success, and an explanation of the events that help them focus on productive problem-solving.

Attitudes

With an attitude to excel, overcome obstacles, attain a high standard, and accomplish something difficult (Murray, 1938), students are able to persist. This need to achieve is what drives or motivates human behaviour. Students with a high need for achievement can often overcome serious challenges in their efforts to succeed.

A number of studies have focused on the characteristics of successful achievers. High achievers tend to set goals of moderate difficulty and to avoid goals that are either too easy or too difficult (McClelland, Atkinson, Clark, & Lowell, 1953). (More on goal-setting will follow in Chapter 5). Motivated by their fear of failure, unsuccessful students tend to set goals that are too easy, which can be easily accomplished. They are also known to set unrealistically high goals (Geen, Beatty, & Arkin, 1984). High achievers also attribute their successes and failures to effort, persistence, and hard work, whereas the low achiever is more likely to perceive success and failure as due to luck, the influence of other people or the ease/difficulty of a task (Weiner, 1989). Finally, high achievers are those who devote more physical and psychological energy to the academic experience (Astin, 1997), and are more motivated to invest effort into the task (Palmer & Cochran, 1988). This makes sense, given their high motivation to achieve, which translates into more dedication to accomplishing academic goals.

Successful students motivate themselves by recognizing the value of particular assignments and using their past successes to build their self-confidence. When appropriate they use either intrinsic (i.e., internal reasons for learning) or extrinsic motivation (e.g., grades, money) to get themselves on track. They use past experiences on particular assignments to assess their probability of future success.

As you view the task set before you, you will likely deliberate regarding the extent to which you think you will succeed or fail at the task. If you have experienced success in completing similar tasks in the past, you are more than likely to have a high sense of self-confidence in completing the new task. If, on the other hand, you experienced failure in completing the previous task, your self-confidence in completing the new task will be affected, potentially reducing your sense of self-confidence for this type of task. One key to becoming successful is to experience success. Thus, many students will sign up for easier, more manageable courses as a means of earning high grades and boosting their sense of self-confidence in learning at the university. However, keep in mind that university education in general is challenging, and successful students focus on strategies that help them achieve in challenging circumstances.

Closely related to the self-confidence involved in doing well is the hope of success, or fear of failure (Atkinson, 1964). These two important yet conflicting factors motivate a student to try harder to ensure success, or motivate the student to avoid the task because of the fear of failure. Successful students are hopeful for successful outcomes. This hope is the driving force that keeps them persisting, even during challenging tasks, and helps them to accomplish their goals.

Attributional styles

Also linked to self-confidence and achievement is the student's explanation for being either successful or unsuccessful (Försterling, 1988; Weiner, 1986). **Attributional style** is the reason you give for explaining your successful or unsuccessful outcome. A successful experience on a task, such as a mid-term exam, may be viewed as due to any one of many reasons. The most common include task ease, ability, effort, or luck. The reasons you identify for your success affect how much more effort you invest into a similar task in the future. As seen in the Cognitive Reframing model on page 82, students who believe they are successful as a result of luck, the difficulty or ease of a particular task, or because of genetic predispositions, are less likely to try harder next time. Why? Well, each of these reasons is not controllable by the student—"I can't change how easy the task might be next time," "I can't change fate or luck," and "I can't change my ability that I have inherited from my parents." Given that each of these reasons or causal inferences is uncontrollable by the students, it is more likely that they will be less motivated to do well in the future. However, making an effort-causal inference for success is different. Effort is something that we all can control. Hence, a student who makes an effort attribution is more likely to be highly motivated to try harder in the future—"I did well because I studied hard." When students focus their reasons for doing well on effort, they increase their chances of success (Försterling, 1988; Weiner, 1986, 1988). So let your next successful academic achievement be one you attribute to your effort.

The same also holds true for an experience of failure. Why did I fail? Was it because the test was too difficult, the professor was inadequate at teaching the material, the content material was too complex, I just don't have what it takes to process this content, or because I did not study hard enough? Here again, as seen in the bottom panel of the Cognitive Reframing model, students who commit to making uncontrollable explanations, such as failure due to luck, task difficulty, poor instruction, or lack of ability, are less likely to be motivated to try harder in the future for similar tasks (Weiner, 1986). It just does not pay to do something if you feel you have no control over the outcome, so your motivation to do well is substantially reduced. However, by attributing your failure to a lack of effort, your motivation to try harder the next time is increased. Why? You can control the amount of studying you do prior to taking the next exam. Hence, your motivation to do well is increased, even though you have experienced failure.

As an aside, experiencing a number of failures and trying to infer lack of effort for each one may be hazardous to your self-confidence. There are some tasks that we simply do not have the abilities to complete. For instance, I was a very fast runner in high school. I tried out for the football team, but was encouraged not to continue. I weighed only 130 pounds. I could have tried as hard as possible to advance to being selected as a team member, but my chances of making the team were more related to my weight than my ability to run fast. If I could have gained more weight, I might have been successful. However, weight gaining was something I could not control, even though I tried hard. Thus, there are certain circumstances that are truly beyond our control where inferring a lack of effort might be detrimental to our self-confidence.

Take a moment to reflect back to the last time that you did poorly on an assignment or exam when getting a good mark was really important to you. How do you compare to the two extremes seen in "A Cognitive Strategy of Successful Students" on page 82? To what extent are you emulating the attributional style of the successful student?

Successful students are not the only ones who benefit from this type of thinking. A number of at-risk university students have also benefited academically from changing their inadequate attributional styles, such as luck, task difficulty, professor, or lack of ability to more functional attributional styles, such as lack of effort, through a simple process referred to as cognitive reframing or attributional retraining (Abry, 1999; Försterling, 1988; Perry, Hechter, Menec, & Weinberg, 1993; Van Overwalle & Metsenaere, 1990; Weiner, 1986, 1988). Their success was based on a simple procedure outlined in "Cognitive Reframing: A Change in Perception" on page 83. When repeated daily, this procedure can easily be adapted to change a student's way of making causal inferences for daily outcomes of success and failure. By applying this new way of thinking, you will increase your chances of success not only at your academic tasks, but also in all areas of life, including sports, fine arts per-

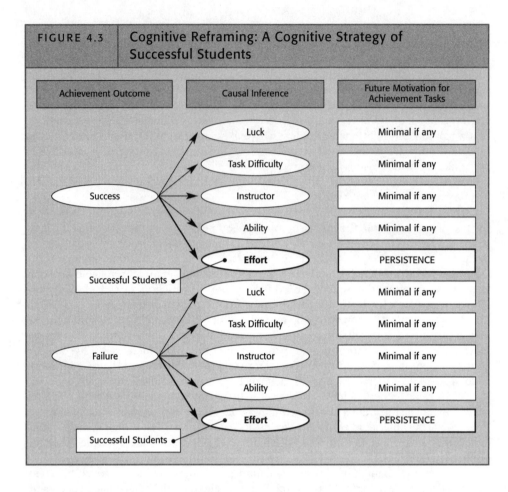

FIGURE 4.3 — Cognitive Reframing: A Cognitive Strategy of Successful Students

Achievement Outcome	Causal Inference	Future Motivation for Achievement Tasks
	Luck	Minimal if any
	Task Difficulty	Minimal if any
Success	Instructor	Minimal if any
	Ability	Minimal if any
Successful Students →	Effort	PERSISTENCE
	Luck	Minimal if any
	Task Difficulty	Minimal if any
Failure	Instructor	Minimal if any
	Ability	Minimal if any
Successful Students →	Effort	PERSISTENCE

formances, social life, etc. So what are you waiting for? Take a lesson from the successful students and apply it to your own way of thinking about your performance outcomes.

Another critical element in focusing effort toward achievement is effective goal-setting that focuses on the steps toward completing assignments and learning tasks. Most successful students focus on six common goals known to improve the transition from high school to university:

1. developing academic and intellectual competence;
2. establishing and maintaining interpersonal relationships;
3. developing an identity;
4. deciding on a career and lifestyle;
5. maintaining personal health and wellness; and
6. developing an integrated philosophy of life (Upcraft & Gardner, 1989).

These goals reflect the identity development of the academic and social self, which is the focus of this text. In making a task an important goal, students increase their motivation to complete it successfully and have higher expectations of performing well. Students who have higher expectations of performing well are also more likely to do better than students who have lower or no expectations (Mayo & Christenfeld, 1999). Thus, goal-setting is a critical element in succeeding. Chapter 5 is dedicated to exploring successful goal-setting.

Cognitive Competencies

To become a successful student you must develop the cognitive or thinking skills required in university. These academic skills include knowledge structure, thinking and problem solving, and learning strategies (McKeachie et al., 1986). Knowledge structure includes how a student organizes and represents knowledge, and will be discussed in greater detail under "During the Class: Learning from Lectures" in Chapter 7. Thinking and problem solving involve the various applications of learning, from the transfer of learning, to problem solving, to critical thinking. Each of these important strategies will be the focus of Chapter 10. Learning strategies include cognitive strategies, learning about learning, and resource management strategies. These will be discussed next.

To improve your learning effectiveness it is useful to enhance your abilities in three areas: cognitive strategies, metacognitive strategies, and resource management strategies. Cognitive strategies include rehearsal, elaboration, and organization (McKeachie et al., 1986), and form the focus of Chapter 7. **Metacognitive strategies** include those involved in reading a text efficiently. They include planning strategies such as setting learning goals, skimming, and generating questions; monitoring strategies such as self-testing, attention-focus, and test-taking; and regulating strategies such as adjusting reading rate, re-reading, reviewing, and test-taking (McKeachie et al., 1986). Each of these strategies will be further detailed in Chapter 7. Resource management strategies will be discussed in more detail below.

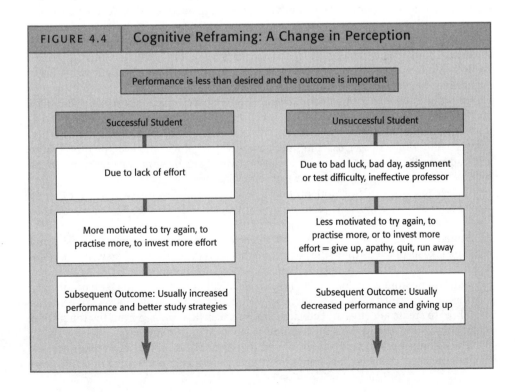

FIGURE 4.4   Cognitive Reframing: A Change in Perception

Performance is less than desired and the outcome is important

Successful Student	Unsuccessful Student
Due to lack of effort	Due to bad luck, bad day, assignment or test difficulty, ineffective professor
More motivated to try again, to practise more, to invest more effort	Less motivated to try again, to practise more, or to invest more effort = give up, apathy, quit, run away
Subsequent Outcome: Usually increased performance and better study strategies	Subsequent Outcome: Usually decreased performance and giving up

Of significance to the learning strategies are the resource management strategies. One of the major challenges facing a first-year student is the overwhelming number of responsibilities accompanying the transition to university. Most students who leave university do so because they do not know how to deal effectively with all of these responsibilities. Key to their demise is the lack of focusing or knowing how to focus on the tasks set before them. These inviting challenges become distractions, thwarting the student from achieving success. For instance, when you applied for university, your dream was one of completing some sort of a degree within the next three to four years. This is an excellent start and is often referred to as "converting your dreams into goals," as explained in Chapter 5. However, as you enter the first weeks of classes, you discover aspects of university life that can overwhelm or confuse you. Using the resource management strategies of successful university students can help to direct your focus. These include time management, study-environment management, effort management, and support of others (McKeachie et al., 1986).

Manage your time

These skills are highly effective for increasing your success as a student. Successful students know how to effectively and efficiently use the minimum amount of time to get the most amount of work accomplished while still having the time to enjoy a meaningful social life. Given its significance in the success of your academic endeavours, Chapter 6 is dedicated to aspects of time management: highlighting planning, monitoring, and feedback.

Organize your study environment

Of significance to study-environment management are the abilities to establish a defined study area, to make it conducive to studying, and to organize the area. A student's study environment is a very important aspect of his/her learning efficiency (Deece & Deece, 1979). It is of great importance to establish a consistent place for studying. This can be in the library, study hall in the dormitory, the student's room, or the kitchen table. Although the location is not as critical, the key is that it is a place where a student can quickly engage in focused studying, free from any distractions.

In order to ensure an area conducive to studying, the successful student identifies and knows how to reduce and eliminate the distractions. For most students, simple distractions include things such as clutter, telephones, televisions, access to the Internet, active chat or e-mail messages, computer games, video games, and even pictures. These are simple in the sense that you have control over them by simply unplugging them, turning them off, making them inactive, or removing them.

To become a successful student, find a place that has few distractions. Your study area should be free of posters, pictures, and any distracting visuals. The next step is to remove the clutter and create a clean space for your academic projects.

Manage other distractions. Turn off the telephone ringer and let the answering machine take its place. Turn off the command that alerts you when you have new e-mail, and let your word processor take full command of your computer's RAM. Remove the computer game from your computer and replace it with reference management software (e.g., Endnote or Procite) known to increase your paper writing skills. Successful students know how to create effective and efficient study spaces that are free from the things that potentially distract them, allowing the mind to focus on important tasks.

The next element in study-environment management is organization. The successful student has all the necessary things for studying close at hand: writing utensils, word processor, paper, resources, and references. This includes having binders or folders for each class and for each assignment. These are stored in user-friendly binders, boxes, or even filing cabinets that are easily accessible and easy to find. As you come across new ideas and supporting literature for different assignments or papers, these are noted, filed accordingly, and referred to when studying. By organizing your study area, the time spent finding important things is reduced, your studying efficiency is increased, and your learning is enhanced.

Practise Self-Management

One way of motivating yourself is by focusing on improving your ability to manage your effort, mood, self-talk, and self-reinforcement (McKeachie et al., 1986). Each of these helps the student maintain a good internal, or affective, state that is healthy and productive for learning efficiency.

Effort

Successful students put a lot of effort into their studying. Sure, there are those who spend little, if any, time studying. However, these individuals are few, and have certain abilities or experiences that most other students wish they had, including photographic memory. This describes a mere one percent of the student population and is rare among first-year students. For the 99 percent of us who are less than brilliant, or gifted, we need to put in a lot of effort to come out with success. Hence, every hour of in-class learning requires on average a *minimum* of one to two hours of extra effort in the form of studying, reading, and researching. The exciting news is that with each passing hour comes the acquisition of new knowledge. With each repetition of an idea comes a stronger thought, etched into the brain's long-term memory.

Effort also translates into repetition. Tasks are repeated, papers are rewritten, ideas are reread, and concepts and theorems are repeated and memorized. Your brain is a muscle that also needs exercising. Think of university as a sports camp, where coaches are training you to compete in the Olympic Games. What sets Olympic medal winners apart from other athletes is sheer determination and dedication to perform over and over again. They put in hours improving their strength and agility in order to perform the sport to its utmost perfection. As an academic, you have entered the intellectual arena. You spend countless hours training in the academy, developing your strongest muscle, the brain. You exercise daily, like the Olympic athlete, by putting maximum effort into all your courses. You begin as all athletes do, with short, easy exercises to minimize fatigue on your brain. This may translate into a minimum of one hour of studying per course taken, each day for the first week of classes. As you develop your thinking muscle, you also develop more efficient ways to do thinking tasks. So by the time you have completed the course, your mind has been strengthened beyond what it was capable of doing at the beginning of the course. You can breeze through difficult theorems. You are able to understand the nuances of a new language. Remember not to take this for granted. You developed your thinking power and now you are able to master more.

The determination to persist also requires effort, even during times of difficulty. This is best described as "staying on task," commonly referred to as persistence. It is all part of setting realistic goals and striving to meet these goals. Determined to accomplish their goals, successful students continue to focus their efforts on specific tasks relevant to completing the requirements on time.

Mood and Self-Talk

As mentioned earlier, the successful student takes an optimistic perspective on learning. He/she sees each class, lecture, reading assignment, laboratory exercise, quiz, test, and exam as a means to increase learning. This positive view is critical to enhancing learning. It helps the student remain committed to the task. When the tasks become overwhelming, the successful student finds ways to remain optimistic. During stressful situations, the successful student does not fall prey to fatalistic thoughts, such as attributing the outcomes of performance to luck, task difficulty, or a rigid professor. Rather, they apply more effort, persistence, and repetition, to strive onward, toward successful completion of the task. This often involves a lot of positive self-talk to reduce and eliminate any destructive thoughts (Bandura, 1982; Dansereau, 1985), such as those associated with students who have high test anxiety.

Reinforce Productive Actions

When intrinsic motivation is lacking to complete the task at hand, successful students use extrinsic motivators to help them persist. Intrinsic motivation is the internal drive or desire to complete the task because of your interest or curiosity to do so. Extrinsic motivation refers to completing tasks through the use of rewards or reinforcement. Successful students will creatively convert meaningful distractions into rewarding, extrinsic motivators. For instance, think of the tasks that bring you pleasure. You may enjoy talking to your friend on the telephone, watching television, reading a book, listening to music, or playing video games. Take these distractions and make them part of your learning reinforcers. Set aside a small segment of your day to reward yourself for completing certain academic goals. For instance, after every hour of reading, writing, or studying, reward yourself with 10 minutes of any one of these reinforcers. The key here is to ensure that only a small portion of time is given after the completion of a task to the enjoyment of these reinforcers. If you allow these reinforcers to occur prior to completing the academic task, or prematurely before the set hour, or if you allow them to reinforce you for longer periods than initially set out, they in turn become even stronger distractions, making it even more difficult to get focused.

Chart Plans and Progress

Another extrinsic motivator for many successful students includes setting up charts in a visible place but not too close to the area of studying, where they might become another visual distraction. As each task is completed, it is indicated on the chart with a check. As tasks are completed, more of the chart is visually completed, providing a sense of incredible accomplishment for the student. Remember to use large paper so that numerous tasks can be recorded. At the end of the semester, you will be amazed at the number of tasks you completed. Once complete, this chart, in turn, can motivate you to focus on the tasks required during the next semester. By referring to it often, you will be reminded of the success that all your effort produced.

Support of Others

Using the support of others is the last resource management strategy that students need to have control over. This includes knowing how, when, and where to seek and obtain help from the professor, from peers, from study and peer learning groups, and from tutors. Often referred to as "practical intelligence" (Sternberg, 1985), successful students are aware of when they need help with new ideas, theories, or formulae that are complex or difficult to understand. They are able to identify the resource providers. As mentioned earlier in this chapter, this begins well in advance of taking classes. Successful students have effective communication strategies to engage in discussions with each of these resource people. The successful student has also connected with the professor and other students. Peer help or peer tutoring, as seen in study groups, can facilitate student achievement (Webb, 1982). These students have also met with the teaching assistants and are aware of all other resource people, such as tutors, resource librarians, and writing advisors. As a result, these students are also more likely to be successful and feel higher levels of confidence and competence.

Academic Abilities

The final contributing factor to the academic self-concept includes the academic abilities of reading, note taking, and writing term papers. Each of these is a valuable and fundamental indicator of the academic concept of the successful student. Successful students have found strategies that enhance their reading, note-taking, and term paper writing abilities. These strategies are presented in Chapters 7 and 8.

It's More Than Common Sense

Increasing Your Effort to Improve Academic Performance

Dieter J. Schönwetter, Ph.D.
University of Manitoba

I was your average student in undergraduate school. I had to work hard at getting good marks. Whenever I received a poor grade on an assignment or test, I would immediately think that I was a poor student and that I would not amount to anything. Fortunately, things changed. For one of my psychology courses, I read an article that explained how students deal with failure in their university courses. I was so intrigued by the article that I began searching for more literature on this topic. What was so fascinating about this issue was that the perceptions a student has about his/her performance may have a direct impact on his/her future motivation to persist at a task and achieve success (Försterling, 1985). Wow! My dream to achieve was rekindled! I just had to make a minor adjustment in my thinking and take full control of my learning. All I needed to do was to change my rationale for doing poorly, from being a poor student who lacked ability, to insufficient effort and/or lack of success strategies. It made such a difference in my studies that I became more interested in this topic and eventually dedicated my graduate training to understanding this phenomenon. Today, I encourage and train children, athletes, undergraduate students, future professorate, faculty, and even fine arts performers to adopt this way of thinking.

"Silver Bullet" or Just Common Sense

What is so fascinating about cognitive reframing or attribution retraining is that it is common sense. Attributions are the causal reasons people give for success or failure for almost any achievement outcomes: sports, fine art performances, academic endeavours (Hyllegard, Radlo, & Early, 2001; Weiner, 1989). The performer assesses his/her achievement as either successful or not, reacts in a related emotional manner (i.e., either positively or negatively) in response to his/her judgment, and searches for the reason that caused the outcome (Weiner, 1989). If the outcome is of importance to the performer, then the cause selected for explaining the success or failure outcome has important and distinct effects on the performer's future achievement expectations and emotional reactions (Wong & Weiner, 1981).

These in turn, jointly determine the performer's subsequent achievement-related performance. Attributions are the specific types of reasons people give for the causes. For instance, ability, task difficulty, luck, and sufficient effort are generally the four major perceived causes of achievement performance (Weiner, 1986). The cause that the performer attributes to his/her achievement outcome has a direct impact on his/her emotions, future expectations to do well at the same task, and motivation which influences subsequent achievement (Weiner, 1989). This is especially thought to be the case when the person is pursuing an important goal.

"An Attribution Model of Achievement Striving" shows how each of the causes directly impacts a performer's emotions, future expectations, and motivation to persist at the task. The example involves a student whose mark on an exam is very important to gain entrance into an academic program of choice. If the student perceives that the last test outcome was successful and attributes that success to ability or sufficient effort, he/she is more likely to experience pride, competence, and satisfaction (Weiner et al., 1971) and have an increase in confidence that he/she will do equally well in the future. If success is attributed to ability alone, it will give the student a sense of overconfidence for future tasks and will result in minimal, if any, practising or studying. Effort will provide a more accurate reflection of confidence and encourage the student to continue working hard for the next achievement event. However, task ease or luck attribution will lead to feelings of gratitude and uncertainty as to future expectations of doing well (Stojanowska, 1999; Weiner, Russell & Lerman, 1979). Both of these are not controllable by the student, and thus their expectations for doing well in the future are uncertain, and the motivation to prepare for similar tasks in the future is not seen as necessary, given that the task will likely be easy again, or the student may once more experience luck (Weiner, 1986).

What happens if the student perceives the outcome as a failure, or lower than expected? Again, if the outcome is of significant value, the student's emotions, future expectations, and motivation to persist at the task are directly

FIGURE 4.5	An Attribution Model of Achievement Striving (adapted from Weiner, 1989)				
Outcome	**Reason**	**Emotion**	**Future Expectancy**	**Motivation**	**Persistence and Intensity**
Success	Ability	Competence	High	Low	Low
	Effort	Pride	Low	High	High
	Task ease	Gratitude, hope	High	Low	Low
	Luck	Surprise	Low	Low	Low
Failure	Ability	Shame	High	Low	Low
	Effort	Guilt	Low	High	High
	Task difficulty	Anger, fear	High	Low	Low
	Luck	Surprise	Low	Low	Low

impacted. For instance, a student who has failed and attributes the failure to lack of ability or insufficient effort will likely experience feelings of guilt, shame, and resignation (Mizuno, 1998; Weiner et al., 1979). Lack of ability, because it is often viewed as uncontrollable, will cause fear of future failure and potentially lower the motivation to persist studying for future achievements. However, lack of effort is the most conducive attribution. The student will more likely have hope (Weiner & Litman-Adizes, 1980) for doing well again in the future because the outcome was related to a lack of effort, something that a student can easily change by studying harder or finding a better study strategy (Perry, 1991; Weiner, 1986). The other two attributions, task difficulty or luck, are more likely to make the student feel a sense of hopelessness and fear (Weiner, 1986) that future performance tasks might not be achievable and thus, there is little sense in putting in any extra effort.

Based on research, successful students demonstrate stronger effort attributions for both success and failure, are more likely to persist in the face of difficulty, and to try more efficient studying techniques than less successful students (Van Overwalle, 1989; Van Overwalle, Segebarth, & Goldchstein, 1989). Moreover, combining effort attributions with efficient studying techniques gives the successful student the edge during tests. These students are also more likely to benefit from the teaching of effective professors (Perry, 1997a, 1997b; Perry, Hechter, Menec, & Weinberg, 1993; Schönwetter, Perry, & Struthers, 1993; Schönwetter et al., April 13, 2001; Schönwetter, Walker, Taylor, & Cameron, June 2001).

So the next time your important exam result is perceived as successful or less desirable than you had initially expected, take the lead of the successful student and make a sufficient or insufficient effort attribution, respectively. Don't stop there. Combine your attribution retraining with effective studying strategies to enhance your learning (Robertson, 2000). Follow this up by continuing to prepare for the next test or assignment, finding new and more effective ways to study by visiting the professor, by asking tutors and teaching assistants for advice, and by consulting the Learning Resource Centre.

Success Strategies FOR STUDENT MASTERY

Self-awareness
What do I know about my own manner of dealing with failure or with success?
I've learned that my strengths in each of the following are:
    Optimism…
    Curiosity and interest…
    Anxiety…
    Making causal attributions for success and failure…
Can I describe the mastery capabilities I would like to develop?

Self-confidence
To increase my confidence in my ability to be more optimistic I will…
To increase my confidence in my ability to engage with others more confidently I will…

Self-concept
Actions I can take to add to my on-task behaviour or persistence are…
Actions I can take to gain greater control of my learning are….

Chapter Summary

To develop the motivational attitudes and aptitudes to sustain your effort to achieve at university requires becoming aware of how to use your current competencies and develop others. Knowing how to foster within yourself attitudes of optimism, curiosity, interest, and achievement orientation is critical to your success. Developing the habits and actions for effective learning gives you the sense of personal control that makes you successful.

Overall, looking at the various student characteristics that identify success, many of these areas have a lot to do with students' effort. How much of yourself you invest and how you focus your effort will determine how successful you will be in university. Effort is the result of what you feel (affect), what you do (behaviour), and how you think (cognitions). It is under your control and can be adapted to fit your situation. Each of the successful strategies outlined in this chapter, and those to come in the following chapters, are skills, or attitudes that most students can control. As you begin to apply and adapt these different attitudes, behaviours, and cognitions, it will take effort. Sometimes it will work; other times it will not. Here again, practise what successful students do, and persist. Part of your success lies in your determination to become successful, your desire to discover what makes you learn more effectively, and the application of this new knowledge about yourself. Each one of the studying strategies in this chapter can enhance your potential for success. By attempting to make these strategies personal habits you can become a successful student.

Finally, knowing about all of these strategies is the first step in becoming successful. Of importance is putting to practice all that you have read. Applying all these different actions and attitudes will not only increase your chances of success at university, but will also impact all other areas of your life. You are more likely to get better grades, to complete courses and programs of study, to receive awards and scholarships, to enter graduate school, and to get a career that not only pays well, but also provides you with more satisfaction. Above all, this will result in a desire for the satisfaction of life-long learning.

Exercises

REFLECT–ACT

The following Reflect–Act exercises are designed to enhance your self-awareness and self-understanding through the process of reflective thinking, analysis, and productive action. These Reflect–Act exercises focus on the affects, behaviours, and cognitions that are related to your success in your academic journey.

Reflect   Rank your courses from most interesting to the least interesting. Next, keep a log of how many hours you spend for each course for a minimum of two weeks. What are your observations? Note the relationship between interesting courses and the effort you expend on the course.

Act   Make a list of other courses that you would be interested in taking and use this list as a reference for next semester's registration.

Reflect   Describe differences in your actions between those courses that interest you and those that do not.

Act   Identify specific changes you can make in your study strategies to increase your interest in the courses that are less interesting. Or identify your least interesting course. Adopt one study strategy that can improve your engagement in this course. Practise this.

Reflect   Identify five characteristics of your favourite athlete or performer.

Act   For each of their characteristics, list a parallel characteristic of a successful student. Note the incredible similarities between the two.

Reflect   Reflect on the types of attributions you generally have and their impact on your own persistence.

Act   Select one attribution to change during the week and observe its impact.

Reflect   Think about the strategies you are already using that make you successful academically and personally. What are some of the factors that inhibit your ability to be successful? Which ones can you control? Which ones can't you control?

Act   Describe actions you can take to make changes and increase your success at university. How will you make these changes in order to increase your success at the university?

Reflect   Identify ten of your greatest distractions. Take this top-ten list and begin to find ways to reduce their impact on your life.

Act   Is there any way that you can eliminate these, to the point where they are no longer distractions, but potentially rewards—as something to look forward to that's entertaining after the completion of an academic task?

GROUP DISCUSSIONS

What are the characteristics of professors you like? Compare your list with others in your group. Are there any commonalties? Develop a list of the top most-valued characteristics of professors from a student's perspective.

In small groups of four people, come up with the following resources and discuss them with each other to increase your success strategies.

1. Find the local listings of course and professor evaluations for your university. Identify the best professors based on high ratings of organization and expressiveness. Include professors who have won teaching awards. Plan to take some courses with these excellent professors.

2. Identify the resource people who students can access for each course. Include your peers, your relatives who have successfully completed these courses, the teaching assistants, the course tutors, the professor, etc. Create a list of their names, their contact numbers, their available times, and how they can be helpful to first-year students. Place this list on the wall above your desk as a reference list when you need to seek help. Also, ask your professor for access to reference materials that will provide you with additional resources to explain the course content matter. These are often placed on reserve in your library.

3. Find all the satellite colleges near your university that offer similar courses for credit. Are these courses available to off-campus students? Would you be able to register for courses at these institutions and still receive full course credit at the university? Consider signing up for at least one, and maybe more courses at these smaller institutions.

APPLY TO LIFE

1. Think back to your last successful academic assignment (e.g., test). What emotions best define your response to the mark that you received? Now think of the reason behind why you did so well. To what did you attribute your success (e.g., easy task, luck, excellent professor, ability, my effort)? Based on this attribution, are you more willing to put in more effort for similar tasks in the future? If it was due to anything other than effort, consider cognitive reframing below.

2. Think back to your last failure. What emotions best define your response to the mark that you received? Now think of the reason why you did so poorly. To what did you attribute your failure (e.g., difficult task, luck, lousy professor, lack of ability, lack of effort)? Based on this attribution, are you more willing to put in more effort for similar tasks in the future? If it was due to anything other than lack of effort, consider cognitive reframing below.

3. *Cognitive Reframing:* Successful students attribute their successes and failures to effort or lack of effort, respectively. You can adapt this way of thinking by going through the following procedure listed in this chapter. Note that the most important thing is to change your attributions to effort or lack of effort.

GOALS:
Getting *On A* Learning Success Path

chapter 5

**Co-written by Michael Doyle, Ph. D.
and Lilly J. Schubert Walker, Ph. D.**

A goal is a dream with a deadline.

Questions

What do I want to learn to complement what I already know about my own effectiveness in achieving the goals I set for myself?

What is the most essential aspect of goal-setting?

Which goals are most important for me to determine?

Objectives

- Understand the importance of goals.

- Develop personalized goals that foster development and accomplishment.

- Design specific types of goals with the use of the STAR model.

Student Success Portrait

Reaching for Success

Krista L. McKay
The University of Manitoba

"Success is the result of perfection, hard work, learning from failure, loyalty and persistence." Colin Powell

Success by one definition is the gaining of wealth and fame. However, when you are a university student, being successful is measured in different terms. As a student, being successful means getting an A on that paper that you spent many long hours working on, or doing well on your final exams. Being a first-year student can be very discouraging. A person has to learn how to survive in an environment that is unfamiliar. Having completed my first year at the University of Manitoba, I have learned to survive and I have also learned a few lessons on how to become a successful student.

Being a student who has already been there, let me tell you what I have learned. When beginning a new class, be open-minded and have a positive attitude. Find out what type of learner you are—knowing that can open doors, and it will help you succeed at studying. Learn how to manage time effectively—study during your spares. One thing I cannot stress enough is do not procrastinate; quality work comes together over time. Another key thing is communication, with your professors and your fellow classmates—trust me, it helps! Professors love students who ask questions; even if you're too shy, do it after class or during office hours. Test-taking can become very stressful; try to minimize stress by preparing—study a week in advance. Do not cram the night before; try to get a good night's sleep. If you do not know the material one hour before the test, you are not going to know the material at all. My last piece of advice is try to ignore the temptation to skip classes; it is easy to do, but it only takes one class to fall behind for the rest of the term.

Everybody is at university for different reasons. Some of you may not know what it is yet. Don't worry, you will figure it out in time. It may not be easy, but who said university was going to be easy? Take things in stride and do not "freak out" about the small things—remember, it could be worse. Having goals to work toward is challenging and rewarding. It also makes things a whole lot easier. Knowing what you want to do keeps you focused and determined. Although it may take you a while to reach your goal, at least you did it. You are the one with the power to make that goal a reality. To reach a goal is to be considered successful.

If you can survive the first year of university, you can do just about anything. A person can follow anyone's advice, but to really be successful is to have experienced university yourself. Don't worry, you will survive!

"I will survive." Gloria Gaynor

Everywhere you turn these days, someone is talking about the importance of setting goals, of knowing what you want in life, of taking the time to explore your options and choices. It seems to be the thing to do in the new millennium. Using common sense, it probably is helpful to have a direction and blueprint to help determine where you are headed and when you have arrived.

But where is the evidence that setting goals is helpful and productive? When you listen to disheartened or confused students, you will hear them lament that everywhere, it seems, there are other students who are simply lucky. Success comes easily to them. They note that the lucky students appear to waltz into opportunities with seemingly little planning. This contrasts with their own experience where in spite of their efforts they are not as successful or as focused as they desire. In fact, most of their energy is focused on searching for direction. So what, in particular, is different about these two types of students? A major difference between them is their ability to set goals.

To know how to set goals, you must know the difference between goals and desires. Goals are different than desires or wishes. A **goal** is viewed as a purpose to which a person is unalterably committed (Crabb & Allender, 1984). A goal is within the person's control. Goals are objectives toward which you can work, such as completing a course project on time. A desire is something that a person wants to happen, but cannot make happen. A desire is beyond one's personal control.

What if you have difficulty setting goals? What can you do, if in spite of your best efforts it seems that you are unable to set goals? How can you do more than just entertain the importance of goal-setting? In all likelihood you must be convinced about the value of goal-setting and you must find out for yourself how to create goals that work for you. This chapter will assist you in learning about the relationship between goal-setting and university success. It will help you understand the practical impact of goal-setting on achievement, satisfaction, and persistence. Further, it will help you learn about the types of goals you need to set to be able to handle the developmental transitions that are a part of your university experience.

Research on Goal-Setting

Research demonstrates that those who set goals for themselves have different experiences than those who do not set goals. Tinto (1997) has written extensively on the importance, or necessity, of setting goals and lists three major outcomes of that venture. Goal-setting fosters persistence so that students successfully complete tasks. It increases students' motivation so that they stay on track, and it enhances their ability to regulate their own behaviour so that they can focus on the actions that promote success.

Tinto (1997) has explored the factors that interact to produce success in university and has found that the more invested one is in the post-secondary environment, the greater the likelihood of persistence in academic endeavours. Based on this research comes the observation that students who set goals experience greater acquisition of knowledge and skills necessary, not just for mere academic survival, but for thriving in the post-secondary environment. To succeed in this new, sometimes foreign environment, most students must change behaviours, skills, attitudes, routines, and values (Allgood, Alvarez, & Fairbanks, 2000). University can be "a make it or break it" experience in which those who are ready can adapt goal-setting strategies to focus their actions toward success. Others must either learn how to do this or experience the overwhelming stress that a lack of goal-setting produces.

Because goals clarify relevant tasks to be performed and help students direct their efforts persistently, goals are motivational (Locke, Shaw, Saari, & Latham, 1981). As students choose to participate in higher education activities they experience an increase in motivation and desirable developmental outcomes (Kaufman & Creamer, 1991). Taken further, students who set goals develop an intrinsic motivation to do well, learn how to regulate and monitor their progress, and further develop a sense of their ability to complete academic tasks (Lan, 1996). Indeed, this is an important connection, as your motivation as a student is related to many factors, not the least of which is the belief that you are capable of developing the cognitive skills necessary to learn and succeed (Greene & Miller, 1996).

Using Goals to Manage the Transition

Allgood and his colleagues (2000) investigated the relationship between first-year experience and the importance of major educational goals. They concluded that students prepared to commit to personal goals were more likely to be committed to developing the skills that would ensure their adjustment and success. Goals increase motivation, aid in persistence, avoid crises, and facilitate the development of self-efficacy.

Tinto (1993) describes this process of adaptation to university as follows. Within the first few weeks of university you will experience a process wherein you will either find your place in the post-secondary environment, or depart prematurely. You will progress through three stages of adaptation: separation, transition, and incorporation. As you leave behind familiar relationships and study strategies (separation), it is critical to develop new approaches to learning and to find a new place of belonging (transition and incorporation). Successful students positively adapt to the new environment, whereas others may falter as they experience difficulties and disillusionment that lead to giving up or loss of confidence. The developmental challenges you must overcome during your first year of university can be understood as either crises or transitions (Birnie-Lefcovitch, 2000). Crises are perceived as disruptive, while transitions are viewed as expected changes for which you can prepare. Both alter the way you view yourself or your world. The personal and academic goals you develop can assist you in progressing through the stages of adaptation and managing the changes you will experience.

How do we account for differences found in first-year students between those who persist and those who do not? Importantly, students who are comfortable establishing goals use the events they experience during their transition as the basis for their goal-setting, while those who construe their transitional events as crises fail to take actions to help them succeed. Additionally, Braxton, Brier, and Hossler (1988) have discovered that lack of awareness, emotional factors, and dissatisfaction with the institution are significant reasons why students do not persist and ultimately withdraw from university. It is apparent then, that some students are not prepared for, or are not competent to adapt successfully to the academic and personal demands of university. Somehow, these students have not developed an accurate sense of their self-efficacy (Bandura, 1977, 1986) and are unprepared to pursue self-exploration. Inherent in this situation is the inability of some students to engage in risk-taking, to adjust their study skills, and to set appropriate goals.

The self-discovery process of increasing your awareness of the interactive influence of goals on academic success can be useful for you as you develop strategies for managing the challenges and adapting to the demands of university. Your answers to the self-appraisal questions in Chapter 2 provide you with an initial assessment of your goal-setting capabilities. Learning more specific details about the process of designing goals that promote personal achievement will improve your probability of success as a university student, which will result in a greater sense of self-confidence. With practice and guidance you can become more confident in your goal-setting capabilities, effectively delineating specific academic and social goals that will ensure your success in managing the developmental tasks of university.

Academic Goals

Now that you are aware of the importance of goals, what kinds of goals should you develop? What are the outcomes you wish to attain? You will soon learn that different kinds of goals affect you differently. Some goals will focus you specifically on mastering the course content. Other goals will assist you in refining the skills that make you a more effective learner. One of your major priorities is to do well in your academic program; thus, figuring out how to develop the course goals, competency goals, and career goals that fit your program, will ensure that you achieve your overall objective. All of these outcome goals relate to one another. However, to understand the unique impact of each of them it is useful to examine them individually.

Course Goals

Course goals are specific goals set to ensure that you master both the content of the courses, and the learning processes that will increase your effectiveness in handling continuing courses. They also help you maintain your motivation so that you are able to persevere even when you experience problems. Course goals detail the content you desire to learn and the outcome you identify as signifying your success.

What will make you successful in your courses? One factor of importance is satisfaction. Pike (1991) has found that satisfaction has a great impact on students' grades and their tendency to stay in school. In other words, your frame of mind can influence your academic performance, as measured on your transcript. Satisfaction is also associated with your ability to generate a purpose for persisting in university.

Dissatisfied students often wonder why their grades are lower than expected, and why they lack drive or energy to apply themselves. What they soon discover is that they lack a goal to help them feel satisfied about their efforts. They must learn the practical steps for documenting goals, both short-term and long-term, understand the value of issuing personal challenges to meet certain specific steps along the way, and accept the lesson that goals change over time as priorities are shifted (Paul, 1996). They must learn to establish goals related to the reading, writing, and test-preparation tasks associated with each course.

How can you develop satisfaction? It emerges through developing strategies for managing your academic workload, as well as focusing on personal goals (Garland & Doyle, 2000; Paul, 1996). Goal-setting is seen as a method to offset the potential for drifting through your academic experiences without a direction. To-do, or to-have, lists (Garland & Doyle, 2000) are used to help you focus on the active management of your workloads and academic responsibilities. Your goals help you avoid the susceptibility to distraction, and reduction in motivation that accompanies drifting.

What should you be learning in your courses? Determine what you want to learn in each course in which you are enrolled and identify the criteria you will use to assess your learning outcomes. You are enrolled in this course because the information will be useful for you. Thus your course goals will reflect the utility of the content of the course as well as your expected performance as measured by grades. In addition to setting goals so that you adequately learn the information presented in each course, it is useful to set course goals that focus on personal growth. When you reflect on your university education you will discover that post-secondary education is much more than the sum of the collection of courses and grades (Cochran, 1978). Because education is the development of the whole person, growth is much more than knowledge acquisition and skill development, and thus, it must focus on personal change. In fact, it has been said that "increased skill or know-how without personal change is like dancing without enthusiasm" (Cochran, 1978).

Productive course goals reflect your anticipated areas of academic growth as well as the necessary skills and personal changes that will allow you to effectively manage your academics in the context of multiple jobs, family expectations, and recreational activities.

Competency Goals

Having an interest in something is different than being competent in it. From an academic perspective, being competent implies possessing the ability to process academic tasks in an effective manner. Specifically, it means you need to know how to study and handle the myriad of school tasks, but it also means knowing how to deal with incomprehensible or complex content. Successful students have the confidence to raise their hands in class, acknowledge that they do not understand, and request clarification. When you are able to discern your level of knowledge and whether or not you know something, you develop a realistic sense of confidence in your ability levels. As further support, research findings suggest that those who develop goals experience increased motivation and an increased use of suitable learning strategies (Tuckman, 1996).

As you become more knowledgeable about goals you will learn that different types of goals produce different outcomes. Because students want to know which goals are the best ones for ensuring their academic success, researchers have investigated this question (Albaili, 1998; Dweck & Leggett, 1988; Vermetten, Lodewijks, & Vermunt, 2001). They have discovered that the type of goal that works best depends upon the learning situation and the student's personality. Furthermore, they have determined that there are two major types of goals that affect how you learn and achieve academically: **mastery goals** and **performance goals**.

Mastery goals, also called learning goals or task orientation, are focused on the acquisition of new skills or the growth of a knowledge base. According to researchers, individuals with mastery goals tend to focus on the intrinsic worth of learning, including understanding and mastering academic principles (Ames & Archer, 1988). These students place tremendous value on personal effort as the way to produce positive outcome. They focus on deep processing (Marton & Saljo, 1997), or on a meaning orientation toward learning (Entwistle, 1988). Deep processing has been defined (Craik & Lockhart, 1972) as using higher order thinking in order to develop a conceptual understanding of complex constructs. Meaning orientation is a desire to gain greater understanding of concepts and ideas that are personally relevant.

Research has found that students with mastery goals develop the higher order critical thinking and cognitive strategies that make them more successful as students. They learn how to organize and integrate academic concepts, develop thinking strategies for analyzing their learning, and attain higher academic achievement (Schraw, Horn, Thorndike-Christ, & Bruning, 1995). Because mastery goals help students develop learning processes that facilitate greater understanding of material (called deep processing skills), they become more capable of understanding complex concepts (Kong & Hau, 1996; Schmieck, Ribich, & Ramanaiah, 1977). Thus, it appears that when students process course information through procedures such as developing outlines, comparing and contrasting techniques, and critical thinking, they increase both their academic abilities and their ability to master or learn material. They are also more likely to be actively and cognitively engaged in the material. Students who utilize deeper processing techniques such as personalization, visual imagery, and mnemonics, increase their level of personal awareness and their ability to self-regulate and delineate personal goals.

Of import is the observation that mastery situations enhance intrinsic motivation and persistence (Bergin, 1995). In other words, feeling successful in regards to a task usually results in increased internal satisfaction, which leads to increased motivation as well as stronger persistence to complete the task. As we know, the impact of persistence is pervasive on satisfaction and personal investment, which increases the potential for involvement in one's post-secondary home.

By contrast, performance goals (also called ego orientation) are concerned with an external validation of one's competence or ability, relative to the performance of others. Students who set performance goals focus on proving how much they know by demonstrating higher grades than their fellow students. The grade, or outcome, is the focus of their efforts. They are motivated by looking good in comparison with others and are motivated to work hard in order to obtain external rewards (e.g., others' approval, higher grades).

The learning strategies of students who develop performance goals tend to focus on surface processing such as memorizing (Marton & Saljo, 1997), or reproducing (Entwistle, 1988). For example, students rely on focusing their attention on specific facts and pieces of unrelated material and use rote or verbatim memory to retain the information. These students believe that they are productive based on the sheer amount of time spent memorizing their books. Their demise becomes apparent during tests when they grapple with attempts to recall from memory information that was not learned effectively.

Researchers have generally found that mastery goals are superior to performance goals, with the exception of highly competitive and achievement-oriented students (Vermetten et al., 2001). Performance goals also work well in class situations when students are being marked on the curve. Performance goals help students focus their efforts on meeting the specific demands of a course, whereas mastery goals focus on attaining competencies by developing an understanding of concepts as well as refining the skills that will make them student scholars. Becoming a student scholar occurs when you learn to increase both the depth and breadth of processing information (Doyle & Garland, 2001) through academic support programs or learning seminars. Mastery goals increase your efficiency in your study skills and reduce test anxiety. Because mastery goals help you learn better, you increase your academic performance and add to your confidence as a learner. Mastery goals enhance your self-esteem and increase your involvement and investment in your education.

Career Goals

Alongside academic demands and goals are issues concerning the choice of a potential career. Career goals allow you to imagine a better life. These goals focus your creative energy. They direct your future. Identifying career goals can help you plan your university program, discover your personal interests, and develop greater satisfaction with your university experience (Crozier, Dobbs, Douglas, & Hung, 1999). As you learn how educational and career information relates to your own personal goals, you are better able to define goals that motivate you.

Goals that motivate you are called **purpose goals** and represent the desired outcomes you are intending to achieve (Harackiewicz, Barron, & Elliot, 1998). For example, some students seek career paths where they can help other people while others describe their purpose as protecting the environment. This contrasts with **target goals**, which are the methods you use to achieve your objective. For instance, students can help others as a social worker, or in the field of medicine, or through non-career related volunteer activities. Generally, purpose goals are significant because they provide the motivational energy for accomplishment and persistence.

Later in this text you will learn to develop greater awareness of your career goals and direction. You will develop a confidence in your ability to determine your career direction. You will learn how dealing with the new demands of university is an avenue to a career, and also an experience that shapes who you are as a person. Just as self-esteem will emerge as a developmental issue for you during your years in university or college, feeling involved in your academic home should contribute to your ability to address and elucidate career goals. As you develop practical career goals related to your academic interests, you begin to take charge of your life.

Social Goals

As you discovered in the initial chapters of this textbook, your success in university is influenced by both academic and social factors. Clearly, as you increase your personal and social investment in your university, you increase your probability of success. As you learned in Chapter 1, your level of self-confidence is a powerful variable that directs your level of energy and helps you to invest in your university experience. Empirical evidence demonstrates that students can enhance their self-confidence in their ability to learn by adapting meaningful learning strategies (Greene & Miller, 1996). Researchers have found that social and personal goals as well as academic and vocational goals have a significant impact on students' achievement (Shen, 1997). It has also been observed that goals, by necessity, change and shift in importance as students move through their education.

Of particular importance is the level of affiliation you feel with your academic home and whether you feel as if you belong. To feel a part of your educational and social experience affords the opportunity to personally invest and become anchored in what you are doing. Here is where it gets cyclical: the greater the level of your social integration, the more likely you are to invest in institutional goals, which further increases your likelihood of continuing in your education and developing your social self. The development of your social self provides you with the personal attributes to persist, and remain focused on your academic and career goals.

It is critical, then, that you be able to articulate social goals that will further enrich your experience in your university. These goals work hand in hand with your academic and career goals to ensure that you offer yourself the most robust and well-rounded education possible. How do you set social goals? What types of activities can facilitate the achievement of your social goals?

As previously noted, your level of self-confidence will be a major force in directing your social energy. When you feel good about yourself, you are more likely to consider interacting with other people. Feeling good about yourself occurs when you are involved in your community, and are healthy and productively focused.

Getting involved starts early as you participate in orientation exercises. In becoming involved and preparing yourself for new, unfamiliar opportunities, you gain a chance to expand and develop your social skills from those that were effective in high school. You begin the process of responding to the demands of a more independent learning environment. Friends and meaningful relationships provide a major source of personal affiliation and help to determine whether you will explore the campus environment and discover further avenues for growth. Try setting a practical goal of meeting new people in each of your classes each semester. In doing this, you increase your personal network on campus and increase the potential for discovering valuable activities.

Find a group, organization, or activity that interests you. Set a goal of joining at least one new club or participating in one new activity each semester, even if it is not the ideal or most relevant activity. Do not procrastinate by telling yourself you can do it later. You won't, and then the opportunity to affiliate is subsequently hindered. Become physically active. Join an intramural team or enrol in an exercise class as a means of meeting others, as well as investing in your own physical health. An important means of becoming involved on campus is to seek part-time work as a research assistant or staff member. Besides offering some form of remuneration, in itself a motivator, working on campus expands your knowledge of the institution and provides you with an opportunity to contribute to research projects being conducted at your university.

You will also notice that when you feel connected to your educational experience, you will be more prepared to manage the responsibilities that are related to the diverse roles you assume as a university student. An important aspect of becoming autonomous and independent (Chickering & Reisser, 1993) is to make your own decisions and goals regarding health, financial priorities, family expectations, and lifestyle preferences.

Setting goals for engaging in physical activities will not only add to your sense of self-confidence and personal health, but can provide the opportunity to meet other students. As you set goals for becoming more physically active you will find that your involvement in these activities adds to your energy, reduces stress, and improves your ability to manage academic demands, so that you are successful in achieving your potential.

Just as taking control of your health fuels your success, so does taking control of your financial priorities. Learning to budget so that you are not overextended is a skill that allows you to focus on your academic responsibilities rather than be distracted by financial worries. One of the advantages of developing connections with other students is that you can sometimes share resources, allowing you to more effectively manage your finances.

Juggling family expectations and making lifestyle choices are important aspects of developing the social supports that are necessary for success in university. Some of your goals in these areas will be negotiated with others as you strive to manage both the personal and academic arenas of your life. Designing social goals that build on your current skill levels adds to your competencies and thus develops the critical components that ensure success in your post-secondary life.

Creating Goals that Work

You are now ready to use the goal-setting process to develop goals that are meaningful and personally relevant. Use the self-development model on page 102 to design your plan for developing goals that will enhance your development. Although you may begin with a general idea of what you would like to accomplish this year, the STAR model designs the details what will become your success plan. You will quickly discover how the combination of academic mastery and performance goals, coupled with career, personal, and social goals, adds to both your competence and confidence as a student. Your goals provide you with direction and are supplemented by an action plan to ensure that you achieve your desired outcome. You will learn how to increase the probability of success by setting goals that are reasonable, gradually building confidence in your ability to achieve. Your success in developing goals that challenge, but do not overwhelm you, will ensure that you develop new capabilities, and build a set of personal expectations about your own ability to perform at the level you desire. The timeframes you set as part of your goal-setting process provide an opportunity to evaluate your ongoing progress. This self-mastery, as well as feedback from others, provides you with the necessary information to judge your own effectiveness in attaining your goals. When you use the feedback, you

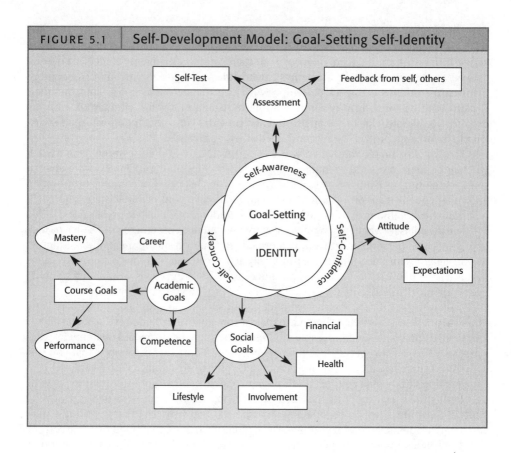

FIGURE 5.1 | **Self-Development Model: Goal-Setting Self-Identity**

reinforce productive actions, and correct unproductive actions, thus adding to your capabilities as a student scholar.

You will recall that Maslow (1970) described a hierarchy of basic needs that motivate individuals. These needs provide the basis for your goal-setting. Consider a situation in which you are hungry. Your immediate goal is to find a means of satisfying that hunger. Your response to fulfilling that need is influenced by the nature of the situation and your own resources. As the nature of the situation changes, your responses change. In a situation in which you experience hunger, your response will be different, depending upon whether you are sitting in a restaurant with money in your pocket or lost in the Australian outback with a group of fellow survivors. Your resources include both the capabilities you have to meet that need, and the confidence that you will be able to use those capabilities effectively. At times throughout your university experience, you will realize that the needs that are dominant in determining your goals vary. You will also begin to comprehend how influential these needs are as a source of motivation. The different goals you establish in order to be successful in university are reflective of these needs. Each of your goals will assist you in directing your effort and action. Whether or not you are successful in attaining these goals depends upon your ability to develop and articulate achievable goals, clarify your expectations, design your action plan, and utilize your feedback loop (Stark, Shaw, & Lowther, 1989).

STAR Model

Goals are the objectives you are trying to accomplish (Locke et al., 1981). Think of goals as dreams with deadlines. Generally perceived as aims or intentions, goals guide your achievements. Your ability to ensure success in achieving your dreams is directly related to your ability to design relevant goals. Thanks to the extensive research efforts investigating the factors that are necessary for goals to be effective, it is possible to provide you with the specifications for creating successful goals. Successful goals are **S**pecific, **T**estable, **A**ttainable, and **R**elevant.

Specific

It is important to avoid the common mistake of developing goals that are general, abstract, and vague. Not only are these goals difficult to measure, but they do not help you focus your effort. Making a goal specific requires developing a clearly defined action statement that leads to a particular outcome (Locke et al., 1981). Specific goals are clear and concrete. The amount and type of specification depends on the context. However, it has been demonstrated that when students develop detailed goals in specific arenas they feel less overwhelmed and more confident about their ability to succeed (Stark et al., 1989). The clarity of a goal relates to how adequate it is for a particular purpose (Frewin, 1977). As you learn to develop clear, specific goals, you eliminate the ambiguity in your goal aspirations. For example, once you learn to focus a general goal such as "succeeding in a course," to a more specific goal of "allocating a defined amount of time to complete a particular task, and thus attaining a grade of 80 percent on your first exam," you are able to clearly measure whether or not you have succeeded in achieving this goal. In addition, you clarify that a general objective, such as success in a course, is actually a series of specific sub-goals that, if completed, will produce the successful outcome you desire.

Testable

In order to measure whether or not you have achieved your goal, you must develop a goal that you can adequately assess. Therefore, an effective goal must be testable. Goals are more than wishes or desires. Effective goals must be stated in terms of actions that can be measured. Testable goals have **time limits**. Without time limits, goals are of little value. Time limits provide a focus for evaluating whether or not you have achieved the objectives you desire. Time limits provide the feedback loop in which you will evaluate your success in achieving the goal. Generally, short-term goals provide the opportunity for frequent, reinforcing feedback, and may include more concrete objectives. They may also be sub-steps of a larger, long-range goal. Long-range goals can focus on broader, developmental areas, and are generally more abstract and imprecise (Stark et al., 1989).

Attainable

Goals motivate you to strive for something better. Goals are designed to encourage achievement as they encourage you to reach beyond where you are now, to learn and do more. Your success is related to how attainable the goal is. A goal is attainable if you have an ability level to achieve the goal, are prepared for the goal, and can manage the difficulty of the goal. The degree of difficulty is an important criterion. With the right amount of difficulty, you are motivated to pursue the goal and able to develop the attributes that will fuel a successful performance. Over 500 studies have supported the general thesis that specific, difficult goals lead to higher success rates than easy goals. Do your best goals, or no goals (Locke et al., 1981). Setting attainable goals allows you to build your confidence as you develop greater competencies.

Relevant

Goals must be relevant. When goals are important, valued, and useful, individuals feel more interested and committed toward investing the effort to achieve them (Locke et al., 1981). Relevant goals are personally meaningful and important. Because they are meaningful they provide a sense of personal control in which you direct your effort. They create an incentive that encourages you to persist (Bandura, 1986). Relevant goals reflect your personal priorities and passions. When you personally develop your own goals and design the strategies for fulfilling those goals, you are more committed toward achieving them. When individuals set their own goals, they achieve higher levels of performance than when goals are set or assigned by others (Locke, Frederick, Buckner, & Bobko, 1984). The more personally relevant goals are, the more likely you are to invest continued effort toward achieving them.

Exercise 5.1 SUCCESS SKILLS: DREAMS AS A STAR GOAL

Think about one of your dreams. Describe this dream in the form of a STAR goal.

Using the STAR model you can develop goals that are motivating and measurable. An important factor influencing your effectiveness in achieving these goals is your expectations regarding them. Two types of expectancies will influence your success: outcome expectancies and efficacy expectancies (Bandura, 1986). Outcome expectancies are the results you expect as a result of your actions. Efficacy expectancies are your perceptions of whether or not you will be able to do what is necessary in order to achieve these goals. Both of these expectancies influence your dedication and determination to achieve your goal.

To ensure that you achieve the goals that you have identified, you must plan deliberate actions to ensure that your goals are more than just desires or wishful thinking. This action plan includes the activities that you will do to ensure your success. As you increase your ability to identify specific actions that you can take, you improve the likelihood that you will achieve success. For example, instead of stating that you should allocate ample time for studying, it is better to specify that this week you will increase the amount of your reading and preparation time in each of your courses by two additional hours. Rather than simply stating that your goal is to earn an A in a course—a desire—you provide details regarding study strategies you will practise that can facilitate this desired outcome. Perhaps you would like to improve your level of physical fitness. Outlining the specific actions (e.g., attend aerobics three times a week), for how you will accomplish this is a critical component of your plan.

To assess whether or not your goal plan is succeeding, you need feedback. Feedback is necessary to keep you on track. Feedback can occur by monitoring your own behaviour, judging the effectiveness of your actions, and assessing how well you are doing in pursuit of this goal. Another source of feedback is the evaluation of others. Feedback can be reinforcing or corrective. As a result of feedback, you must evaluate your actions in relation to your desired goals. This evaluation can provide the impetus for continuing in the current direction, or it can signal a turning point at which you choose new goals, or change your outcome expectations.

Consider the parallels between your academic journey and a self-guided trek up a mountain trail. As you climb the trail to get to your destination (i.e., purpose goal), you travel through heavily treed mountainous landscape. Depending upon your preparation and previous experience (i.e., competencies), your comfort and confidence regarding your ability to navigate the terrain varies (i.e., expectancies). Depending upon your abilities, you will select different paths (i.e., outcome goals), and use different strategies (i.e., mastery goals), to get to the place you want to be. If, as you travel, you come across a rapidly rushing stream, your immediate goal (i.e., short-term goal), is to get to the other side. You must now choose from several options, and depending on the conditions, time, immediate safety, and your personal needs, you will make different choices. You may choose to detour, to wait for help, or to use the natural environment as stepping stones (i.e., subgoals). The actions you take to get to the other side are influenced by the feedback you receive. In accomplishing your aim of arriving at the end of the trail, you engage in the goal-setting process.

Your university education provides a number of paths that will lead to your future. To assist you in navigating the process it is useful to begin by choosing a destination (i.e. purpose goal). The additional goals (i.e., outcome goals), depend upon the experience and expertise you bring. You may need to develop new competencies (i.e., mastery goals) to help you more effectively manage the demands you will face in the environment. With the use of the STAR model you can develop goals that are personally motivating and accurately measurable. These goals will be supported by a series of deliberate actions you will take (i.e., action plan), so that you will accomplish your goal. Because your confidence in your ability to succeed depends upon the expectancies you have about university (i.e., outcome expectancies), and your own judgment about your ability to achieve these outcomes, you must develop goals with these factors in mind.

Be honest in your self-appraisal and make certain that your goals provide the motivational supports that are necessary for your success. Along the way you will gather feedback through self-evaluation and evaluation from others that will help you determine how well you are doing relative to your goals. This may provide the corrective action you need to remain on track to your ultimate destination.

The following framework is based on the goal-setting information from this chapter. It is intended to assist you in developing your own goals for succeeding in university. Review this framework and use it along with the STAR model for developing your own success plan of relevant goals.

> **Purpose goal:** Primary reasons for attending university or taking this course
>
> **Outcomes:** Academic and social goals
>
> **Performance goal:** Course goals
>
> **Mastery goal:** Competency goals
>
> **Actions:** Specific activities
>
> **Expectancies:** Ideas for maintaining motivation and interest
>
> **Feedback:** Evaluation from others and self-awareness

Example of Student Goals

Purpose goal: Because I want to get into a professional school I plan to complete my first year of university with a B+ average (April 30, 2003).

Outcomes: To earn a grade-point average of 3.5 to 4.0.

Performance goal: To get an A in my first-term history course (Dec. 2002).

Mastery goal: To learn the basics of writing a history term paper (Dec. 2002).

Actions: To prepare for the mid-term exam I will take a practice exam two weeks before the scheduled mid-term. I will read 150 pages of literature each week.

I plan to commit 3 hours/week to the details of writing a term paper. In week one I will choose my topic and obtain three references.

Expectancies: Because I like the course content and usually earn top grades in this area, I expect that I will be motivated to read regularly.

Feedback: My professors' feedback on my written work can inform me about aspects of my writing that I need to improve.

Exercise 5.2 SUCCESS SKILLS: DEVELOPING GOALS

To begin your personal goal-setting process it is useful to reflect on the hopes and dreams that influenced your decision to attend university. Your dreams and future aspirations can be your starting point. Use them to describe your purpose goal. Then select one of your courses and design both mastery and performance goals for that course. Remember to make each goal specific, testable with time limits, attainable for you, and relevant to your needs and desires. Think carefully about the activities that will ensure your ablility to achieve these goals, and think about the expectancies you have for your own success. Finally, identify the sources you will use for feedback that can help you identify whether or not you are progressing as you desire.

Purpose goal: Some of my primary reasons for attending university or taking this course are…

Outcomes: When I think about my academic and social activities relative to this course, I want to achieve…

Performance goal: In this course I expect to…

Mastery goal: To become a better student in this class I will need to develop the following competencies…

Actions: I will engage in the following activities as a way to reinforce my efforts to achieve my goals…

Expectancies: To motivate myself and maintain my interest in this course I will…

Feedback: To increase my own awareness of my progress I will…

To get feedback from others I will…

Setting a goal is the beginning ... achieving the goal is the victory. To achieve the victory you desire, you can incorporate the information you have learned through your reading and your initial self-assessment (Chapter 2) to design the details that will define your goals for the upcoming year. An important detail will be to develop a time management schedule for ensuring your success in accomplishing these goals. Through including both academic and social goals in your plan, you enhance the probability of success as you benefit from the synergistic effect of these two arenas on your self-confidence. Incorporating the essential elements of the STAR model allows your goals to become meaningful and motivational. Thus, you will be able to proceed purposefully and persistently on the path that is your future. Most importantly, your goals are the essential elements of the plan that ensure that today's dreams become tomorrow's accomplishments.

It's More Than Common Sense

Setting Goals to Improve Academic Performance

Gerard H. Seijts, Ph.D.
Richard Ivey School of Business, University of Western Ontario

Goal-setting theory (Locke & Latham, 1990; Pinder, 1998) is considered to be one of the most effective motivational theories. The theory states that specific, challenging goals, either assigned or self-set, plus a high sense of confidence in attaining them, are the impetus for high performance. The positive effect of specific, challenging goals on performance has been demonstrated in numerous areas, including educational, business, and sports settings. Both individuals and groups can benefit from setting goals (Locke & Latham, 1990; Seijts & Latham, 2000).

Goal-setting theory is a practical theory in that it provides clear guidelines (e.g., set goals that are specific, measurable, attainable, and time-based), for individuals as to how performance can be improved. Unfortunately, individuals and groups may downplay the importance of goal-setting because they believe that almost everyone sets goals. This assumption is faulty because the core concepts underlying effective goal-setting often are not systematically applied (Locke & Latham, 1990; Seijts, Taylor, & Latham, 1998). For example, many people who perceive themselves as effective goal setters (e.g., students, instructors, business people, and sports athletes) fail to engage in behaviours that characterize successful goal-setting processes. Instead, they are observed to set vague or unreasonable goals, to have low commitment to goals, and to seek feedback only irregularly, if at all. The main tenets of goal-setting theory are as follows.

First, specific, challenging goals lead to higher performance than the setting of abstract goals such as "doing one's best." This is because specific goals (e.g., get an A for the term-paper), help define what constitutes an acceptable level of performance. Abstract goals, in contrast, allow individuals to give themselves the benefit of the doubt in evaluating their performance as a success. In the absence of a specific, challenging goal, individuals have a tendency to assume that their performance is better than it actually is, and hence do not always give their maximum effort while working on a task.

Second, given goal commitment, there is a linear relationship between goal difficulty and performance. The higher the goal, the higher the performance, and it is only when individuals reach the limit of their abilities that the linear relationship between goal difficulty and performance levels off (Seijts, Meertens, & Kok, 1997). Goal-setting does not work if the goal is totally beyond one's reach. Goals thus need to be realistic or believable to have a positive effect on performance. However, performance does not necessarily drop when goals become impossible. As long as individuals try to get as close as they can to the goal (e.g., because the goal has relevance to them), performance will be high. Nevertheless, commitment becomes harder to obtain with increased goal levels. Individuals need to have positive outcome expectancies of goal attainment (i.e., tangible or intangible results of achieving the goal), as well as a high sense of confidence to commit to specific, challenging goals.

Third, feedback is a necessary but not sufficient condition for goals to have an effect on performance. For example, individuals who are progressing at a slower rate than required to meet the goal, need to know this in order to be able to adjust their effort level, or to look for more effective strategies to attain the goal. If individuals do not receive feedback from sources (e.g., course instructors, peers, and team projects), they need to engage in feedback-seeking behaviours. The most effective feedback allows individuals to make adjustments so that they can grow and develop their skills. At the same time, however, providing individuals with feedback on their performance in cases where they do not have a specific, challenging goal in mind has little effect on performance.

Committing oneself to specific, challenging goals does not always lead to an improvement in performance. Research has shown that when a task is novel and complex, such as when an individual is in the process of learning how to perform the task (e.g., how to master textbooks, maximize the learning from lectures, or prepare for and write exams), performance decreases when a specific, challenging goal is set. In these situations where people have not yet learned the appropriate strategies for performing a task effectively, additional strategies are needed in order to succeed (Latham & Seijts, 1999; Seijts & Latham, 2001).

Performance on novel, complex tasks can be enhanced through the setting of proximal goals, learning goals, or both (proximal learning goals). Proximal or sub-goals divide the task into a series of smaller and controllable opportunities of modest size that produce visible results. A learning goal challenges individuals to formulate strategies to accomplish a task.

The setting of proximal goals (e.g., specific goals for mid-term grades, quizzes, term papers, and class participation, which, in turn, contribute to overall course grades) provides individuals with clear markers of goal progress and reduces the risk of self-demoralization that can occur when current accomplishments are measured against a distal or end-goal. Proximal goals in conjunction with a distal goal provide individuals with additional, specific information about performance that is not present when a distal goal alone, such as an overall course grade, is set. That is, inherent in proximal goals is an increase in performance feedback that can be crucial for altering strategies while maintaining effort and persistence to attain the distal goal.

In educational and business-like contexts, suitable task strategies are often not known and must be discovered through problem solving and trial and error (e.g., how to research a topic and develop a class presentation on the research, or how to implement innovations in organizations without creating resistance). A high sense of confidence is required to remain committed to the goal. Setting proximal goals and seeking performance feedback can assist individuals in facilitating the learning process in educational (Bandura & Schunk, 1981) and business-like (Latham & Seijts, 1999) settings.

It is tempting for individuals to focus on task outcomes such as course grades and GPA alone, even when obstacles and setbacks are encountered. The focus on such outcomes is often a function of competitive processes in the classroom, others' expectations, and several other factors. Grades, no doubt, are important to one's career. But is this exclusive focus on outcomes a proper or smart one? For example, what would happen if we directed our attention to learning rather than task-outcome achievement, at least in the early stages of learning how to best perform the task? That is, what would happen if we would attempt to work smarter (e.g., discover and implement task or course-specific strategies), rather than harder?

In a series of studies, Gary Latham, a professor at the University of Toronto, and I examined the effects of specific, challenging outcome goals and specific, challenging learning goals on a complex task (Seijts & Latham, 2001). The findings have important implications for students. The results we obtained suggest that, on tasks that are novel or complex, the assignment of learning goals (e.g., discover and implement strategies that will help you to master the task successfully) lead to higher goal commitment, higher confidence in mastering the task, and higher performance than the assignment of outcome goals (e.g., course grade). Similar research in educational settings has found that setting outcome goals on complex tasks such as solving math problems can trigger apprehensions of failure that, in turn, lower self-confidence in mastering the task (Bandura & Schunk, 1981). These findings together suggest that rather than emphasizing outcome goals on tasks that are perceived as complex, students and instructors should emphasize learning goals. Such goals stress discovering means (e.g., talking to the instructor about his or her expectations, and asking others to critique one's report) to achieve the desired outcomes: mastering the task and obtaining good grades. This should be helpful information for first-year students as they try to discover during the first few months in university what will, and will not, work for them.

Goal-setting has a positive effect on both motivation and learning (Seijts, 2001). Research has shown that outcome goals should be set when motivation is the issue (i.e. when individuals have the abilities and knowledge required to perform the task). In contrast, it would prove useful if individuals adopted proximal goals or learning goals when the requisite knowledge to perform the task is lacking. All goals—outcome, proximal, and learning, should be specific and challenging to have a positive effect on task performance.

Self-awareness
Important personal characteristics that will help me achieve my goals are…

Self-confidence
Past experience has taught me that I can achieve my goals when I…

Self-concept
The goals that work best for me are…

Chapter Summary

Goal-setting, an essential component of academic success, is the focus of this chapter. The chapter explains the importance of both academic and social goals as essential for easing the transition into new situations. The chapter describes the complex interrelationship between course goals, competency goals, and career goals, as significant factors influencing success in university. Readers learn to differentiate between mastery and performance goals. Introduction of the STAR (specific, testable, attainable, relevant) model to goal-setting, along with practical exercises, assists students in developing appropriate goal-setting skills.

Exercises

REFLECT–ACT

The following Reflect–Act exercises are designed to help you increase both your self-awareness and self-understanding so that you are able to develop productive plans for yourself. Constructive goal-setting begins by thinking reflectively about your aspirations and attitudes. As you reflect on your experience, integrate those insights with the new information you have learned. Then, use this information to develop actions you can undertake that will ensure success in achieving your goals.

Reflect   Each year brings different dreams. As you think about your life thus far, what have been some of your most important dreams? Have any of your dreams come true? Which ones? What are some of the reasons why those dreams came true?
Act   Learning from this past experience, identify one action you can take now to make today's dreams come true.

Reflect   In considering your future, it can be productive to determine specific examples of both your goals and your desires. How do you distinguish the difference between them?
Act   Identify the activities and actions you associate with goals versus those you associate with desires.

Reflect   Describe the three most important dreams you have for your future. Since dreams are goals with deadlines, reframe these dreams as goals. In composing your dreams use the STAR model.
Act   For each goal, identify a specific action you can take as an initial step toward achieving your goal.

Reflect   What encourages you? What discourages you? What motivates you?

Act   Now that you have identified your self-motivators, plan how you can use this information this week to focus your academic activities.

Reflect   Name your favourite hero. What are the characteristics that make this person successful? What actions does this individual take to ensure that he/she achieves his/her goals?

Act   Describe actions you plan to take to model this behaviour.

GROUP DISCUSSION

1. Brainstorm the major factors that interfere with students' success in achieving their dreams.

2. Identify the major differences between individuals who appear to achieve their goals and those who do not.

3. Sometimes students are required to take courses in order to gain admission to a particular professional faculty. These entrance courses are often not intrinsically motivating for some students. Provide examples of how the information on goal-setting can help students overcome the motivational problems that they experience.

4. In which courses are students more likely to set performance goals rather than mastery goals? What are the benefits and risks associated with these two types of goals?

APPLY TO LIFE

Now that you understand the importance of course goals, competency goals, and career goals as tools for achieving success, you can use this information to design detailed plans for progressing toward attaining your dreams. Use the following questions to more clearly discover your capabilities in developing meaningful goals.

1. As I review the information I have gathered through my self-monitoring and self-reflection exercises, I can describe three personally important goals that I must achieve in order to attain the success I desire.

2. In analyzing the information I have learned in this chapter about goals, what can I do to improve my chances of success?

3. Can I describe specific information that I am learning about goal-setting that I believe will be particularly important to me in the future? What should I do differently than I have done previously? How will goal-setting influence my actions? What are the most important ideas I have learned? How do I think that I might use them?

Managing Time and Life in Terms of Academic Success

chapter 6

"Time is the coin of your life. It is the only coin you have and only you can determine how it will be spent." Carl Sandberg

---

Questions

What do I know about my own ability to manage time?

How might information on time management be personally useful?

What would I like to learn about time management?

Objectives

- Ensure academic success through effective time management.
- Understand the nature of my workload.
- Eliminate counterproductive patterns that interfere with success.
- Clarify my personal priorities.
- Establish a balanced lifestyle.

Student Success Portrait

Making the Most of My Time at University

Holly White
Memorial University

Attending university can be a very challenging transition, I know it was for me. My success, like yours, depends on my outlooks and my actions. I am enjoying my first year because I decided that instead of becoming stressed out and overwhelmed by this new experience, I would get involved and find out exactly what my university had to offer me. I was amazed by the results. There are so many different opportunities in which to get involved and so many programs to ease the transition for first-year students. Over my first two semesters, I have participated in orientation and found work on campus coordinating student activities. I volunteer three hours a week off campus and participate actively in both the Debating Society and the English Society. I have volunteered throughout the term in programs that are aimed at facilitating the incoming first-year students' transition to university. Recently, I ran in the Student Council Elections for the position of Arts Representative, and I was the only first-year student to get elected. Although I value my extracurricular activities, my academic performance is also a priority. I am a university scholarship student and have worked hard to maintain very good grades. I am proud of my academic accomplishments and I am certain this is strongly credited to my involvement and time management.

There are days when it seems like there is so much to do that the day will never end. Instead of freaking out, overwhelming myself and retreating into inactivity, or turning off the alarm and going back to sleep, I try to manage my time effectively. It is so easy to get caught up in how much I'm supposed to do that it's possible never to accomplish anything. One thing that works well for me is, at the beginning of each day, to write a daily list of things to do, as well as develop a schedule for the day. My daily schedule lists things like going to class, volunteering, and any other activities that have a set time during the day. My daily list clarifies objectives such as writing an essay, going to the bank, or making phone calls. Then I integrate the list into my schedule so I have a plan for accomplishing all I want to do. On weekends, after I write my list, I tape it to the wall and highlight it, making it more difficult to escape what has to be done, and more rewarding to cross off the things I accomplish.

Another important part of time management is making priorities. Everyone has different priorities, whether they be academic, social, or personal development. As time progresses, it is normal for different things to take priority. For example, when I have two important activities, a mid-term next week, and a volleyball tournament two weeks later, studying may take precedence over physical training this week, and that could reverse next week. Usually, I find it easier to complete my highest priorities first, and let everything else slide to the back burner, but many will suggest to do your least-liked things first and get them over with so you can spend the most time on what is most enjoyable. Like everyone else, there are days that if my list seems too long, I get overwhelmed, and it is easy to crawl into bed and try to sleep my work away. However, I know that this doesn't get the job done, but sometimes the rest helps me get the energy I need. I believe that the best thing to do when I get overwhelmed is to take a break. This may work for you too.

From my experience, attitude and perception play a huge role. I studied really hard for my last psychology mid-term, but my mark was below average. Instead of seeing this mark as a failure, I saw it only as merely an obstacle. I convinced myself that I could overcome this challenge and get a super-high mark on my next mid-term. In the opposite situation, if I do really well on a paper, or receive recognition for my creative or organizational skills, I delight in the feeling of personal accomplishment, congratulate myself on a job well done and reward myself. If you can see disappointments as challenges, not failures, and credit achievements to yourself, not flukes, life becomes much easier to handle and definitely less stressful.

Although academics are fundamental to university success, it is very important to have a healthy balance in life. That is why I am involved in activities outside of the classroom. Volunteering gives me an opportunity not only to do something I like and help others, but also to get off campus and away from university-related stress. Out of sight, out of mind, I guess. Then, after this break I can go back with a clear head, and in the right mindset to accomplish my goals. I love being busy and on the go. Participating and being involved gives me a healthy balance between school books, socializing, and interacting. In my opinion, social growth is as important as academic growth. I strongly suggest that you get involved! Find something that interests you—universities have a lot to offer, so don't feel as if there is nothing there for you. Get into it, experiment, find out more information, try something new. Who knows, you may make lifelong friendships and discover a new passion in life. A well-rounded education should consist of acquiring academic skills, social skills, and personal development skills. These are supposed to be the best years of our lives! Getting involved and making each moment count will ensure this happiness.

Time management umbrellas life. It shelters you from feeling overwhelmed by pressures of studying and work. It is easy to procrastinate, so set goals, accept challenges, and credit your achievements. Write a "to do" list, organize a daily schedule—anything to keep you on track. Get involved, partake in extracurricular activities and always remember that you are your number one priority. Hopefully, some of the tips that work for me will also work for you. I am having the best time of my life, and I hope that your time at university is as enjoyable as mine.

Attending university is a signal that you are at the threshold of your future. With your future before you, you have the freedom and the responsibility to spend your days as you choose. Hoping to make these the best days of your life, you are committed to achieving the success that you desire, and are excited about your plans for taking charge of your life and your time.

For many, the transition from high school to university comes with a new freedom. You have probably already discovered the freedom you have as a university student to do what you want to do, when you want to do it. Your arrival at university brings you the thrill of succeeding on your own, coupled with the responsibility for self-direction that is associated with independence. No longer are others telling you what to do and how to do it. You have control over your life, your educational program, and the way in which you manage your own time. Being independent and succeeding on your own is one of the benefits of being a university student.

For most of you, parents or teachers are no longer structuring your time. Within the limits of the availability of specific classes, you design your own timetables and study schedules. You are also free to schedule your work hours, time with friends, and time for recreation as you see fit. Because you are responsible for your own learning, you will soon discover that professors are not interested in whether you schedule time for studying or completing the assignments. They just want to see your finished product. What freedom! What responsibility!

Effectively managing your time is not just an important challenge of university, but of life. Critically mastering this developmental task requires knowing how to adapt to new demands (Chickering & Reisser, 1993; Kuh, 1993). Previously, you may have achieved reasonably high grades by cramming your studying into the night before the exam, or by finishing assignments at the last minute. You may be so accustomed to a tightly packed, prearranged schedule that the freedom and lack of structure of university makes you feel uncomfortable. It is quite possible that because others have controlled much of your previous study time, you may not know how to schedule study time effectively for maximum productivity and personal fulfillment. Whatever your previous time management experiences, you will most likely need to make some adjustments in order to create the balanced lifestyle that will ensure your success at university.

The way in which you perceive and use time is influenced by your personality and past history. Glancing around the classroom does not reveal how each of your fellow students manages time differently. However, once you get to know others, you may find that the person sitting next to you spends a great amount of time thinking about his/her future, devotes efforts to planning, and schedules time carefully in order to achieve his/her goals. This contrasts with another student sitting in front of you who lives spontaneously, and spends most of his/her time socializing rather than studying. Just as some individuals appear well-organized and adept at making those time-management systems work, others look hassled, chaotic, and rushed. While some individuals are planners who anticipate possibilities and potential problems, others are responsive, adaptable crisis managers. Like you, these students' values, culture, and past successes determine their time-management practices, and influence the strategies they will need to develop in order to meet their immediate and long term needs.

To enhance your probability of success, it is especially important to understand your time-management preferences. One source of information to assist you in determining your preferences are your answers to the Self-Assessment test featured in Chapter 2. Another is to reflect on the impact of your cultural values and family traditions on your attitude toward time. Within the Canadian mosaic there are many views about the nature of time that are exhibited through attitudes and actions. Your attitude is revealed through phrases such as "live today fully as if it were your last," or "take time each day to sit, listen, and be one with nature," or "don't put off to tomorrow what you can do today." It is influenced by the importance placed on achievement (i.e., academic accomplishment), versus the significance of family, social, and community relationships (i.e., social connections). It is shaped by the environment in which you live. Thus, the time preferences of individuals who value the immediacy and convenience of 24-hour shopping available on the Web contrast sharply from those folks who plan their lives in accordance to the rhythm of the seasons. Understanding the nuances and complexities of your attitude toward time can assist you in developing strategies for adjusting to the time demands expected at university.

As you continue reading this chapter, you will add to your understanding of your own self-management capabilities, identify the strengths of your personal time-management style, and focus efforts on eliminating problem areas that cause you stress or difficulty. These steps prepare you to add to your competencies, which give you control of your time and life. With this control, you add to your confidence levels, relative to your ability to manage the developmental tasks of university (Chickering & Reisser, 1993). Learning how to use your time-management capabilities to manage the academic and social tasks of university will provide you with increased awareness of the strategies that work for you, as you begin to establish personal control of your time. The more you invest in the process of taking control of your time through increased self-awareness and self-discipline, the greater will be your competence to confidently determine your success .

Why Is Time So Important?

What do we know about time management? It has been well established that effective time management is associated with higher academic performance as measured by grade point averages (GPA), higher self-ratings of performance, higher satisfaction with one's life, and less confusion about one's roles and responsibilities (Britton & Tesser, 1991; Macan, Shahani, Dipboye, & Phillips, 1990). In fact, Britton and Tesser (1991) have demonstrated that effective time management is more important in determining grades in university than is high school academic achievement. In other words, one of the most important factors in determining university success is the development of good time-management skills.

Equally important, however, is the perceived control of time. When university students perceived that they had more control over their time, they reported less role overload and ambiguity, and a decrease in tension. They experienced greater satisfaction with their life (Macan et al., 1990; Metzner & Bean, 1987). As students learned to increase their control of time, they also increased their GPAs, and their satisfaction ratings for their academic performance. Especially significant in many of these findings, perceived control of time was more important than the specific behaviours of time management. In other words, there is no right way to manage your time at university. There are many ways, and finding the right way for you is important in giving you the sense of personal control that is critical to your success.

Finding the best way to schedule your time can add to your success. Sooner or later you will discover that time, like money, is a resource for you to manage. How you spend it or invest it will affect your future. Your success in figuring out your time-management style, and using it to manage the demands of university, will add to your feelings of confidence regarding your capabilities to assume the responsibilities of university. You can enhance these feelings of confidence even more by strengthening your current skills, and by adapting the information and insights you learn to be better able to manage the open structure, demanding workload, competing requirements, and conflicting demands of university. By adding to your competencies, you become confidently in-control of your time and life.

The time plan that you design may be quite different from anyone else's. This is related to the important difference in the time demands of various types of students. For example, non-traditional students, who have commenced their post-secondary studies at a higher age than most, often have very different time demands than traditional students, who have commenced their university education immediately following high school. This is due to the responsibilities of family and work that are associated with their stage in life. Some individuals have assumed that non-traditional students have greater time-management problems than traditional students (Blaxter, Dodd, & Tight, 1996). However, researchers (Melichar, 1994; Trueman & Hartley, 1996) have found that non-traditional students have better time-management skills than traditional students, and are rated higher on completion of assignments, initiative, organizational skills, concentration abilities, common sense, and responsibility.

Figuring out your style is achieved through self-reflection, comparison, and analysis. You can begin by taking a moment to reflect about how you spend time. How would others describe you? How does your cultural background influence your perception of time? Are you perceived as efficient or inefficient, organized or disorganized, deliberate or spontaneous? What habits do you have that affect the way you approach time? What are your typical thoughts about time? Take some time to write a brief description of the way in which you manage time. Once you have an initial description of your style, you can add to it by comparing your approach to one of the four typical time-management approaches of university students. Each of these styles presents an integrated description of a general time orientation. It includes a description of time preferences and associated thoughts, feelings, and actions. Review the following four personal styles; compare them with your self-description of the way in which you spend time, and select one that most closely describes you.

Personal Styles

The following personal styles reflect four characteristic ways of managing time. Important studies (Myers, 1980; Provost & Anchors, 1987; Walker, 1988) have identified distinctive factors that differentiate individuals' time habits. These factors are attitudes such as confidence, locus of control, and need for achievement; emotions such as fears; thinking patterns; and actions. Because individuals vary in their approach to time based on a complex combination of characteristics, these descriptions provide a synopsis to help you understand the interaction of attitudes, feelings, cognitions, and behaviours in patterns of time management.

Perfectionist

Time is important to the perfectionist who is focused on doing all one can do to create future success. Never satisfied with the status quo, perfectionists are dreamers who take control by setting high goals for themselves. Because excellence is important to them they can have difficulty discriminating the amount of time that should be spent on a specific task versus the amount of time a task requires. Their tendency to spend too much time on each task means that they do not have enough time to perform at the level they expect. Their future focus involves continually imagining possibilities. They have great expectations of what they can be, and their lofty aspirations motivate them. However, the expansiveness of their goals and the lack of concrete plans to achieve these goals can present problems for perfectionists. Their fantasy world can also be an escape pattern that interferes with their success.

Perfectionists dislike the ordinary and fear mediocrity. Their thinking patterns are filled with "should" statements that focus on performing well. Typical thoughts of perfectionists include desiring to be more responsible or doubting their own abilities to achieve. Much of their time is spent feeling dissatisfied, in spite of achieving success, and worrying about not being as good as they should be.

Postponer

Postponers live for the moment. For them, time is to be experienced and enjoyed. They view the future as an extension of life as they experience it now, and often act as if there is no tomorrow. Their need for pleasure, fun, and excitement keeps them searching for the unusual. Because they fear monotony and boredom, postponers direct their thoughts to fostering excitement and avoiding responsibility. They often run out of time because of inadequate planning. Typical thoughts include, "It's just a small test," I've got lots of time," or "I'll start studying after my favourite television program."

Postponers fatigue and frustrate easily. Their short attention spans interfere with their ability to concentrate and study for long periods, and they must learn how to adjust their study strategies to give themselves the diversity and variety they need. They lack self-discipline and a sense of responsibility, and are therefore more apt to succeed when others direct, structure, or supervise their activities. They are responsive and able to manage immediate demands, but have difficulty anticipating future problems or planning for the long term. When given a chance they will choose fun over studying.

Politician

Making time for friends, family, and social encounters is a major priority for the politician. They are motivated by a need to belong and be liked by others. Whenever possible they will devote time to socialize. Anxious to please others, they often spend time doing what others want them to do, rather than what they want or need to do themselves. Because they are drawn to many social situations and are busy doing what they believe will please others, they are overextended and experience time pressures.

Adept at social interaction, politicians perceive themselves as confident and able. However, their self-confidence is invested in the opinions of others. They sometimes wonder if they measure up, so feedback from important people is particularly salient. Typical thoughts include, "I'm concerned that I will let others down," or "It's hard to stay focused, especially when my friends want me to go out with them." Because of their need for approval from others, their time is not their own and they have difficulty setting limits and choosing their own priorities.

Punisher

"What will be will be" is the fatalistic approach of the punisher. These individuals feel little control over their lives. Often pessimistic, uncertain and self-critical, they are especially aware of their past failures and inadequacies. Their focus on the past negatively affects their view that the future will be any different.

Inefficient and inconsistent, they are acutely aware of other's capabilities. Often they see themselves as not good enough. Typical thoughts include, "I can't measure up, everyone I know is better and more successful than I am," or "nothing ever works out for me." With their attention on the success of others, coupled with their self-deprecation, they easily become overwhelmed by negativity and discouragement. This leads to feelings of shame and inadequacy, and an undermining of their own ability to manage time effectively.

One of the four personal styles should fit you better than the others. You may also see yourself as an overlap between some of these personality styles, depending on the situation you are in. As you match a personal style to a picture of how you work, study, and function, you will begin to notice the interplay of your needs, feelings, thoughts, and habits on the ways in which you manage your life and your time. Your selection of one of these styles will help you understand more clearly which aspects of the university workload you will find easy to manage, as well as those you might find more difficult.

Managing the Workload

Most students acknowledge that their greatest personal challenge at university is to learn how to manage their time more effectively (Weissberg et al., 1982). Because the workload of the university is so demanding, and the tasks are of differing lengths, complexity, priority, and clarity, students are confused about how to most effectively manage the different time demands that university places on them. To master these time demands, students must become proficient at planning, pacing, prioritizing, personal control, and problem solving.

Planning

This is probably the first time in your educational career that you are responsible for planning how you will manage all of your learning and life responsibilities. Although your course outlines provide information regarding the material that you must learn, you must figure out how to most efficiently fit your courses, study sessions, assignments, social time, work responsibilities, recreation, and daily living activities into a schedule that fits your personal style and priorities. Planning involves designing a blueprint for success by determining long-term expectations, detailing short-term action plans and organizing your time into a personalized schedule that works for you.

Planning involves setting long- and short-term goals that ensure that you achieve the academic and personal success to which you aspire. This requires that you set specific academic, personal, social, and lifestyle goals and develop a specific plan for attaining these goals (see Chapter 5). In this first year of university it is best to define long range within the timeframe of the first term or first year of university. An important part of planning is a periodic review in which progress toward achieving the goals to which you have committed yourself is assessed.

All plans will succeed only if you are effective at scheduling your activities. By now you have probably discovered that time is a limited resource. As you strive to do all you want to do, you need to find enough hours in the day. Scheduling helps you structure activities to make the most of your time and ensures a healthy mixture of academic, social, and personal activities. Scheduling, however you do it, allows you to be in control of your life. The more that you incorporate concrete actions into your personal approach to organizing time (such as making "to do" lists, keeping time logs, evaluating your daily schedule, setting priorities, completing the tasks you have identified as important, and planning for the unexpected), the more proficient you become in mastering the elements of effective time planning.

Pacing

By adopting the plan you have developed for yourself, you may begin to discover that it is taking you much longer to complete academic assignments than you had anticipated. This means that you will either need to adjust your schedule or to improve your pacing.

Pacing is the ability to effectively and efficiently manage the workload of university. You are not alone in this discovery. Most university students underestimate the time that it will take them to complete assignments. Even some of your professors have difficulty with this. You can improve your pacing by developing the learning efficiency skills that are included in this course, and by changing your workload balance. Too much of one activity, not enough variety, and inappropriately investing too much time on tangential assignments are all workload issues that, once adjusted, will improve your pacing. Pacing requires you to schedule the proper balance of study, work, recreation, physical activity, and social interactions so they match your personal style of time management.

Priorities

With all the competing demands for your time, you have choices to make about how you will spend your time each day. Like it or not, each action you take is the result of a decision you have made. Your decisions generally reflect your priorities at the moment, but they may not reflect your long-term priorities. Effective time managers first clarify their long-term priorities, then commit themselves to engage in actions that support these important life goals. Once you establish for yourself the priorities that matter most, you are better able to focus on activities that support those priorities and avoid the distractions that could interfere with your success.

Perceived Control

Being in control of your time is critical to your sense of mastery. Strategies that help you gain a sense of control include engaging in activities that are fulfilling, improving your ability to manage your daily tasks, and eliminating activities that hamper your effectiveness. Research (Britton & Tesser, 1991; Macan et al., 1990) has clearly demonstrated that when students take control of their time, they feel less overwhelmed by trivial and unimportant tasks. They are able to say no to distracting activities and refrain from unproductive actions that interfere with their success. Because they are clear about their priorities they do not experience the inner conflict and confusion that is associated with feeling out of control, ambivalent, and indecisive. Your plans for changing elements of your personal style that interfere with your achievement, or replacing non-productive thoughts that feed your fears, with motivating thoughts that keep you focused, are productive ways for gaining personal control.

Problem Solving

Discovering your own best strategies for managing time is a process of experimentation and evaluation. Although you can avoid some of the common pitfalls that hinder the progress of many university students, you will soon learn that effective time management is best learned through practice and problem solving. Effective problem solving happens when you analyze your use of time, design strategies for improving your efficiency, eliminate some of the patterns in your personal style that reduce your effectiveness, understand the common problems you need to overcome, and invest effort in becoming better. Effective problem solving provides you with a blueprint for change.

Another aspect of effective problem solving involves anticipating the problems you may encounter. Knowing which task, such as writing papers, preparing for exams, and reading textbooks, are easy for you, and which ones are more challenging, is a beginning. Developing an awareness of typical problem areas that most university students experience can help you plan strategies for avoiding these potential difficulties.

It all works together. Research (Feather & Bond, 1983) has demonstrated that those students who have identified an overall sense of direction in their lives, which they have used to establish long-range plans, and a daily schedule of activities for accomplishing their priorities, feel in control of their lives. These students are also more efficient in their study habits, are happier, experience fewer physical problems, and are more optimistic about their future success.

You have probably developed competencies in some of these areas of workload management, and are deficient in others. As you begin to develop your strategies for managing the workload of university, your personal style helps you gain an appreciation as to how you can proceed. Because you know that your personal needs and priorities affect the way in which you plan and schedule, your strategies for managing the workload will build on the time-management competencies you currently possess. For example, if you are a dreamer, with important long-range plans, you can use this capability to plan for short-term successes as you improve your ability to pace more effectively. Or if you are socially oriented and stimulated by variety, it is important to avoid long periods of solitary study, and to schedule discussion into your study sessions.

Common Problems

Researchers (Eison & Holtschlag, 1989) have identified the most common time-management difficulties of university students. These include academic goal-setting, work overload, poor planning, inadequate speed, distracting activities, and procrastination. These problems evolve from students' inability to successfully manage the university workload issues of planning, pacing, and priority setting. Academic goal-setting is related to students' problems in establishing long and short-term priorities for themselves. It often results from students' indecision about their future direction and lack of awareness about career options. Workload problems are evident in students' inability to master their academic course material and accomplish other responsibilities. Difficulties with work overload are due to the tendency of students to overextend themselves, to remain indecisive about their personal priorities, to experience difficulties in establishing limits and to hesitate in asking for help with their academic problems. Poor planning results from students' preference for living in the moment, which hinders their commitment toward developing time schedules that focus on productive activities for attaining their goals. Because many students are more comfortable completing one task before starting another they have difficulty planning the components of large assignments, or changing gears so they can manage the diverse assignments of their university courses. Those students with inadequate speed read too slowly, have difficulty comprehending complex material, and are not accustomed to managing the increased volume of work that is expected at university. Over-involvement, an inability to set limits, lack of assertiveness, and work commitments can all interfere with a student's main priority—academic achievement. The most common problem that negatively affects students' academic success is procrastination. Students who procrastinate have difficulty starting their studying, avoid attending classes, experience problems in completing assignments on time, and generally put off those activities that are necessary for doing well.

Counter-Productive Patterns that Interfere with Success

Procrastination

Procrastination, the act of postponing and delaying needlessly, is a pervasive problem affecting over 70 percent of university students (Ellis & Knaus, 1977). This pattern of avoidance affects both male and female students equally, and increases throughout their undergraduate years (McCown, Johnson, & Pretzel, 1989). In fact, many university students assume that because procrastination is such a common practice, it is simply something they must live with. The typical outcomes of procrastination are lower grades (Rothblum, Solomon, & Murakami, 1986), course withdrawals (Welsley, 1994), stress (Blunt & Pychyl, 2000), increased health risks (Baumeister, 1997), and interpersonal conflict (Day, Mensink, & O'Sullivan, 2000). Over 52 percent of students have reported that procrastination has become a serious problem for which they have sought help (Gallagher, 1992). It was not until these students discovered the detrimental effects of procrastination on their academic standing, their effectiveness as students, their ability to get into their preferred program of study, or the quality of their lives, that they decided they needed to address this problem.

It is quite possible that you may experience more than one form of procrastination. Students procrastinate about their activities (i.e., task avoidance), and their decisions (i.e., decision avoidance). There are five different forms of procrastination with various levels of severity. These include academic, life routine, decisional, neurotic, and compulsive procrastination.

The first and most common form of procrastination is **academic procrastination**. This is defined as the last-minute preparation of term papers or cramming for examinations (Hill et al., 1978). A second kind of procrastination, known as **life routine procrastination** (Milgram, Sroloff, & Rosenbaum, 1988), is the difficulty some individuals have in scheduling the timing of normal, recurring chores, such as paying bills or washing dishes, and doing these regularly so that they get done. Both of these forms of procrastination are related to the avoidance of tasks. The reasons individuals avoid these tasks may be related to the nature of the task itself or to the individual's needs and fears regarding the task. A third form of procrastination is **decisional procrastination**, the inability to make timely decisions in a variety of social, academic, and personal situations (Effert & Ferrari, 1989). Indecision leads to lack of motivation and lack of action. For example, students who avoid choosing the topic for their research paper cannot focus on getting the background materials, which provide the basis for the written report. The nature and importance of the decision, as well as the decisional style of the procrastinator can lead to avoiding decision-making. **Neurotic procrastination**, familiar to many first-year students, is the tendency to postpone major life decisions such as choice of a career path or academic major (Ellis & Knaus, 1977). For example, when students lack a career focus they often experience difficulty selecting appropriate courses. A more serious type of procrastination is **compulsive procrastination**, which is decisional and behavioural procrastination in the same person. This individual wavers in their decision-making so that at one moment they attempt to follow one course of action, then they change their mind and attempt another.

Why is procrastination so relevant and common among college students? Researchers have discovered that causes of procrastination are as varied as the individuals who procrastinate. Procrastination patterns relate to both the academic and social self-concepts of students. Sometimes people procrastinate because of the nature of the task. They find the workload or assignment to be distasteful, too difficult, confusing, overwhelming, or uninteresting. At other times, the procrastination is related to the motivational style of the individual. For some, procrastination has become a habit (Ellis & Knaus, 1977), while for others it is described as a dimension of their personality (Lay, 1997; Milgram et al., 1998), or a coping strategy utilized to preserve feelings of self-worth. Researchers who have examined the causes of procrastination have found that it is related to low self-esteem, anxiety, and depression. It is also related to perfectionism (Flett, Blankenstein, Hewitt, & Koledin, 1992), disorganization (Schouwenburg & Lay, 1995), low conscientiousness (Lay, 1997), motivational problems (Senecal, Koestner, & Vallerand, 1995), learned helplessness (Covington, 1993), and irrational thinking (Ellis & Knaus, 1977). It becomes clear that both the nature of the work tasks and the nature of the attributes of the students interact to produce a tendency to procrastinate that can be self-defeating.

Tasks

For some individuals the nature of the task influences whether or not they will procrastinate. If students perceive a task to be unimportant, uninteresting, difficult, too complicated, or confusing, they may easily become distracted by other more pleasurable activities. If students feel frustrated, bored, or resentful, a task can easily be perceived as aversive. The more aversive students perceive a task to be, the greater the tendency to procrastinate (Pychyl, Lee, Thibodeau, & Blunt, 1999). When students do not feel in control of their projects and do not see the relevance or value of the project, they are more likely to procrastinate.

Many students have difficulty starting a task, while others procrastinate the closer they get to the completion of a task (Blunt & Pychyl, 2000). The reasons and motivations that fuel procrastination change depending on the stage of a project. In the initial phases of a project, students are required to be more actively engaged in decision-making, planning, and structuring. To ensure progress and avoid procrastination during this initial stage, students must find their project or assignment to be personally meaningful, important, or enjoyable. Personal investment in a project helps students avoid procrastination. During the action stages, when students are working to complete a project, control, organization, independence, and certainty are important. If students feel disorganized, uncertain, and hassled, it becomes easy to give up and abandon a project. During the final stages of a project, students' fears of evaluation can adversely affect their ability to complete a project. Thus, when students are problem solving the reasons for procrastination and are developing their own approach to eliminating the problem, they must plan their solutions based on the nature of, and stage they are at in, the task they are planning to complete.

Styles

For a large number of students, procrastination is a motivational problem fed by emotions and thoughts. Sometimes procrastination makes students feel good, as putting off a difficult or distasteful task protects their self-confidence and allows them to engage in activities they find pleasurable (Silver & Sabini, 1981). At other times, students feel negative emotions as their guilt, discouragement, and inadequacy adversely impact on their ability to succeed personally and academically (Walker & Stewart, 2000). Because procrastination is a complicated response to fears of personal inadequacy, students vary in the expression of their feelings. Some students express worry and anxiety, while others are discouraged and depressed. In contrast to the manifestation of these negative feelings, there are some students who experience positive feelings of overconfidence, which also lead to procrastination. The interaction between students' feelings and procrastination becomes even more complicated by their personality.

The challenge of understanding how various aspects of one's personality affect procrastination has the potential to uncover important links that can help students develop personalized coping strategies for managing their procrastination. Various researchers have investigated the relationship of personality factors, such as impulsivity, self-absorption, energy levels, social orientation, self-esteem, and emotionality, to procrastination. These researchers (Day et al., 2000; Lay, 1987; McCown et al., 1989; Solomon & Rothblum, 1984), have used these factors to identify and classify different styles of procrastination. Although their categories differ, their combined typology has identified five distinct patterns of procrastination. These include anxious, academically unsure; depressed; self-engaged, independent; socially overconfident; and rebellious.

Anxious, Academically Unsure   These students experience high levels of evaluation anxiety because they lack academic confidence and are overly concerned about their ability to meet the high standards that they set, or that others set for them (Day et al., 2000). They often express anxiety about examinations, and have difficulty preparing adequately and performing well. These students experience a cycle of self-destructive feelings, where lack of confidence fuels worry and anxiety, which in turn fuel procrastination, which then fuels self-doubt. To eliminate the negative emotional cycle produced by their fear and anxiety, these students require help with anxiety-management strategies, such as graduated goal-setting, relaxation, and cognitive reframing (see Chapter 7).

Depressed   Socially sensitive and academically insecure, these students react to their concerns about success, and their fears of failure with discouragement, low energy levels, and depression (Lay, 1987; Solomon & Rothblum, 1984). They are low in both social and academic confidence. Due to their low energy levels and inactivity, these students experience little success, and therefore, do not develop confidence in their ability to manage academic demands. Treating the depression is an important aspect of assisting them; thus, consultation with professional counsellors and physicians regarding the best treatment approach is important. Medication as well as a cognitive-behavioural treatment often helps them gain academic confidence and competence as they overcome their feelings of discouragement.

Self-Engaged, Independent   Socially unconcerned and ambivalent about their own academic success, these students are not responsive to the expectations of others (Day et al., 2000; Lay, 1987; McCown et al., 1989; Solomon & Rothblum, 1984). Independent and self-absorbed, these students have difficulty finding sources of motivation to keep them on task. Self-engaged and ambivalent, they need help in understanding themselves and discovering an inner source of passion and academic confidence. Helping them design their own system of self-management and personal rewards will add to the autonomy they value. These types of students are best helped by counselling with professionals who can assist them in discovering a personal focus for their university career.

Socially Overconfident   Extraverted, other-directed, academically unconcerned, and socially confident, these students spend time in social and impulsive activities (Day et al., 2000; Lay, 1987). Also described as socially-focused, optimistic students, they overestimate their academic competence and their ability to complete tasks within appropriate time frames. Their procrastination is related to overconfidence, coupled with unrealistic personal expectations. Although they may never seek help, as they do not often perceive procrastination as a problem, socially overconfident students could manage their impulsivity by developing shorter deadlines and reinforcing their own performance when they work in small spurts. They would also benefit by organizing their work so that they are involved in collaborative work-study sessions.

Rebellious   A few students react to social expectations regarding their academic performance by passively resisting (Lay, 1987). Although this pattern is less common than the other patterns, these individuals, in response to external demands, either quietly refuse to complete academic assignments or actively engage in competing, alternative, non-academic activities. Some theorists (Milgram et al., 1988) have hypothesized that because these individuals are resentful about the demands imposed on them by others, they react with a passive-aggressive strategy of procrastinating. Rebellious students can be helped to eliminate some of their self-defeating behaviours by seeking professional counselling. Once they have developed greater self-understanding, they may benefit by developing more effective communication skills and personal management skills.

As researchers (Day et al., 2000; Lay, 1987; Milgram et al., 1988) have uncovered these five patterns of procrastination, they have also sought to understand the complex relationships between feelings, with their accompanying thoughts, and the resulting actions that are associated with procrastination. Their goals have been to assist students in developing an understanding of the multidimensional nature of their procrastination patterns, so that with analysis and assistance they can develop appropriate coping strategies for dealing with procrastination.

If you are a procrastinator, understanding your pattern of procrastination provides you with strategies that can help you take greater control. Whether or not you are willing to change your own procrastination pattern depends on your motivations and patterns. Some procrastinators are unconcerned about their procrastination; they see it as just a minor inconvenience and a pattern that does not usually affect them too much. If you fit this pattern you will probably not be motivated to change. Or if you are satisfied with mediocre grades and accept that your procrastination is a pattern you have learned to live with, you will have no reason to invest in changing yourself. On the other hand, sometimes the stress and worry associated with procrastination become the motivating reasons for you to seek help in changing your behaviour (Day et al., 2000).

Stress

Researchers (Rocha-Singh, 1994; Solberg, Hale, Villarreal, & Kavanagh, 1993), have identified three major types of stress experienced by university students: **academic stress**, **financial stress**, and **social stress**. Academic stress includes situations when students experience difficulties in managing academic tasks such as taking tests, writing papers, or reading assignments. It may also include problems in time management, or difficulties in effectively applying study strategies in order to handle the more demanding workloads of university. Financial stress is associated with the pressures that students experience related to financing their education. It includes worries about the cost of their education, problems in paying for tuition and/or the living costs associated with attending university, and difficulties in managing their money. Social stress refers to stress related to dealing with their peers, family, or faculty. It can include isolation, problems in establishing new friendships, or getting along with those who are different from you. It also results from conflict with family regarding personal preferences and priorities, and the discouragement that occurs when you are unable to understand and learn from your professors.

When students become overloaded with too much stress they react with a variety of cognitive, emotional, and somatic symptoms. These symptoms fall into five general categories: depression, sleep problems, overeating, irritability, and physical complaints such as headaches, gastrointestinal difficulties, or heart palpitations. Although these symptoms can be signals alerting students to the importance of managing their levels of personal stress, sometimes the symptoms themselves become problems that require solutions (Ryan, Solberg, & Brown, 1996).

Stress has been associated with increased susceptibility to illness, difficulties in decision-making (Rawson, Bloomer, & Kendall, 1994), problems in concentration and thinking (Solberg et al., 1998), negative academic outcomes (DeMeuse, 1985), and becoming worn out (Cope & Hannah, 1975). Therefore, to increase your probability of success it is useful to develop strategies for managing stress. Lazarus and Folkman (1984) have identified two categories of stress-management strategies, *emotion-focused* and *problem-focused* coping. Some strategies such as relaxation, exercise, and cognitive reframing reduce the emotional effects of stress. Other strategies (such as lifestyle management, academic skill development, and eliminating ineffective time utilization) focus on solving problems.

One of the most important strategies for eliminating the detrimental effects of stress and improving students' performance and problem-solving capabilities is to help students feel in control of their time (Nonis, Hudson, Logan, & Ford, 1998). As students gain control of their time they are better able to concentrate, pay attention, make decisions, and solve problems. Each of the strategies in this chapter is designed to assist students in gaining control of their time. One approach for reducing stress in your life is to select and use the strategies that best serve your needs and personal style, giving you the sense of personal mastery you desire.

A second strategy for reducing stress is to ensure that you have a healthy mixture of activities that nurture, sustain, and challenge you. The better able you are to maintain a healthy lifestyle, the less stress you will experience. The three rules of balanced living are: recognize your rhythm, renew yourself routinely, and reflect regularly. University challenges you to discover your own best rhythm to maximize your effectiveness. Differenciating between your peak performance times and the times when you need additional stimulation is important for learning how to use your own rhythm for the greatest personal advantage. Determining the mixture of activities that keeps you motivated and engaged is a vital aspect of knowing your own rhythm. This also includes establishing a regular pattern of sleep, which refreshes you. To make the best use of your own rhythm, you must renew yourself through regular rituals of exercise, fun, social encounters, leisure, and relaxation. Routine renewals involve investing in your own mental and physical fitness by designing the appropriate combination of activities that will help you maintain your motivation, focus, and dedication. Successful students understand the value of regular exercise as a means of improving their stamina and building reserves so that they can better handle personal and academic demands. By including pleasurable, interactive and relaxing leisure (Iwasaki, 2001) in your plans, you provide yourself with an important source of stimulation to counteract the boredom and fatigue associated with concentrated activity. To complement the energy you gain through activities, you need reflective activities to calm and rejuvenate you. Reflection, or meditation, provides the vehicle for letting go of the worries and concerns that can sometimes overwhelm you. Reflection can be a formal or informal process. You may choose to engage in formal meditative practices such as yoga, tai chi, prayer, or journal writing, or more informal contemplation that occurs during a regular evening walk or warm, relaxing bubble bath.

Developing Your Personal Plan

To begin the process of managing your own time in the best way, you must develop a personal plan that reflects your abilities and priorities. This plan will incorporate the knowledge you have learned about the demands of university, as well as your own self-management abilities. Two approaches that will help you gain the self-awareness that is essential for developing the best plan for you are critical self-reflection, and self-monitoring.

Critical **self-reflection** and personal assessment provide the basis for the self-discovery cycle that allows you to become a master of your own time. By using both self-reflection and self-monitoring you are able to develop the attitudes and actions that give you the personal control you desire. Initially engaging in an honest self-appraisal of your attitudes, patterns of time use, problem areas, and procrastination tendencies provides you with an awareness of your personal approach to managing time. By deliberately exploring the influence of your cultural values, family traditions, and typical attitudes toward time, you will gain a perspective that will allow you to more clearly understand your time-management patterns

This awareness is further enhanced through the discovery process of monitoring your actual time usage. The data you collect can teach you about yourself. Once you have a clearer picture of your own capabilities as a time manager you can begin the process of building a time-management identity that will ensure your success at university. Several exercises are included to assist you in adding to your competencies and confidence as you follow the steps of developing a time-management plan. These exercises include developing a plan, practising skills, and defining problem-solving difficulties in order to develop the self-disciplinary skills that are necessary in university. By understanding the personal and social factors that influence you (i.e., social self-concept), and adding competencies (i.e., academic self-concept), you increase your ability to manage your time effectively. This success leads to enhanced feelings of self-confidence that in turn allow you to use your time-management self-identity to your greatest advantage. Because you have developed greater self-confidence, you then willingly seek additional opportunities for adding to your abilities. Thus, your time-management plan becomes a vehicle for self-development and university success, as presented in the Self-Assessment Cycle for Time Management on page 128.

Self-monitoring, or observing yourself through systematic recording, planning, and analysis, provides you with information about your real self, as well as any academic or personal areas that are problematic. Self-monitoring begins with observation. Careful observation is best achieved through a process of time-logs, term plans, and weekly timetables. The picture you see of yourself through the lens of the self-monitoring process becomes the focal point for you to develop your personalized approach to time management. After you have collected data, self-reflection and critical analysis enriches your understanding of the factors that influence you. Through this self-discovery process you discover both the actions and attitudes that enhance or detract from your success. Your focus is to identify actions that give you greater personal control and self-direction. Especially important is to understand the attitudes that have influenced your choices of

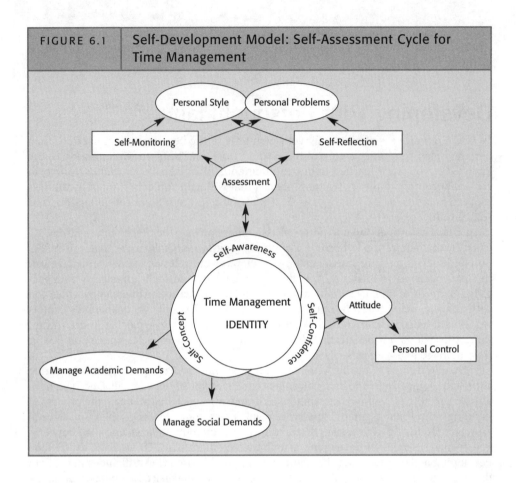

FIGURE 6.1 | Self-Development Model: Self-Assessment Cycle for Time Management

particular actions, and to uncover the thoughts or feelings that have added to, and detracted from your sense of confidence about your abilities as a self-manager. Self-monitoring provides important data, and self-reflection provokes you to uncover factors that influence motivational levels. These dual processes provide the basis for you to determine your self-direction and efficiency.

Time-Logs

To know yourself, you must observe and analyze yourself. To truly gain heightened self-awareness, you must become a critical observer of your own behaviour. This appraisal is best accomplished through a self-monitoring approach in which you observe and chronicle your actual time use. Surprisingly, how you think you spend your time is often far different from how you actually spend your time. Curious? We invite you to test your perception against reality. Complete the time-log on page 129, recording the important information about your time spent, hour by hour and day by day. By using a time-log to record how you actually spend your time during an entire week, you are able to gain insight about your time preferences and priorities.

FIGURE 6.2 | **Time-Logs**

	Sunday	Monday	Tuesday	Wednesday	Thursday	Friday	Saturday
DATES							
6:00 a.m.							
7:00							
8:00							
9:00							
10:00							
11:00							
12:00 p.m.							
1:00							
2:00							
3:00							
4:00							
5:00							
6:00							
7:00							
8:00							
9:00							
10:00							
11:00							
12:00 a.m.							

Self-reflective observations:

Attitudes that influence my activities:

Actions that I can take to improve:

Once you have completed a time-log of one week of activities, you can engage in the process of critical self-analysis. Begin by classifying your time allocation into one of the four categories of typical student activities: academic (e.g., classes, study time, labs), social (e.g., family, friends, clubs, church, relaxation, fun), personal (e.g., work, fitness, volunteer activities), and maintenance (e.g., sleeping, eating, household tasks, commuting). To add to your understanding of this information consider what attitudes, such as thoughts or feelings, have been important in your decisions to allocate time as you have. Create a graph or pie chart that visually demonstrates your time use. This visual representation will assist you in identifying the proportion of time you invest in these four areas.

Use the information you have learned through this self-monitoring process to increase both your competence and confidence as a time manager. By identifying and continuing productive activities, you build an increased confidence in your ability to manage your own time in order to meet your priorities as a student scholar. Once you have summarized the information gathered through your time-logs you are ready to begin the process of effective time allocation: planning and problem-solving.

Planning

Effective planning involves matching your priorities to your allocation of time. You, like most university students, have many competing priorities in university. Your priorities may include succeeding academically, making friends, becoming involved in the university, having enough money, and capably managing your home, family, and living responsibilities. Each of these priorities requires a commitment of time. However, some of them are more important to you than others. Thus, effective time management relates to making choices about which of these priorities are most important for you, and ensuring that you allocate adequate time for them.

Effective time management involves investing time in your priorities. This requires setting limits, saying no to some activities, avoiding time wasters, and engaging in important, personally relevant activities, rather than being distracted by seemingly urgent demands. It also requires avoiding the problems of over commitment that occur when you overextend yourself by becoming involved in too many activities.

Develop an Academic Success Plan

One unique challenge of university is scheduling and planning your academic and personal priorities. Because university is an open, unstructured system, it is your responsibility to develop a schedule that fits the academic requirements of your program with your own aspirations, abilities, and attitudes. This includes the scheduling of all due dates for term assignments, tests, projects, and lab reports; the scheduling of additional academic activities such as reading, preparing, and reviewing for examinations; finding answers to difficult problems; writing papers; searching the library for resources; and reviewing material with study groups. The scheduling of the social and personal priorities that you value complements this. Your first step in effective scheduling includes developing a term plan for all of your assignments. This will be supplemented with weekly plans of activities, and daily "to do" action lists.

Step 1: Create a Term Plan

Your term plan, as seen in the example on page 131, is the big picture. It includes your assignments and your personal priorities for the academic term. Because this term plan provides the framework for you to succeed in making the most of your time at university, it must include your priorities for achieving the goals to which you aspire. This plan is a preview of the responsibilities and activities for which you are accountable in the upcoming months. This means, of course, that you will describe the academic assignments for which you are responsible, as well as other important commitments and priorities. For example, if you are an athlete who is expected to train daily, then this is one of the commitments you will include in your term schedule. Or, if you have a job on campus for a particular number of hours per week, then you will include this information as well. You may volunteer regularly at a local crisis line; if so, you would also include this in your term plan.

The term plan gives you a general overview of all your activities. It allows you to see how all your responsibilities fit together. Importantly, it also helps you avoid potential problems, as you will be able to identify times when you have overlapping demands and limited time availability.

Step 2: Develop a Weekly Timetable

Your term plan will be supplemented with a more detailed schedule of activities—a weekly timetable—that will ensure that you are progressing regularly in your reading and writing assignments, and are prepared for unscheduled and scheduled exams. These weekly timetables, as seen on page 132, also include the other activities that are important to you. You will begin by filling in all of your fixed, prescheduled activities such as class times, commute times, regular appointments, and study times. After you have completed this general weekly schedule, make as many copies of this timetable as there are

FIGURE 6.3	Term Plan

In order to see the entire view of the first-term workload, review the course syllabi of all of your courses. Complete the following weekly summaries of the assignments, tests, reports, and other deadline-related activities.

Week	Course	What's Due	Other Priorities
1.			
2.			
3.			
4.			
5.			
6.			
7.			
8.			
9.			
10.			
11.			
12.			
13.			

weeks in the academic term. If your term is 13 weeks long, you will have 13 individualized timetables that will provide the basis for your time-management plan.

To personalize each of the weekly timetables, refer to your master calendar for the due dates of particular assignments during the various weeks of the term. Add this information to each of the weekly timetables. Working back from these assignment dates you can use your awareness of your own academic skills to estimate the amount of time that you will need in the weeks preceding these due dates in order to ensure your success. Schedule these hours sequentially in the preceding weeks to allow you to prepare adequately.

University is an environment in which most of your learning will occur outside of class. It is an environment in which you are responsible for supplementing the information from the lectures. Most university professors recommend that students study a minimum

FIGURE 6.4	Weekly Timetable						
	Sunday	Monday	Tuesday	Wednesday	Thursday	Friday	Saturday
DATES							
6:00							
7:00							
8:00							
9:00							
10:00							
11:00							
12:00							
1:00							
2:00							
3:00							
4:00							
5:00							
6:00							
7:00							
8:00							
9:00							
10:00							
11:00							
12:00							

of two hours for every hour in class. This **two-for-one rule** is a guideline for ensuring that you allocate the necessary time for reading and synthesizing information, which leads to mastery. However, you may need to adjust this recommendation based on your ability level in a particular class, your efficiency, and your grade aspirations. It is better to overestimate the time that you need than to underestimate it. When you underestimate time, you run out of time, feel rushed, and are unable to perform. If you overestimate time, you will be able to use the extra time to reward yourself with activities that are fun and pleasurable.

University researchers have also discovered that students are more efficient if they use **distributed practice.** Distributed practice involves spacing studying time over several shorter time periods rather than one long period. This means that it is much better to study a subject for one hour on each of three nights rather than study that same material in a block of three hours. Distributed practice reduces fatigue and avoids boredom. It keeps you working at peak efficiency. Distributed practice includes time for small study breaks between hours of study sessions. Scheduling short, five- to ten-minute breaks as part of a regular study session provides both an intellectual and physical refreshment that can add to your efficiency and effectiveness.

Step 3: Develop Daily "To Do" Action Lists

Your daily "to do" action lists, as seen in the example on page 134, are one of the best ways to take control of your time, and add to your feelings of confidence regarding time mastery. In composing these lists, focus on the activities that you need to do in order to ensure your success in your personal priority areas. This list reminds you to focus on the important tasks of the day. You develop this list by reviewing the information in your time plan and your weekly schedule. If you have scheduled that you need to read 50 pages in your psychology text, obtain three new references for your term paper, and arrange with your friend to get notes from a particular class, then these are some of the items that compose your daily action list. Remember to include in your daily action lists those lifestyle priorities which are important for maintaining your motivational levels, such as swimming for an hour or having lunch with your friend. To build self-confidence and self-mastery, acknowledge each successful completion of the tasks on the list.

Planning not only gives you confidence in your ability to succeed, but also provides the specific framework for developing the time-management competencies that will make you successful. However, knowing how to schedule time is only the beginning. Ensure success by actively "working your plan" through focused actions and attitudes that increase your efficiency. Continue monitoring and evaluating your activities each week. Use the feedback to clarify how well you are achieving your goals and priorities, and to problem-solve any factors that are hindering you.

Problem-Solving

The time-log provides a picture of the way in which you allocate time. To understand the information presented in the time-log it is productive to analyze particular aspects of your time-management processes. Productive problem-solving promotes enhanced feelings of self-confidence and self-discipline because it provides opportunities for you to develop the personal management skills that add to your sense of academic competence. With effective problem-solving techniques, you can eliminate time-wasters and problem patterns that detract from your ability to manage your time. Problem-solving skills save time and promote the development of strategies for personal peak performance and time efficiency.

FIGURE 6.5 | Daily "To Do" List

	Academic Tasks
1.	
2.	
3.	
4.	
5.	

	Social/Personal Tasks
1.	
2.	
3.	
4.	
5.	

	Household Tasks
1.	
2.	
3.	
4.	
5.	

	Other Tasks
1.	
2.	
3.	
4.	
5.	

Attitudes: Thoughts that encourage me:

Attitudes that defeat me:

Actions: What I do well:

What I need to do:

Time-Wasters

Though you may be quite different than the student sitting next to you in class, one characteristic you share is that you both waste time. Almost everyone wastes time. Once you learn about the activities that keep you from doing what you need to be doing, you are able to eliminate your personal time-wasters. Typical time-wasters can include watching television, day-dreaming, commuting, over-organizing one's desk in preparation to study, snacking, computer activities, worrying, running around, inefficiency, telephone calls, long coffee breaks, and partying. Becoming aware of your own "time-waster" patterns presents you with the potential for finding more time in your schedule as you discover significant amounts of time that could be better utilized.

Time-Savers

Equally important to avoiding time-wasters is figuring out how to save time. Saving time can occur when you combine activities such as studying with friends, as a means of meeting your social and academic needs, or using spare moments in a typical day for reviewing material—such as while you are waiting in line at the bank machine. You can learn from the experience of successful students, who through courses such as this one, discover a variety of study techniques that in the long run save them time.

Task Analysis

The time-logs provide information regarding your success in accomplishing the tasks you have identified as important. An appraisal of the tasks you do, the tasks you avoid, the tasks you easily master, and the tasks that are demanding and difficult will provide important information for designing strategies for increasing your effectiveness.

Peak Time

Most individuals have times when they are more effective than other times. These peak times relate to your personal time-management style. Peak times are the periods during the day when you feel the most efficient and when you accomplish your best work.

Purposeful Self-Control

Figuring out the complex combination of your own thoughts, feelings, and behaviours, as they affect the ways in which you use your time is an important phase of problemsolving. A critical step in effective time management is to practice reflective thinking about your own approach to managing time. This includes analyzing your own irrational beliefs or cognitive distortions that lead to problems in making the most of your time and energy. It requires figuring out how to use your own positive feelings for motivating yourself, and for building a sense of personal confidence. As you take control of your time, you are able to eliminate the negative feelings that interfere with your success. Especially important is identifying the actions you can take to ensure that you follow the plans you have outlined for yourself, and that you incorporate the attitudes that will facilitate your perseverance.

Through the two-stage self-discovery process of self-monitoring and self-reflection, you have gathered critical information for developing your own self-management plan. The time-logs provide informative data, and your self-reflection provokes insight. By using these complementary processes you now have the elements of effective self-management. By combining the information you have learned in this chapter with the insights you have learned about yourself, you can develop a personalized plan for managing time. This plan will recognize your personal time-management style, incorporate priorities that inspire and motivate you, and include strategies for replacing self-defeating actions with productive alternatives (i.e., steps that you believe you can accomplish). Because your plan is based on an honest, realistic self-assessment of your capabilities and motivations, it is a plan that ensures you will gradually make the changes you need to make in order to become increasingly self-reliant and self-disciplined.

Becoming self-disciplined is an ongoing developmental process. Daily, you will add to your ability to master those habits that ensure success, by following and adjusting your time-management plan throughout the term. By committing to practise the strategies that ensure you efficiently manage the workload, while sustaining a balanced lifestyle, you will add to the capabilities that make you autonomous and successful. You will also add to your confidence, enabling you to encounter difficulties fearlessly, find solutions, and make advancements. Effective time management builds on the goal-setting skills you have previously learned as well as the self-regulation and motivational strategies that keep you focused. Allow yourself to learn through the self-discovery process that teaches you about your time-management capabilities and challenges. As you add to your self-awareness, direct your attention to the actions and attitudes that promote growth into self-mastery.

Day by day you choose your destiny by the decisions you make and the actions you take. You know how to make university the time of your life. Now, just do it.

It's More Than Common Sense

Procrastination

Clarry Lay, Ph.D.
York University

In 1986 I published my first research article on procrastination. The topic was a natural for me, and I was not the first psychologist to study my own foibles. Since that time I have conducted more research and have counselled university students who see their own tendencies to procrastinate as a problem. One continuing aspect of the research is a personality scale we developed to measure trait procrastination (Lay, 1987). You can complete the questionnaire yourself to see where you stand. Although some of us may be specialists in putting things off, most procrastinators do so in many aspects of their lives. Over the years I have built up some understanding of why people procrastinate and how to counter this behaviour. These are some of my reflections. First of all, time management is important, but it will not be the complete solution for procrastinators (Lay & Schouwenburg, 1993). You will need to consider other elements in bringing about self-change. There are some aspects of why we procrastinate that are complex, and elusive, and, of course, to change requires a level of self-discipline that we may lack at the moment. This is not to discourage anyone, however. To procrastinate less does require a lot of talking to ourselves in special ways, ways that we can all learn and incorporate into our lives. It also involves the development of a clearer, consistent sense of who we are as individuals. A new colleague of mine, Ian McGregor (1998), has developed a theory of identity consolidation. He indicates that any inconsistencies in self-concept interfere with self-regulation processes. Because procrastinators experience wide discrepancies among their goals, intentions, and actions, they are highly likely also to experience inconsistencies in their self-concept. They are likely to dwell on the inconsistencies, at the expense of doing what they ought to be doing. A good look at who you are, what you want, and what you stand for, is a great beginning.

Beyond this, there is a bottom-line of lessening the extent to which you put off your intentions. It is an obvious, but effective point, nevertheless. Most simply put, you need to spend more time doing what you ought to be doing, working on high-priority tasks. This is the obvious part, but an important starting point in terms of what you say to yourself. Of course, because the hours in the day are limited, this means that you are going to have to give up spending time on less important tasks and activities. Identify these and then ask yourself if, indeed, you are willing to give up much of the time you spend watching TV, exploring the Internet, talking to friends on the telephone, or whatever. If you are not, then you really do not want to change. In addition, when you make plans (Gollwitzer & Brandstatter, 1997), make them as concretely and as detailed as possible ("I will begin to work on this task at 11:00 a.m. tomorrow morning"), including where you will be ("I will be at the library"). It also helps to mentally rehearse all the steps that you plan to go through to fulfill your intentions and reach your goals (Taylor, Pham, Rivkin, & Armor, 1998). This is similar to imagery-training by athletes. Then (and this is the key), recognize that the plans you make are obligations to yourself ("you ought to," not, "wouldn't it be nice if I did"). We are not talking about goals here, but rather plans for action. You need to become more responsible to the plans you make to reach your goals. Finally, and of extreme importance, you must place yourself in the location where you work best—you must simply spend more time there (for me it is my office and not my home). Of course, there is some balance that needs to be reached here; you cannot spend all of your time in one place. Nowadays that right place is more difficult to manage, and you will need to arrange it in special ways if you can. For example, Internet access may still be available, and the cell phone in your pocket will be an added temptation. All the more reason to engage in constant reminders to yourself. And the payoff all along the line is simple, and very worthwhile. Do what you intend to do (based on what you need to do), and you will feel better, especially about yourself.

If you are an optimist by nature, don't change. This in many ways is a great perspective to have on life. But remember that optimism in the hands of a trait procrastinator can be a detriment rather than a benefit (Lay, 1988). Optimistic procrastinators can all too easily revise their best intentions, believing that the planned six hours of study can now be done in two hours, so why not go out with friends for awhile! If you are a procrastinator, you will need to temper your optimism.

Another psychological liability that many procrastinators seem to have is a lack of organization in the way they think and remember (Lay, 1987). Procrastinators are sometimes as likely to forget their plans for the day rather than avoid them. You are likely to get home and forget that you were supposed to go to the library earlier today to get books for tonight. I know of no cure for this scatteredness, except to structure your intentions and goals in ways discussed in this chapter.

Finally, don't make excuses. There are some popular interpretations of why people put things off that simply have not stood the test of research. If you think that you procrastinate because you are such a perfectionist and want your essay to be perfect before you hand it in, and put off working on it because it can't be perfect, and so what are you supposed to do—think again (Flett, Hewitt, & Martin, 1995). This is probably not the reason, although it sounds awfully good, and how could we fault someone who wants to do a perfect job? Think again, as well, if you believe that you can only work under pressure and love the "high" associated with your last-minute, frantic endeavours. This is probably not the case. Don't mention that your fear of failure leads you to procrastinate. You procrastinate because you lack conscientiousness (Lay, 1997). To change, remember to tell yourself "I will," and really mean it. Not "I may," or "I hope," or "wouldn't it be nice if," I started to study at 6:30 p.m. tonight until bedtime. To begin, put this book down for ten minutes, get a hammer and a nail, and put the framed poster in your room up on your wall—you remember, the one that has been sitting there for three months now. And then get back to the high-priority tasks.

Success Strategies FOR EFFECTIVE TIME MANAGEMENT

Self-awareness
I've learned...

Self-confidence
To increase my confidence in my ability to manage my time I will...

Self-concept
Actions I can take to gain greater control of my time are...

Chapter Summary

Time management is perhaps one of the greatest challenges to the new university student. Filled with practical tips and exercises, this chapter introduces readers to strategies for managing the time demands of university. It outlines a number of common time-management problems that university students experience, and offers concrete suggestions for planning the academic term activities, prioritizing commitments, and overcoming difficulties. It presents the reasons for students' procrastination, defines various types of procrastination, and offers suggestions for eliminating patterns that produce procrastination and stress. The emphasis is on proper time management as a means of achieving a balanced and healthy lifestyle.

Exercises

REFLECT–ACT

The following Reflect–Act exercises are designed to help you develop increased self-awareness of your time-management effectiveness through the process of reflective thinking, analysis, and productive action. Self-reflection encourages you to consider the information you learn and the data you collect, in order to increase your self-knowledge and to better manage your time.

Reflect   Imagine that you are a time-management expert who has been asked to review the time-logs, schedules, and plans that a student has given to you. (Use your own time-logs for this exercise). Analyze these logs to provide a list of five important recommendations that this student could use as a focus for productively improving their effectiveness in university.
Act   Select which recommendations you are willing to work on and develop a plan for following through.

Reflect   Describe three or four of the most common situations in which you procrastinate. In a chart, classify whether the factors that produce these procrastination patterns are related to the task or to your personal attitudes and attributes, such as your thoughts, feelings, or actions. For each factor, describe a possible solution that would help you eliminate that component of your procrastination pattern.
Act   Choose one or two actions you can take to prove to yourself that you are curbing your tendency to procrastinate.

Reflect   Consider the two-for-one rule of effective studying. Assess your own hours of study time by adding up the amount of time you invest in studying. By comparing your study hours to this guideline, are you satisfied or dissatisfied with the number of hours that you are investing in study? Using data from several sources such as your grade aspirations, academic skill levels, and the difficulty and demands of your courses, develop your own rule of effective study. In other words, what is the ratio of hours studied to class time hours you believe you should follow in order to optimize your success at university?
Act   Design a study schedule for the next week, following your rule of effective study. Monitor your success in your ability to meet your goals. How does your ability to successfully use your rule add to your feelings of self-confidence and self-control?

Reflect   Review the information you have collected through the self-monitoring exercises. To assist you in analyzing the information you have gathered, use the following three questions to determine some of the factors that influence the way you use time. What do I do? What is behind what I do? What can I do to take control?
Act   Use your answers to these questions as the basis for designing two to three specific actions you can take in the upcoming week as a means of taking more control of your time and your life.

Reflect   You have learned that your attitude (i.e., self-confidence), and your actions (i.e., academic competencies) interact to influence your ability to manage your time successfully. Think about the actions and thoughts you currently use to enhance your self-confidence as a student.
Act   Add to your current levels of self-confidence by developing two or three specific actions you can take that will strengthen your feelings of personal confidence.

GROUP DISCUSSION

1. Explore and discuss the major time problems of university students. Identify the reasons for these problems. Through discussion and consensus, rank order the top five time problems and provide possible solutions.

2. Different students have dissimilar time demands and assorted challenges to overcome in order to effectively manage all their priorities within the time available. Describe the differences in time demands of traditional students compared to those of non-traditional students such as single parents.

3. In addition to attending university full-time, many students work on and off campus. Explore the relationship of employment to effective time management and university success. If students attending university full-time choose to work, estimate the optimal number of hours that is reasonable for them to work, and yet maintain satisfactory academic performance.

4. Identify the most common time-wasters and time-savers of university students. Using this information, provide five guidelines that first-year students can use to enhance their time-management capabilities.

5. Describe the time-management factors or situations that produce stress for first-year students. Identify approaches students can take to manage their stress levels so that they do not feel out of control.

APPLY TO LIFE

Now that you have developed an understanding of the importance of planning in effective time management, you can use this information to enhance your own performance. Use the following questions to more clearly discover your strengths and limitations as an effective planner.

1. As I review the data I have gathered through my self-monitoring and self-reflection exercises, what are the planning activities that I perform well?

2. In analyzing the information I have learned, what can I do to improve my chances of success?

3. Are there specific skills that I am learning now that I believe will be particularly important to me in my future? What are they? How do I think that I might use them?

Developing
Effective Learning
Strategies

chapter 7

Tell me, I forget. Show me, I remember.
Involve me, I understand. Ancient Chinese Proverb

Questions

What are the basic strategies that enhance learning in and outside of the classroom?

How can I apply them to my learning?

How do I get the most learning value from my textbooks?

How do I take effective notes?

How do I increase my study efforts?

How do I get the most out of learning with peers?

Objectives

- Developing student identity through managing the academic tasks of university.
- Understanding critical learning strategies such as reading, note taking, and learning with others.
- Applying these critical learning strategies.

Student Success Portrait

It All Comes Down to HIPS

Heather Francis
The University of Manitoba

Having been a student for most of my life, I have learned how to be successful in my studies. Here are some of my tips for success. It all comes down to "HIPS."

The most important aspect of doing well in school is *hard work*. It is true that some people are able to do well simply because they are geniuses, but not all of us have the IQ for MENSA membership (check out www.mensa.org if you are interested). Fortunately, you can learn how to do well in school. This book is full of helpful suggestions for you. However, if you just read about doing well, and memorize the points for your exam, you will have missed the whole point of this course. Take a hint from someone who knows—you have to work hard in order to get a good grade. When your instructor gives you an assignment, do not look at it with the idea of doing the least possible work. Put your best effort forward. If Professor Smith asks you to find at least five references for your paper, find ten! If she asks you for a minimum of three pages typed, go for four! Unless your professors specifically ask you not to exceed a certain number of pages, always strive to provide them with a little bit more. Never put your paper in 18-point font simply to fill space. (Believe it or not, this has been done!) Professors are not stupid, and can spot a student trying to do as little work as possible from a mile away. Hard work will pay off in good grades.

Sometimes it can be very hard to motivate yourself to work hard in a course that is boring. First of all, as mentioned in this textbook, you should strive to select courses that you will enjoy. If that is not possible, it is possible to modify a course so that it becomes *interesting*. Having an interest in the subject matter makes a world of difference in both your attitude toward the course and in the effort you bring to it. Here is an example from my life that will help you to see how to accomplish this. In my third year of university, I had to take a philosophy course. I was less than thrilled at that prospect. However, I found a way to incorporate my field of interest—gerontology—into the course. The class assignments asked us to construct a variety of arguments for and against certain issues. Most of the time, we were free to choose our own topics. Can you guess what I chose as my topic? Suddenly, a course that had appeared irrelevant was allowing me to further my knowledge in my own area of interest.

Relationships with *people* are also key to being a successful student. When I attended Providence College, I was part of a study group that met before each of our psychology exams. We took turns explaining different terms and concepts to each other, which really did help us to remember the material. Meeting as a group also meant that we were less tempted to quit studying than if we had been in our own dorm rooms, with our beds close at hand. We actually had fun studying! There are other important people to connect with at university besides your friends—your professors. Take time to introduce yourself to your professors—suddenly you begin to see them as people who are there to help you, and not just faces in the classroom. You will probably find most of them very helpful and open to you. In fact, they are a virtually untapped resource. When you are faced with an assignment in Professor Brown's class, arrange an appointment to meet with him and discuss your ideas. You will probably leave the meeting with a number of resources (books, journals and Web sites) that Professor Brown was more than willing to share with you, not to mention a preview of what he thinks about your topic. Suddenly, you are light-years ahead of your classmates and are zooming toward finishing an A paper. Establishing relationships with your professors can also have long-term benefits. When your interests coincide with a professor's interests, you may be able to participate as a volunteer in research projects he/she is conducting, giving you a jumpstart on graduate studies if that is your goal. It would also be a good idea to check out any mentor programs your university may have, especially if you plan on studying at a graduate level.

My final tip is to *stop to rest.* You are not Superman or Wonder Woman. If you do not take breaks in your study periods, as well as whole blocks of time off, you will most likely crash and burn. Set reasonable goals for yourself. Do not tell yourself you will read that 300-page novel for English by 8 p.m. tonight. In all probability, you will not even start reading. In my first year at college, I told myself that I was going to finish all of my second-term assignments during reading week. Talk about impossible!

Learning Defined

What is learning? Educational researchers are intrigued with how successful students learn. In fact, learning is of such importance that many of the social sciences are dedicated to exploring and further understanding the secrets of the mind, especially in relation to the concept of learning (McKeachie, Pintrich, Lin, & Smith, 1986). The most recent trend in cognitive research and educational advice is viewing students as active learners who process knowledge and construct their understanding, as compared to passive recipients of teaching (Barr & Tagg, 1995). Active learning includes an awareness of your own learning abilities; the requirements of the university learning environment; the effective techniques in reading, note-taking, lecture-learning, and test-taking that can enhance learning; the value of self-regulation on academic performance; and the importance of social connection to the learning process. Throughout this chapter you will learn strategies that define active learning.

Learning is defined as a set of behaviours that indicate how people learn and adapt to their environment (Myers, 2001). In other words, it is the actions that students take to survive in university. As such, learning strategies are thoughts, feelings, and behaviours that a student intentionally uses to gain new knowledge (Weinstein & Meyer, 1991). Learning is all about taking control and is only limited by the amount of effort applied. How you learn is influenced by various cognitive, affective, and physiological factors. The thinking you use, along with a positive attitude can enhance your learning efficacy. And your state of alertness adds to your learning capabilities.

As seen in the following self-development model, your learning identity involves all three dimensions: self-awareness, self-confidence, and self-concept. Each of these dimensions is critical to the success of students in university. Self-awareness provides

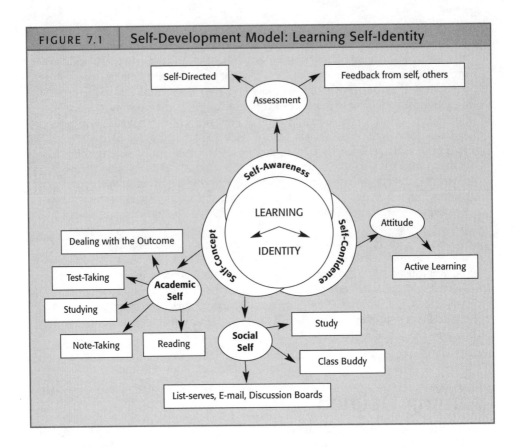

FIGURE 7.1 | Self-Development Model: Learning Self-Identity

you with an understanding of your competencies relative to the expectations of university. Self-confidence is the positive attitude that you take in learning. Self-concept involves all the strategies that enhance learning, both the personal and the social. Let's explore each of these below and see how you can adapt them.

Self-Awareness

Successful students are aware that the expectations of university are different than those of high school or college. Most significant is the learning environment of the university, including larger classes, lectures, required readings, varied assignments, and multiple-choice examinations.

The Learning Medium

In larger classes of 200 to 400 students, many students have difficulty identifying and focusing on the most important material provided in the lecture. Add the required readings of 40 to 100 pages of text, and suddenly it can be overwhelming. Given the large classes, complex multiple-choice exams often replace assignments as an efficient method to provide students with grades. So how do successful students deal with these new expectations? There are various strategies that almost any student can adopt to become one of the top scholars.

The unfortunate thing is that many potentially successful students are unaware of these strategies and thus, are less likely to fulfill their goal of graduating. For most successful students, it involves a combination of persistence and key learning strategies.

Self-Directed Learner

The university places the responsibility of learning directly on the student, whereas previously, teachers guided and coached students in completing assignments, and warning them about upcoming projects and tests. In university, tasks are completed based on self-initiative and self-direction. This includes reading the assigned chapters prior to classes, completing the assignments as required, and studying for each course. Peers become accountability partners, helping each other meet goals. As indicated in the chapters on goal-setting and time management, these successful students create goals and use their time to meet these goals. As a result, students' self-initiative rewards them with achieving the tasks required by their courses.

The successful student constantly assesses the effectiveness of learning skills in facilitating success in university. This includes monitoring the comprehension of increased reading speeds, assessing the note-taking strategies that enhance retention rates for exams, appraising research strategies that produce scholarly papers, and evaluating study skills that yield high scores on exams. Awareness of one's competencies is an important strategy that the successful student uses. By constantly assessing one's skills in comparison to the skills of successful students, and where possible, adapting new skills and modifying existing skills, success becomes more likely.

Let's take a look at the various learning strategies that successful students use. As we go through each of these, take a moment to assess your own learning strategies in comparison to the ones used by successful students. Celebrate the similarities that you discover and take active steps to adopt the strategies that you are lacking.

Self-Confidence

The self-confidence of successful students is based on a positive attitude toward the course and professor. It also comes from experiencing success in similar types of learning situations. Moreover, confident students are those who take full responsibility for their learning by using active learning strategies, in and out of the classroom.

Self-confidence of successful students is often based on their attitude toward the subject matter and the professor. Chapter 4 identified successful students as generally optimistic. The material learned is made relevant. Self-confidence is also built on past experiences of success in academic situations. Previous success provides the successful student with the confidence to try new ideas that are related to the ones mastered earlier.

Responsibility as a Learner: Active Learning

Successful students also demonstrate a high level of responsibility for their learning. Fueled by strong self-confidence, successful students are more likely to persist in their learning, using more effort, as described in Chapter 4, and adopting an active stance as learners (Weinstein & Meyer, 1991). This not only includes spending a greater proportion of time engaged in learning activities, using effective learning strategies such as taking notes, and being actively involved in class and group discussions, but also includes applying the most effective strategy in each learning activity. For instance, an effective note-taking strategy is more than just copying the lecturer's words. There are efficient methods that enhance how one takes notes. The active learner is aware of these efficient methods and actively engages them in all learning strategies. And the payoff is rewarding—a greater level of learning (Pascarella & Terenzini, 1991).

As active learners, successful students use a variety of strategies to enhance the learning of new material. These learning strategies can be grouped into two distinct types: the personal and the social. Personal learning strategies incorporate activities to take charge of your learning, and to be actively engaged in the learning process. Social learning strategies involve sharing learning responsibility with others. Active learners have a number of successful strategies that they use prior to class, during the class, and following the class. These include reading, note taking, studying, and researching. Each of these strategies will be defined in this chapter, with specific examples to help students adopt the most appropriate strategies for increasing their learning efficiency.

Self-Concept: Academic Self

The academic self is based on a host of different personal learning strategies that students can adopt to enhance their learning. Refer back to the subscales in Chapter 2 to identify which areas you already excel in, and the areas in which you require additional development. Specifically, look at the Learning from Lectures, Reading and Comprehension, Test-Taking, and Learning Strategies scales. Each of these scales identify important learning strategies for the three time periods that relate to the time of class: prior to, during, and after class.

Prior to Class

Successful students begin their learning prior to attending class. For the most part, this can be equated to the preparation for a journey. I enjoy canoeing in the pristine wilderness of northern Manitoba. However, before venturing on the journey, I prepare. Of importance is the knowledge of where I will be canoeing. A detailed map provides all the necessary information—where the rapids are, where the hidden falls are, and the side of the river on which I will need to portage. This is identical to preparing for class. Successful students have a good understanding of where they will be journeying, cognitively speaking. They prepare by planning ahead, pre-reading, and consulting the course outline.

Consulting the Course Outline

Successful students consult their course outlines in anticipation of where the professor will take the class. The course outline provides the specific topics in the order in which the topics will be covered in class, as well as the corresponding textbook readings needed to understand the material. Access to this material provides basic clues as to the important content, the focus of the lecture, and possible examination items. This preparatory strategy is often referred to as a cognitive map. A brief overview of what is to be covered in class enhances successful students' development of a cognitive map, or set of expectations of the cognitive journey on which the professor and the class will embark.

Familiarizing Yourself with the Content Material—Reading

With an idea of what to expect for the class, the successful student begins to prepare for the journey. As a canoeist, this involves preparing by learning the details on the map. I need to mentally prepare myself for all the different types of moving water, from rapids to waterfalls. This will be life-critical once I launch the canoe in the water. One wrong move and I could end up dumping my canoe with all my gear, or even worse, losing my life. For the successful student, this means learning the details of the upcoming lecture. The most important strategy related to this is reading the assigned chapters in the text prior to the class. Becoming an academic reader demands increasing one's reading efficiency, expanding one's vocabulary, and developing learning strategies for effective content mastery.

Before continuing, take the Reading Comprehension Test below and see how you rank.

Reading Comprehension Test

Survey your present reading habits by completing the following questionnaire.

By assigning yourself a number between 1 and 6 (answer 1 if you ALWAYS agree with the statement and 6 if you NEVER agree), answer the following questions to give yourself an idea of your present effectiveness as a reader. Be honest with yourself and give yourself credit where credit is due.

Do you...	Always Agree					Never Agree
1. Enjoy reading?	1	2	3	4	5	6
2. Feel that you read well?	1	2	3	4	5	6
3. Spend more time reading than watching TV?	1	2	3	4	5	6
4. Set goals for yourself at the beginning of each reading-study session?	1	2	3	4	5	6
5. Set time limits for yourself at the beginning of each reading-study session?	1	2	3	4	5	6
6. Have a clear purpose for reading before you start?	1	2	3	4	5	6
7. Adjust your reading speed to suit the materials you read?	1	2	3	4	5	6
8. Pre-read a chapter or book before you read it?	1	2	3	4	5	6
9. Search for the main ideas in what you are reading?	1	2	3	4	5	6
10. Use underlining or highlighting to identify important information?	1	2	3	4	5	6
11. Write notes in the margin of your text?	1	2	3	4	5	6
12. Make use of graphs, tables, and pictures while reading?	1	2	3	4	5	6
13. Keep your mind on what you are reading?	1	2	3	4	5	6
14. Put what you've read into practise?	1	2	3	4	5	6
15. Remember what you have read?	1	2	3	4	5	6
16. When you meet a word that you don't know, do you try to determine its meaning from the way it is used in a sentence?	1	2	3	4	5	6

Scoring: Your score will be somewhere from 1–96. Scores from 1–24 demonstrate a mastery of reading; 25–48, strong reading skills; 49–72, growth is definitely needed; 73–96, seek out additional reading resources from Student Resource Centre. Note the scores on each ranked 1 and 2—these are your strengths when it comes to reading. Note the scores on each item ranked 5 and 6. These are your weaknesses and require attention in order for you to excel as a reader.

Successful students tend to have a positive yet critical attitude toward their reading as reflected in a high score on the Reading Comprehension Test. They are eager to learn new ideas, yet they carefully test new ideas with evidence.

Textbooks are one of your major learning resources. Your texts are substantially different from those encountered in high school. Characteristics such as idea density, technical vocabulary, patterns of organization, and the necessity of background information all define the university text. However, successful students find ways to get the most from their texts. They employ active strategies to increase their reading efficiency. As seen in the Reading Strategies figure below, these strategies are threefold, occurring prior to reading, while reading, and after reading.

Prior to Reading

Before reading the text the successful student prepares by first finding a quiet place with minimal distractions (see Chapter 4). Once settled in a good reading environment, the student takes an active and purposeful approach to reading. Before reading, you should know what you want to accomplish. You plan a reading goal. Your purpose is situation-

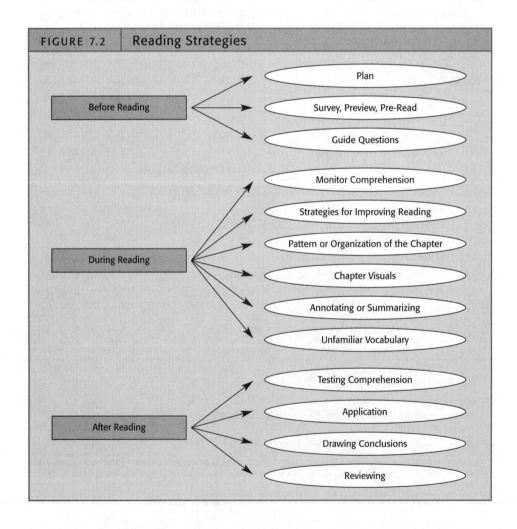

FIGURE 7.2 | Reading Strategies

specific. For instance, when reading a magazine article on "squeegee kids" your purpose is to learn more about the extent of the problem, while your purpose in reading a sociology text chapter may be to locate facts and figures about the causes, effects, and extent of "squeegee kids." Your purpose for reading should be as specific as possible. While reading this chapter, you may focus your purpose on discovering the strategies of learning that will make you a successful student.

With a purpose in mind, successful students survey, preview, or pre-read the text. In preparation for reading the chapter, it is helpful to establish a cognitive map of where the author(s) wants to take the readers. Surveying and previewing the chapter by focusing on the chapter headings and subheadings will set a purpose for reading. You will get a sense of the author's direction and an understanding of the layout of the chapter. As you look at the different headings and subheadings, you are likely to activate prior knowledge of things related to the chapter. Making connections to past learning is critical in strengthening your memory. Also, formulate questions to guide your reading by turning headings and subheadings into questions. For instance, for a sociology heading titled "Methods of Studying Society," you could ask, "What are the methods of studying society?" By engaging in this activity, your inquisitiveness is energized and your mind is primed to engage in the content.

Time for Application

Take this chapter and do a quick mental preview. Look at all the headings and subheadings. Do you have any predictions as to what the best reading strategies will be? How has your experience prepared you for reading? What have you heard from others about reading efficiently? Access your prior knowledge about this chapter by asking yourself, "What do I already know about this topic?"

Now that you have had a chance to preview and make a few predictions, your mind is much more prepared for the content. Preparing expectations and knowing your purpose for reading the chapter is the mental preparation required to enhance your reading of most texts. Set a purpose for your reading by asking yourself, "What are my reasons for reading this?" Is it for pleasure, for developing background knowledge, preparing for an exam, or writing a paper? Follow this by matching your purpose with a specific reading strategy such as memorizing details, reading for main ideas, or skimming to get the gist of the material. Pre-read by beginning with the introduction, reading each major heading and subheading, looking at pictures, charts, or graphs, reading the first sentence after each heading, and then reading the summary or last paragraph. This will provide you with a good overview of what to expect as you read. Now you are ready to begin reading.

While Reading

Successful students use a number of active strategies. These include monitoring comprehension, utilizing strategies to improve reading, looking for the organization or pattern of the text, highlighting or underlining, annotating the text, and dealing with the unfamiliar vocabulary in context.

Monitoring comprehension involves checking to see that your reading speed allows you to understand what you have just read. The Types of Reading table identifies various types of reading. The trick is to select the rate that works best in each situation. In reading a text, you will want to focus on normal or study reading. This will provide you with the maximum speed for the retention of information for future recall, which is especially helpful when preparing for an upcoming lecture, or for the test that follows. Monitoring your comprehension is accomplished by seeing how well you can answer the guide questions you created prior to reading the chapter. Some texts provide study questions and/or key terms. If you are able to answer these questions and to define the key words, you have successfully comprehended the material in the chapter. Monitor your comprehension continually and adjust your reading speed to the complexity of the material. More effort is required initially in developing a good understanding of the material, thereby eliminating the need to relearn it again in the future.

Another strategy to deal with difficulties comprehending is to read the material aloud. This activates a second sense— hearing—to process the material. Remember from Chapter 4 that combining seeing with hearing increases your learning. Also, rephrasing what you have just read often helps to solidify the material. You are elaborating the material, and are thereby beginning the process of creating your own understanding. Take the ideas in the paragraph and try to say it in your own words and apply it to a personal experience. This strengthens the new idea to an already strong memory of a certain event. For instance, as I am reading about new, effective time-management strategies, I try to make connections to time-management strategies that I have personally used. This personal connection to the new material being read solidifies my comprehension of it. During an exam situation, questions about the new time-management strategies are easier to recall, since I have associated them with my personal memory.

Utilizing Strategies to Improve Reading

Making changes in your reading speed to accommodate your comprehension of the material is a very important reading strategy. If you discover that you are reading too slowly, which is a common obstacle for first-year students, you can easily set a reading strategy into action, whereby you set goals for reading a little more each day in a given time allotment, and for learning the new terminology so that reading becomes easier. Set reading goals and monitor your progress. You should notice a gradual increase in reading speed as you progress into your academic term. This is expected, given that you are becoming more immersed in the discipline and developing reading abilities. It is very

TABLE 7.1	**Types of Reading**		
Method of Reading	Range of Speed	Purpose in Reading	Types of Material
Careful or analytical	under 100 wpm	Detailed comprehension: analysis, evaluation, critique, memorization	Poetry, argumentative writing
Normal or study reading	150—250 wpm	High comprehension and high recall	Textbooks, library research
Rapid or casual reading	250—400 wpm	Moderate comprehension of main ideas, entertainment, enjoyment, general information	Novels, newspapers, magazines
Accelerated reading	above 600 wpm	Overview of material, rapid location of a specific fact or new material	Reference material, magazines, novels, nonfiction
Skimming	1000 wpm	Overview of main ideas by reading first sentence of every paragraph	Texts, reference material, magazines, novels
Scanning	2000 wpm	Searching for specific details	Looking for specific type of information

much like learning how to rollerblade. The first day, you might be fortunate enough to keep your legs straight and refrain from hurting yourself. But as you progress, your speed and agility improve. As you increase the amount of reading you do, you begin to increase your reading speed, as well as your ability to process and comprehend the material.

Uncovering the Organization or Pattern of a Chapter   Another effective strategy is to discover the organization of the chapter by creating a cognitive map, or an organizational layout of the information that you are learning. The Self-Development Model on page 144 is an example of the organizational structure of a learning identity. Note that without this figure, the explanation of this model would be quite complex. However, by visualizing how the various elements of this model (e.g., active learning, note-taking, writing tests), are connected to the learning identity, the easier it is to comprehend. If the text you are reading is well organized, you may use the organizational structure of the chapter to enhance your learning of the material. Take the outline of the chapter and create a visual cognitive, or mind map connecting all the sub heads to the main concept of the chapter. When it comes to learning the new material, information will be processed much quicker, and recall of the information will be enhanced. Again, it is like canoeing. By having a good understanding of the map, landing spots before rapids and waterfalls are much easier to identify, increasing the success of canoeing. So too, a good understanding of the layout of the chapter alerts you as to what to expect, and increases your reading rate and comprehension of the material.

Engage in the Visuals of the Chapter   While you are reading, try to engage in the visuals of the chapter. We are 90 percent visual learners and tend to remember things when they are associated with visual stimuli. First, look at the visuals provided in the chapter. Try to understand how they fit with the text. Associate specific ideas in the text with each visual. This will substantially improve your memory of the idea.

Highlighting   Highlight key words with different colours. Again, remember the visual association. For me, red is associated with urgency and reserved for highlighting the most important ideas. Green is used to highlight important explanations, definitions, or examples of the very important (red) things. Use up to four colours, ensuring consistency with the colour and the colour's significance. Also critical is the amount you highlight. The key here is to be frugal, highlighting only important material. Although many first-year texts encourage students to highlight from 15–25 percent of the text (Gardner & Jewler, 1997), the key is to know what is important (Kiewra, 1989; Kiewra, Mayer, Christensen, Kim, & Riskh, 1991). After the first two lectures, successful students are aware of what the professor thinks is most important, and use this in guiding their highlighting.

Annotating or Summarizing   Annotating or summarizing the text is an effective active learning strategy for processing new information. After a paragraph is read, the student explains it in his/her own words—in an annotated, or a shorter, more concise format. A good understanding of the ideas provided in the paragraph might mean just writing the key words down. Complex material requires summarizing the material in short sentences. This is extremely useful in that you are actively reading, taking existing information from a text, and rewriting it in your own words. It is a good test of your understanding of the material. As you continue to do this, you strengthen the processing of this material and thereby increase the potential for remembering it in the future.

Above all, reading takes mental energy. Thus, it is very important to take breaks to provide a time to re-energize. Most students have a high comprehension rate when reading between 45 and 60 minutes. After this time period, a short 10-minute break allows students to renew their energy before proceeding to the next section or chapter.

After Reading

After reading the chapter actively, it is time to recheck comprehension, apply new information, make connections, and summarize. Once again, as you did during the reading of the chapter, it is crucial to ensure that you understood everything that you read. There is a variety of ways for testing your comprehension. First, use the questions that you created during the previewing of the chapter. Next, use your chapter outline and your annotations to see if you understand the material based on your paraphrasing of the text. Use any questions provided in the text to check your comprehension. If you are able to provide answers for each, then your comprehension is strong. However, if there are any questions about the content, these areas need more attention. Flag any material that is difficult or confusing by placing a red mark beside it and writing the question in the margin. During your next class, ask the professor for clarity.

Another key strategy to increase your comprehension and retention of the material is to apply the new material. Apply what you have read by asking yourself "How does this relate to other topics in the course?", "How does this relate to my life?" or "What practical application can I make with this new information?"

Making mental connections, such as concept maps or charts of the material in the chapter also strengthens your memory of the new information. For instance, taking the material read so far, there are a number of ways of connecting it cognitively to form a visual that makes the material easier to remember. As seen in the Concept Map on page 153, a visual representation of what you have learned so far enhances your reading of the chapter material, and helps you to remember it. In looking at a visual representation, or concept map, you have further strengthened the retention of the material in your mind.

Pulling ideas together is another active strategy. After each section, capture the idea presented. Once you have read the entire chapter, summarize the chapter content in less than five statements. Your chapter outline will help guide you in summarizing.

Review by summarizing what you have learned in the chapter. This is accomplished by reviewing your concept maps and by answering your guide questions. The more often you review the material, the stronger the memory retention of the material. Reviewing is a critical strategy for being prepared in class and for the final examination. Moreover, it provides you with the necessary knowledge for future applications in the real world.

Psychologists and educators have developed several models to assist students in refining their reading capabilities. Probably the most commonly used is the SQ3R model (Robinson, 1946). You will often find this model in the preface of many social science textbooks. The acronym stands for Survey, Question, Read, Recite, and Review. "Survey and Question" is synonymous with the "prior to reading" strategies listed above. "Reading" is the active approach taken in highlighting and annotating. "Recite and Review" incorporate the strategies utilized after reading. Once you adopt these strategies, you will notice improvements in your reading speed and comprehension, often rewarding you with free time. However, do realize that it takes commitment and effort to begin.

During the Class: Learning from Lectures

Because most first-year courses are taught in large lecture sections, students are expected to be efficient at recording new information. This involves effective listening skills, an efficient system of note taking, and an awareness of the relationship between the informational content and diverse academic questions.

The purpose of the lecture is to highlight important concepts and content. Thus, only a few major points are selected and highlighted. Often, professors will spend time explaining the ideas to make them clearer. In the case of introduction courses, a general survey of the field is given. One can expect very little details about the topic. To maximize your learning from a lecture, preparation, active learning, and post-class review are essential.

Before the lecture it is useful to anticipate the content and focus of the presentation. Refer to the syllabus for pre-lecture reading assignments and read before class. Use the syllabus to anticipate the content of the lecture. Also useful is to anticipate possible exam questions that this lecture might address. Moreover, develop an awareness of the lecture style, including the organizational style and thought patterns of your professor. As you will discover in Chapter 11, students and professors alike have varying learning styles, which include different organizational and thinking strategies. Knowing about your professor's style improves your learning and prepares you to take more efficient notes.

Attend class regularly and arrive early to get the best seat. After all, your classroom hour is costing you an average of $87.50 per minute (an estimated cost including tuition and government contributions). Think back to the last concert you attended. Did you

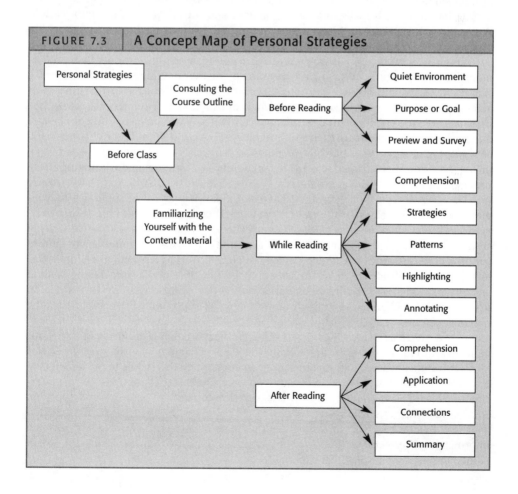

FIGURE 7.3 | A Concept Map of Personal Strategies

arrive late to take the seat furthest from the stage? Well, successful students view the lecture in a similar manner. Having worked hard at paying tuition, they want their money's worth. So they sit in the front, in an area often defined as the "golden T." Why? Because of its proximity to the professor. There are fewer distractions in this area and the student has better eye contact with the professor. Moreover, professors often establish greater rapport with these students and take teaching cues from them (Feldman, 1997).

Once in the "golden T," successful students actively engage with their professors by "SLANT"ing, or **S**itting up, **L**eaning forward, **A**sking questions, **N**odding and smiling, and **T**racking. Sitting up and leaning forward provides the physiological posture necessary for your body to continue supplying the brain with the maximum amount of oxygen required during sitting. Asking questions keeps you focused. Nodding and smiling encourages the professor to teach to you, and increases your commitment to remaining alert. Finally, tracking the movement of the professor increases your blood flow and compensates for the challenge of sitting in one place for a long period.

Note-taking has been mistakenly viewed by many as the transmission of information from the professor to the student with minimum processing—passive and inefficient learning. Assuming the role of a stenographer and copiously transcribing every word that is uttered by the professor produces little learning. A better approach is to become an active note taker. This involves a process of developing understanding of a subject based on active listening, interpretation, and organization of the information. When it is appropriately utilized it keeps students involved in the teaching-learning process (Hult, Cohn, & Potter, 1984; Kiewra, 1983).

A critical factor in active learning is active listening. Active listening involves preparing, encoding the words, clarifying the meaning of ideas, observing professorial clues for significant ideas, and asking questions. Successful students engage in the process of active listening during note-taking. Given their prior reading of the material, these students are able to spend less time taking notes and more time engaging in the process of integrating the new ideas into their well-established cognitive maps of the chapters read. New information is integrated with the material previously read. Once completed, note taking then provides a resource for studying, writing, comparing, and combining classroom information with the text material.

The Cornell Note-Taking Method has been identified as one of the most efficient methods because it allows students to consolidate their learning. This note-taking strategy was developed in the early 1950s at Cornell University as part of a study on increasing students' retention of material learned in a lecture (Pauk, 1968). A number of studies confirmed the effectiveness of this strategy in comparison to a number of other note-taking strategies (Feldman, 1997). As seen on page 155, the Cornell Note-Taking Method encourages students to rewrite the material in their own words, organize the material in a logical fashion, highlight what the professor views as important, and to summarize the material learned.

Active note-taking also includes making connections between ideas and previous material learned, as well as elaborating on the ideas presented by giving real-life examples. Here students listen to the examples given in class and then come up with their own examples. Writing the material into your own words means that you have some understanding of it. This is where your previous exposure to reading the text is so important. You can now integrate what you hear during the lecture with the ideas you have read in your text. By doing so, you are strengthening the association of new ideas with existing information. These connections can be made using cognitive maps inside the "Main Points" of the Cornell Note-Taking template.

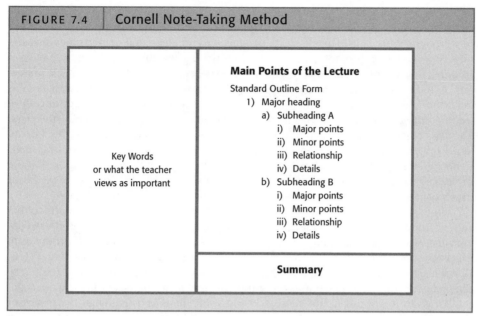

FIGURE 7.4	Cornell Note-Taking Method

Key Words
or what the teacher
views as important

Main Points of the Lecture

Standard Outline Form

1) Major heading
   a) Subheading A
      i) Major points
      ii) Minor points
      iii) Relationship
      iv) Details
   b) Subheading B
      i) Major points
      ii) Minor points
      iii) Relationship
      iv) Details

Summary

Based on Pzuk, Walter (1962). *How to Study in College.* Boston: Houghton Mifflin.

Key to annotating the lecture notes is to do so in an organized and logical fashion. Outlines are designed to organize information by encouraging the identification of major concepts, providing supportive evidence and stating the relationship between points. The standard outline form and the decimal outline form are the most common. Both are supported by most word processing software, and thus allow for ease of note-taking with a laptop.

Organization is also important in keeping notes. Successful students date and number their notes so that they are easy to follow. Accompanying handouts are dated as well and entered into the note binder in chronological sequence. They use their best handwriting in order to decrease the amount of confusion in trying to decipher the notes later. Some students opt to write notes on their laptop computers.

Predicting Future Test Items—Clues

In the ideal world, you learn for the sake of interest and invest learning in the areas that appeal to you. However, in the academic world, there is another side to learning; a competitive process that rewards students for knowing how to get excellent grades. When it comes to high grades, marks often rely on what the professor thinks is important, and not what the student finds of interest or significance. So the successful student, although enjoying learning for the sake of gaining personal knowledge, also becomes an expert in uncovering what the professor thinks is important. This importance bias of the professor is what will often guide the selection of material presented in class, the criteria and content expected in assignments, and the type of content covered on a quiz or exam. In the classroom, the successful student, like a detective, looks for clues that tip off important information.

Most obvious to the student are the professors' verbal clues such as "this is important," "this will be on the next test," "a major aspect is...," "most important...," and "a key point to remember is...." The repeating of concepts and ideas, and written clues also signify importance. If the professor spends time writing the material down or having it recorded in hard copy form and presented, there is good reason to believe that it is important. A number of organizational clues, such as lecture outlines, class objectives, lists, generalizations, cause and effect, and comparison and contrast demonstrate importance. The lecture outline becomes your road map as to where the professor will be taking the class. The class objectives are the learning goals that the professor wants you to master. Lists of items presented in class are considered important, otherwise they would not be mentioned. When the professor refers to one item causing another item, or any time that the professor engages in a comparison of two or more ideas, make note. Whenever a professor uses any of these techniques, make sure to signify this as important in your notes.

Other clues less likely to be noticed are mannerisms of the professor. Mannerisms that suggest importance often include an increase in energy or excitement, increased eye contact, and raised voice intonations. Content specialization is also important. If unsure as to the professor's special interests, listen carefully for his/her biography on the first day of class. Check his/her Web site for additional clues. Also, conduct a search of material published by the professor, using his/her name as the author. You might be amazed at what you discover.

Thus, an important tip for success in academic life is knowing what the professor finds important. Successful students use clues to highlight their notes as indicators of professor importance, and are fairly accurate in predicting assignment or test items. These students use their notes to study intelligently. However, what you as a student find important will be most important for your life. The key here is to remain balanced. Find ways to increase your learning for the sake of your inquisitiveness while at the same time, knowing what is important for you to succeed.

After Class

After actively learning prior to class through reading, and during class through active note-taking, successful students engage in a variety of learning strategies after class. These include studying and preparing for a test or exam.

Study Strategies for Mastering Course Material

Studying is defined as the active processing of information that involves **attending**, **acquiring**, **organizing**, and **integrating** information into memory (McKeachie et al., 1986; Weinstein & Mayer, 1986).

Attending

Successful students are able to select the important or key information by flagging material that has been presented in assigned readings and lectures. Then they transfer that information to their working memory (McKeachie et al., 1986). Key are the skills of being "alert" and "selective" to the information that is seen as important (Corno & Mandinach, 1983).

Acquiring

Once the content has been selected as important, the student works on acquisition by transferring this information from working memory into long-term memory. This involves making sense of what the new material means and linking it with previously learned material (McKeachie et al., 1986; Weinstein & Mayer, 1986). To understand new material, students seek clarification from professors, tutors or fellow students, or consult their textbooks for further information. Once the meaning is derived for the information being presented, the student can effectively and efficiently process it into his/her memory for future recall.

Rehearsal strategies are also useful in acquiring new information. For example, if you are learning a list of words, reciting them is probably the most efficient method for long-term memory (Weinstein & Mayer, 1986). If the learning tasks are more complex— such as learning the material from your text or from your notes—shadowing, or reading the material out loud, rewriting the material into notes, highlighting key text, as well as making notes in the margins of texts all increase your long-term memory of the information (Weinstein & Mayer, 1986). However, rehearsal strategies are only effective in recalling the information. If you are interested in processing the information at a deeper level, then you need to combine your rehearsal strategies with some form of organization and elaboration of the content.

Organizing

Your working memory is information that is actively being processed, but not to a level that can produce strong memories for examination purposes. A student needs to take important content and commit it to memory through active construction or organization. Construction engages the student in making connections among ideas in his/her working memory, using concept maps, or coherent and organized outlines (Weinstein & Meyer, 1991). There are a number of efficient organizational strategies available to the student. These involve **chunking**, **mnemonics**, **selecting main ideas**, **defining hierarchies,** and **integrating**. Chunking involves the grouping of words or ideas into categories that reflect some common and meaningful element (Myers, 2001; Weinstein & Mayer, 1986). For instance, if you are learning about the different types of motorcycles, you can group them into meaningful chunks, so that you have off-road types, touring motorcycles (e.g., Honda Gold Wing), racing, and classics (e.g., Triumph). By grouping the material you are learning, you are actively processing the content information. Of significance here is the fact that the average person is able to remember up to seven groups of material. That is why our telephone numbers, licence plate numbers, and many of our credit card numbers have seven digits, or up to seven groups of digits. Moreover, if your chunking can be made visual, such as a concept or cognitive map, the retention of the material improves. So the next time you are chunking, or grouping material into meaningful clusters, find ways to place this organizational structure into a concept map.

The use of mnemonics is also an effective organizational strategy. Developed by ancient Greek scholars to remember lengthy speeches and passages (Myers, 2001), mnemonic devices include both acoustic and visual codes such as acronyms, and taking the first letter of each word in a list and creating a new word or jingle. Many musicians will recognize the following jingle as the order of sharps in music: "Father Charles Goes Down And Ends Battles." The first letters of each word represent the notes F, C, G, D, A, E, B. Mnemonics have been demonstrated to increase the memory of lists of words or ideas (Myers, 2001).

When trying to increase your memory of more complex material, such as the information from your text chapter, students who are able to select the main ideas and connections in the chapter are more likely to do well in examinations of the material. Of importance here is the ability to identify the main idea of the text. Chapter headings and summaries provide clues as to the main idea of the chapter. Once identified, students begin to analyze the remaining chapter text to see how the other ideas in the chapter connect with the main idea. This includes networking, whereby students identify the different types of links between the text ideas and the main chapter ideas, such as definitional links, empirical or supporting links, or contradicting links (Dansereau, 1985).

Creating hierarchies is another organizational strategy known to increase students' memory (Waldrop, 1987). Here students who organize material into a few broad topics, and further subdivide the topics into more refined ideas and concepts are able to reconstruct the memory of the material during examinations. Most often, textbook chapter outlines can be consulted for a hierarchical structure of the content. For instance, the Concept Map of Personal Strategies on page 153 demonstrates how a student can organize the present study into a hierarchy or a concept map.

In the final stage, the student integrates the new information with material previously learned and experienced (McKeachie et al., 1986; Weinstein & Mayer, 1986). Integrating means adding personal experiences and information to the new material in order to help strengthen the learning of it. For instance, attributional retraining becomes more meaningful when you apply it to a personal situation, in comparison to just reading and memorizing it. Studies demonstrate that students who elaborate by associating personal experiences with words in a long list, tend to remember more of these words than students learning the same list of words via memorization, or through organization of the words into hierarchies (Craik & Lockhart, 1972).

Learning from the text by reading, paraphrasing, creating analogies, creating notes, explaining, asking questions, and finding answers are all cognitive strategies that engage the student in active elaboration of the material being read (Weinstein & Mayer, 1986). As explained earlier in the section on reading strategies, each of these strategies is helpful in integrating and connecting new information with previously processed information (McKeachie et al., 1986).

Taking Control of Your Learning

So far, we have covered the cognitive characteristics predicting the success of university students. However, of equal, if not more importantance, are the internal operations of your mind. Many refer to these as cognitive characteristics, or metacognition. Cognition includes the various things that occur in our brain, whereas metacognition refers to knowing how you best use your brain to increase your learning. The most effective metacognitive strategy to improve your success as a student is self-regulated learning (Bandura, 1986; Naumann, 1999). It allows you to take control of your learning by *planning, monitoring,* and *feedback utilization* (Bandura, 1986).

Successful students are known to engage in more planning than non-successful students (Pressley, 1986). Planning activities include goal-setting for reading, studying, and researching; skimming and creating questions prior to reading the chapters; and conducting a task analysis of a problem prior to solving it (McKeachie et al., 1986). Key to the success of the student who uses planning is anticipating the best strategy to accomplish the task at hand efficiently and effectively.

Monitoring allows students to track their performance and adjust their activities to ensure success (McKeachie et al., 1986; Weinstein & Mayer, 1986). Monitoring includes recognizing distractions and making alternative plans to eliminate them, testing one's comprehension of reading material, and matching time limits on tests to the value of the question.

Feedback provides the student with valuable information as to the extent to which they comprehend the material. Feedback is a continuous process that helps the student fine-tune his/her learning strategies to provide the best possible strategy to enhance learning (Brown, Bransford, Ferrara, & Campione, 1983). This could include making changes to their reading speeds, consulting the professor on material, or analyzing exam questions so as to modify ineffective learning strategies to more effective ones.

Self-regulated learning is crucial. Successful students are continuously planning, monitoring, and using their feedback to guide them in improving their learning strategies. As they do so, their learning strategies become efficient in meeting the learning goals set out. Self-regulated learning is critical in university given the diversity of courses, diversity of professors, and the diversity of research material available for each content area.

Putting It All Into Practice

As shown, successful students incorporate a number of cognitive and metacognitive strategies while studying. Most studying occurs on a daily basis, and over many short periods rather than all at once. As a result, the student's memory trace, or strength, is increased. For many successful students a consistent studying pattern includes the following. The first five minutes are used to set the studying goals for the next 40 minutes. Once the goals are set, the student focuses on the studying task at hand, such as reading, selectively highlighting, and/or intense writing. After the 40 minutes are up, the student reviews what he/she has done for approximately five minutes and follows this with a ten-minute break. After the break, the cycle begins again and continues until the student's studying time is complete. An important strategy is to ensure that the next cycle of studying focuses on a topic unrelated to the first, thereby providing the mind with a totally different set of ideas. For instance, studying for a psychology course is followed by studying for a science or mathematics course. By studying different rather than overlapping course material (e.g., psychology and sociology, which overlap), the student is less likely to become distracted by overlapping content, a known phenomenon that often causes more confusion than learning. Studying consistently in small chunks is more effective in increasing a student's memory than studying intensely for longer periods of time (Craik & Lockhart, 1972).

Test-Taking Strategies: Tests Are Performances

A test is defined as an "appraisal" or "the systematic basis for making inferences about learning and development of students" (Erwin, 1991). In other words, a test is a form of classroom research whereby the professor systematically attempts to investigate the relationship between teaching and learning in the classroom (Cross, 1990). In creating an exam, the professor's goal is to make it a valid, fair, and trustworthy judgment about the quality of the student's work (Thorndike & Hagen, 1995).

What Do Tests Measure?

Tests are created with a plethora of purposes in mind. These include tailoring the test to the learning goals of the course, establishing grading criteria and marking standards, helping students acquire skills and knowledge that they need, assessing student learning over time, shaping student motivation, providing students with feedback to learn from mistakes, communicating students' learning to other students and other audiences, and for using results to plan future teaching methods (Walvoord & Anderson, 1998). As seen in the figure on page 160, tests help students identify their strengths and weaknesses with regard to the content material, help motivate them to study, and provide a learning opportunity as well as a career assessment (McMillan, 1988).

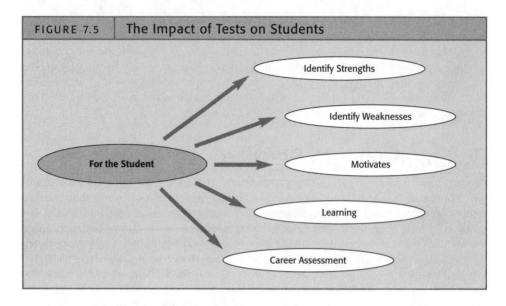

| FIGURE 7.5 | The Impact of Tests on Students |

Identify Strengths

Identify Weaknesses

For the Student

Motivates

Learning

Career Assessment

Although the intentions of test designers are noble in attempting to meet each of the above goals, tests in and of themselves are not true measures of what is learned in the course. Neither are they measures of personal worth or intelligence. Tests are only indicators of how well students will do on the exam. In the ideal world, the best test of your learning would be to follow you around for the next two to five years and observe how well you apply what was learned in class. However, since this is not economical in our age of education, a more efficient means to measure learning is the testing of information the professor identifies as important. Thus, demonstrating your learning of material depends upon your ability to predict, understand, and know what the professor thinks is important.

Study Strategies for the Appropriate Exam Type

As seen in Figure 7.5 above, there are a number of behaviours that lead to being a successful test-taker. See how well you score on these predictors of successful test-takers.

Improving Your Test Results

If you're concerned about your score on this test, you may want to check and see if you are following practices that lead to success. Can you answer "yes" to each of the items below?

Answer each item below as either "true" or "false"

1. I read the assigned chapter the day before the lecture on the chapter material.

2. I allow about one hour for reading each assigned chapter so that I can read it slowly and thoughtfully.

3. I read to find out "why?" in addition to "what?" because I really want to know how to be an effective student.

Tests and exams can be divided into a number of categories. These include time, content, value, and response type. Time or duration of the material is either cumulative or non-cumulative. Cumulative means that the exam will include all previously learned material, usually beginning from the very first class. Non-cumulative means that the exam will only focus on a certain section or module of the course, and that material learned earlier is not required for the exam. Type of content is also of significance for being successful. Many professors provide clear outlines as to what content is expected on the exam, based on the importance of the content stressed during the class lectures. Review classes prior to the exams provide clues as to what a student can expect on the exam. Moreover, successful students are usually able to find copies of previous years' exams from which to study. These are usually found on the professor's Web site, on reserve in the library, or on file in the department. The value of the exam indicates to the successful student how much time to budget for studying. If there are two exams, one worth 40 pervent of the course and the other worth only 5 percent, the successful student allocates more time to the more valuable exam.

Exams can also be divided into two categories, *objective* and *subjective*. Both of these types of exams require different approaches to studying, and different types of responses by the student. The objective type of exam includes multiple choice, matching, true-false, and fill-in-the-blank questions. For instance, the objective test has the answer as part of the question. It is just a matter of selecting the most appropriate multiple-choice response, matching the correct word or phrase with the appropriate stem, or determining whether the statement is true or false (Thorndike & Hagen, 1995). To ensure success, the student needs to be able to identify the correct responses. Thus, the studying strategies aimed at strengthening the student's recognition of the material are most beneficial. This includes having a good understanding of the content material.

Successful students are also "test-wise," employing test-taking strategies to help identify clues in the test. For each item, begin by reading the question and underlining the keywords in the question that have a significant effect on the meaning of the question. Strike out irrelevant or filler words that detract from the main point of the question. Then, with the possible responses still covered, write down what you think is the correct answer.

Proceed with revealing the possible responses and make the appropriate selection. If the answer is different from the one you wrote down and difficult to determine, then employ the process of elimination, striking out contradictory and obviously incorrect responses. In the process of matching, begin by making connections between the easiest matches and then move on to the more difficult ones. If the question is still not answerable, ask for clarification. If the answer is still unachievable, mark the question with the intent of returning to it later. Often the answer becomes apparent later as a result of working on other questions. Spend your time wisely, never dwelling too long on any question.

Part of being test-wise is looking for clues, including keywords, grammatical connectors, and even response length. Keywords provide one clue. Beware of negatives, specifically those presented in not so obvious ways. For instance, "all of the following are found in psychoanalysis *except*...." Second, where there are choices that represent combinations, such as "A and B only" or "Any two of the above," begin by separating the items in the combinations. Look at each item independently. If both are correct, then the combination is most likely. Third, in a true/false test, make sure that the entire sentence is true. Even a small part, if incorrect, renders the entire sentence as false. Fourth, take care in answering statements that contain absolutes such as "never," "none," "always,",or "only." In most cases, these are generally false. Grammatical connectors are also valuable clues. The process of creating an exam often provides opportunities for minor grammatical errors. For instance, a test question with the article "an" requires that the correct response have a vowel as the first letter. If the question implies that the answer has more than one element or is plural, responses that are singular can be eliminated. Fifth, the length of the response often indicates the economic skills of the exam writer. Most professors creating exams are time-conscious and try to find ways to minimize their efforts in designing exam questions. Thus, a correct response will usually be the one with the most detail, whereas each of the other "filler" responses might be derivations of the correct response with fewer details. So if in doubt, it is very likely that the longest response is the correct one. Finally, when you cannot determine the correct response, make an intelligent guess. However, before doing so, improve your odds and eliminate as many incorrect or unlikely answers as possible.

Subjective, or constructed response exams rely on short answer, essay, open-book, take-home, and problem solving types of questions (Thorndike & Hagen, 1995). In order to prepare for these tests, you need to have the ability to construct the answer from a limited, and often clue-less question. In other words, you will need to have a thorough knowledge of the material in order to recall the information. Recall is different from the recognition required in the objective test in that the material needs to be memorized and readily available. Given that most subjective responses require a paragraph or an essay response, the successful student uses a more intensive studying strategy to try to gain an overall comprehension of the material. Here, concept maps and organizational strategies are useful in processing large amounts of material into meaningful memory. During the exam and prior to reading any of the questions, the successful student jots down all the concept maps that he/she has studied. By doing so, the student is ensured that the material is written and not potentially lost as a result of the effects that test anxiety has on the student's memory. Once on paper, the student begins the exam.

Here too, the successful student relies on an exam-writing strategy. Above all, successful students manage their time for test writing. They allocate enough time to formalize an outline and then begin the writing process. Second, the writing is done as legibly as possible and is always double-spaced. This allows for making changes later, as well as drastically improving the "user-friendliness" of the paper for the reader. Professors tend to give a higher grade when the writing is neat and easier to read. Third, the student creates an outline of what he/she is about to write, often referring to the concept maps that he/she has written at the beginning of the exam. Fourth, and of great significance, is the defining of any key terms in a question. For instance, a student asked to write an essay comparing and contrasting the different types of exams would begin by identifying each of the types of exams—defining, and providing an example of each before comparing them. Fifth, the essay is written as if the student were trying to teach a person who has never heard of the idea before. Each element is defined, described, and exemplified without assuming any knowledge on the part of the reader. With the remaining time, the student edits the essay to ensure that the grammar is correct, that sentences make sense, and that ideas are correctly portrayed. Finally, the student ends by finding a catchy title for the essay to capture the interest of the professor.

Coping with Exam Anxiety

Very common among first-year students is exam anxiety. Fortunately, if detected early, there are ways to reduce it. First, you need to identify the source of the anxiety. Is it the content—something that you find very complex and thus feel anxious about? Is it the professor who keeps trying to motivate the class to learn by scaring them with the potential of a surprise quiz at any time during the class period? The key to coping is to discover what causes the anxiety. The next step is to monitor your response. As your feelings of anxiety are aroused, are you able to monitor and potentially reduce them by taking longer breaths? Are you able to mentally remove yourself to your favourite hideaway momentarily until the anxiety lessens? Each of these techniques can be used to reduce the anxiety. Finally, seek the advice of professionals. Many university campuses have excellent workshops that help students deal effectively with exam anxiety. Most of these are offered free to the student. In cases where the anxiety is severe, professional help is also available through Counselling Services. By successfully identifying, monitoring, and getting help, you are able to break free from the negative effects of exam anxiety.

Dealing with the Outcome

When you get your exam back, celebrate your achievements. If they are less than expected, deal with your emotions first. Ideally, give your self at least three days before approaching your professor. This gives you time to think rationally rather than react emotionally. Analyze your performance and prepare to discuss the examination material. You can tabulate the scores, check for accuracy in marking, and ask for clarification.

If you are going to challenge the mark, provide a strong, clearly written argument with excellent supporting documents, such as the reference and page number of the text that supports your answers, even attaching a photocopy of the evidence with full reference. The stronger your argument, the greater your likelihood of success in changing a grade. In meeting with the professors, be respectful, polite, and succinct. Ask questions using **"I" messages**. Practice what you plan to say. You may use such statements as "I want this to be a learning opportunity…" or "I found a potential error…" or "In my reading of the material, I noticed a discrepancy…." The professor is more likely to accommodate your request. Any time that you make the professor feel defensive, such as accusing him/her of a poor test, or a poorly written question, he/she is more likely to become defensive, and the opportunities for grade improvements diminish quickly.

In the event of not being fairly heard, you can seek help by consulting with the staff in the Student Advocacy office at your institution. These trained professionals will provide you with excellent ideas and strategies regarding how to have your concerns accommodated. Finally, remember that the potential for doing well is in your control. By applying more effort with the best learning, reading, and studying strategies, you will be able to increase your chances of becoming successful. Above all, learning at the university is usually the result of your effort, not because of task difficulty, luck, or ability.

Why Study When You Can Cram?

Wouldn't it be nice to minimize all studying? What about cramming? Cramming involves studying hastily for an imminent exam (Merriam-Webster, 1986), and seems to work for some students. Well, it is possible to do well if cramming is conducted in a rigorous manner. However, the results are at best, poor. If you get caught in a situation where you have just a few hours to prepare, you might try rigorous cramming.

Key to cramming is avoiding all distractions during the time that you are studying and up to the time at which you write the exam. Given that your memory of the material is going to be superficial, a simple distraction, such as listening to other students just prior to entering into the examination room, is powerful enough to eliminate any material that you might have crammed. So ideally, find a quiet area away from all potential distractions. Study before you sleep. Sleep is crucial, and studying prior to sleeping will allow your mind to continue cycling the material while sleeping. As soon as you wake up, review what you have crammed the night before. Continue doing so right up to the time of the exam. Avoid having any conversations about the anticipated exam with other students. Use earplugs, and find a seat away from other students so that you are not distracted when they begin to leave earlier from the exam. This too, can cause you to become anxious and further reduce your superficial memory. When you hand in your exam, set reasonable expectations regarding your possible grades.

Once the exam has been completed, go back and revisit your studying strategies, modifying them so that studying on a daily basis becomes a priority and not something that is left to the last minute. Take a lesson from the sponge. A sponge increases its absorption ability when it has initially been saturated with moisture. For instance, take a dry sponge (ideally a sea sponge), and a sponge that has been soaking in water. The dry sponge represents the student who has not studied all semester. The totally wet sponge represents the student who has studied consistently. Wring out the wet sponge. Take a glass of water and pour it onto each sponge for 12 seconds, representing the 12 weeks in the semester. Notice that the sponge that is totally dry cannot take in as much water as the sponge that has been totally wet. Like the sponge, you learn more if you prepare, than if you rely on cramming for tests.

Social Self: Integrating Social Skills in Learning

Learning can become a meaningful enterprise when shared with others. Recall from previous chapters the importance of social learning. It provides a sense of belonging, creates a sense of community, and provides training for valued skills in the work place, such as team work. There is an incredible increase in learning when you do it with others. Let's explore each of the strategies involving others in learning.

Study Groups

The first and most effective way to learn with others is in study groups. The goal of a study group is to advance the knowledge of everyone in the group. Group members not only share content information, but also effective studying strategies. Group size should be between three and four people. This will enhance your ability as a group to identify incongruent ideas and cause you to research the topic more. Any group with more than four people reduces the chance for you to contribute meaningfully.

Together, the group is more efficient at predicting the exam criteria. When ideas are complex, the group can provide more details, given that each member might be viewing certain aspects of the content material more than the others. Also, when difficult content arises, it is more likely that at least one group member may understand the complexity, and thereby extend the learning of the group. Moreover, if further resources are needed, a group can distribute research responsibilities for gathering the details of the course material. In other words, each person in the group can be responsible for finding more details about specific components of the chapter—further enhancing the knowledge.

Finally, a group of peers can also provide important and valuable feedback on writing assignments. During the preparation of a research project, the student often becomes so involved in the process that he/she fails to see minor grammatical or content errors. Feedback by one or two other peers in the study group can make the difference in a grade. However, in having others read your material be careful to avoid problems of plagiarism. Ensure that all members of the group do their own independent projects.

"Buddy" or Support System

Another advantageous method of social learning involves a buddy system. It is possible, for unforeseen circumstances, that you might miss one or two classes. To avoid missing information and ensuring that you are up to date on class assignments, you can arrange with a fellow student in the class to take notes and save handouts. This system works when both people are committed. If either of you is absent, the other will obtain the information, and you will contact each other through e-mail or telephone. Missing too many classes, however, can adversely affect your performance as you miss the active learning that is such a critical component of successful learning.

In some cases, professors encourage collaboration in projects. Although it takes a little more effort in delegating responsibilities, group projects can be exciting and very meaningful. People who share common tasks are also more likely to develop stronger relationships. Group projects require that all contribute equally. One way to ensure equal distribution of work is to have a written contract set in place that all group members agree to. Clarifying the responsibilities and commitments for all, the project can move ahead as planned.

List-Serves, E-mail, or Discussion Boards

Another strategy involving others, yet not involving face-to-face contact, would be the use of modern technology for discussion. E-mail or list-serves between interested students in a class can also enhance your learning. Here you can join in on active conversations that deal with the class material, and keep apprised of the questions and answers students have. Some professors support active list-serves, or discussion boards where students can communicate with one another and get advice from the professor and/or the teaching assistant. This can also be used to enhance your learning of material that was presented in class, and to hear how other students understand the material.

As shown, there are a variety of ways to learn with other people. If you choose your learning partners well, you will be able to increase the efficiency with which you presently study. However, be aware not to spend all your effort studying with others. There is a fine balance between studying alone and studying with others. The best method is to prepare on your own for the group tasks. Thereby you get the best of both worlds. And remember, the more that you are involved in teaching the material to others, the stronger your retention will be.

Throughout this chapter, you have learned that your learning identity involves three dimensions: self-awareness, self-confidence, and self-concept. Each of these three dimensions is critical to your success as a student in university. Self-awareness provides you with an understanding of your competencies, relative to the expectations of university. Self-confidence is the positive attitude that you take in learning. Self-concept involves all the strategies that enhance learning, both the personal and the social. Each of these three dimensions requires your active learning. In other words, to be a successful student, you need an awareness of your own learning abilities; of the requirements of the university learning environment; of the effective techniques in reading, note taking, lecture learning, and test-taking that can enhance learning; of the value of self-regulation on academic performance; and of the importance of social connection to the learning process.

It's More Than Common Sense

Learning to Learn: The Importance of Metacognitive Skills

Michael Doyle, Ed.D.
John C. Garland, Ph.D.
Memorial University of Newfoundland

In the Fall of 1997, the University Counselling Centre at Memorial University of Newfoundland instituted UCC2020: Cognitive and Affective Learning Strategies (Doyle & Garland, 2001). The central goal of this credit course is to improve the overall learning skills of the students who take it. This includes cognitive skills, such as improved study and learning strategies, as well as more affective skills such as the management of time, stress, and test anxiety.

The Student Learning Experience

The course presents students with an array of cognitive and affective learning strategies that include two main learning tasks: master a large number of cognitive and affective learning strategies, and implement these strategies in their courses. Critical in the selection of these strategies is the opportunity for students to become more aware of how they process academic information. This self-monitoring, or metacognition (Flavell, 1979), involves the ability to reflect upon one's thinking, and has been described as the foundation for understanding text (Nist & Holschuh, 2000). Students learn how to actively monitor and regulate their cognitive processes, as well as to increase their awareness of study strategy usage.

In this course, students learn a broad range of cognitive learning strategies. These include memorization techniques such as chunking, imagery techniques and classical mnemonic techniques, broader learning techniques such as hierarchical organization, and learning systems such as SQ3R and MURDER (Doyle & Garland, 2001). They are also taught affective strategies such as time management, stress management, test-anxiety reduction, increased positive self-talk, self-monitoring, and self-coaching activities (Doyle & Garland, 2001).

Students' progress in the course is assessed by their performance on a standardized battery of tests. These include: the Nelson-Denny Reading Test (NDRT) (Brown, Fishco, & Hanna, 1993), the Test Anxiety Scale (TAS) (Sarason, 1956), and the Inventory of Learning Processes (ILP) (Schmeck, Ribich, & Ramanaiah, 1977). The NDRT is an objective test designed to measure vocabulary, reading rate, and reading comprehension. The TAS measures the amount of reported test anxiety, and the ILP organizes students' reported learning strategies on four sub-dimensions: deep processing, elaborative processing, fact retention skills (or confidence), and methodical study. Students complete the same battery of tests toward the end of the semester and receive objective feedback on their term changes.

Each student uses the results of the pre-test evaluation to design their personalized plan for improving their learning abilities during the term. Throughout the term, students reflect about their learning success and record their progress in using various cognitive and affective strategies in a learning journal. The journal gives each student a record of changes over the semester and provides an opportunity for them to evaluate the efficiency of various techniques. Researchers have demonstrated the usefulness of learning journals in enhancing students' awareness of their cognitive processes during learning tasks (McCrindle & Christensen, 1995), and are seen as promoting the development of metacognitive skills. Toward the end of the semester, students present to the rest of the class examples of techniques they have found useful in their studies.

While the course tends to use a lecture format, the course developers have constructed a number of in-class activities that lead students to try out various strategies in small groups. These include exercises in employing study systems and mnemonics, relaxation exercises, and completing and discussing a learning-styles inventory (Kolb, 1981). As UCC2020 is a credit course taken for a grade, examinations form a significant portion of the final evaluation for each student.

The results of data collected on these students indicate that these students improve significantly in their reading and learning abilities (Doyle & Garland, 1999). In particular, on the NDRT, students demonstrate increases in reading comprehension and reading rate. On the ILP, students report increases in deep processing strategies (e.g., categorizing, organizing, critical thinking); elaborative processing strategies (e.g., personalizing and increasing the meaningfulness of academic material); and the quantity of study and attention to details. Further, students report significant reductions in test anxiety.

A longitudinal study in which students from the initial three semesters were followed, for a period extending from two semesters prior to taking the course to two semesters after the course, demonstrated increases in grade levels. The most general result observed is that for those students who completed the course successfully (85 percent), there appears to be a direct benefit on the grade percentages attained for those students whose prior averages ranged from the C+ to F levels. Specifically, the increase is in the order of one-half grade for C student to a full grade for D/F students.

Taken together, the outcomes of this course demonstrate that students can increase the efficacy of their study skills by experimenting with, reflecting on, and adopting more effective methods of study. Evaluation studies demonstrate the potency of adopting cognitive and affective approaches to studying. Specific techniques that enhance success include reflecting upon available strategies, generating good comprehension questions during reading, developing an awareness of the text structure, externalizing thinking, and using effective study skills. These strategies can provide students with a heightened sense of control over their studies that can lead to improved study skills.

Success Strategies FOR EFFECTIVE LEARNING

Self-awareness
I've learned that my strengths in each of the following are:
    Reading…
    Active listening…
    Note-taking…
    Studying with diversity…

Self-confidence
To increase my confidence in my ability to read more efficiently I will…
To increase my confidence in my ability to listen more actively I will…
To increase my confidence in my ability to take notes more efficiently I will…
To increase my confidence in my ability to study efficiently I will…

Self-concept
Actions I can take to gain greater control of my reading are….
Actions I can take to gain greater control of my active listening are….
Actions I can take to gain greater control of my note taking are….
Actions I can take to gain greater control of my studying are….

Chapter Summary

Learning is defined as a set of behaviours that enhance performance and achievement. Students are encouraged to take responsibility for their own learning, and develop active learning skills from their first perusal of the course outline, to writing the final exam. A variety of techniques are identified as elements of successful strategies for effective learning. These include increased self-awareness of reading, note-taking, listening and exam preparation strategies, and developing self-confidence in one's ability to satisfactorily use these different strategies in various situations, in order to master material. The chapter features a number of actions that students can take to ensure greater control over the mastery of material. Understanding and practicing these skills will enable students to master course materials and take control of their learning.

Exercises

REFLECT–ACT

The following Reflect–Act exercises are designed to help you develop increased self-awareness of your learning effectiveness through the process of reflective thinking, analysis, and productive action. Self-reflection encourages you to consider information you learn, to increase your ability to know yourself and manage yourself.

Reflect   After having completed the reading survey on page 147, where do you find yourself on the continuum of being an efficient reader to being a mediocre reader? Which items did you score low on? Why?
Act   Take the time to develop your reading efficiency by first addressing the low scores on the reading survey.

Reflect   Think about the different types of reading you enjoy doing. What speed do you use for each type of reading? Which one gives you the most understanding of the material? Which type of reading gives you the most pleasure?
Act   Select the most appropriate reading speed from the Types of Reading table on page 150 that will strengthen your learning efficiency for each course text you need to read this semester. Create a chart to demonstrate the progress of reading you accomplish over the semester to encourage you to continue reading.

GROUP DISCUSSION

1. List the differences between your high school texts and your university texts.
2. Create a list of common note-taking problems associated with lectures. Beside each item create a recommended solution for the problem.
3. Make a list of tips that students should follow before, during, and after a lecture to assist their learning.
4. Explore and discuss the potential cues and clues that indicate the material presented by the professor during a lecture is important and may be on the exam.
5. Compare your notes from the last class with each other. Discuss how you as a group can increase your efficiency in note taking.

APPLY TO LIFE

Now that you have developed an understanding of how to increase your efficiency in reading, actively listening to lectures, taking notes, getting involved in study groups, and being prepared for discipline differences, you can use this information to enhance your own performance. Use the following questions to more clearly discover your strengths and limitations as a learner.

1. As I review how I have formerly read texts, what are my strengths in reading? Where do I need to improve, in terms of my reading, in order to succeed at university?
2. Assess your note-taking skills. Describe your areas of competency and identify areas for improvement.
3. In your next week of classes, apply the Cornell Method of Note-Taking. Compare your former style of note-taking with the Cornell Method. Which one will be easier to study from?

4. Using the self-development map on page 144 as a guideline, create a concept map that links all the major ideas of this chapter. Notice how much easier it is to remember a visual of this chapter than to look at a set of notes.

5. Choose a chapter, or section of a chapter, from any text you are presently studying. Create a summary outline reflecting the overall content and organization of the chapter, or section you have selected. Next, draw an idea map reflecting the overall content and organization of the chapter, or section you have selected (suggestion: choose material that will be most helpful in your studies).

Communicating Effectively

"It's not only what you say, but also how you say it."

Finding your way is enhanced by your ability to *Communicate Effectively* with others. Your success on your educational journey is influenced by your ability to seek direction, ask appropriate questions, inquire, clarify your understanding, and demonstrate your knowledge. In finding answers and listening to others, there will be times when you understand and other times when you do not. Sometimes when you seek to be understood, others do not hear you, misinterpret your message, or simply do not comprehend your words. You soon discover it's not only what you say, but also how you say it that makes the difference between effective communication and ineffective communication. To communicate effectively, either through writing or talking, involves engaging in an interactive process of sending a message and responding to that message.

Communicating effectively involves expressing your ideas so that both you and your message are understood by others. Effective communicators connect with people. They are able to interact effectively because they know that effective communication involves a reciprocal process of interchange, understanding, and feedback. Therefore, in communicating, whether it is through writing or talking, you must consider three major factors: what you have to say, how you say it, and to whom you are saying it. In developing your skills as an effective communicator, whether as a writer or a presenter, you will discover the factors that can benefit or interfere with your ability to communicate. You will develop an awareness of the common processes in planning and delivering your message and the strategies that can ensure that you possess the writing and presentation skills that add to your capabilities as a communicator. Both communication processes involve developing a clear understanding of your topic or message, using a well-designed medium to deliver your information, and recognizing the needs and demands of the audience so that your message can be understood. In the following two chapters you will discover basic information regarding the process of communicating through writing and talking. You will learn strategies you can utilize to improve your own communication capabilities.

There are many types of writing that you can use to communicate various ideas and information. In fact, the exercises throughout this textbook have encouraged you to write in various formats. At times you have written to express your reactions, analyze your experiences, provide information, summarize ideas, or persuade others. Through these processes you have been able to communicate your ideas and your perceptions. In many of your courses you will be required to write an essay, a research paper, or a book review. To succeed in writing these formal academic assignments, it is useful to learn the process of writing and master the important details that are required. You will learn strategies for focusing the topic and purpose of the paper, engaging in the developmental process of constructing a paper, and ensuring proper documentation so that the format of the paper meets the requirements of the academic course area. You will learn the basics of academic writing that are important to achieving success in university. By using the information provided in the writing chapter you will improve your ability to communicate to others through your writing.

There are times when you strive to communicate with others by speaking. Whether or not you are heard depends on the way in which you deliver your message, and the nature of your message. It also depends on the attitudes and needs of the individuals who are listening to you. Presenting yourself and your ideas to an individual or to a group requires you consider your message, the process of delivering the message (i.e., medium), and the audience to whom you are delivering the message. In the chapter on talking with others you will learn how to enhance your capabilities with two types of oral communication: interpersonal communication and information dissemination. You will be provided with the basic information for improving your capabilities to talk effectively with others through formal presentation processes or informal interactive processes.

There are a number of measures that can be used to assess your progress on your educational journey. One significant indicator of how successful you are is your ability to communicate effectively with others. Your ability to communicate effectively is evidenced as you demonstrate your competencies, express your ideas authoritatively, assert your needs, reach out for resources, ask for what you need, and connect with others. By enhancing your diverse communication capabilities you are better able to progress further toward your destination.

chapter 8

Academic Writing

K. Lynn Taylor, Ph.D.

"Quality writing is a combination of art and craft, of style and mechanics, and it can be mastered." (Reynolds, 1982–83, p. 41)

Questions

What are the characteristics of quality academic writing?

Are there skills I can develop that will enhance my abilities as a writer?

What are some of the things I need to do in order to develop as a writer?

What are some of the strategies I can use to become a more effective writer?

Objectives

- Become more aware of your own abilities as a writer.
- Identify areas in which you need to develop your writing.
- Develop a better understanding of the requirements of academic writing tasks.
- Identify specific writing strategies used by successful academic writers.

Academic Integrity

Brandy Usick
The University of Manitoba

An important aspect of becoming a university student is being aware of and knowing "all the rules." One of the most important rules governs academic integrity. Students are expected to be honest in their academic work, and this includes not cheating (i.e., using a cheat sheet or glancing at a neighbour's paper while writing a test), and not plagiarizing (i.e., failing to reference the work of others).

Students may be found to be academically dishonest for a number of reasons. As a former undergraduate student in a large faculty, I understand how students may wonder how a professor could ever catch a cheater in a class of 200, or identify a plagiarized paper from a large stack of essays. Some students give in to temptations that allow them to cut corners and save time, instead of doing their own work. Other students are overwhelmed by the pressures they are experiencing; increasingly, students are leading complicated lives balancing many responsibilities within and outside of school. Sometimes a student may feel they have no other choice but to copy their roommate's essay from last year, or download a paper off of the Internet. In some other instances, students may not even be aware that they have broken the rules until they get caught.

One of the ways students navigate themselves through this process of higher education is by relying on the wisdom of other students who offer advice and anecdotes. Sometimes the advice directs the student to obtain copies of old exams because a particular professor always recycles test questions. The advice might be in the form of passing on an institution's legend. For example, a group of students who had access to exam questions before the test date and didn't get caught. Studying from old exams is usually a smart way to prepare for tests—if the instructor made them available.

Your job as a student is to use your personal integrity to decide what to do if ever presented with ethical dilemmas. Sometimes these conflicts manifest themselves in ways you may not anticipate. For example, you have likely been encouraged to form study groups. But what happens if your study group works through an assignment together and you are all later charged with inappropriate collaboration because you were instructed to hand in independent work? Or what if you find out that an assigned essay topic is one that you wrote about last year, and on which you scored an A? Did you know submitting the same paper twice could be considered duplicate submission? You are expected to submit new or original work for each course requirement. So, in order to make good ethical decisions, more often than not you need to know the expectations of your instructors, and that means asking questions and thinking critically.

For graduate students, the consequences of violating the academic integrity policy are more serious because graduate students are held to higher standards. I realize now, more than ever, the importance and integrity of citing the sources of all ideas, or expressions of ideas. Of course I have always been careful to cite my sources; I became citation savvy before I submitted my first university essay.

But now that I am conducting research of my own, I understand how devastating it would be to have my own work plagiarized.

So, why should you heed my words of wisdom? Not only have I had the experiences of undergraduate and graduate study, but I am also a Student Advocate who assists students with any number of concerns and thus, I have become more keenly aware of the consequences of academic dishonesty as a Student Affairs professional. One aspect of my work is to assist students who are being investigated for academic dishonesty. Through my job, I have heard of many different cases of academic dishonesty and many different "excuses" for violations. The cases which I feel are the most unfortunate are those in which the students inadvertently plagiarized, or who unknowingly worked too closely with others. By this, I mean that if the student had been aware of the rules, they would not have been in this situation. I have witnessed students being investigated, and when they receive the devastating news of a penalty. Penalties can range from a warning, to zero on the assignment, to an F in the course, to a suspension or expulsion. From one student to another, and from someone who has " been there," be academically honest!

One of the main ways people in academic communities communicate is through writing. Perhaps this is why it is difficult to find a course that does not require some kind of writing task. At times, it seems like you are constantly asked to demonstrate your knowledge and abilities by writing about them. However, writing is about much more than demonstrating what you know. Writing helps you learn by challenging you to think more deeply, make more connections, and discover new information and skills (Frederiksen & Dominic, 1981; Hilgers, Hussey, & Stitt-Bergh, 1999; Strode, 1991). Students themselves say that writing is good practice for thinking, for organizing, and refining ideas (Hilgers et al., 1999). Although it may seem obvious, one of the skills you develop through writing is the ability to write more effectively. What is not so obvious is that students who do not consciously plan to learn from their writing experiences often learn a lot less than they could about writing, and the things they write about. This chapter will focus on helping you to become more aware of the academic writing process and to use this awareness to grow as a writer and a learner.

If you find academic writing the most challenging part of being a student, you are not alone. Many of your professors, who engage in academic writing as part of their daily work, still find academic writing difficult, and often have moments when they lose confidence, suffer from "writer's block," or genuinely dislike the writing process (Boice, 1990). However, these same professors have learned strategies to get past these moments and, in large part, that is what learning to be an effective writer is about: finding the strategies that work for you. This chapter will identify many of the strategies that work for other people. Your challenge will be to experiment with them in your own writing to discover how they can work for you. Efforts to develop your writing are well worth the trouble; effective writing is critical for academic success and it is a skill that is also in high demand in the workplace. The Conference Board of Canada identifies written communication as a fundamental employability skill needed "to enter, stay in, and progress in the world of work" (*www.conferenceboard.ca/nbec*). The time and effort spent developing yourself as a writer are good investments in both your academic and professional careers.

The emphasis on "developing yourself" as a writer is intentional. To a great extent, writing is a process that you learn on your own, more than it is a process that someone teaches you (Emig, 1981). This is because academic writing is the product of complex interactions among what you know about a topic, new information learned from research, critical thinking, the writing process, the particular situation, and personal characteristics of the writer (Frederiksen & Dominic, 1981; Kennedy & Smith, 1994). As a result, there are no simple recipes for how to be a successful writer. However, we do know a lot about the processes commonly used by effective writers. For instance, writers who plan their research and writing process spend less time on the task, are more successful, and find writing less difficult (Kellogg, 1990; Torrance, Thomas & Robinson, 1994). More specifically, first-year students who know how to identify quality information relevant to the task and who organize that information well, produce the highest quality writing (Risemberg, 1996). Experienced writers also engage in repeated phases of planning, writing, and revising at different times in the writing process, and the sequence of these phases is unique for each task and for each writer (Emig, 1981; Flower & Hayes, 1981; Kennedy & Smith, 1994). Across these phases, we know that a major difference between successful and unsuccessful writers is the amount of revising they do to elaborate, restructure, and refine their writing (Nold, 1981). The purpose of this chapter is to introduce you to some of these strategies and skills so that you can apply them in your own writing.

Writing and the Self-Development Model

In many ways, our written work tells others not only what we know, but also who we are as people: our interests, our passions, and our personalities. As seen in the self-development model for writing on page 177, to be a successful writer, it is essential that you develop a "writing identity." Your personal writing identity will continue to develop throughout your career, but will always consist of a familiar set of components, which follow.

Self-awareness   This is the degree to which you are aware of your own skills and writing development needs, and the demands of individual academic writing assignments. You began articulating this awareness when you completed the social self-concept assessment in Chapter 2. In that assessment, you described the degree to which you are a good writer, use correct spelling and grammar, understand the differences between informal and academic writing, and know how to avoid plagiarism. In this chapter, you will be challenged to build on that awareness and to appreciate more fully the nature of academic writing tasks.

Self-confidence   This is the degree to which you believe that you have the skills and abilities to be successful in academic writing, have strategies to use in your writing and know when to use them, and have conscious control over your writing decisions while completing a task. Your confidence in yourself as an effective writer is a key factor in your success as an academic writer. Zimmerman and Bandura (1994) demonstrated that self-confidence positively influences the writing goals students set, their commitment to achieving these goals, and the effort they devote to a writing task. Not surprisingly, these behaviours resulted in higher writing achievement. To have this kind of confidence in your writing, you need to have effective strategies for monitoring your writing activity and judging its effectiveness, for making decisions about what strategies to use in a given situation, and for using self-talk to keep yourself motivated and on track (Zimmerman & Bandura, 1994). This chapter will challenge you to build your self-confidence as an academic writer by developing some of these strategies.

Self-concept   This is the degree to which you see yourself as an academic writer, and can use your knowledge and writing skills to engage yourself and other people in academic work. Developing your writing self-concept depends first, on how well you can integrate the roles, attributes and abilities of effective academic writers into your own writing experience, and second, on the development of your own academic writing "voice." Lloyd-Jones (1981) defined the writing voice as the writer's relationships to the information being communicated, and to his/her audience. This chapter will challenge you to develop the kinds of personal connections with both content and audience that are essential for effective writing.

Writing is a complex task that benefits from the active application of all elements of the self-development model. Elements of that model will be used to organize the remainder of the chapter.

Self-Awareness of Academic Writing

Self-awareness with respect to writing consists of being aware of both the demands of academic tasks and your abilities as an academic writer. Knowing what is required in academic writing tasks includes understanding several critical differences between oral and written communication, between academic and informal writing, and between different kinds of academic writing tasks. Knowing your own abilities as an academic writer

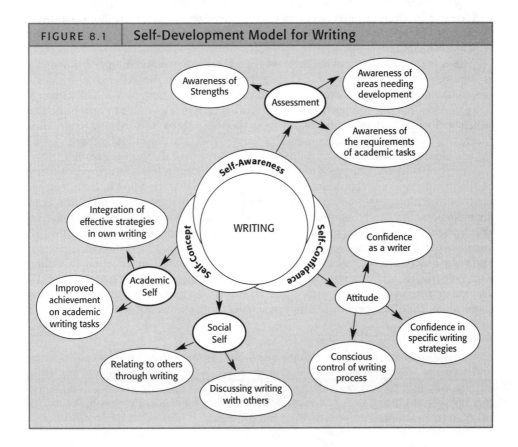

FIGURE 8.1 | Self-Development Model for Writing

includes an accurate assessment of how well you are equipped to participate in the academic writing process, and your personal goals for developing your academic writing. Both dimensions of self-awareness are essential to success in academic writing.

Understanding Academic Writing Tasks

Oral Versus Written Communication

Most students are adept at conversation and often assume that their oral communication skills will translate into effective academic writing. There are a number of reasons why this is not a valid assumption. First, the dynamics of conversation include verbal and non-verbal expressions that clarify what we wish to communicate. The use of tone, expression, and emphasis help to insure that our communication is received as intended (Green & Morgan, 1981). For instance, depending on where the emphasis is placed, think of the meanings this simple phase can have.

"Are *you* really going to do that?"

"Are you *really* going to do that?"

"Are you really going to do *that*?"

If you were to add a non-verbal gesture such as a raised eyebrow to any one of these communications, your doubts about the person, the likelihood, or the action would be even clearer. In addition, oral communication is often face-to-face, providing opportunities to judge the reactions of the listener or even to interact with the listener to check his or her understanding (Green & Morgan, 1981).

Many of the advantages of the dynamics of oral communication disappear when you are limited to expressing yourself in writing. The challenge for the writer is "to compensate for the reader's disadvantage of not being able to interact with him or her" (Green & Morgan, 1981, p. 177). You need to think of writing as a very one-sided conversation in which you must anticipate the reader's possible responses and misunderstandings (Reynolds, 1982–83). In written communication, the demands for carefully chosen wording and clear explanation at every point far exceed those in oral communication.

A second difference between oral and written communication is structural. In many conversations, you often approach a topic in a gradual way by building to your point. In contrast, the most common communication pattern in written communication is to state the point first, and then provide the details (Green & Morgan, 1981). It is also true that written communication needs to be more structured, generally. To be most effective you need to have a clear audience and purpose in mind (Click, 1996), and then help that audience understand your message by giving an overview in the introduction, by stating each point clearly, and by reviewing your main points at the end (Green & Morgan, 1981). The importance of connecting with your audience is vital in both oral and written communication. The differences lie in how you achieve those connections.

Academic and Informal Writing

A second distinction that is sometimes overlooked is the difference between informal and academic writing. Just as oral communication does not translate well into academic writing, you need to be aware that more familiar forms of **informal writing**, such as letters and journal entries, usually do not meet the criteria for **academic writing**. A number of criteria characterize academic writing and distinguish it from other kinds of writing.

Perhaps the primary characteristic of academic writing is that it builds on the work of others (Misser, *www.wlu.ca/writing/handouts/whatisit.pdf*; Slattery, 1994). As a result, almost every academic writing task will require research to find information that you will use in your work (Simon, 1991). Each of your points should be supported by credible sources of evidence and these sources should be accurately represented in your work (Kennedy & Smith, 1994). If there are competing points of view, you should acknowledge them and demonstrate why you have taken the position you have (Elder & Paul, *www.criticalthinking.org/university/unistan.html*; Simon, 1991). In contrast to information presented on television, in newspapers and magazines, academic writing not only uses previous work in an area, but also identifies for readers each piece of information from another source that was used to support a position or explain an issue (Kennedy & Smith, 1994). Although this practice is intended to acknowledge the contributions of others, it also strengthens the work of the writer by providing credible support for points made and assists the reader by providing direction on how to locate more information on the topic (Harris, 2001).

A second characteristic is that academic writing frequently demands that you integrate your own thinking with the work of others (Kennedy & Smith, 1994). This requirement raises a number of questions. What if your own thinking is similar to the work of others? (Even if you independently came to the same conclusion, you must acknowledge the earlier work.) How do you clearly delineate your own interpretations and ideas from the work of others? (Clearly identify all facts and ideas from other sources by using quotation marks for direct quotes or by indicating the source of paraphrased/summarized material. The remainder will be taken to be your own work.) How do you indicate the sources you use to develop your work? (Different disciplines use different systems, but there is a standard system of notation that must be learned for each group of disciplines.) By clearly indicating the work of others and your own insights, you demonstrate the quality of your research and your own thinking.

A third characteristic of academic writing is that your work should represent a well-evidenced personal position as opposed to a personal opinion. One of the common ways academic writers communicate this difference is by not using the first person (I, we, us), in presenting their work (Buckley, 1995). Instead, a more formal tone focusing attention on the research that supports the work is achieved by using author's names, directly (e.g., "Taylor (2002) contends that..."), or pronouns such as "one," or "they." Phrases that communicate a systematic analysis such as "It can be argued that" often replace "I think." All of these writing conventions are intended to communicate that your work is based on strong evidence, and not on personal opinion alone. However, like many things in academic communities, these conventions vary across the disciplines (and sometimes within a discipline!), so check with your professors about the ones you should use in individual courses.

A fourth characteristic is that academic writing should demonstrate logical reasoning. Your points should follow each other in a progression that makes sense to the reader and supports your argument (Elder & Paul, *www.criticalthinking.org/university/unistan.html*; Simon, 1991). Within your argument, you should present your evidence in ways that build your arguments, and explain any evidence that may seem contradictory (Elder & Paul, *www.criticalthinking.org/university/unistan.html*; Misser, *www.wlu.ca/writing/handouts/whatisit.pdf*). In presenting your arguments, you should know that even though one alternative is to build your evidence and then state your conclusion, the preferred form of academic argumentation follows a pattern of making your point and then presenting the evidence (Duffin, 1998). This contrast in style is raised as an interesting gender issue by Topping (1995), who observed that males tend to intuitively use the preferred format for academic writing (and receive disproportionately higher grades), whereas women tend to build to their points gradually (and receive disproportionately lower grades). If you are going to use a different pattern of argumentation than the preferred format, you need to be clear about your approach. Test your understanding of this by completing the following exercise.

Exercise 8.1 INFORMAL WRITING VERSUS FORMAL WRITING

Bring to class two examples of your writing. One piece should be an example of formal writing, such as an exam, an essay, a research paper, or a book review. The other should be an example of informal writing such as journal assignments, poetry, or a personal opinion piece. Working in small groups, review the similarities and differences between these two forms of writing.

Kinds of Academic Writing Tasks

Even within academic writing, there are different forms of writing tasks (Simon, 1991). One of the most common forms of academic writing is the essay. In an essay, you step into the role of an expert to communicate information or a point of view to a particular audience (Buckley, 1995). The purpose of your essay may range from describing and explaining, to interpreting, to comparing and contrasting, to arguing, to evaluating (Gardner, Jewler, & Robb, 1995). Especially in exam situations where time is constrained, it is important to quickly recognize the purpose of your writing task. For instance, describing involves presenting information at face value, while interpreting implies explaining the meaning of something beyond a simple description, to insure that even a non-expert reader understands it. Analysis implies going beyond the information presented by breaking it down into its component parts to explain why something might be so, whereas evaluation involves developing an opinion based on specific criteria and the evidence available. Arguing is characterized by taking a particular position on an issue and supporting it with the evidence you have accumulated in your research (Gardner, Jewler, & Robb, 1995; Kennedy & Smith, 1994). Clearly understanding your purpose is essential to success in essay writing (Click, 1996).

Two specific variations on the essay are the book review and the research paper. In a book review, you are frequently asked to describe and evaluate a book for an audience you assume has not read the book. A book review usually entails a brief summary of the main points or events in the book, and your assessment of the book's strengths and weaknesses, illustrated with examples (Buckley, 1995). In contrast to the book review, which involves a deep analysis of a single source, a research paper usually involves gathering information from a variety of sources and points of view, and synthesizing the information to provide a comprehensive view of a particular topic. The task of documenting where you obtain information is especially challenging in a research essay, because there will be many different pieces of information to organize. To differing degrees, academic writing requires not only effective communication through writing, but also efficient management of a complex planning and organizational process. Please complete the following exercise.

Exercise 8.2 ESSAY QUESTIONS

Select a topic from one of your courses. Develop three different types of essay questions that could be asked about that topic. In what ways would the requirements for each question be similar, based on general requirements for academic writing? In what ways would the requirements for each task be different, based on the particular demands of the task?

Question	Task Requirements in Common with Other Questions	Task-Specific Requirements
1.		
2.		
3.		

Self-awareness of your own abilities

In addition to an awareness of the requirements of the academic writing task, it is also important to be aware of your own abilities and developmental needs as an academic writer. Building on the items explored in Chapter 2, how would you assess your own capabilities in the areas identified in the table on page 182 on a scale of 1 (not at all descriptive of you) to 5 (very descriptive of you)? Would you add any categories to this table? As you continue reading, look for strategies that could help you develop in some of these areas of your academic writing.

Figure 8.2   Self-Assessment of Writing Abilities

Self-Assessment Item	Not At All Descriptive		Somewhat Descriptive		Very Descriptive
	1	2	3	4	5
I consider myself to be an effective writer.	1	2	3	4	5
I know how to find the kinds of information needed to complete academic writing tasks.	1	2	3	4	5
I know how to evaluate the kinds of information I find for its credibility and relevance.	1	2	3	4	5
Once I have completed the preliminary research for a task, I know how to organize that information into an outline for the writing task.	1	2	3	4	5
I usually spend enough time planning a writing assignment to ensure that I have a clear focus when I begin writing.	1	2	3	4	5
I have a clear picture of who the audience for my paper is before I begin.	1	2	3	4	5
I have a clear picture of the position I wish to take before I begin writing.	1	2	3	4	5
I make a timeline for completing the writing assignment before I begin.	1	2	3	4	5
I formulate a clear thesis statement (one or two sentences summarizing the purpose of my assignment) before I begin.	1	2	3	4	5
When I am writing, I know how to use quotes directly from my sources.	1	2	3	4	5
When I am writing, I know how to correctly paraphrase information from sources.	1	2	3	4	5
I know how to avoid plagiarism.	1	2	3	4	5
When I am writing, I am aware of when I need to revise my writing or find additional information.	1	2	3	4	5
When I stall in my writing process, I motivate myself to find a way to solve the problem and not to give up.	1	2	3	4	5
When I finish the first draft, I spend time revising the structure and content of my assignment.	1	2	3	4	5
I know how to organize my thoughts efficiently to answer essay questions on exams.	1	2	3	4	5

Self-Confidence in Academic Writing

To develop your self-confidence as an academic writer, you need to acquire effective strategies for conducting research, producing writing, and motivating yourself when writing becomes difficult. Of equal importance is the development of your ability to consciously use these strategies to manage your writing process (Zimmerman & Bandura, 1994). This section of the chapter outlines some of the strategies used by successful academic writers. If what you are doing now is not helping you to reach your academic goals, experimenting with some of these practices in your own writing is definitely worth a try.

Planning Ahead

The academic writing process begins well before the first word is written. The research on student writing demonstrates that one of the biggest differences between effective and ineffective academic writers is the time they spend planning (Torrance et al., 1994). Failure to invest enough effort in planning is a common source of problems (Hunter-Carsch, 1990). One kind of planning that helps inexperienced academic writers, in particular, is to construct a timeline for major assignments such as research papers (Kennedy & Smith, 1994).

Kennedy and Smith (1994) recommend that you begin with the due date for the assignment and work backwards, being careful not to underestimate the time you need for research. For a ten-page research paper that requires a minimum of ten book, journal, and Internet resources, with no more than four sources in each category, the timeline outlined on page 184, would help you schedule your work in a realistic way. This is a good situation in which to apply the STAR model of goal-setting from Chapter 5. For each major stage in the writing process, you can make your own **S**pecific, **T**estable, **A**ttainable, and **R**elevant "to do" list to guide and motivate your work. Examples of these more specific tasks are provided under the "complete first draft" phase in the sample timeline.

Finding Information Sources

Once you have a realistic timeline in place, you are ready to begin the research that characterizes academic writing. In some respects, finding information has never been easier. Information technology provides the tools to readily search for information on almost any topic. However, technology also makes the information selection task more challenging. It is quite possible that you will locate more information than you can possibly use. As a result, you will have to select the best information sources by evaluating the quality of many different kinds of information (Ward, 2001). Effective academic writing requires a high degree of information literacy. Information literacy is "the ability to define a problem, find information to solve the problem, evaluate the information, and use it effectively" (Ward, 2001, p. 922). Some of the skills you will need to find, evaluate, and use information effectively include:

- defining what specific information you need;

- knowing where to look for that information;

- knowing how to search for information;

- assessing the quality and relevance of the information you find (based on factors such as author, source, date, evidence, etc.);

- organizing the information you find; and

- acknowledging where you obtained your information (Association of College and Research Libraries, 2001).

The reference librarians in your university library are the experts in information literacy, and if you ask for their assistance, you will learn a lot about finding and using information effectively.

TABLE 8.1	Sample Timeline for a Research Paper	
Target Date	**Task and "To Do" List**	**Date Completed**
Due date	Submit paper	
Two days before due date	Complete editing *To Do List:*	
Four days before due date	Complete revisions *To Do List:*	
One week before due date	Complete first draft *To Do List:* 1. Note any gaps in information 2. Note any missing reference information 3. Complete needed research tasks	
Two to three weeks before due date	Begin drafting the paper *To Do List:*	
Three weeks before the due date	Outline the paper and a preliminary thesis statement *To Do List:*	
Three to four weeks before the due date	Locate research materials, make and organize notes, and determine if your information is sufficient to complete the task *To Do List:*	
Four weeks before the due date	Decide on a topic for your paper *To Do List:*	

Adapted from Kennedy, M.L., & Smith, H.M. (1994). *Reading and writing in the academic community.* Englewood Cliffs, NJ: Prentice-Hall.

Avoiding Plagiarism

When you use the work of other people to support your own academic writing, it is critical that you know how to acknowledge that work, using accepted conventions. Otherwise you could be accused of plagiarism. **Plagiarism** is "the unacknowledged use of another person's work, in the form of original ideas, strategies, and research, as well as another person's writing, in the form of sentences, phrases, and innovative terminology" (Spatt, 1983, p. 438). Plagiarism is a serious offence in academic communities. Students found to have committed plagiarism can suffer consequences that include a zero on the assignment, failing the course, suspension from a program, or in serious cases, expulsion from the institution. It goes without saying that blatant plagiarism such as downloading a paper from the Internet is cheating (and students should be aware the chances of being caught are high, since professors can easily search the Internet to find where you obtained the paper, or even sections of a paper). However, plagiarism often occurs because students do not understand how to correctly report and acknowledge the work of others in their academic work.

Kennedy and Smith (1994) identify three ways in which the work of others is commonly used in academic writing: quoting, paraphrasing, and summarizing. Direct quotations should always appear in quotation marks or in the case of longer quotations, as blocks of text that are clearly indicated as quotations from another source. Each quotation should be identified by its source, including the specific page on which the quotation occurs. You should never take a quotation out of context or alter it to change its intended meaning simply to support your argument. Such behaviours betray the work of the authors and, as such, are considered to be dishonest (Kennedy & Smith, 1994).

Because academic work requires interpreting and integrating the work of others rather than simply reporting it, it is more likely that you will either **summarize** or **paraphrase** that work rather than quote it directly. A summary is a concise statement of the main idea expressed in a section of text, described in your own words and including a citation. In contrast, paraphrasing is when you interpret, in detail, a specific section of the work of another person in your own words, to better explain it to a particular audience. Although it is used extensively in academic work, paraphrasing is often misunderstood. To avoid plagiarism, Kennedy and Smith (1994) suggest that you meet several criteria when you paraphrase:

> Change the vocabulary, sentence structure, and order of the ideas.
>
> As a guideline, the differences between the original and paraphrased texts should be extensive enough that they do not have three consecutive words in common.
>
> Always cite the original source.

To illustrate the differences, consider the following quotation, summary, and paraphrase based on the preceding paragraph.

> **Quote**   *Because academic work requires interpreting and integrating the work of others rather than simply reporting it, it is more likely that you will either **summarize** or **paraphrase** that work rather than quote it directly. A summary is a concise statement of the main idea expressed in a section of text, described in your own words and including a citation. In contrast, paraphrasing is when you interpret, in detail, a specific section of the work of another person in your own words, to better explain it to a particular audience (Taylor, 2002, p. 185).*

Summary   *While paraphrasing describes, in detail, the content of someone else's work in your own words, a summary simply states the main point of that content (Taylor, 2002).*

Paraphrasing   *Two common ways to use the work of others in academic writing are paraphrasing and summarizing. Paraphrasing involves a detailed description of information from another source, whereas summarizing communicates only the main idea. In both cases, you have the freedom to interpret information in a way that your audience will understand. Even though you are not quoting directly, you should always cite the source of your information (Taylor, 2002).*

If the paraphrase and the original texts are too similar, you have plagiarized because you have used the words of the original author as your own, rather than quoting them. If your paraphrase is distinct, but you do not cite the source, that is also plagiarism, because you have failed to acknowledge the ideas of the original author. If you are uncertain about how to avoid plagiarism, your reference librarian or your professors can help you. As can be seen in the table on page 187, there are also excellent Internet resources on this topic.

Standard Methods for Acknowledging the Work of Others

Because building on the work of others is one of the defining characteristics of academic writing, academic writers have developed standard systems that clearly identify where specific ideas came from, and that direct other interested persons to these same sources. Unfortunately for people who are learning the craft of academic writing, there is no single system for citing the work of others; each group of disciplines has its own preferred "style." Even within a discipline, different professors sometimes use different styles, so be sure to ask each of your professors what style you should be using.

The humanities (areas including English literature, history, and philosophy), tend to use the Modern Language Association (MLA) style. MLA style signals the source of an idea by clearly naming the author(s) in the text, either as an integral part of a sentence ("Taylor argues that…") or in parentheses ("The fact that students do not know how to correctly acknowledge the work of others in their academic work is one cause of plagiarism (Taylor)."). These references in the text direct readers to look in the "Works Cited" list at the end of the paper to find complete information on each source used.

In the social sciences (areas including sociology and psychology), the preferred system tends to be the American Psychological Association (APA) style, which includes both the author's name and the date of publication or a Web site address for each reference in the text. In APA style, authors can still be acknowledged as an integral part of a sentence ("Taylor (2002) argues that…") or in parentheses ("The fact that students do not know how to correctly acknowledge the work of others in their academic work is one cause of plagiarism (Taylor, 2002)."). A reader can then use the name(s) and dates in the text to find a particular source on the list of references at the end of the document.

A third major kind of referencing system is used in scientific fields where references are signaled by a bracketed or superscript number in the text, as in the Council of Biology Editors (CBE) system. For instance, in this numbered system, authors can be acknowledged as an integral part of a sentence ("Taylor[1] argues that…") or by a superscript ("The fact that students do not know how to correctly acknowledge the work of others in their academic work is one cause of plagiarism[1]"). The particular reference can be found by consulting the numbered list of references at the end of the document.

TABLE 8.2	Online Writing Resources
Location and URL	**Highlights**
The University of Victoria *web.uvic.ca/wguide/*	This site has a huge selection of excellent handouts on a broad range of academic writing topics. The site is easy to search and many documents have internal links, making it easy to find the information you need.
The University of Toronto *www.utoronto.ca/writing/*	The Writing Support Centre provides excellent advice on many aspects of academic writing in concise and specific handouts on individual topics. Internal links between topics make it easy to move from one resource to another.
Wilfrid Laurier University *www.wlu.ca/writing/*	This site provides a mix of original resources on different writing topics and links to other useful sites. Resources include advice on specific types of assignments (e.g., book reviews and lab reports).
St. Cloud State (The Write Place) *leo.stcloudstate.edu/#online*	This site features excellent resources on the use of grammar. It also allows you to search from a long list of phrases describing everyday writing challenges, making it user-friendly.
Purdue University *owl.english.purdue.edu/* *handouts/index2.html*	This site provides a comprehensive set of academic writing resources, including resources for ESL learners and exercises on grammar, punctuation, and paraphrasing. There are also links describing how to avoid plagiarism, complete with clear examples. A notable feature of this site is an extensive set of resources on résumé writing, and writing required in job searches.
Indiana University *education.indiana.edu/~frick/* *plagiarism/*	This site features a plagiarism quiz that helps you learn how to quote, summarize, and paraphrase the work of others.

In addition to acknowledging the work of others in the text of your academic writing, you also are required to tell the reader where the information you used can be found. Different referencing styles require that you format your reference list following specific guidelines. These guidelines ensure that the information for each reference is complete, and that the information is presented in a consistent way. "Understanding Reference Styles," on this page illustrates some of the differences between the different styles.

Exercise 8.3 UNDERSTANDING REFERENCE STYLES

Working in small groups, carefully examine these three references for a hypothetical book. What information is included in each reference? In what ways do the MLA format and the CBE format differ from the APA format?

APA

Adams, J. L., & Brooks, K. M. (2000). *Helping students develop as writers: Strategies and resources.* Halifax, NS: Learning Resources Press.

MLA

Adams, Jane, and Ken Brooks. *Helping students develop as writers: Strategies and resources.* Halifax, NS: Learning Resources, 2000.

CBE

1. Adams J L, Brooks K M. *Helping students develop as writers: Strategies and resources.* Halifax NS: Learning Resources Press, 2000. 364 p.

Based on this brief introduction, you can see that each style is unique. You will need to consult a current edition of the style manual recommended by the professor in your course, or visit one of many useful Web sites, to obtain more specific information on using different styles to format your academic writing.

Style Manuals

American Psychological Association. (2001). *Publication Manual of the American Psychological Association* (5th ed.). Washington, DC: American Psychological Association.

Council of Biology Editors. (1994). *Scientific Style and Format: The CBE Manual for Authors, Editors and Publishers* (6th ed.) New York: Cambridge University Press.

Gibaldi, J. (1999). *MLA Handbook for Writers of Research Papers* (5th ed.). New York: Modern Language Association of America.

Examples of Web Resources on Academic Writing Styles

MLA

www.english.uiuc.edu/cws/wworkshop/bibliography/mla/mlamenu.htm

APA

www.english.uiuc.edu/cws/wworkshop/bibliography/apa/apamenu.htm

Numbered references
wisc.edu/writetest/Handbook/DocNumCitations.html

The Writing Process

Although there is no exact recipe for producing quality academic writing, we do know a lot about the strategies used by successful academic writers. These strategies can be organized into four major stages that characterize the writing process in most academic writing tasks: pre-writing, drafting, revising, and editing (Emig, 1981; Flower & Hayes, 1981; Kennedy, Kennedy & Smith, 2000). **Pre-writing** includes developing a clear understanding of the task, gathering information, reading and taking notes, organizing and making connections between different pieces of information, summarizing the main point of your paper in one or two sentences, and outlining a plan for the task. **Drafting** involves implementing your plan to create a written document. During the drafting phase, you may return to the pre-writing stages as you discover gaps in information or realize a need to refine your plan. **Revising** entails a critical analysis of your draft: its content, organization, and evidence. A important question to ask at this stage is to what degree you have achieved the goals of your writing task. **Editing** involves a careful assessment of the technical aspects of writing such as punctuation, grammar, and spelling (Flower & Hayes, 1981; Kennedy, Kennedy & Smith, 2000; Nold, 1981). While most people think of the drafting phase as "writing," research demonstrates that it is attention paid to pre-writing and revising strategies that can provide the most leverage on improving your writing. Because of their potential to improve your academic writing, pre-writing, revising, and editing will be explored in more detail.

Pre-Writing

Pre-writing is essentially a planning stage. Research shows that on the whole, you save time and find writing less difficult when you invest time in planning (Torrance et al., 1994; Risemberg, 1996). Conversely, a common source of writing problems is a failure to spend enough time planning (Hunter-Carsch, 1990). The first step in pre-writing is to establish a focus by selecting a topic, a purpose for writing about that topic, and a particular audience for whom you are writing (Hilgers et al., 1999; Kennedy & Smith, 1994). Establishing your focus bridges the gap between your general ideas and research, and communicating those ideas clearly in academic writing (Flower & Hayes, 1981). In the pre-writing phase, a clear focus narrows your topic to make it manageable and helps you select and use information efficiently.

Gibson and Killingsworth (1991) recommend that you choose a topic that is interesting and for which you can find research sources. The next step is to identify the scope and main points of the topic, and to explore its possible interest to a particular audience. These decisions help you to establish your writing "voice" for the assignment—i.e., how you want to be seen by your audience (Lloyd-Jones, 1981).

Once you have a focus, you are ready to begin gathering information. The ability to find and organize quality information that is relevant to your writing task is the strongest predictor of the quality of your writing (Risemberg, 1996). Your note-making strategies are critical at this stage. When gathering information, Procter (2001) suggests that you should clearly indicate your sources, noting all of the information you need to provide a reference. When you make notes, you should clearly indicate if the information you record is a direct quotation (note the page number), a summary, or a paraphrase, and leave space for your own thoughts as you compile your notes. If you record your notes on separate sheets, individual pieces of information can be more readily grouped and organized to create an outline to guide your writing.

At this point you should be able to further refine your focus by writing a tentative thesis statement: one or two sentences that sum up the main point of your paper (Buckley, 1995). This statement should become the focus of your drafting process.

Revising

One of the major differences between skilled and unskilled writers is the amount of time devoted to revising (Kennedy & Smith, 1994; Nold, 1981). Revising involves more than minor editing and can include changes in the organization of your writing; shortening or elaborating sections of text; clarifying which ideas came from your research and which are your own; sharpening your focus; and improving the cohesion and flow of your writing (Kennedy & Smith, 1994; Nold, 1981). Revision takes place constantly as you plan and draft a writing assignment, but it is particularly important that you also set aside time for revision when the first draft is complete. However, sometimes it is hard to examine your own writing critically for how it can be clarified and strengthened. Exchanging papers with someone in your class or having someone else give you feedback on the completed draft of your paper is one way to gain a fresh perspective on the quality of your work.

Editing

Editing may be the simplest part of the writing process, but it is often overlooked by students. The editing stage focuses on the small details of writing: spelling, punctuation, sentence structure, grammar, and proper use of a particular presentation style such as MLA or APA. At this point, it is helpful to read your paper aloud in order to "hear" your writing as your readers will (Kennedy, Kennedy & Smith, 2000). The time you spend on editing is worth the effort. You have probably noticed that teachers are very efficient editors, and a good editing job on your part will be appreciated and rewarded with higher grades on your assignments.

Self-Concept about Writing

Your self-concept as a writer will grow and change throughout your career. With a little effort, you can greatly increase the development of your writing self-concept with each academic writing experience. Developing your writing self-concept requires being more self-aware of your writing processes and of the demands of the task at hand. It also requires that you have confidence in your writing strategies and in your ability to use those strategies consciously. There are two ways in which you can use increased self-awareness and self-confidence to optimize the development of your self-concept as a writer. First, each time you consciously integrate writing strategies in your own writing or feel the satisfaction of improved achievement on academic writing tasks, you create a learning opportunity for yourself. Second, when you communicate with other people through your writing, and when you revise your work or discuss revisions with another person, you are actively developing your writing self-concept. As you reflect on your own work or discuss writing with others, remember that writing development is optimized if you use the strategies discussed in this chapter to assess how they are helping you first, to achieve success on the task, and second, to develop as a writer (Perkins & Salomon, 1989; Petraglia, 1995).

Bringing It All Together

One way to increase your self-awareness and self-confidence with respect to writing is to use an assessment framework to evaluate and revise your own writing. Frameworks such as the one shown on pages 191–3 also can be used for peer assessment, when you request feedback from or give feedback to another writer. This particular framework was generated by a large group of professors from different disciplines, and contains advice that is relevant in many different discipline areas. If you use it systematically, it will help you become more critically aware of the writing process and how you are developing as a writer. Engage in the exercise on page 194 and take advantage of the peer review process.

FIGURE 8.3 A Framework for Self/Peer Assessment

Letter Grade	Research	Logic/Organization	Analysis/Integration
A	• used a variety of information sources • most sources were relevant, authoritative sources • sources reflected most contrasting viewpoints • discussion of viewpoints was supported well	• clear thesis statement • logical flow • clear progression of ideas building on a central theme • clear transitions between paragraphs and ideas • effective use of transition statements and linking statements	• original interpretation or application of information (A+) • critically analyzed information • integrated information by applying information/discussing implications
B	• used a variety of information sources • at least 2/3 of the sources were relevant, authoritative sources • sources reflected a number of contrasting viewpoints • most viewpoints were supported well	• thesis statement is present, but not specific • logical flow • general progression that builds on a central theme • some transitions between paragraphs and ideas • under-use of transition statements and linking sentences	• some analysis of information • presented analysis, but did not integrate it fully into argument • thesis is not entirely clear, but argument can be followed • opened the door, but failed to drive the point home
C	• limited variety of information sources • about 1/2 of the sources were relevant, authoritative sources • not all major contrasting viewpoints were considered • viewpoints were stated with minimal or inconsistent levels of support	• thesis statement unclear/hard to find • logical flow is not always evident • lacks progression but expresses ideas that support an argument • 1 or 2 tangents that distract from main ideas • under-use of transition statements and linking sentences	• analysis lacking or off track • overlooked critical information in analysis • have to work to follow argument • generally lacked integration/original thinking
D	• few relevant information sources • minimal variety of information sources • little contrast in viewpoints • viewpoints generally lacked solid support	• no clear thesis statement • lacks logical flow • lacks a progression of ideas • frequent tangents that distract from main ideas • generally lacks transition statements and linking sentences	• overlooked critical information • faulty analysis • can't follow argument • no original use of information

FIGURE 8.3 Continued

Letter Grade	Research	Logic/Organization	Analysis/Integration
F	• little evidence of research/references used • presented a very narrow view • viewpoints lack solid support	• lacks thesis statement • ideas are scattered, disjointed • lacks logical flow • no obvious progression of ideas • lacks clear transitions	• weak research • no critical analysis • no apparent line of argument

Letter Grade	Answers Question/Makes Argument	Writing Style	Structure
A	• clear definition of audience • makes the point • relevant to stated purpose • follows through on thesis statement • backs up with powerful evidence	• few spelling/grammar mistakes • consistent use of tense and person • use of creative expression • typed, professional appearance • accurate use of style manual • acknowledges all sources, contributors	• intro states purpose, is explicit and grabs attention • intro clearly states the thesis statement • body reflects intro, shows logical progression • body contains research evidence • body contains the major expected elements • body paragraphs are well-integrated, connected • conclusion summarizes, integrates, and discusses implications
B	• audience identified, but not a clear focus • good evidence • evidence relevant to purpose • shows thought and analysis, but lacks clear focus or follow-up on thesis statement	• spelling/grammar mistakes begin to interfere with reading flow • minor changes in tense/person • generally good use of style manual— some inconsistencies • some inconsistency in the typed format • incomplete acknowledgments	• intro states purpose and grabs attention (2/3 of A) • intro states the thesis statement • body reflects intro, shows logical progression • body contains research evidence • body contains the major expected elements • integration of ideas is less obvious, not as well connected • conclusion summarizes, integrates, and discusses implications, but less clearly than A (2/3 of A)

FIGURE 8.3 | Continued

Letter Grade	Answers Question/ Makes Argument	Writing Style	Structure
C	• audience unclear • purpose generally addressed, but with weak evidence and argumentation • weak evidence of thorough analysis and thought	• frequent spelling/grammar mistakes • inconsistent in tense and person • typed, but not professional in appearance • inaccurate use of style manual • acknowledges direct quotes, but not all sources, contributors	• intro states a purpose, but lacks a clear thesis statement • body generally connected to intro • body contains research evidence, but progression is not always logical • body lacks some of the major expected elements • integration of ideas is less obvious, not as well connected • conclusion summarizes or repeats intro, but fails to integrate/discuss implications
D	• no sense of audience • point not explicitly made, have to work to see it • noticeable lack of evidence • unconvincing argument	• frequent spelling/grammar mistakes • inconsistent in tense and person • handwritten, with explanation • misuse of style manual • failed to acknowledge a number of major sources, contributors	• intro does not indicate purpose or thesis statement • body contains unconnected ideas • body reads like a series of short-answer questions • sentences and paragraphs are not well integrated or connected • conclusion does not reflect the paper, and/or is too brief
F	• no sense of audience • point not made, or irrelevant to purpose • little evidence for argument • failure to make argument	• frequent spelling/grammar mistakes • inconsistent in tense and person • handwritten, no explanation • ignored style manual • fails to acknowledge many or all sources, contributors	• lacks a clear introduction or thesis statement • rambles without obvious structure • contains information, but it is not organized to form a clear position or argument • sentences and paragraphs are not integrated or connected • conclusion is very brief or missing

Figure 8.3 is based on a framework generated by faculty members who participated in a workshop on "Grading Students' Writing: Achieving Consistency, Perceptions of Fairness, and Learning," University of Manitoba, Winnipeg, MB, November 30, 1995.

Exercise 8.4 PEER REVIEW

Form a "writing consultation" group with two or three other students. Each member should bring to the group the first draft of an assignment he/she is working on, together with a self-assessment based on the chart on pages 191–3.

Group members can review the assignments of others, using the same chart to give feedback on how the assignment might be revised to improve its focus, organization, or writing style.

When Writing Does Not Come Easily

If you make your plan and do your research, but just cannot put your ideas on paper, you are not alone. Even experienced writers such as professors and novelists go through periods when the writing does not come easily. Writers often experience difficulty in getting started on a writing task, but "writer's block" can happen at any point in the process (Reynolds, 1982–83). Successful writers learn how to use self-talk, goal-setting, and writing development resources to sustain progress on their writing (Risemberg, 1996).

Perhaps the most powerful tool you have available to "unblock" your writing is how you respond when you get stuck on a writing task. In his research on professors' writing, Boice (1990) found that most people, including successful writers, first respond by thinking negative thoughts about the task or about their abilities as writers. However, productive writers notice what they are doing and change their self-talk to thoughts such as "I can get unstuck—I have done it before," "What is the problem here?" or "I will work on another part and come back to this later." Successful writers use positive self-talk to keep themselves motivated and to strategize about how they can change what they are doing to be more successful (Boice, 1990). Sometimes simply clearing your mind so you can focus on the task enables you to resume your writing (Hunter-Carsch, 1990).

If your writing difficulties lie more in the mechanics of writing, there are many resources available to you. Your campus will almost certainly have a Learning Resources Centre or a Writing Centre where students can receive help in developing their writing. Many writing centres provide on line resources and make them widely available through their Web pages. The table on page 187 highlights only a few of the excellent online writing resources available. In addition, your university libraries and campus bookstores will have a number of useful books on academic writing.

Academic writing is a complex task. Your writing process will involve interactions among what you know about a topic; new information gained from research; your ability to analyze, organize, and apply information; your personal interest in the topic and the task; and your ability to communicate through writing (Frederiksen & Dominic, 1981; Kennedy & Smith, 1994). This chapter has challenged you to explore the nature of this task and how you can develop your own academic writing skills by increasing your self-awareness about academic writing. It has also described some of the strategies used by successful academic writers that you may find helpful as you develop your own academic writing ability. However, your increased awareness and strategic knowledge will have an impact on your writing only if you consciously apply this knowledge when you write. Finally, you need to remember that becoming an effective academic writer takes practice and that every assignment is an opportunity to develop your skills further. As the Greek philosopher Epictetus (55–135 AD) advised, *"If you wish to be a writer, write."*

It's More Than Common Sense

Effectively Using Library Resources

Trina O'Brien Leggott, MLS
University of Manitoba

As a Reference Librarian, I am interested in meeting students early in the research process because I know the value of efficient, effective research skills. I know too, that with the balancing act many students have to perform between classes, work, family, and extracurricular activities, I often see them when they are rushed, stressed, and only interested in the end result.

The skills required for effective library research are often components of courses designed to enable students to integrate successfully into university life. Effective library research skills are critical for success in university. The elements of the Introduction to the University course reflect the steps taken as one researches a term paper or project. Increasingly, "librarians teach students how to identify, use, and critically evaluate the use of information" (Chiste, Glover, & Westwood, 2000, p. 6). While the research process will vary depending on the subject, there are certain steps necessary to all research projects. Now more than ever, however, it is the evaluation phase of the research that is significant as a student learns to become an effective researcher. Not only are the resources of the library available to the student, but doors to other libraries are open via the Internet, where a plethora of Web sites beckon the student with their promise of easy information through the magic of cut-and-paste wizardry.

According to Troutman (2000), "in most cases, the problem is not finding information—we are inundated with it, both in print and electronically—rather, it is teaching our users how to discover, evaluate, and use appropriate information." (p. 621). Many libraries offer step-by-step guides to the research process through their Web sites. Many faculty members have developed partnerships with librarians to introduce the students to the resources relevant to their discipline. Many librarians provide workshops on searching their catalogues or the databases to which they subscribe. These workshops are generally free and are offered numerous times, particularly at the beginning of term. Take them! If the material covered is not clear, go back for another session, or go and talk to a librarian.

Skills such as setting goals and objectives, time management, identifying and managing stress, learning styles, note-taking, studying, critical thinking, and concept mapping are integral components of a course designed to integrate students to university life. Coincidentally, they are skills that are germane to the research process as well. This is the same research process that is essential to a successful university career, and to producing an information-literate individual. The American Library Association (1989) describes an information-literate person as one who "must be able to recognize when information is needed and has the ability to locate, evaluate, and use effectively the needed information."

As a librarian I feel it is extremely important that these skills are part of an undergraduate's education. Many of my colleagues too, feel that "as the creation of, organization of, and access to information are becoming more complicated and convoluted—and the sheer amount of information available is increasing at an incredible rate" (Chiste et al., 2000, p. 6), these skills are essential. One of the best ways to polish a skill is to practise it. Each new paper presents an opportunity to be exposed to new ways of finding information. Successive papers build on and augment these skills as more detailed research is required.

The first step, once you have decided on a topic, is to do background research in order to become more familiar with the area. Good sources of information at this point include encyclopedias or subject dictionaries, thesauri, subject bibliographies, maps or atlases, or book reviewing sources. Once you have acquired some basic knowledge on your topic, it is time to proceed to subject indexes or databases to search for journal articles. In some cases your professor will ask that you must have a specific number of books and/or journal articles. As you proceed with your literature search it is important to remember that the first five articles you find may not be appropriate to your topic, so it is important to provide yourself with more than enough sources to choose from. Also, some of the articles that you find may be unavailable at your institution or simply be unavailable to you at the time you need them.

Once you have accumulated your research material it is important to read and to critically evaluate it. Does the article or book contribute to your knowledge of the topic? Does it support the argument you wish to advance? Are there areas of the article that you wish to quote in your paper? At this point, it is extremely important to maintain a complete record of the sources that you plan to use in your final draft. It is not a pleasant experience to come into the library the night before a paper is due to search for incomplete bibliographic information. Should you be using Internet sources, it is equally important to keep accurate records so you can find the site again. In addition, you will want to include the date you accessed at a site, since information may be added or removed from a Web site at any time.

The practice of evaluation is constant throughout the research process. It is important to remember that you need to evaluate the quality of a resource with regard to your own purpose and information requirements. Sometimes evaluation is unconscious, as you discard books or journal articles based on title alone. More often, as you peruse the table of contents, the abstract, or read through an article and decide it adds nothing to the information you wish to present, you make a conscious decision not to use it. Evaluating journal articles and scholarly texts may be a matter of determining their appropriateness for your paper as they have probably already passed the scrutiny of an editorial board.

Evaluating Internet resources can be a much trickier proposition, but fortunately there are guides to assist you. The Web site "Doing Research from a Distance" offers a section on evaluation, and Harris provides a very good article on evaluating scholarly resources on the Internet (*www.virtualsalt.com/ evalu8it.htm*). It is necessary to question constantly, to keep yourself informed, and to know when to ask for assistance.

Self-awareness

The most useful things I learned about my own writing in this chapter are …

Self-confidence

One strategy that I will definitely use to become more effective in my writing is …

Self-concept

The academic writing skills that I believe will help me succeed in university are…

Chapter Summary

Writing is the basis for good academic communication, but is often a source of great difficulty for university students. In order to become a strong academic writer, you must develop an awareness of both your own abilities and the processes and expectations of academic writing. This chapter provides information and exercises so that students add to their self-confidence in their writing abilities and develop the competencies that make them effective writers. The chapter outlines four stages involved in academic writing (pre-writing, drafting, revising, and editing), and assists students in using these processes to improve their academic writing by providing tools such as timelines, self-assessments, and on line resources.

Exercises

REFLECT–ACT

The following Reflect–Act exercises are designed to enhance your self-awareness and understanding of the academic writing process, and to help you identify specific actions you can take to develop as a writer. Like the academic writing process itself, these tasks will require you to integrate your own writing knowledge and experiences with some of the ideas presented in this chapter that might be new to you.

Reflect   Academic writing is a complex task, in which you need to coordinate the integration of existing knowledge with new information, the organization and use of that information for a particular purpose, the communication of your message through writing, and the management of your own motivation and progress on the task. Few people are born with this broad skill set.

Act   Based on your self-assessment of writing abilities (page 182), can you identify two areas in which you would like to improve your academic writing process? Using the STAR model for goal-setting from Chapter 5, create at least one personal goal in each of these areas. Place these goals in a location where you will be reminded of them whenever you are working on academic writing tasks.

Reflect   One of the most demanding and stressful kinds of academic writing takes place in an exam context. In these situations, you are challenged to make the most of what you know under tight timelines. One of the common mistakes people make is to skip the prewriting stage and launch right into the drafting process, thinking they do not have time to plan. Planning is critical to all academic writing tasks, but especially during an exam, where planning saves time by helping you organize both the information you have available and how you will present your ideas.

Act   Select a possible examination question. Demonstrate in your work the outline that would guide your answer, specify the information you would be using to answer the question, and present a concise thesis statement that would focus your writing. Attempt to answer this exam question within a timeframe.

Reflect   Think about some of the feedback you have received on your academic writing. If you have a recent essay available, examine the comments that are written on it. Are these comments related to any of the strategies discussed in this chapter?

Act   Make a list of strategies that would help you respond to at least three pieces of feedback you have received.

Reflect   Most writers have a specific area that is a writing "soft spot"—an aspect of writing that requires the most development. Can you identify a soft spot in your academic writing?

Act   Beginning with the Internet resources identified on page 182, find at least three writing resources that can help you reinforce your soft spot. How, specifically, will each source help you?

Reflect   Those little conversations we have in our own minds while we write can either hinder or help our writing process. Even effective writers go through stages where they are very self-critical about their writing, and these periods are often associated with low writing productivity. Writing is hard work, and sometimes you have to psyche yourself up to do it, or to get past a place where you just cannot seem to put words on paper. One of the characteristics of productive writers is that they engage in more positive self-talk when they get stuck in the writing process. They have the same negative response in the beginning, but they notice what they are saying to themselves and switch their self-talk strategies to thinking more positively about how to solve the problem.

Act   On your next few academic writing tasks, keep records of the kinds of things you say to yourself when you are writing. A simple count of negative, neutral, and positive statements is one way to do this. Identify the negative comments and change them so you are able to coach yourself through the rough spots in your writing process or to keep yourself motivated.

GROUP DISCUSSION

1. Based on the responses of different group members to the self-assessment of writing (page 182), describe the common areas of writing weaknesses students share. Then identify resources that students may use to eliminate these weaknesses.

2. One of the challenges of academic writing tasks is that they come in many different forms. To be successful, you first have to identify clearly what the task is. Sometimes you just have to demonstrate your knowledge by telling it. Other tasks require you to compare, argue, analyze, outline, evaluate, or explain. Select a topic such as student

success at university, academic honesty, or writing effectively. Provide examples of the information you would present if you were asked to compare, argue, analyze, outline, evaluate, or explain.

3. Plagiarism is one topic that receives a lot of attention in discussions of academic writing. Almost all academic writing tasks require you to use the work of others as evidence to support your own work and to acknowledge where, exactly, those ideas came from. Many students are unclear about how to properly use the work of others when they quote, paraphrase, or summarize from different sources. Develop a list of the questions your group has about how to properly cite the information you use.

4. There are many excellent resources available on the Internet to help you develop your writing. You can help each other benefit from these resources by choosing one that has been particularly helpful to you, and teaching other members of your group what you have learned from it.

APPLY TO LIFE

This chapter outlined a number of writing strategies used by successful academic writers. One of your challenges is to discover the ones that can make a positive difference in your own academic writing. Perhaps the following questions can help you focus on specific ideas you can use.

1. Based on the writing developmental needs you identified earlier in the writing self-assessment, can you identify a specific skill or strategy you will now use to address each of these needs?

2. What sections from the Self/Peer Assessment Framework will you consult most closely when revising you own work?

Talking with Others

chapter 9

> "It is the providence of knowledge to speak, and it is the privilege of wisdom to listen."
>
> Oliver Wendell Holmes, Sr.

Questions

What are my abilities as a communicator?

Are there strategies I can develop that can improve my ability to communicate effectively with others?

What are the successful strategies of presenting effectively?

How can presenting information formally in class be made easy?

Objectives

- Provide an overview of the fundamental elements of communication.
- Provide information on sending messages.
- Provide specific skills for effective listening.
- Highlight effective presentation tips.

Student Success Portrait

Communicating Effectively

Christine Adams Stubbs
The University of Manitoba

Strong communication skills are important in all facets of life—you use them every day. Effective communication skills have helped me in being a successful student, in my personal relationships, and in my work as a student advisor for University 1. Like any skill, communication skills need to be learned. I would like to share some of the knowledge I have gained, and I hope you can learn something from it. There are three key components of communication skills: spoken words, listening skills, and body language.

Spoken Words

When I started university, I rarely asked questions or challenged people for fear of not being liked. I was a poor communicator. I learned that to be successful I needed to get over this fear. I realized that I needed to ask questions if I didn't understand something, because if I didn't, I was the one who would suffer. It took awhile, but I realized that part of a professor's job is to help students outside of class. In a class that I was struggling in, I had a professor who spent many hours outside of class helping me. I did much better in the course than I would have done without his help. In this situation and many others, I have had to approach people who make me nervous, or speak in situations that make me uncomfortable. I have more confidence if I enter these situations prepared and know what I am going to say.

I have also learned that if I am angry or hurt by someone it is okay to share this with him or her. This is particularly effective when I address the true issue, and explain to them how it makes me feel. I do this by using "I" statements, for example, "I feel hurt when you are not honest with me." It is also okay to share my opinions. Everyone might not agree with me, but I have something to contribute, and people can learn from me, just as I can learn from them.

Finally, when speaking, I need to pay attention to the tone of my voice. Tone can contribute meaning to what is said by adding emotion. I have learned that when I explain something and it is not understood, I tend to get frustrated with the listener and myself. In these situations, I tend to speak louder, even though this does not help. The listener is not hard of hearing. Now that I know this about myself, when I find myself getting frustrated, I take a breath and start over again. I am conscious not to raise my voice in attempting to get my point across.

Listening Skills

In university, I learned the value of talking to people outside of my friendship group, the value of opposing opinions, and the value of listening skills. University provides an opportunity to interact with people of many different backgrounds, experiences, and viewpoints. When interacting, it is always important to listen with an open mind. Even if the opinion presented is different from your own and even if it does not change your opinion, it provides a great opportunity to learn and grow as a person.

For a successful interaction, it is important that the speaker know that I am listening and am interested. Thus, I need to listen attentively. I do this every day in my job as a student adviser, and in my personal relationships. I maintain eye contact with the speaker, nod my head, ask for clarification when I do not understand something, and to ensure that I have understood, I repeat what I think they have been saying.

Body Language

Successful communication requires more than paying attention to the words spoken. A key component is the body language of the person speaking and of the person listening. Body language can tell you a lot more about the interaction than the words do. I touched on this when I talked about listening skills, and how I maintain eye contact and nod my head when people are speaking with me. This lets the speaker know I am interested, and gives them encouragement to continue.

It is important when I am the speaker to think about how others perceive me. That includes how I am dressed, my facial expressions, how I hold my body, and if I appear nervous or confident. I need to maintain eye contact with the listener to keep them part of the interaction, and ensure that they are listening. If they are not listening, then I know I need to try and get them involved more. I have learned to read other people's body language. I see students on a daily basis and sometimes the words they speak contradict what their body language is telling me. This is my cue to question them, which results in a much more meaningful interaction.

As I said at the beginning, communication is a skill that takes practice. I am still learning, and still make mistakes. Effort, practice, and self-awareness have made me a better communicator. By learning about communication, and learning more about your strengths and weaknesses as a communicator, you can develop your communication skills—something that will help you in all facets of your life.

Communicating well connects you with others. In the past chapter you discovered critical information about communicating through writing. Some of this information will be useful in developing strategies for presenting information through oral presentations. Presenting information formally in the classroom, teaching others, or reporting findings at academic presentations at conferences is known as dissemination. The second type of oral communication is known as **interpersonal communication** and focuses on forming relationships with others. Before proceeding with this chapter, find out what your communication skills are like by reflecting on your scores on the Communication and Connection with Others subscales in Chapter 2.

Communication Defined

Effective communication is usually perceived as the exchange of thoughts or ideas. According to *Webster's Dictionary*, communication is "a process by which information is exchanged between individuals through a common system of symbols, signs, or behaviours." Communication is an active reciprocal process of sending and receiving messages. The symbols or signs include words and nonverbal cues such as gestures or facial expressions. These will be further explored as we look at models of effective communication, self-presentation, active listening, and public presentation skills.

Returning to our model, our relational identity is based on communicating effectively with others. As seen in self-development model on this page, self-awareness involves your ability to identify your strengths and your weaknesses as effective communicators. By increasing your awareness of the nature of the communication process and learning about the factors that influence both the sending and receiving of information, you become better equipped to communicate formally and informally. This includes effective listening and speaking skills. As you increase your communication skills, you increase your confidence in your ability to connect with others. Your self-confidence is based on your ability to relate to others, your comfort and ease in presenting information, and your competence as a presenter. By adding to your competencies to express yourself you are able to overcome hesitancy or fear that detract from your self-confidence. Your success in connecting with others reinforces your confidence in your own abilities as a communicator. Your relational identity is influenced by your social and academic selves. The social self is your ability to interact with others on a social, interpersonal, and intimate level whereas your academic self is your ability to communicate clearly to others in formal presentations. In designing formal presentations, the presenter considers both the purpose of the presentation and the characteristics of the audience. All these aspects are important in defining effective communication, which in turn, define our relational identities.

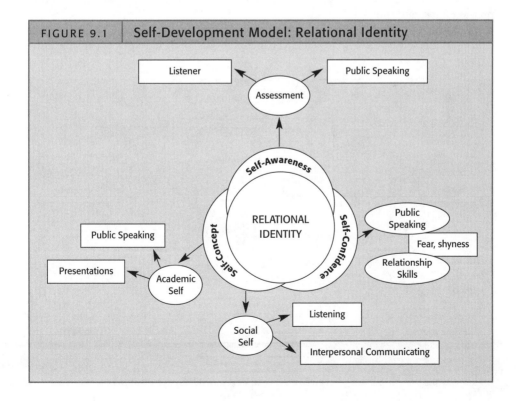

FIGURE 9.1 | Self-Development Model: Relational Identity

Model of Effective Communication

Of the various communication models identified in the research literature, the most frequently cited one belongs to Maletzke (1963). As seen in his model on this page, Maletzke has identified five important elements in effective communication: the speaker, the medium, the message, the listener, and feedback. The speaker presents his/her message through a medium, such as an oral presentation, hoping that the listener will hear the message as originally intended and convey what has been heard through some form of feedback. Each of these important components of effective communication is further defined below.

Self-image, personality, social support, and assumptions of the audience all influence speaking. The self-image is based on previous speaking experiences. Good experiences create a strong self-image, whereas poor experiences weaken it. A speaker's personality also influences speaking. For instance, extroverts, as compared to introverts, tend to enjoy public speaking. Social support provided by peers throughout the presentation includes encouragement during trial runs, subtle feedback during the presentation, and valuable advice for future considerations. Finally, the speaker's assumptions of the audience guide the choice of words and illustrations used to get the message across. Each of these factors, in turn, influences how speakers present themselves and their message.

The **message** is a set of key ideas that the speaker desires the audience to appreciate, understand, and apply. It can be informational—providing important novel facts, creative—inviting the audience to help develop new ideas, or motivational—challenging change. Regardless of the format, the speaker focuses on one relevant point. The **medium** is the channel through which the message is conveyed such as oration, interpretive dance, or drama.

A number of factors influence how a listener interprets the message. Those listeners with a positive self-image tend to listen with an open mind and are willing to consider con-

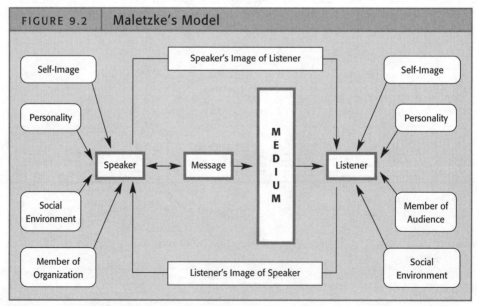

FIGURE 9.2   Maletzke's Model

Adapted from "Maletzke's Model," Maletzke, G. (1963). *Psychologie der Massenkommunikation.* Hamburg: Verlag Hans Bredow-Institut.

troversial topics and others' viewpoints and experiences. Listeners with a critical personality tend to be resistant to persuasion and skeptical of others' ideas. When the listener is part of a group, there is compelling pressure to support the opinions of the group, whereas when not part of a group, the listener has the freedom to accept or reject the information based on independent opinions. The expertise of an audience directs responses from inquisitiveness to criticism. The social environment also invites certain expectations: a nightclub invites entertainment, while an academic forum invites debate and evidence. Thus, a variety of factors influence how the presented material is understood.

Given that the "only meaning a sequence of language has in the real world is the meaning the listener understands it to have" (Elgin, 1996), a speaker needs to be aware of how his/her message is interpreted. Feedback provides valuable information. Immediate feedback during the presentation occurs through nonverbal and verbal responses. Eye contact often reveals the interest levels of listeners (Wolfgang, 1984). Scrunched furrows and tightened cheek muscles indicate confusion (Hoff, 1992). Crossed arms may imply offence. Verbal responses such as applause, laughter, sneers, comments, and questions all add to the immediate feedback (Hoff, 1992). Delayed feedback is given through presentation evaluations. A word of caution: nonverbal feedback is not generalizable across all cultures. In some cultures it is disrespectful to look into the eyes of another. Thus, one needs to be sensitive to these cultural differences. How one makes the most of these to enhance communication will be discussed later in the chapter.

Developing Skills as a Speaker: Self-Presentation

As you have discovered, the process of communicating effectively with others involves becoming aware of your own abilities as a sender and receiver of information. As a sender of information, your verbal and nonverbal messages add to or detract from your ability to communicate. The words and sentence structure employed, the tone of voice used, and the non-verbal gestures displayed are all part of the message that you send. Your effectiveness as a communicator is based on an understanding of how your own patterns of communication facilitate an effective transmission and the recognition of your own abilities and limitations.

One factor that affects communication skills is **sex-role socialization**. Men and women are known to communicate differently (Glass, 1992; Tannen, 1990). Men use more forceful gestures, sit further away in conversations, speak in a lower-pitched voice, avoid eye contact, interrupt others frequently, and use loudness to emphasize points. Women use more fluid gestures, take up less physical space, lean forward in conversations, speak rapidly, look directly at others, allow others to interrupt them, speak in higher-pitched voices, articulate more precisely, vary their tones when speaking, and use pitch and inflection to emphasize points. The verbal messages of men and women also vary. Men use direct, declarative statements, give more command terms, tend to be blunt, and focus on solving problems. Women engage in more self-disclosure, make more tentative statements, use more emotional verbs, compliment others, are diplomatic, and focus on understanding others. The goals of communication also differ. Men tend to be task focused, confront others, and engage in report talk, whereas women are maintenance-oriented, strive to preserve relationships, value connections, and engage in rapport talk (Tannen, 1990). Knowing these differences assists you in understanding others and in developing important skills that enhance your communication.

Interpersonal communication improvement is dependent on an awareness of your own personal patterns. Effective communicators articulate their thoughts, feelings, and beliefs in direct and appropriate ways. They understand differences in communication approaches and employ strategies that facilitate understanding. Strategies they use include **S**tating their needs directly, **E**mploying "I" language, **N**oticing nonverbal cues and **D**iscussing differences in the ways that individuals express and perceive information (**SEND**).

Stating Needs Directly

Effective communicators take charge by using language that is precise, concise, and effective. They value honest expression of their feelings, are comfortable describing their needs, and are able to ask for assistance. They use declarative statements appropriately and offer their opinion and ideas freely. They use feeling and idea words to describe experiences. They recognize the problems associated with indirect communication and strive to improve their own capabilities to deliver clear, articulate messages that others can understand.

Employing "I" Language

In assuming responsibility for communication, one of the important steps is using "I" language. "**I" language** allows communicators to take responsibility by specifically stating needs, asking for clarification, or using accurate descriptors that present a personal viewpoint or reaction. With "I" messages, communicators speak directly, rather than hint or expect others to know their needs or expectations.

Using "I" messages avoids one common area of miscommunication—"you" messages. Often using "you" messages makes the listener defensive. This is especially true if those messages are accompanied with generalizations such as "never" or "always." In situations in which communicators are sharing their views about their own experience, providing feedback, or exploring areas in which miscommunication is occurring, "I" messages facilitate the communication process. They assist the communicator in avoiding interruptions, finishing thoughts, clarifying perceptions, and discussing the consequences of various types of behaviour. In situations in which a speaker provides feedback to another, there would be three parts to this "I" message. These "I" messages involve stating clearly how you feel, identifying a situation or behaviour that has produced your reaction, and describing specifically the consequences of the behaviour that you are experiencing. For example, when someone interrupts you when you are speaking, a proper "I" message might be, "I feel irritated when you interrupt me as I am unable to present my viewpoint effectively."

Noticing Nonverbal Language

Effective communicators know the importance of looking at others when they are speaking, monitoring their nonverbal cues, using appropriate language, and varying intonation appropriate to their message. They are careful to use a relaxed, open-body posture (e.g., looking at others, hands at sides, leaning forward), eliminate detracting gestures, and avoid ending sentences with upward inflections. They have developed an awareness of their own nonverbal messages so that they are able to use hand gestures, head nodding, facial expressions, and smiling to complement rather than detract from their verbal messages. They have an appreciation of the differences in communication patterns that are the result of socialization and cultural differences. They use this information in understanding the impact of their nonverbal message on others. Effective communicators strive to use nonverbal behaviours that reinforce their competency and indicate their interest in others.

Discussing Differences

Given that many factors influence the communication process, effective communicators ask for information as a way to avoid potential problems and to help clarify situations so that mistakes and misperceptions do not occur. Requesting feedback illustrates respect for the listener and demonstrates an understanding of the interactive nature of effective communication. Asking for information allows individuals to explore others' perceptions, analyze similarities and differences in viewpoints, discuss disparities, and determine options for gaining greater understanding.

Effective communicators assume responsibility for ensuring that others understand the message they have sent and respect the interactive process of communication. They anticipate the reactions of others, value the diversity of perceptions that others have, and know that clarification is a vital component of the communication process. Because they recognize differences in individuals' perceptions of messages, they seek feedback regarding their messages. They value both their own messages, and the messages of others, using strategies to engage others while asserting their own views.

Developing Abilities as a Listener

Listening is fundamental to being an effective communicator. By mastering listening skills, the speaker can more fully communicate to others. Listening is different than hearing. While *Webster's Dictionary* defines hearing as "perceiving or apprehending through the ear," listening is defined as "hearing something with thoughtful attention." Thoughtful is explained as "given to heedful anticipation of the needs and wants of others." Attention is the "selective narrowing or focusing of consciousness and receptivity." Thus, **active listening** is an active process of attending to others, acknowledging their concerns, validating their importance by striving to empathetically understand what the other is trying to say. It is an activity that Considers another's needs and experiences, it Affirms others, it Restates feelings, and it Empowers self-understanding (CARE).

Considering Another's Needs and Experiences

According to many psychologists, the purpose of listening is to have contact with and know the world around the other person, and to bear witness to another's expression (Brizee, 1993; Huggett, 1988; Nichols, 1995; Riediger, 1992; Tournier, 1984). It involves acknowledging the other by freeing the person from the solitude of his/her own heart and lightening the other's load. In its most profound moment, it reaches the hurt behind the expressions of hostility, the resentment behind avoidance, and the vulnerability that makes people afraid to speak and afraid to truly listen. When a person is able to verbalize his/her thoughts, thereby externalizing them, he/she is able to look at them from a new perspective. Otherwise, the "un-listened" person's thinking remains trapped and he/she feels "How can I know what I think until I hear myself say it?"

Affirming Others

Active listening also requires that we affirm others by acknowledging their importance and appreciating their point of view. When you attempt to listen attentively—so that you are able to walk in another's moccasins, you are affirming someone by acknowledging the person, their uniqueness, and their story. It requires that you try to place yourself into the other person's situation, taking on all the circumstances, as well as the history that the person brings to the listening setting. For instance, a student who has just received a poor grade may have a history that is associated with poor marks. This history is key to active listening and provides a deeper understanding of the feelings, thoughts, and behaviours that are connected to the person's talk with you. By knowing that this student's parents might have very high expectations, by knowing that marks are important for the student's self-esteem, and by knowing that anything less than an A is perceived as a failure, as a listener, you have more closely taken on the perspective of this student. Through adopting the perspective of another, you are more able to identify with the person's feelings and thereby support, as well as validate his/her feelings. Active listening at best requires us to actively and imaginatively become immersed into the other person's situation— affirming the frame of reference different from our own.

Restating Feelings

Active listening helps to clarify a speaker's thoughts (Dunn, 1983) by encouraging the speaker to be honest with him/herself while being heard. As a speaker, this may be the first time that we are given a chance to hear what we think or feel, and thereby solidify who we are and why we do what we do. In essence, the active listener becomes a mirror, reflecting the speaker's thoughts, feelings, and actions. By active listening, we improve the accuracy in the speaker's responses to the listener, and affirm the speaker's thoughts, thereby acknowledging his/her personhood (Dunn, 1983). This, in turn, gives rise to a healthier self-identity.

Empowering Self-Understanding

Sharing life's victories with a listener sustains a sense of significance in the need for being appreciated. It nourishes and fortifies our sense of who we are. When we celebrate life with another, it becomes more of who we are. During overwhelming life circumstances, active listening provides inner strength. Failing an exam, the tragedy of a broken relationship, the death of a loved one, or the realization of an incurable illness are more bearable when someone listens. It provides a sense of security, an opportunity for healing, and clarity as to what is felt. It is through the listening of another that the journey to self-understanding begins. Thus, listening provides the necessary expression and clarification of thought and feeling as it nourishes and fortifies the sense of self-worth. It allows a source of healing and the releasing of pent-up bitterness that hinders relationships so that the complexity and importance of the relationships are more clearly understood. It also sustains a sense of significance in the need for being appreciated and recognition that there is someone-there-for-us. Finally, it allows individuals to express themselves honestly and to learn about themselves (Augsburger, 1982; Brizee, 1993; Drakeford, 1967; Nichols, 1995; Tournier, 1984).

Active listening is a powerful tool. It is so powerful, that "listening shapes us whereas the lack of listening twists us" (Nichols, 1995, p. 19). So why aren't more people harnessing the power of listening? Because it requires a selfless and giving attitude, an attitude that is foreign to most people and requires immense effort. For most of us, we do it when it is convenient or when we anticipate reciprocity. But for the most part, we miss out on the opportunity to experience active listening, either as a speaker or as the listener. As a result of the lack of a selfless and giving attitude, we often experience communication breakdown.

How to Become an ACTIVE Listener

There are a number of ways to enhance your active listening skills. These include Avoiding ineffective listening strategies, Communicating feedback, Transferring and Imitating others, being sensitive to non-Verbal cues, and Embracing a broader awareness.

Avoiding Ineffective Listening Strategies

Some of the factors that interfere with an ability to listen include an individual's need for detail, tendency to hypothesize about individual motives, and a desire to relate your own experience (Drakeford, 1967). Sometimes a need for too much information results in asking questions before the individual has completed his/her thought. By too quickly adding your empathetic response and a quick solution, the individual may feel misunderstood and apprehensive about sharing any more thoughts. Labelling an individual also thwarts the potential for change and reduces him/her to the confines of the label. If perchance the conversation happens to enter an area that is too close to a personal issue, it is possible that feelings of defensiveness can affect effective listening abilities. Be aware of these common pitfalls, and wherever possible, attempt to avoid them.

Communicating Feedback

Only after we have given the other a chance to be heard, may we begin to let them know what we think they are trying to tell us. Once they have been heard, we need to act on the next step of active listening: promoting understanding by providing explicit feedback of what we have just heard. In order to promote understanding, we need to communicate two levels of meaning: the meaning that is being conveyed by the speaker's words, and the interpretation of the relationship between this meaning and the associated posture, tone of voice, facial expressions, pauses, gazes, and gestures. The feelings behind the message are critical! We need to listen to the tone of voice and emotions that are being expressed. The simple act of taking time to restate the other's position in your own words while asking him or her to correct or affirm your understanding, has the potential to transform the listener. What this requires is being skilled in the art of reply—in other words, becoming a verbal mirror not only for the words spoken, but also for the emotions displayed. As a result, the speaker discovers him/herself anew.

Transferring and Imitating Others

Probably one of the most effective ways to develop your listening skills is to be mentored by an effective listener. Observe individuals who are good at listening, such as counsellors, social workers, and human resource professionals. You develop your listening skills while being listened to by effective listeners. Transfer the effective listening techniques that make you feel heard and validated as a person.

Nonverbal Cues

An active listener also focuses on the face, body language, and emotions—or nonverbal cues—emitted by the speaker (Florence, 1983). The face can be very revealing. Dark concentric circles under a person's eyes may reveal depression, whereas happiness or contentment is often reflected in a smile or a bright face. The eyes, often referred to as the windows of the soul, portray pain, hurt, fear, excitement, or joy. Body language, such as hunched shoulders, often reveals heaviness. Perceptivity to nonverbal cues enhances understanding.

Active listening also requires nonverbal responding, or allowing the speaker to determine the course of communication. There are few if any interruptions. The listener, in attempting to understand, follows the speaker by appropriately nodding, shaking the head, moving the eyes, wrinkling the forehead as if to agree with the speaker, reflecting or mimicking the emotions of the other, and otherwise coaxing him/her to continue sharing. These nonverbal ways of listening validate and encourage the speaker. A willingness to understand the other through an acceptance of the other's feelings, an affirmation of the other's emotions as real, an attempt to feel with the other, and a willingness to share the other's feelings, increases the interpersonal trust between you.

Embracing a Broader Awareness

Preconceived expectations often interfere with what is being communicated. For instance, students who overconfidently assume knowledge about a given topic are less likely to listen actively to the professor. To their dismay, they often discover too late that their assumptions are not supported by their professors—as evidenced by the incorrect answers on a given exam. Another common oversight by many students is the dependence on their rich history of relating to knowledge experientially. For example, at one time, many of us believed that Santa Claus existed. What seemed like common sense may at best have been a stereotype or even a bias that may not have had circumstantial or conclusive evidence. Students who continue to hold tightly to their beliefs may often have difficulty listening to the knowledge presented by others. One of the more difficult elements of active listening requires us to suspend our agenda, preconceived expectations, and experiential knowledge in order to hear the other person. For the most part, we are expert "**competitive conversationalists**" (Nichols, 1995). At a moment's notice, we are able to launch into a conversation, totally ready to share our story before acknowledging what the other is saying—jockeying for a chance to be heard.

In summary, active listening is an act of self-transcendence, a skill that one masters little by little, that focuses not on our desires but on the needs of the other. When applied to its fullest, listening is powerful. As Brizee (1993) stated: "To listen to another person is to offer a gift. To listen with caring to another person is to offer a gift of awareness. To listen with acceptance to all facets of another person is to offer healing. To listen with patience for new ways to see the past events of another person is to offer a gift of freedom. To listen with reverence for new becomings emerging within another person is to offer a gift of grace."

By practising the principles of effective interpersonal communication you have a framework for establishing meaningful, trusting, and caring relationships with others. As you add to your ability to share with others, express yourself, clarify misunderstandings, and listen to others, you gain increased confidence in your communication capabilities. This increased confidence allows you overcome any barriers that may be interfering with the give and take of the communication process. Increased confidence allows you to attempt new skills and reach out to others. While success in communicating to others and knowing you are understood by them adds to your self-confidence. By applying the information you have learned on interpersonal communication, you will experience the synergistic effect that increased confidence and competence have on your ability to connect effectively with others.

Presentations: What Am I Getting Myself Into?

A very important skill to acquire as a scholar is the ability to disseminate information through oral presentations. As a student, you will find a variety of settings where you will be asked to publicly communicate what you know. This may include informal and impromptu, or formal and well-prepared presentations in class or at academic conferences. These are opportunities to advance the knowledge of your audience members. You learn information and in turn, share it with others—critical components of transferring and further developing knowledge.

You can improve your presentation skills through knowledge and effort. In this section, we will focus on understanding what an effective presentation is, presenter self-awareness, the elements of an effective presentation, how to prepare for the presentation, and how to use the evaluations of your presentation.

For the most part, a **presentation** is a "commitment by the presenter to help the audience do something." Simultaneously, throughout the presentation, the audience is evaluating the presenter's ability to deliver—to make good on the commitment" (Hoff, 1992, p. 6). As a presenter, you make a commitment to your audience. So your first task is to identify a goal for your audience. This could be to expand their knowledge, to persuade them to believe your evidence, or to change their minds. If you want to prove that bottled water is no safer than tap water, your goal will be to persuade your audience that this is true. If it is to promote change, such as changing people's drinking habits, your information must generate action. The content you choose must be relevant to your audience. Crucial to your commitment as a presenter is the ability to focus on a specific point that the audience can use. The best way to do so is to be prepared and to select information that is already important to the audience. The presentation then analyzes the information and sharpens it. It brings it even closer to the audience's real needs, ending with a single point that audience members can take with them.

Presenter Self-Awareness

A confident presenter knows his or her presentation skills. Your confidence is based on your past experiences speaking in front of people. Great experiences reinforce your confidence, whereas challenging experiences may harm your confidence. As you read the various elements of presenting, compare your skills with those of successful presenters. Celebrate the ones that you can identify with and take the effort to adopt those that are not currently part of your skills, so that your confidence as a speaker is enhanced. Identify any fears that are associated with public speaking and learn from the list of anxiety-reducing strategies that follow. Finally, enlighten yourself with the successful presentation strategies, adding them to your presentation skills.

Elements of Presenting

There are a variety of public speaking texts addressing a variety of different presentation styles. However, as seen in the flow chart on this page, the most common presentation style for academic audiences can be organized into three major elements with complementary activities: *prior*—content preparation, material preparation, rehearsal and revision, preparing the environment; *during*—oral presentation and managing interaction; and *after*—feedback (Davidson & Ambrose, 1992; Locke, Spirduso, & Silverman, 1998; Renfrow & Impara, 1989; Taylor & Toews, 1999). Each of these is critical for an effective presentation and will be further explored.

Prior to the Presentation

Prior to the presentation, learn by attending other academic presentations and by identifying the effective methods and strategies used therein. Gain wide exposure to effective presenting by observing a wide variety of academic speakers, noting effective strategies such as appearance, delivery, props, and tone of voice, and applying these to your own repertoire. Next, prepare the content and materials that best address the requirements of the presentation and the needs of the audience. In the previous chapter you learned how to write papers for specific audiences and purposes. Preparing for presentations includes some of these same skills and strategies.

Determine the Presentation Criteria

What is it that is required from you as a presenter? Your course outline will provide these in the form of presentation marking criteria. Most times, these criteria are very similar to those found in professional presentations, including content, time limits, delivery format, use of audiovisuals, and meeting the needs of the audience.

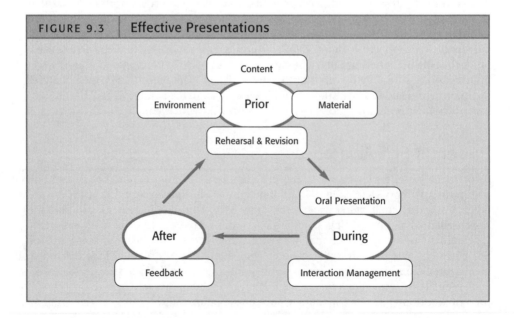

FIGURE 9.3 | **Effective Presentations**

Critical Time Duration

A successful presentation is completed on time or just short of it. The audience responds more favourablly to presenters who end before their allotted time. Order of presentation is also important. If at all possible, request the very first spot on the agenda. Your content is new and your presentation is evaluated first—setting the standard against which all other presenters are compared. Thus, being first has its merits, especially if you are well prepared to address the needs of the audience.

Assessing the Audience

As a presenter, you are making a commitment to the audience to provide them with new information. You are best able to make good on that commitment when you know who your audience is, their knowledge levels, their needs regarding the topic, and can anticipate their reactions (Locke et al., 1998). Background research is helpful. Ask the professor what content would be most meaningful. Ask your peers what they would like to hear, and what their needs are concerning the topic. This way you can ensure that your presentation will not be too simple, boring, complex, or confusing. You want to be able to challenge the audience at their point of need. Remember, your goal is to engage and interest your audience.

Anticipate the reactions that audience members may have to your content. If it is something controversial, such as capital punishment, be prepared to know both sides of the argument. If it is conflicts with common sense, such as drinking tap water, be prepared to defend the material with current empirical data. Once gathered, the background information on your audience can provide you with meaningful criteria that will guide you in developing your presentation. Applying the criteria effectively will assure your audience that you are committed to them.

Organizing the Presentation

Just as you organize your paper, so too, your presentation needs to have some sort of organization. Select the central idea of your presentation, often referred to as the thesis, and focus on this throughout your presentation. As with an excellent paper, you want to introduce your audience to your topic, provide a body of knowledge to support your thesis, and then conclude with some form of application for the audience.

Creating a Script

Once the content is written, focus on creating a script that will guide you in presenting the material to "say the right things, about the right topics, in the right order" (Locke et al., 1998, p. 135). Use discrete strategies that minimize reading and increase eye contact with your audience. Memorizing your content provides you with the greatest freedom. However, most presenters find a sense of security and added confidence in having some form of notes nearby. When relying on a manuscript, print words in 18-point font and use only the top third of the paper. Referring to the top third of the paper is easy to see and almost parallels your audience's eye level, giving them the impression that you are not reading. Even more effective are 3×5 cards highlighting key points. With the cards in hand, you have more freedom to move. Another successful strategy is to use presentation visuals such as overheads or computer presentations. Use key words that provide an aid for the audience yet cleverly guide your presentation. Whatever form your guide takes, ensure that it provides you with the most confidence and ease as you refer to it when presenting. Pay attention to details such as the size of type font for your readability and numbered pages to keep you on track. Also, provide smooth and discrete movement of the guides from one to the next. Papers can be moved from one side of the lectern to the next. Rotate 3×5 cards from the front of the stack to the back. The key here is to make smooth, dance-like movements that enhance the presentation.

Preparing Material: Visuals, Handouts, Supplementary Material

Given that most people are visual learners, visuals are vital for effective presentations. Ideally, pace your visuals so that you have one for every one to threee minutes of presentation time. Visuals should only include important information, and be used sparingly and appropriately. If it enhances understanding then it is worth showing. Be very critical as to how many to use. Too many can be distracting. Also, try to use the aid in a limited manner, where at all possible, blocking or removing it from the view of the audience. This is to ensure the continued curiosity and inquiry of the audience. Leaving an aid up too long will invite continued inspection and further distraction (Locke et al., 1998). When using an overhead, sequentially block material, releasing it at opportune times during the presentation.

One of the most important visuals should include the presentation objective(s) and an outline of the key points. This prepares the audience as to what can be anticipated. Moreover, the audience will perceive you as well prepared and well organized. Other visual aids that could be included as part of this presentation are photographs, posters, models, tables, figures, graphs, outlines, diagrams, and demonstrations.

Finally, content-appropriate humour is also an effective presentation supplement. Use it to introduce the topic, especially when you are one of many presenters and you need to help the audience make a mental transition from previous presentations. If used appropriately, humour can open up the audience and make the presenter more accepted. Often this takes the form of a cartoon that best illustrates the content to be presented.

Rehearsal: Practice and Revision

Before going onstage or standing in front of an audience, successful presenters spend time practising. There are three types of practising: silent reading, solitary speaking, and trial runs (Locke et al., 1998, p. 138). Each of these methods increases your confidence and provides you with opportunities to refine the content of the presentation. Begin with silent reading to become familiar with the material. Then allow for opportunities to speak out loud, in order to help refine the sound of your presentation. Finally, invite others to be present as you practise, in order to get their constructive criticism to enhance your presentation.

To experiment with timing and with the mechanics of presenting, solitary speaking in front of a mirror is useful. Take note of your gestures, eye contact, facial expressions, and body movement. Ensure that your gestures parallel your content. For instance, when listing a group of ideas, use your fingers to represent the first, second, and third ideas. Given that your audience reads from your right to your left, ensure that your gestures proceed in the same direction. For eye contact, train your eyes to move smoothly, panning the entire room. Listen to your voice intonation. Does it parallel the importance of your content? Focus more energy on the important points. Record your presentation and play back for feedback on what to improve.

Once you feel confident about your presentation, invite family, friends, and even content experts to participate as mock audiences. Trial presentations add to your confidence, further refining your content, helping test the appropriateness of aids, and making you aware of potential audience reactions such as questions. As you present, ask your audience members to provide constructive criticism, focusing on your gestures, eye contact, facial expressions, and body movement. To what extent does your presentation style parallel the content being presented? Next, have your audience reflect critically on what you say. Are there any logical inconsistencies? Is there any inappropriate or overly technical jargon? Are there any difficult concepts that require further explaining or defining? Are there ways that the ideas can be stated in a more concise manner? How appropriate are your aids? Is there a better way to demonstrate the idea visually? Is there a better figure or chart?

Most critical is your behaviour as a presenter. Ensure that any distracting behaviours are brought to your attention. Too often a potentially powerful presentation is distracted by some bizarre behaviour, such as jingling keys or coins in a pocket. Once identified, write in bold print on your presentation cards: **DO NOT PLACE HAND IN POCKET**.

Finally, encourage your mock audience to log their thoughts throughout the presentation. For instance, during your introduction, were they interested, curious, bored? When you presented the main point, did they feel convinced or compelled to disagree? Ensure that the responses felt by your audience are the ones that you intended. If not, revise your presentation. Have them also list questions to help you anticipate audience questions in your formal presentation. Prepare responses for each of these potential questions.

As with any stage performers, your presentation becomes more effective with each successive repetition. The more effort you put into the presentation, the more confident you will be. Anxiety usually occurs as a result of the audience responding to your lack of preparation. The more you use these successful preparation strategies, the more prepared you will be for your presentation. As with all excellent things, successful presentations require lots of effort and the help of others.

Preparing the Environment

Important to an effective presentation is the environment. Maintaining room temperature at a constant 18 degrees Celsius and providing continuous air circulation will keep the audience alert. A semi-circular seating arrangement invites most audience members to feel a part of the presentation, given that they can see the faces of their peers with minimal effort (Kolb, 1994). This format makes it less likely to conceal audience incivilities (e.g., distracting behaviours). Also, a clean room with neatly arranged chairs sends a strong signal of preparation and order, so take the extra time to ensure that the room is organized and clean.

Next, test your voice. Does it carry well in the room? Do you need to raise the volume? Remember that sound is absorbed by people in the room, so you will need to remember to speak louder when your audience is seated. Whenever possible, minimize facing your back to the audience, but when it's necessary, remember to increase your voice volume.

Check that the equipment has arrived and is functioning. Pull down the screen to ensure that it is functional and has no surprising messages inscribed on it. Get training on any new equipment so that you handle it expertly. Be prepared. If the data projector or computer fails, have a set of transparencies ready to pull out and use.

Handouts provide a professional touch to the presentation, especially when they are in place at each seat before the audience is seated. As with anything an audience has access to, ensure that the handouts are user-friendly, spell-checked, and professionally copied without any flaws. Remember, your evaluation will also be based on how well you have created your handouts.

A successful presentation includes having a well-prepared environment. Attention to details such as room temperature, seating arrangement, sound, functional presentation technology, and handouts adds to the confidence of the speaker. Take time to ensure that each of these is adequate before your presentation. Both you and your audience will feel more comfortable and you will have fewer reasons to feel stressed.

During the Presentation

Once you are very comfortable with your content, it is time to present. The most important element of the presentation is presenting! This requires a number of key elements: appearance, stance and gait, speaking style, taming nervousness, and eye contact.

Appearance

Dress is important to your audience. It sends a message that they are important enough to you that you would consider being well groomed, wearing a set of clean clothes, and dressing up. Studies have shown that people who are dressed well and groomed well are more liked and are judged more favourably (Feingold, 1992). Being somewhat extreme, such as a major change in hair fashion, or some outrageous article of clothing may in itself be very distracting to the audience. Unless your topic deals with the content of fashion, dress moderately and appropriately.

Stance and Gait

When it is your turn to present, move toward the lectern with a slight bounce, moving a little more quickly. The audience will interpret this behaviour as belonging to someone important and valuable for them to listen to. Next, begin by standing behind the lectern. Once you feel confident, move toward the audience. This speaks volumes. First, you appear confident about the content. Second, you feel comfortable with the audience and begin to move into their circle. Third, your body is in full view as compared to being hidden behind the lectern or podium, and becomes one of your most powerful and essential multimedia tools. Stand tall and display your confidence. Have your hands dance the gestures required to drive home the points of your presentation. Move ever so slightly around the front of the room to entice audience members to follow you. This again keeps the audience attentive and alert. Find a balance between gracefully moving your body and hands, while continually maintaining eye contact with each member in your audience. As you do so, you will strengthen the engagement of your audience with your content material. The more you use your body to communicate, the more persuasive your presentation potentially could be! However, keep in mind balance. There is always the possibility of too much movement producing distraction.

Speaking Style

Key to any effective presentation is a physical, content-related change of voice. It involves intonations, volume, and crescendos. As the message becomes more important, the voice should become more emphatic, more excited, and louder. Be enthusiastic about your topic and you will win your audience's attention (Schönwetter, 1993).

Taming Nervousness

Many speakers experience nervousness about presenting. Often referred to as stage fright or communication apprehension (Beatty, Balfantz, & Kuwabara, 1989), it adds to feelings of embarrassment, fear of the audience's reactions, and heightened self-consciousness (Ayres, 1986, 1992; Booth-Butterfield & Booth-Butterfield, 1986). To reduce these feelings and add to your confidence, avoid calling attention to your nervousness by mentioning it. Find support groups to learn strategies for coping more effectively (Beatty, 1988; Connell & Borden, 1987). Reduce apprehension by changing the seating arrangement to the u-shaped format that facilitates greater connection with your audience (Bowers, 1986). Learn strategies for lowering your anxiety (Hamilton & Parker, 1993). Most anxiety is caused by ineffective speaking strategies or inadequate preparation. For instance, many students use poor introduction strategies that encourage more anxiety (Beatty et al., 1989). To reduce anxiety, use presentation strategies that help divert attention, such as handouts and visual aids.

Prior to presenting, take a short walk to help reduce your anxiety. Next, if waiting for your turn to present, let your hands dangle so that the blood can move down the arms. This helps to reduce your anxiety. Take deep long breaths, but do so quietly. Ensure that you are not sitting cross-legged. There is a good tendency for one of your legs to fall asleep and this adds to the stress as you get up to present and realize that you have no control of your sleeping leg! Above all, do not visualize your audience as naked. This may be more distracting to you.

Also and ideally, find ways to harness the nervous energy into excitement and energy for the presentation. Eliminate distracting behaviours. There is nothing more humourous and distracting than observing a speaker jingling keys or grabbing the lectern and displaying white knuckles. Find discreet ways to harness your energy. For instance, if you need to do something with your fingers, practise touching your pointer finger to your thumb. This behaviour can be done with your hand at your side and conducted in a manner that draws little attention from your audience.

Eye Contact

Eye contact is critical. Most cultures in North America require that the speaker communicate with his or her eyes. Be sure to look at all people. Many presenters have a favourite side of the audience and focus too much attention to that side. Audience members on the other side often feel left out and are more likely to provide less favourable evaluations. Also, if you have friends in the audience, have them sit at both sides of the auditorium so that you are more encouraged to look at the entire audience. Attempt to make eye contact with all members of your audience in a smooth, sweeping fashion, moving from the left to the centre to the right and then back to the centre and then to the left. As you do this, you are more likely to engage your audience in your presentation, encouraging them to listen to what you have to say.

Also take note of the audience's facial cues and body language. If you observe boredom, increase your enthusiasm and eye contact to win these people back. If facial cues indicate confusion, revisit your last point and provide more clarity through another example or a visual. A successful presenter is in tune with the audience's facial feedback. Take in the cues from your audience and try to address them during your presentation.

The Presentation Sequence

The first 90 seconds of any presentation are vital to the success of the following minutes (Hoff, 1992). It is in these initial 90 seconds that a speaker develops important rapport with the audience. Once established, rapport potentially energizes the speaker and provides the first and lasting impression on the audience. As a speaker, plan your first 90 seconds with a short personal story, content-appropriate humour, or a current news event that introduces your topic. Have this material memorized so that you can maximize your eye contact with every audience member. As you recite the story, joke, or news event, scan the room for audience approval and note who is smiling at you. These are your **refueling** centres (Hoff, 1992). Later, when you feel a lack of confidence, their smiling and approving faces will re-energize you to continue. For example, it was said of a well-known speaker that during his talk to a large audience, he began to lose his confidence as a result of the audience's negative facial cues. However, near the front of the auditorium was an elderly man who, for whatever reason, provided the speaker with the most positive facial cues. By the end of the presentation, the guest speaker had regained his confidence and the support of the audience as a result of constantly refueling by looking at this older gentleman. After the presentation, the guest speaker questioned the host about the man in the front row. He wanted to thank him for his support. The host responded, "Oh, Joe—he's stone deaf."

In those first 90 seconds, a speaker can often win over most of the audience simply through eye contact. A positive and attentive audience will reinforce your presenting behaviour and increase your energy to present to the point where you may experience a speaker's rush. The positive rapport that you have with your audience, coupled with an excitement about your content material, gives way to a release of endorphins or pleasure hormones in your body. During these pleasurable times, it is often difficult for the speaker to stop speaking. It becomes exciting and very rewarding! And it all begins by setting the stage in the first 90 seconds.

After the first 90 seconds, deliver the content as best as you can. Begin with a quick overview of what you will be presenting. This is usually best accomplished by providing the audience with an overhead of the presentation objective or thesis statement and an outline of the ideas that you are going to present in the remaining time. Remember to be clear in presenting your content. Ideally, launch into your topic by providing definitions and examples. Deliver the main point(s) concisely with the appropriate rationale and empirical support.

In the final 90 seconds, draw your presentation to a close by carefully reviewing the essential points and providing the audience with something that they can take with them. This may be a challenge to change a way of thinking, an invitation to further explore the topic, or a practical solution to apply in everyday life. Then close by thanking the audience for their time.

After the Presentation

Managing the Interaction that Follows

If your presentation was successful, you can anticipate a flood of responses from your audience members. So what is the best way to respond and to manage the interaction that follows? First, nod your head toward the audience member who is anticipating to respond. As a presenter, you have some level of authority of the topic. The nod is one of approval, which not only invites the audience into a dialogue with you, but also sends a strong signal to other members of the audience that you are willing to respond to their interactions and that you will respond in an orderly way. If there are many responses, there is always the potential of people talking out of turn. Your approving nod to the first and each successive audience member will help approve the dialogue and order of responses.

Second, ensure that you understand the question before responding. Sometimes a trick question is asked to make you look foolish. Rephrasing the question to the person ensures that you understand the question. If the question is not clear, use your authority as a speaker to ask for clarification. This demonstrates you are concerned with appropriately addressing the audience member's need. If a question includes a number of items, each of which requires a separate answer, take time to address each item. If after answering the first part of the question you forget the second, take confidence in asking the person to repeat the question. This does not reflect poor listening skills as a speaker, but rather a genuine concern to understand the specific issue of the audience member. In the eyes of the audience, it further demonstrates your effective ability to respond confidently.

Third, always anticipate a question that may be difficult for you to answer. Overconfident presenters make the mistake of providing answers to every question, even questions about which they have no knowledge . Most audiences usually have one content expert. An overconfident presenter usually challenges these experts whose responses often unwittingly demonstrate the presenter's lack of knowledge and shatter the presenter's credibility, both for the moment as well as for any future chance of presenting. A more eloquent response is to be honest with your audience and state that you do not know the answer for that question. Invite comments from the audience. Usually the experts in the audience are more than willing to provide an answer. Otherwise, make a public commitment to the audience member to conduct more research and send a personal response to that person. Your honesty as a speaker enhances your credibility and you have avoided challenging the experts in your audience by inviting them to contribute.

Also of importance, as a speaker, you have some control over the time during which the audience interacts with you. If you are given five minutes for questions, stay within those five minutes. The audience is still holding you accountable for the time, even though it is the audience that is now actively involved in dialoguing with you. If you notice that the time is running out and that there are many more questions, invite audience members to forward their questions to you directly after the presentation via e-mail. This helps to bring closure to the questions, while providing further opportunities for getting a response. In turn, your audience will feel that you have accommodated their needs, even though you did not have time to do this during the presentation. The audience perception is that you cared for their needs, you attempted to address them as best as you could within the time constraints, and that you are approachable afterwards to continue further dialogue. As the presenter, your commitment to the audience has been fulfilled and is reflected in the evaluation of your presentation.

Evaluating the Presentation

A successful presenter is proactive about evaluations. There are four purposes for providing feedback (Book, 1985; Edwards, 1990). First, it imparts valuable information about the audience's reaction to the presentation. Second, it provides suggestions and solutions for improving. Third, it can motivate and increase the confidence of the speaker. Fourth, it offers information about the speaker for further self-understanding and development. Each evaluation should be seen as an opportunity to improve and build on one's strengths. Just as a diamond requires cuts to reveal its lustre, so too, evaluations provide opportunities to refine one's speaking potential. There are three forms of evaluations: audience, self, and significant others. These evaluations occur throughout the presentation, not only at the end.

Audience evaluations

The audience is constantly evaluating your commitment to them. People who sit forward, lean toward the presenter, follow the presenter, giving positive facial cues such as smiles and nods of the head, are likely indicating a sense of interest in the presentation.

Behaviours such as looking away from the presenter, sullen facial cues, frowns, or scrunched facial expressions may indicate challenged, threatened, uninterested, or even confused feelings about what has just been said by the presenter. Being aware of these immediate feedback cues provides the presenter with opportunities to revisit what has just been presented and either to rephrase the comment with empirical support or clarify a complex point. However, be aware that an audience has the ability to change an "eloquent orator into a halting, hesitating, dry-as-dust talker" (Drakeford, 1967). One thing to remember is that it is next to impossible to please all audience members. Some will challenge you by responding with negative facial cues and body language. If you feel confident, use eye contact to try to win them over. Remember to "refuel" for emotional support.

Invited audience evaluations are also valuable. These can take the form of a short one-minute paper. Ask audience members to spend no more than one minute responding to three questions:

1. What was the most important thing that you learned as a result of my presentation?

2. What question remain unanswered as a result of my presentation?

3. What would you do differently if you were to present the same topic?

The first question provides information on what the audience perceived as important and how well you communicated the information. The second question elicits information on your clarity of presenting. The third question is one that indicates how the audience perceived your presentation overall. Suggestions are good indicators to use, especially if a number of the audience members say the same things. Take note of these. Also, if you presented well, many will compliment your strengths.

A more formal evaluation process by the audience involves a standard checklist of the strengths and weaknesses as seen on page 221. Invite your peers, experts in the area, or a professor to evaluate you as well. Ideally find someone who is encouraging and honest and is known for his or her presentation abilities. Have them provide you with constructive feedback and arrange for them to review your presentation within an hour if possible so that their timely observations can be incorporated into your own experience. This becomes a powerful learning tool for improving and strengthening your speaking abilities.

Finally, take time immediately following the presentation to conduct a self-evaluation. Use the format found on page 221. Take note of all responses people have made during your presentation.

Once you have gathered all the evaluation data, graph your quantitative responses and determine what your average score is for each item evaluated. This would mean adding up all the responses and coming up with an audience score for each item (e.g., use of audio-visuals). Also, find recurring themes in the qualitative (i.e., open-ended) responses. With the use of a computer, you can quickly have each of the responses transcribed into a word-processing document and group all common responses into subcategories. Whenever there are strong recurring themes, these are good indicators of your performance and require your attention.

Once you have had an opportunity to summarize all your evaluations, act on them. Find ways to address the weaknesses. If the audience encourages you to use more visuals, make a note to do so in the future. If your voice was too quiet, print in bold letters on the top of your next presentation: **TALK LOUDER**. Create a file and call it "Future Presentations." Take notes as to what you would do differently next time and file these notes for the next presentation. In preparation for the next presentation, consult these notes for fine-tuning suggestions.

Presentation Evaluation

Name of Presenter: _____ Topic: _____

Please rate the presentation using the following scale:

	Poor			Average				Excellent		
	1	2	3	4	5	6	7	8	9	10
Relevant to my needs										
Strength of material										
Persuasiveness										
Learn anything new?										
Delivery										
Audio-visual										
Overall score										
Total score:										

Comments:

Your Presentation Diary (to be completed ASAP after your presentation)

Name of Presenter: _____ Topic: _____

Please rate the presentation on the following scale:

	Hopeless			Average				Perfect		
	1	2	3	4	5	6	7	8	9	10
Rate overall presentation										
What pleased you about it?										
What are your strengths?										
What are your challenges? How will you address these?										
What was said afterwards by audience members?										
What would you do differently next time to make it perfect?										

As mentioned earlier, a very important skill to acquire as a scholar is the ability to disseminate information. For the most part, it is a "commitment by the presenter to help the audience do something. Simultaneously, throughout the presentation, the audience is evaluating the presenter's ability to deliver—to make good on the commitment" (Hoff, 1992, p. 6). In fulfilling your obligation as a presenter, you need to focus on meeting the needs of your audience members. The most effective way to do so is to focus your effort into the three main elements of effective presentation with complementing activities: *prior*—content preparation, material preparation, rehearsal and revision, preparing the environment; *during*—oral presentation and managing interaction; and *after*—feedback. Meeting these objectives requires effort. The time invested in preparation adds to the confidence that one has during the presentation. The rewards gathered at the end of the presentation reinforce the effort invested, strengthen one's abilities, and direct one to the weaknesses requiring improvement for the future. In presenting, knowledge has a chance to be transmitted to many others, who in turn, can add to the further development of ideas in the academic community.

It's More Than Common Sense

Learning Communication Skills in Group Counselling

Peter Cornish, Ph.D.
Memorial University

Do I belong here? Will I fit in? Will I be able to make new friends? Will I miss my old friends or family members? These are some of the questions new students may ask themselves as they embark on their university experience. Important to this process of making friends is refining communication skills that facilitate making friends.

Social Support and Adjustment to University

A survey of first-year students entering Memorial University of Newfoundland suggests that the second most helpful orientation activities (after campus tours) were those aimed at helping students connect socially (Watton, 2001). In response to the question, "What helped you adjust to university?" the most common response was friends, family, and other students.

Social, psychological, and other behavioural changes have been identified as some of the leading sources of stress among university students (Newby-Fraser & Schlebusch, 1997; Santiago-Rivera, Gard, & Bernstein, 1999). A review of the literature on students at risk academically suggests that the best way to help these students is through group programs that are structured, ongoing, and voluntary (Coleman & Freedman, 1996).

The Power of Groups

Think about the settings in which you have learned to communicate socially. Generally, it has been within a group setting. The impact of groups can be positive or negative. A supportive, open, family environment that also teaches limits, boundaries, and sharing of responsibility is likely to foster the development of healthy relating in the future. Conversely, a highly conflicted, or uncommunicative family environment is likely to impede the development of healthy relationships in the future. A cohesive sports team, on which each member's contribution is valued and roles are well-defined, is more likely to promote cooperation and healthy interdependence among team members. A group that does not respect or value the dignity of the individual will foster intolerance.

While most university students are unlikely to be drawn into groups that are destructive, students who are less assertive or less confident in social situations are more susceptible to negative peer pressure. These students are at greater risk of inadvertently entering into relationships which can become conflicted, manipulative, or even abusive.

Group Learning and Student Development

Professionally-led counselling groups can help students make the social transition from high school or rural living into the much larger, diverse, and urban university community. At the University Counselling Centre of Memorial University of Newfoundland, we offer two groups aimed at improving relationship skills. In our *Assertiveness Training* group, students learn specific strategies for identifying and expressing their feelings and needs in direct and respectful ways. In our *Developing Healthy Relationships* group, students who are experiencing problems in relationships learn to recognize and respond in healthy ways to unique, often complex patterns of communication that develop as more intimate relationships evolve.

In my experience as a group counsellor, first-year students have typically been more interested in our Assertiveness Training group, whereas senior or mature students have been more likely to participate in our Developing Healthy Relationships group. Assertive communication skills are essential for initiating even the most basic relationships. They need to be well learned before healthy, intimate relationships are possible. Having obtained more experience in relationships, along with practise using assertive communication skills, more senior students are in a better position to begin identifying, exploring, and negotiating the complexities of intimate relationships. Some students who begin in first year with assertiveness training return a few years later to delve deeper into relationship dynamics.

Assertiveness Training Group

Do you have trouble asking for things you need? Do you find it difficult to say what you think, want, or feel? Do people take advantage of your generosity? If so, you may benefit from an Assertiveness Training group.

Assertiveness Training was developed first in the 1970s. It is based on human rights principles that hold that all people have the right to express feelings and needs as long as this expression does not impinge on the basic rights of other people. Assertiveness is a skill, and like any other skill, it requires training. One of the first steps in assertiveness training is to learn how to distinguish assertive, aggressive, and passive communication. Assertive communication is direct, responsible, and respectful. Assertive messages often begin with the word "I." For example, "I feel... I need... I think...," are stems for assertive statements. In contrast, aggressive messages are often blaming, exaggerated, disrespectful, and sometimes indirect. Aggressive messages often begin with the word "you." For example, "You always leave the house a mess. You are such a pig!" An assertive alternative would be, "I can't stand this mess. I would like you to take more responsibility for cleaning up."

In addition to learning assertive communication strategies, participants begin to learn to identify rights and responsibilities associated with healthy relationships, and obstacles to assertiveness including negative self-talk. First-year students who are shy, feeling isolated, or unaccustomed to life within a city and large institution may find Assertiveness Training particularly helpful. The skills learned will make it easier to identify and seek the kind of social support that makes a smooth transition from high school to university.

Developing Healthy Relationships Group

What is your track record with respect to close friendships or intimate relationships? Have you noticed any recurring negative themes or patterns in your relationships? Do you wonder where the friendship or love has gone? Are your relationships characterized more by conflict than closeness? Does the phrase "relationships: can't live with them, can't live without them" describe your current attitude? If you answered yes to any of these questions, interpersonal group counselling may be helpful.

Most people struggle with relationships at some point in their lives. One of the first steps to fixing any problem is simply to admit that there is a problem. And when it comes to relationships, the key often lies in recognizing the pattern, or the typical sequence of events that has come to characterize attempts to connect with others. It can be especially helpful to have others point out signs that could be missing in re-enacting these unsatisfying relationship patterns.

At Memorial University, our Developing Healthy Relationships group has been designed by integrating theory and techniques from three well-established methods of counselling (see Cornish & Benton, 2001). Our group counsellors work to create a safe, confidential, sometimes serious, sometimes entertaining, and almost always lively place for exploring, clearly identifying, and replacing old patterns with more fulfilling ones.

The focus on relationships is broad and often includes relationships with friends, romantic partners, roommates, employers, or parents. Students who have benefited from these groups in the past have explored a wide range of issues during sessions including negative self-image, loneliness, expressing anger, difficulties establishing or maintaining satisfying relationships, gender differences, and ongoing conflicts with friends, parents or others.

In contrast to Assertiveness Training, which is more task-oriented and led in a manner similar to a class, The Developing Healthy relationships group is unstructured—process and insight oriented. This means that the focus in the relationships group is on identifying and understanding complex patterns in relationships including the way that group members relate to each other in the "here-and-now" of the group itself (Yalom, 1995). Participants learn to pay closer attention to identifying their own needs, the expectations they hold of others, the actual responses they receive, and how these responses from others affect them.

Conclusion

Effective communication in social, academic, and vocational contexts is central to post-secondary education. This cannot be learned through academic study alone. Communication is learned primarily in relationships with peers and family members.

Depending, in part, on the quality of communication in your family, your community, and with friends you grew up with, you may wish to enhance your university education through group counselling participation. How would you know if interpersonal communication is something you need to work on? If your approach to others (including peers, partners, parents, and instructors) is either passive or aggressive, then you may benefit from assertiveness training. If you have noticed problematic patterns in the way that you relate to people who are close to you, then interpersonal group counselling may also be helpful.

Success Strategies FOR EFFECTIVE COMMUNICATION

Self-awareness

I've learned that my strengths in each of the following are:
   Listening…
   Self-presentation…
   Oral presentation…

Self-confidence

To increase my confidence in my ability to listen more actively I will…
To increase my confidence in my ability to present myself more confidently I will…
To increase my confidence in my ability to make oral presentations more effectively I will…

Self-concept

Actions I can take to gain greater control of my listening are….
Actions I can take to gain greater control of my self-presentation are….
Actions I can take to gain greater control of my oral presentation are…

Chapter Summary

In summary, the ability to communicate effectively is critical to all areas of life. By enhancing your communication capabilities, you achieve greater success as a student, employee, team-member, friend, and partner. Communication is a complex, interactive process of sending and receiving messages. Being able to actively listen to others is a key in becoming successful. Listening in class facilitates understanding and enhances achievements as students. Interpreting and understanding what peers and significant others say enhances relationships and facilitates the meaningful, intimate sharing that builds connection. Complementing your ability to listen is your ability to state your messages clearly and authoritatively so that you are understood. This includes being able to communicate interpersonally and formally through oral presentations. By refining your skills as a communicator, you are able to connect meaningfully with others. Communication is critical to life, providing the energy that is needed to continue the process of inquiry and to share the findings with others. In actively engaging in effective communication we build a true community of academics and a community of social networks that provide us with life-giving energy.

Exercises

REFLECT–ACT

The following Reflect–Act exercises are designed to help you develop increased self-awareness of your communication effectiveness through the process of reflective thinking, analysis, and productive action. Self-reflection encourages you to consider information you learn and data you collect to increase your ability to know yourself and to manage yourself.

Reflect This chapter lists a number of short-circuiting listening behaviours. Which of these most adequately define your listening behaviours?

Act Find ways to change your short-circuiting listening behaviours to more active listening ones. Create a set of goals as to how you will be acting on making these changes.

Reflect Reflect about your personal style of talking with others by listing at least five distinguishing verbal or nonverbal attributes that are characteristic of your style. Determine which of these qualities enhances your ability to send messages effectively and which detract.

Act Select one component of your style that you would like to change. Determine a plan for practising this new communication habit.

Reflect Think about the different types of presentations you enjoyed as an audience member. What characteristics of the presenter made the presentation inviting? Interesting? What type of medium was used to convey the message? What types of props or aids were used? Which ones created the most interest in you as an audience member? Why?

Act In developing a class presentation, select the most appropriate characteristics from the reflection noted above that parallel your personality. Create a list of effective presentation techniques that you would like to use to enhance your presentation.

GROUP DISCUSSION

Look at each of the items that short-circuit effective listening. As a group, come up with examples to illustrate each of these.

1. List the differences between effective presenters and ineffective presenters. Which of the effective presentation characteristics are the most important for group members to adopt? Develop a list of five recommendations for other members of the class to use in preparing for oral presentations.

2. Create a list of common presentation problems or challenges associated with presenting in front of peers. Beside each item create a recommended solution to the problem.

3. Make a list of tips that students should follow before, during, and after a presentation to assist their communication.

4. Explore and discuss the potential clues and cues associated with different emotions as displayed by the audience's different facial features. Make a list of emotions and try to determine what cues a presenter could watch for to predict these emotions in the audience. For instance, confusion, interest, boredom...

5. Partner up with another person. One person is the listener and the other is the speaker. The speaker recounts an exciting life event. After the speaker is finished, the listener replies by summarizing. The speaker expresses whether he/she has been understood. Then switch roles and repeat.

6. Bring to class cartoons representing examples of some of the miscommunications that occur between individuals or read any one of a number of articles in the popular press highlighting issues that lead to miscommunication between men and women. Discuss and identify the most common areas of miscommunication that occur between male and female university students. Describe how differences in communication styles influence friendships, dating, and group student sessions.

APPLY TO LIFE

Now that you have developed an understanding of how to increase your efficiency in listening, self-presentation, and formal presentations, you can use this information to enhance your own performance. Use the following questions to more clearly discover your strengths and limitations as a communicator.

1. As you review how you have formerly listened to others, what are your strengths in listening? Where do you need to improve, in terms of your listening, in order to succeed at university?

2. Assess your self-presentation skills. Describe your areas of competency and identify areas for improvement.

3. In your next week of classes, apply active listening skills as outlined in this chapter. Compare your former style of listening with active listening. Are you discovering the power of effective listening?

4. Consider a situation in which you must ask a professor with whom you have previously not spoken, to re-evaluate an examination. You believe that you deserve a much higher grade, and your friend who wrote similar answers to you received a grade ten points higher than yours. It is your goal to use your most effective communication skills to make this request. Describe what you intend to say and how you intend to say it. Identify particular information about the nonverbal components of your message.

5. You will be preparing a presentation for your class. Make a copy of the "Effective Presentations Flow Chart" and begin fleshing out each of the components of your presentation in preparation for it.

6. After your presentation, take time to have significant others provide you with feedback about your presentation. Also, take the time to reflect on your presentation by completing a self-evaluation. List all the strengths of your presentation and your challenges. Celebrate your strengths with a friend and seek solutions to your challenges for future presentations.

secret Creating Community 4

"Together everyone achieves more."

You are not alone on this great adventure of exploration and discovery. In fact, your success in achieving your greatest ambitions occurs as a result of synergistically combining your own abilities with the contributions of others. Connecting with others provides the necessary support system that allows you to succeed. " We" is greater than "me," thus, learning to come together with others allows you to create a community that sustains and nurtures you. Alone you can do so little, but together you can do so much. Because great feats are only accomplished through working together, it is essential to learn how to create meaningful connections and to overcome differences that may distance you from others.

As technological advances and globalization make the world in which we live smaller, our connections to one another become increasingly important. *Creating Community* requires recognizing the perspectives and contributions of others. Creating community involves valuing cooperation, connecting around shared beliefs and collaborating in order to achieve common objectives. Creating community requires appreciating differences and bridging diverse viewpoints. Differences can be sources of strength that when used expand understanding. And it is by expanding understanding, discovering commonalties, and revealing shared needs that people are able to create the connections that allow them to focus productively toward accomplishing meaningful, mutual goals.

Each person's life experiences provide a prism through which their world is seen. Because you see things not as they are, but as you are, it is particularly important to acknowledge the factors that influence your perceptions of others. To connect to others whose life experiences and perspectives contrast with your own, you must expand your awareness of other cultures, religious perspectives, lifestyle preferences and life experience. By identifying personal barriers such as racism, homophobia, and sexism, you avoid some of the misunderstanding that prevents you from reaching out, connecting with others, and discovering Truth.

Once you discover the capacity of your peers to teach you, class discussions, team projects, learning groups, peer review of writing assignments, and volunteer activities become as important to your development as the more formal classroom learning. By recognizing the role that others play in ensuring your personal success, you can more fully understand the desirability of collaborating with others rather than competing with them. Sooner or later, you too will discover that by working together everyone achieves more.

Enhancing Learning Through Communities

chapter 10

"It takes a community to raise a child."

African saying

Questions

What communities have an influence on me as a student?

How do they influence me?

Are there ways in which I can better access the resources from each of these communities?

How can I establish social networks and use learning groups maximally?

Objectives

- Explore resources on and off campus.
- Identify the importance of building social networks and community.
- Develop relationships that work and connect productively to others.
- Create a sense of community.
- Work productively in groups.
- Understand others.

Student Success Portrait

Being A Successful Mature Student

Myrna Cook
The University of Manitoba

I returned to university in January 2001, as a mature student, wife, and mother of two children, ages three and five. Returning to university was one of the most difficult decisions I have ever made. I had been out of school for ten years and had only my high school diploma. University had never occurred to me back then as a possibility. I married and settled down to raise our children. But circumstances changed and my husband and I decided to move from our small community in northern Manitoba, where we had both grown up. Coming to the city was quite an adjustment, as we were country folk unaccustomed to the ways of city life. We would order pizza and laugh as the deliveryman delivered it to our home. To us this was a foreign luxury—but one we quickly became accustomed to.

There were many such adjustments to be made when I decided to enter university. I had to learn just about everything, from taking a city bus, to finding my way around the university. Even with my map, the university seemed of an enormous size. I also had to struggle with self-doubts and there were many such tormenting thoughts such as: Do I really belong here? Am I intelligent enough to succeed? Can I make it all balance with family considerations and school? The first month was the most stressful but once I got into a routine it felt like the most natural thing in the world. I settled into learning with enthusiasm and eagerly looked forward to my classes. All my earlier doubts vanished; I was now confident in my abilities and determined that I would meet the goals I had set.

This determination was what got me past the difficulties—every time an obstacle was presented to me I faced it, I went over, under, through, or around it. I would keep looking for the answer to a problem until I found it. I learned not to be afraid to ask for help if I needed it from my professors. They were all excellent to me and more than happy to offer their assistance when I had questions about lecture material. When you present yourself to them they see that you are an active participant in your education, and that you are serious about your studies. Professors cannot be mind readers; if you are having a problem you must take the first step and approach them. You will find that the professors are respectful of you as a person; they do not talk down to you or make you feel like you should know the material; they enjoy teaching and are usually more than willing to facilitate you in your learning.

The important thing to remember when returning to university is that nobody can make your dreams come true, but you! Seize hold of your dreams and refuse to be intimidated by circumstances, whatever they may be. Resolve to do your absolute best in all that you do and don't let the odd disappointment get you down. There will be disappointments—be ready for it and accept it. It is all part of the learning experience. I know for me, the first essay that I had to write was overwhelming; I had no idea where to start. I really depended on my professor for that one and it went well. I also had some marks on tests that I wasn't too impressed with. But again, I learned from my mistakes and tried to do better the next time.

There are many difficulties that you will face when you embark upon your new adventure, but I'm sure it will be one of the most rewarding experiences of your life. It will draw strength out of you that you never knew existed. It is both a personal and academic journey you are on and I wish you the best of effort in your studies!

We live in a world of connections. We live, learn, and work beside people. We are part of our community. It is the identification with the community, whether it is our home, school, church, work, or social community that provides a sense of belonging. As the advances in technology and globalization make the world smaller, interdependent, and interconnected, we recognize more than ever that we are citizens of the global community. With this interdependence, cooperation becomes especially important. Finding meaningful ways to work within groups, understand different perspectives, appreciate diversity, and bridge perspectives facilitates greater cooperation. We are increasingly tied to one another economically, politically, and personally. Thus knowing how to develop partnerships, collaborate across differences and foster greater understanding is essential to creating a community that sustains people. Establishing a sense of community is critical, first for success in university and second for success in all of life.

As a first-year university student you are meeting new people, forming new friendships, and developing new connections. You are becoming part of your new community. At the same time your relationships with friends you have had for awhile may be changing as you develop other interests, see each other less frequently and pursue different programs of study. The opportunity to create a new community in university prepares you to hone the skills and strategies that will facilitate your next transition to the world of work. This chapter will assist you in understanding the importance and impact of diverse communities on your personal identity. It will also provide ideas for expanding your awareness and understanding of the perspectives of others so that you are better able to bridge differences and collaborate productively. Moreover, it will provide you with alternatives for gaining the social support that facilitates academic success.

Much of who you are evolves from the relationships you have. Others teach you about yourself. The relationships you have with family, friends, teachers, professors, and employers provide you with important feedback about who you are, skills you have, and personal characteristics you possess. As you learn to interact with these diverse people and forge long, lasting relationships you develop enhanced self-esteem. The social self-development model on page 234 illustrates that finding a sense of belonging and building a sense of community are fundamental elements of a student's social identity. In enhancing and expanding your social identity, you develop competencies that are useful personally and professionally.

Your success in refining your social identity begins with expanding your self-awareness of your current abilities, in comparison with those used by successful students. Your answers to the questions in Chapter 2 provide you with initial baseline information that is useful in assessing your social attitudes and actions. Because your social identity is influenced by your involvement in your community, an important element in your initial self-awareness assessment is to evaluate your knowledge of the resources, support systems, and opportunities available to you in your institution. Once aware you can select how utilizing these can be personally beneficial to you. As you learned in Chapter 1, developing interpersonal competence, which includes connecting with others, appreciating diversity, and engaging in altruistic actions, is one of the developmental tasks in first-year university (Chickering & Reisser, 1993; Kuh, 1993). Your success in connecting to others is enhanced by your attitude toward others and by your abilities.

It is easier to reach out to others when you feel self-confident. Self-confidence is enhanced when you develop attitudes of open-mindedness and acceptance of others regardless of their social status, sexual orientation, or race. The abilities that add to your social identity focus on both your academic and social self-concepts. Through your academic activities you develop knowledge of cultural, social, and global issues that allows you to bridge discipline differences, learn from others, and become an integral part of the global community. Through the social interactions and activities of study groups, team-building training, and diversity-awareness exercises you develop personal competencies that help you collaborate effectively with others. As you progress through this chapter, your awareness of the skills that successful students use, and your ability to identify your own abilities, adapt them, and add others will ensure that you possess the social skills to nurture and sustain vital, diverse, and meaningful relationships.

What is Community?

Community is defined as "a unified body of individuals" where "people with common interests live in a particular area," or "an interacting population of various kinds of indi-

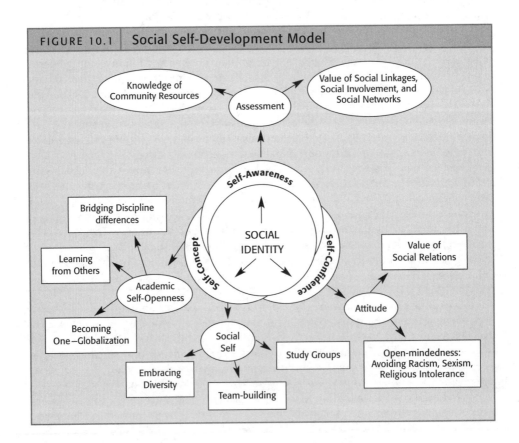

FIGURE 10.1 | Social Self-Development Model

viduals in a common location" (Merriam-Webster, 1986). As a university student, there are various communities that have an impact on your well-being. Successful students are involved in their personal, academic, local, and global communities (Astin, 1997). It is the support services of each of these communities that are so important to the success of the student. Successful students have discovered that involvement in their community adds to their academic advantage. By developing greater awareness of the importance of each community to your personal development, and learning tips for increasing your involvement in communities, you become better able to achieve the success you desire. The following descriptions will inform you of the unique contributions of various communities to your success, thus assisting you in being better able to use the resources they provide.

Personal Community

The personal community is defined as your immediate family and friends. They include your parents, siblings, spouse or partner, children, and immediate circle of close friends. Successful students often have supportive relationships from their personal communities. Sometimes it may involve a number of different members from their personal community, and other times it might only be one member who provides all the support needed.

Influence of Personal Community

Various members of the personal community are known to influence the success of the university student. These include immediate family members, close friends, children, and supporting spouses. The family has been viewed as one of the most important sources of success for college students, particularly in predicting students' personal adjustment (Gurung, Sarason, Keeker, & Sarason, 1992). Studies demonstrate that the socio-economic factors of the family, the amount of communication among family members, and the learning activities of supportive parents have an impact on student learning (Astin, 1997). A students' persistence toward their degree completion is influenced by their personal community (Grosset, 1997). Parents, children, and supporting spouses increase the success of a student (Grosset, 1997). Likewise, peer support and satisfying peer relations are influential in the academic success of students (Astin, 1997). The support provided by a student's personal community has a direct influence on his or her success.

Productive Involvement in Your Personal Community

Fundamental to being a successful student is ensuring that these supportive relationships with members of the personal community continue. For the traditional 18–22-year-old student, attending a university often means moving away from home. Geographically removed from your personal community, it is important that you continue to remain in touch. There are various ways that you can do this. "Snail mail," e-mail, Internet, Instant Messaging, and the telephone provide useful vehicles for maintaining contact, receiving encouragement, and sharing life experiences. Regular visits help you stay connected with the members of your personal community. As discussed in Chapter 8, face-to-face contact is the most effective form of communication. However, regardless of how you keep in touch with your supportive personal community, it is critical that you do it consistently and regularly. In doing so, your support system is continuually updated and can provide more immediate support when you need it.

Although geographic distance may challenge your relationships, it also has the powerful influence of strengthening the most important ones. Separation often allows you to develop new dimensions in your relationship as you establish your independent identity. In some instances, a strained relationship may be resolved through geographical distance. A new perspective may take shape and provide a new way of interacting with one another. Often distance provides the opportunity to mature and the chance to test the values of your parents, thereby providing you with a totally new and healthy perspective of your relationship to those at home. Thus, part of being a successful student is continuing to nurture the relationships already established within your personal community, and re-creating others.

Even students who remain in their home community may notice a change in their connections to their personal community. Striving to manage the demands of multiple roles and achieve academic success often means that there is less time for normal family activities or regular outings with friends. Learning to balance the academic demands with the social support of your personal community is important.

Academic Community

In a community of learners the most important role of faculty members, administrators, employees, and departments is to help students achieve their goals. The academic community is rich with resources that can help you attain the success you desire.

Influence of the Academic Community

The influence of the academic community is demonstrated not only through information that students learn, but also through the relationships that are established, and the many opportunities for social integration. The most common and most effective are the professor-student relationship and the student-student relationship. The professor-student relationship occurs both in and outside of class as professors nurture students' social and academic potentials. Relationships with other academic support people are also important and include student advisers, peer mentors, support groups, club members, sport team members, political members, and religious groups. Student-student relationships are fueled by supportive environments such as study groups, extracurricular activities, and living in residence.

Professor-Student Relationship   A significant part of your involvement in the academic community is your relationships with your professors. Not only are they your potential academic mentors, guiding your development as a student scholar, they can also provide you with direction to summer employment and careers, as well as connections to the global academic community for graduate training, research, and authorships. Professor-student relationships are crucial to student educational attainment. Studies demonstrate that professor-student interactions contribute to students' perceptions of classroom climate and to their sense of belonging (MacKinnon, 1999). They are related to student success and persistence at degree completion (Astin, 1997). A positive relationship with a professor, both in and outside of class empowers students to overcome barriers and achieve academic success (Astin, 1997). Thus, central to your success as a student is an ability to establish and maintain a positive professional relationship with the professor both in and outside of class. For more details, refer to Chapter 8, on developing relationships with professors. Also, complete the exercise on page 237 as your first step in developing relationships with professors.

Exercise 10.1 PROFESSOR INTERVIEW

In groups of four students, create a list of 10 questions that will help you get to know your professor better. For example, ask the professor to relate any of their experiences as students, how many years they went to school in order to complete their degrees, what they would recommend to be successful as a student, etc.

After a list of 10 questions has been established, have your professor preview the questions to ensure that they are appropriate.

In groups of two, approach a professor and ask for an interview. Provide at least two weeks notice of your request.

Get to the interview on time, ask the questions, and thank the professor for his or her time.

Join your original group of four and compare notes on the two professors interviewed. To what extent are they approachable?

Student-Student Relationship   Support from your on-campus friends is likely to predict your sense of belonging, your adjustment, your coping, your perception of the classroom climate, and your successful academic performance (Hertel, 1997; Inman & Pascarella, 1998; MacKinnon, 1999). There are a variety of student-student relationships that are conducive to your success as a student. These include learning or study groups, residence relationships, student advisers or mentors, and friendships formed through involvement in extracurricular activities. For most students, it is these peer connections that become the relationships they most value throughout their university years.

Learning or Study Groups   The student-student relationship in the form of study groups stands out as one of the most effective social networks for successful students. The reason for this powerful dynamic is that study groups provide an increase in success because of the multiple points of view that each group member represents. There are various opportunities for each group member to be a consultant to the rest. As you may recall from the pyramid chart on page 59, there is value in teaching each other as a means of learning effectively. Each person provides various experiences and abilities that can be used to help the other group members. For instance, understanding and reviewing lecture material is more effective as each member brings his or her knowledge, awareness, and perception to the task of synthesizing the concepts together in a study group. Furthermore, writing tasks are enhanced as each member becomes an editor for major research assignments. For successful presentations, the group is a mock audience on which to test new ideas. In the long run, successful study groups advance the efficiency and economy of studying and researching ideas. They are a primary source of encouragement, resources, assistance, and advice.

As students become more integrated with each other, the potential of success for the group grows. For instance, successful study groups, known as "high octane groups," find a balance between friendship and academics that gives them an edge for success (MacKinnon, 1999). Friendship provides the basis for a relaxed atmosphere for learning. The provision of clear guidelines for the rotation of leadership roles within the group allows all group members to see their roles as important for the overall functioning of the group and the success of one another (Woods, 1994). "Other" study groups, where participants are less familiar with each other and more serious initially, demonstrate less confidence, are less proactive, and not as successful (MacKinnon, 1999).

Residence Relationships   Students who live in the university community, as compared to commuters, are consistently more engaged in educational, interpersonal, and social systems through extra curricular, cultural, and social activities that nurture greater levels of cognitive growth (Astin, 1997; Inman & Pascarella, 1998). This includes higher levels of participation in honours programs, extra reading, more studying in a library, or discussing schoolwork with friends (Chickering, 1974). Through the residence living arrangements students form social connections to each other and the institution, as well as valuable interpersonal skills such as communicating with peers, negotiating living arrangements, and accepting other's lifestyle habits.

Advisers or Mentors   An **adviser** or **mentor** is often referred to as "an ally, a friend, someone who takes a personal and professional interest in you" (Kanar, 2001, p. 4). Many successful students become student advisers or peer mentors. They can be influential allies, as some have recently experienced being a first-year student and understand the course demands and social issues that are important. Student advisers provide direction and guidance for important academic decisions about course selection, regulations, section transfer, and class withdrawals. Mentors are more personal, tend to know you better than other academic members, and can provide you with advice as you move through your academic journey. Mentors come in all types: older siblings, graduate students, alumni, and established successful people, and can provide guidance in how to prepare for careers as you venture through the academic landscape.

Friendships through Extracurricular Activities   Another well-documented finding is that social integration in the form of involvement in extracurricular activities has a positive impact on students' critical thinking (Inman & Pascarella, 1998), and is important to overall academic achievement (Kuh, 1993). This includes participation in campus events and student organizations, such as clubs, recreational sports, political organizations, religious groups, and support groups. These activities allow you to practise, to exercise, or to experiment with the material learned in class. In doing so, you extend your learning from the classroom to real-life situations as you expand your friendship network.

One element overlooked by many students is their spiritual side. Regardless of one's beliefs or faith, every person has a religious need (Maslow, 1970). Even the atheist is a spiritual being, holding fast to a belief in atheism. Finding others on campus with similar beliefs provides support and nourishment for the soul. Here too, one can find various levels of resources. On most campuses you can find student faith groups and chaplains who serve as spiritual advisers. These groups provide social activities, discussion groups, and informal support. Consultation, advice and counselling is often available from each of the spiritual representatives. Take advantage of developing your whole being by also addressing your spiritual needs.

Support groups defined as "a network of people to whom you can turn for advice, answer to questions, or boost in confidence" (Kanar, 2001, p. 3), are also important to your success. The university campus provides many opportunities to join various support groups such as the Diabetes Support Group, the Single-Parent Student Group, and Commuter Group. These groups are organized around a particular interest area and provide a variety of informal and formal support.

Although participation in extracurricular activities adds to your success at university, there is also the potential for your participation to detract from your success as a student. Sometimes becoming over-involved leaves too little time for the academic priorities that are important. Unfortunately, this can include participation in athletic events. Studies show potential adverse effects of participating in athletic sports toward academic success (Inman & Pascarella, 1998). One of the biggest factors is the commitment required to perform sports that often overshadows the commitment required to be a successful student. Although it is possible to be a successful athlete and a successful student, the balance requires effort and preplanning to ensure success on both parts. For some students a good compromise is to focus on intramural-type sports, which integrate play with social networking.

By forming various student-student relationships you are able to add to your academic success, personal development, and self-confidence (Astin, 1997; MacKinnon, 1999; Tinto, 1997). Academically, your friends can serve as role models for becoming a successful student and provide access to resources that may enhance your success. Your personal development is also influenced by your relationships to other students. Peers are known to have an impact on students' interpersonal competence, personal values, and overall maturity (Astin, 1997). Moreover, as you have opportunities to exchange ideas with peers, your self-confidence is often impacted, especially through the encouragement of your peers. Thus, student-student relationships are important for your success and should be highly valued.

Productive Involvement in Your Academic Community

Identifying the Resources   Part of successfully accessing your resources in the academic community is knowing who and where these resources are. Although academic communities have campus handbooks and directories, a successful student creates a personal directory of resources and resource people. Create your own directory by completing the exercise on page 240.

Informal Peer Network   Successful students are one of your best contacts for identifying key resources. Seek out students who have completed the course, program, or degree that you are seeking and ask questions about resources. These students have survived various challenges, figured out short-cuts, and experienced success as a result of various resources. Ask these former students about effective resource centres, best programs, best workshop facilitators, and the most helpful student advisers, and make note of these.

Paper and Online Resources   Paper resources such as campus directories, institution calendars, student directories, student handbooks, and student newspapers provide listings of resource people and resource centres on your campus. Make note of the resources that you might need during the year. Next, go online to the university's Web site and conduct a search on the various "help" resources. Make a note or bookmark the URLs for future access.

Resource Centres   Once identified, make a visit to each of these resource centres or resource people to find out the numerous programs, activities or services that may be helpful to you at various stages in your university career, when they are available (i.e.,

Exercise 10.2 PERSONAL CAMPUS RESOURCE DIRECTORY

Create your own campus handbook, checking out all the resources on campus prior to classes, asking questions at all the different centres, creating a list of resource people, finding out what is available to you, the names of contact persons, if costs are involved, and resource offerings.

Resource	Resource People	What is available	When is it available	Cost	Contact
Student Resource Centre	*Adviser X*	*Test-Taking Workshop*	*Oct 19, 2002*	*$10*	*Phone or e-mail*
• admission					
• advising facilities					
• career development office					
• carpool centres					
• child-care centre					
• counselling					
• exchange programs					
• job-placement office					
• library					
• off-campus housing					
• registration					
• security					
• sports facilities					
• student disability services centre					
• student information centre					
• student international centre					
• student learning centre					
• student records					
• student resource centre					
• student union/student centre					
• tutoring & special services					

workshops), and possible costs. Equally important is to identify the best experts and means of contacting them (i.e., telephone numbers and e-mail addresses).

Networking

Networking, a fairly new word established in 1966, is defined as "the exchange of information or services among individuals, groups, or institutions." It is the framework on which you build success with a community. Creating contact, or networking, is your responsibility. By establishing links with others you are able to make your learning environment responsive to your needs for success. Being new to campus can place a certain amount of fear in students. Networking involves reaching out to others in spite of shyness. It reminds you to focus on being interested in others rather than on yourself. Critical to being successful as a new student is to make contact with others in your community by joining established groups or creating new ones.

Participating in Groups

Successful Group Dynamics

Participating in groups is vital for your success as a student. Groups provide the basis for your academic and social success in university. By belonging to various groups you learn about yourself, about others, and about your community. Whether you join an existing group or form a new group, fundamental to making the group successful is an understanding of group development and dynamics. Groups follow predictable stages of development. Knowing these stages can help you make the most of your experience. There are four phases of group development. At each phase, the group develops a more stable sense of its group identity (Kieffer, 2001). These phases include dependency and inclusion, counterdependency and fight, trust and structure phase, and productivity and effectiveness (Wheelan & Tilin, 1999). A useful process for understanding these four phases is to consider their importance in establishing a study group.

The first phase, **dependency** and **inclusion**, describes the dependency of group members on a strong, designated leader as they discuss procedures for ensuring commitment from all members and equality in the distribution of the workload (Wheelan & Tilin, 1999). To ensure that members feel involved and included, it is important to specify the group goals, clarify expectations, and explain procedures. Specific information about attendance, the focus of study sessions, the time duration of the group, and the assignment of roles for activities are part of this stage. Roles include the **climate facilitator**, a person who monitors and evaluates the concerns, needs and frustrations of group members to ensure effective group functioning; the **recorder**, the member who keeps a written account of what happens during the meetings; and the **task facilitator,** the member who keeps the group on task and moving toward the shared goal by checking on the progress of group members.

Next is the stage of **counter-dependency** and fight, defined by disagreement and conflict among members, about group goals and procedures. This is a period in which members may question the procedures previously established and change some of the rules. There may be disagreements in the group. These power struggles are useful as they provide a vehicle for the group to re-evaluate its priorities and establish a unified set of values and objectives that is reflective of the needs of the group (Wheelan & Tilin, 1999). Ironically, it is through conflict that trust and a safe climate are established in which members feel free to disagree with each other. Some members may feel like they want to drop out of the group at this time; therefore, processes to ensure they remain are important for ongoing development. Structured processes to help members move constructively from conflict to renewed commitment are important.

As the group members' communication becomes more open and task-oriented, the group moves into the **trust** and **structure** phase. During this phase, members move toward solidifying positive relationships with each other (Wheelan & Tilin, 1999). They know more clearly the strategies that are working best in improving their studying and learning and have figured out how to use one another's strengths to personal advantage.

During the final stage, **interdependence**, the group feels more like a team. Their meetings are productive, they are clearer in their goals and more effective in ensuring they meet those goals The energy formerly used to resolve issues is now channeled toward goal achievement and task accomplishment (Wheelan & Tilin, 1999). Groups achieving this level, such as "high-octane" groups, produce more than groups at other levels (Wheelan & Tilin, 1999).

Creating Communities with Technology

Commuters and students learning by correspondence share a common challenge with students living on campus—the challenge of networking with others. Given that social integration with others is so important in a student's achievement of success, it is useful for you emulate the activities of your on-campus colleagues by establishing Web study and discussion groups by linking through online platforms such as WebCT or Blackboard. You may also identify resources that can help your success through the Web.

Local Community

The local community is defined as the various organizations outside of the academic community that have an impact on your well-being as a student. These organizations are not only ones that contribute to you as a student, but are also ones to which you contribute. Members of the local community include business professionals, government officials, local community action groups, agencies, and non-profit organizations. Just as you are supported by your personal and academic community, your local community also provides you with volunteer opportunities, part-time employment, career opportunities, mentors, and information.

Getting to Know Your Local Community

There are various sources for identifying your local community resources. These include paper resources such as the telephone directory, local newspapers, journals and newsletters, and local libraries. You can also search electronic Web sites or government and non-profit organization offices, and facilities such as recreation centres, child-care centres, healthcare centres, places of worship, crisis centres, and helping organizations.

Influence of the Local Community

Students have discovered the academic and social benefits of linking their academic learning to their experiences in the local community (Chapman & Morley, 1999). Involvement provides students with expanded social networks, an awareness of the interconnection of local issues to course content, and personal development. There are various volunteer opportunities available, including Big Brothers/Big Sisters (*www.bbsc.ca*); soup kitchens; Meals on Wheels (*www.projectmeal.org*); candy striping at hospitals; visiting the elderly in homes; working for institutionalized children, M2-W2 programs (*www.m2w2.com*); and volunteering with refugees. Benefits include enhanced understanding of course content, integration of theory with practice, an increased awareness of the complex causes of social problems, a heightened understanding of human differences, and improved preparation for the world of work (Jacoby, 1999).

The community provides a variety of employment opportunities. However, there are limitations to the benefits of employment. Working more than 15–20 hours per week and employment that does not parallel your course content can adversely affect academic achievement (Astin, 1997; Inman & Pascarella, 1998; Schoenhals, Tienda, & Schneider, 1998). The reason for this is that employment during university, particularly off-campus work, takes students away from the intellectually stimulating environment of academia, especially in work settings requiring mundane tasks.

Global Community

The global community refers to the opportunities to connect with people from around the world as a result of modern technology and the convenience of travel.

Getting to Know Your Global Community

One way to become more aware of the global community is to participate in travel-study opportunities and international exchanges. Many institutions are connected with other partner institutions worldwide that allow students to register for programs at their home institution and to pay the tuition rates of their home institution, while attending the partner institutions. These opportunities provide invaluable experience as well as connections for future careers and friendships. Above all, these global experiences will stretch your worldview, provide rich and stimulating intellectual growth, expand your social network, and permit an exchange of ideas. Cultural experiences improve students' learning and overall success (Astin, 1997; Inman & Pascarella, 1998).

An ideal place to start preparing for an international exposure is at your institution's international resource centre. Former students often manage these centres and can share their international experiences and give you valuable information. By including international students as part of your friendship circle you will have the privilege of discovering firsthand their culture and their worldview. These international students can provide you with valuable information about their culture, the best institutions in their country, important contacts, and tips about what to anticipate when traveling or studying in their country.

Another way to become aware of your global community is to participate in any one of many international volunteer programs. There are many to choose from, including para-church organizations such as Mennonite Central Committee (*www.mennonitecc.ca*),

Habitat for Humanity (*www.habitat.org*), United Way (*www.uwint.org*), Peace Corps (*www.peacecorps.gov*), OXFAM, and WUSC (World University Service). Many students choose to travel abroad to teach English as a second language and thus learn through this process of sharing, exploring, and mutual teaching. Each one of these opportunities will provide you with valuable life experiences that move beyond the walls of the classroom.

Cultural Awareness: Embracing Diversity

Today's academic community is reflective of globalization as more and more international students are sharing learning environments with Canadians. Globalization provides learning opportunities for exchanging ideas with students from many social, cultural, and religious backgrounds who represent various worldviews. Cultural diversity is defined as the way in which humans are different by virtue of their age, socioeconomic class, ethnicity, gender, physical and mental ability, race, sexual orientation, and spiritual practices (Pascarella, Whitt, Edison, & Nora, 1997; Whitt, Edison, Pascarella, Nora, & Terenzini, 1999).

There are moral, intellectual, and social grounds for all members of the academic community to attend to diversity (Karenga, 1995). Morally, there is a need for mutual respect between learners and educators as individuals. Intellectually, embracing multiple perspectives provides holistic growth through the challenges and contrasts that are brought by a diverse group of people. Socially, it is imperative to actively practise justice and equity among people. Key to embracing diversity is a good understanding and appreciation of cultural differences, a commitment to dealing with the barriers thwarting cultural diversity, and a willingness to embrace and celebrate the value of diversity.

Gaining Cultural Awareness

An important aspect of embracing cultural diversity is becoming fully aware of the differences and the issues. University is a community of diversity, consisting of a variety of different people, all with different needs and services. These include both visible and invisible differences. Within the university there are individuals of different racial and religious origin, people of different ages, sexual orientations, political beliefs, and language.

Gather Information

There are numerous ways to become aware of the different types of cultures within your academic environment. Visit student centres such as the international students group or a non-traditional religious group. Make an effort to meet people who are different from you so that you can learn from them. When considering topics for papers, you may wish to write about areas such as learning disabilities, cultural values, or gender differences— your academic learning about these topics can broaden your awareness. Contact your Equity Office for more information and for workshops that provide education about differences. Check the Web for information. The more you engage in discovering the diversity on your campus, the greater your understanding of others will become.

Become Involved or Immersed

Immerse yourself in a different culture. Find time to get to know others from a different culture. The Aboriginal community has a powerful metaphor that best illustrates this—to walk in the moccasins of the other person. This means trying to fully immerse yourself in the other's situation, rich history, culture, and way of thinking. As you do this, you will discover a wealth of new ideas and new experiences. As you interact and engage with people from diverse backgrounds, you cannot help but become influenced by their thinking, thereby enhancing your limited worldview. Immersion allows you to benefit from the wisdom of other cultures and become better able to look beyond stereotypes and appreciate individual characteristics.

Assessing Attitudes and Actions

In order to embrace cultural diversity, it is necessary to have a good understanding of the attitudes and actions that people have, including your own, toward other cultures. The learning environment of many institutions in Canada is still strongly Euro-centric in focus, rewarding students who think and act consistently with the traditional European model of education. This dominant culture can make you feel either very comfortable, or it can inadvertently or even deliberately exclude you. This cultural perspective can be a barrier to students whose native language is not English, those who prefer alternative ways of knowing and those who are not as experienced with the mainstream culture (Collett & Serrano, 1992). As a result, these students experience any number of the following negative attitudes and behaviours.

Discrimination is defined as the systematic, intentional or unintentional, denial of recognition, power, privilege, and opportunity to certain people based on the groups to which they belong (Collins, 1998; Crawford & MacLeod, 1990). Examples include access to resources, such as computers and classrooms limited only to mobile people, or grades on an assignment, based on how closely the work parallels the professor's worldview.

Stereotyping is defined as the behaviour that influences the expectations of certain individuals (Collins, 1998). For instance, blond-haired people and athletes are inaccurately stereotyped as "dumb blondes" and "stupid jocks," mature students are assumed to be "wise," while Asian students are often perceived as intelligent and gifted in the hard sciences. Each of these actions thwarts the potential of learning not only for the person being discriminated against, but also for all other students who could benefit from the different worldviews. In order for learning to increase, members of the academic community strive to embrace diversity.

Awareness of Negative Attitudes and Actions

In order to embrace diversity and engage in the pluralistic learning environment, the barriers—discrimination, stereotyping, and alienation—need to be removed. Identifying that these barriers do exist is the first step. This requires an awareness of your attitudes and actions, as well as the attitudes and actions of others. Observe yourself. Notice your language. It can be useful to keep a journal and record your observations. Reflect on your thinking patterns in regards to students from diverse backgrounds. It is quite possible that you may find that some of your attitudes and actions reflect prejudices you may not have previously acknowledged. Thus, part of your development is learning alternative attitudes and views. Be aware of common terms that may offend someone, such as "homosexual," "Oriental," "girls," "Indians," and use terms that are more sensitive such as "gays and lesbians," "Asian," "women," "Indigenous," or "Aboriginal." Spend time unlearning the expectations you have that promote discrimination and find new attitudes that will help you embrace diversity.

Taking a Stand

Take a stand against discrimination. Stand up for those being discriminated against. When you hear a racist joke, interrupt the conversation and let the speaker know of the offence. When students are excluded due to their cultural representation, find ways to actively engage them as part of your group. Participation in class discussions is usually dominated by white males, who speak more often and for a longer duration of time than white females and all other students of colour (Sadker & Sadker, 1992). If you are a white male student, do your part to encourage more discussion by your female and non-white peers. If you are not a white male, find ways to become more confident in actively participating in discussions both with your professors and with your peers. When presenting formally or informally, attempt to present material from the perspectives of diverse people.

Requesting Inclusion

If you feel that you and your cultural group are not being fairly represented, request inclusion. If another member of the learning community offends you, let them know this. Ideally, this is best done privately to minimize embarrassment, further alienation, and defensive responding. When you feel shy or find it difficult to discuss your observations with the individual, find a peer who will support you. Approach the person with another student and engage in "I" messages (see Chapter 8), express your concern, give reasons for your own reactions, and ask for understanding and respect. If you have a specific request for a professor, be precise in clarifying your request. In those situations in which you desire specific accommodations to enhance your learning, make certain that you have the proper documentation to support your request. Universities have policies regarding accommodations for assistance in the classroom, so check with the learning resource or learning disabilities centre if you have questions. The goal is to work collaboratively within the community so that you are able to fully participate and engage in the learning process. When appropriate, professors are willing to explore options for accommodating your worldview, your learning style, and your learning challenges through alternative learning and test-taking formats.

Consulting the Experts

In situations where the discrimination continues or is too challenging to overcome, keep a record of all offensive occurrences and behaviours, both verbal and nonverbal, along with the time of day and date on which they took place. Seek guidance from your Student Advocacy Office, Equity Services, or Counselling Centre on your campus. These people are trained to restore the pluralistic learning environment. They will represent you and your cultural group to ensure equity in the learning process. They are also available to educate others through workshops and informational resources.

In the ideal **pluralistic university community**, all worldviews are treated equally and the equity of all members is rewarded. Mutual respect, acceptance, teamwork, and productivity are evident. A pluralistic culture reflects the interests, contributions, and values of all of its members. Differences are celebrated, as they provide a competitive intellectual advantage. Importantly, all members have full and influential participation in the decisions and policies that shape the learning environment. Therefore, the learning climate is safe and secure for both students and professors.

With an awareness of cultural diversity and an appreciation of the differences that you and your peers represent, you can more successfully move forward in embracing these differences. Everyone benefits, as sharing worldviews increases knowledge, and increasing understanding builds community. For you, this knowledge has direct benefits on your academic success and personal relationships (Inman & Pascarella, 1998).

Dealing with Cultural Shock

An important aspect of the experience you may have as you travel to other cultures is cultural shock. Cultural shock is precipitated by the anxiety that results from losing all familiar signs and symbols of social interaction (Arthur, 2001). When a person enters a strange culture, familiar cues are removed. Without these unwritten rules regarding appropriate behaviour, people may experience frustration and anxiety.

Studies show that predictable stages occur when people enter a new culture, country, or environment (Pederson, 1995). International students are expected to go through culture shock. Most first-year university students also experience it. Prime candidates for intense culture shock are first-generation college students, students who performed well in high school with little effort, and students who have moved from a large city to a small college town or vice versa. When the university environment is quite different from the original home environment, traveling through these stages may take longer. For the most part, the length and intensity of each stage varies from person to person. The steps of adjustment are the honeymoon phase, the hostility phase, the humour phase, and the at-home phase.

Honeymoon Phase

The honeymoon stage is usually the most exciting phase. The student is fascinated by and eager to explore the new academic environment. Everything is new. Everything is exciting. There are positive feelings associated with the adventure. However, this novelty does wear off. When the student finally moves into the next phase, it can come as a surprise to those who have made this assumption. Thoughts such as, "I don't know who I am any more," or, "I think I made a mistake by making this choice," are indications that someone is leaving the honeymoon stage of cultural adjustment.

Hostility Phase

The hostility stage is characterized by a hostile and aggressive attitude toward the host culture or country. The student new to the environment realizes the differences between the two cultures and longs for something familiar. He/she finds fault with many things in this culture, especially things that are different from his or her home culture. They may become uncomfortable with the food, the living arrangements, and even the social behaviours. This is often the stage in which stereotypes are formed, based on the hostile and aggressive behaviours often displayed by students going through this stage. The student in this stage may try to escape from the uncomfortable environment. Some individuals long to return home, others drop out of school. Some students become depressed, worried, physically ill, or cope by drinking or taking drugs. An unfortunate outcome in this stage for some students involves suicide. At this stage it is particularly important to find positive alternatives to the feelings you are experiencing.

Humour Phase

In this phase, the person begins to see the humour in the difficulties he or she is having rather than criticizing others for them. During my stay with a gypsy community, I learned very quickly to laugh at my Canadian mannerisms that were very contrary to the acceptable norms. As a new first-year student or a student from a different culture, learning to laugh at the various challenges that you have to face is healthy and allows you to move forward as you meet new cultural challenges.

At-Home Phase

When the visitor embraces the customs of the new culture, the at-home phase has been reached. Anxiety disappears. He or she accepts and begins to enjoy many of the foods, drinks, habits, and customs of the new culture. Once you have arrived at this stage, you will feel comfortable learning in the new environment.

Re-Entry Phase

When a cultural adventurist returns to his or her former environment, he or she goes through a re-entry process, repeating many of the above phases. The student is excited to be home, feels some hostility when it is not the same as he or she remembered it, sees humor in the differences between the two cultures, and eventually feels at home once again in the native culture.

   These steps are often seen in students as they move through the academic culture. Some go through these steps very quickly, keenly adopting the predominant cultural habits and ways of social interaction. These are the successful students. Others struggle with the new expectations placed on them by the academic community. Some experience such high levels of anxiety, homesickness, and depression, even to the point of exasperation, that they return home. Understanding the process of cultural adjustment can reduce the anxiety associated with it. When you are aware that these stages are a normal part of adjusting to a new culture, you may be able to pass through them with less anxiety. A role model (someone who has successfully become a part of a new culture) can be especially effective in easing this transition.

It's More Than Common Sense

Hidden Disabilities and Academic Success

Donald W. Stewart, Ph.D.
University of Manitoba

Our universities are becoming increasingly diverse institutions. Changing economic realities, globalization, and an emphasis on accessibility have all contributed to dramatic changes in who now attends university. As these changes have occurred, however, universities have struggled to keep pace with the increased challenges posed by the unique needs of some of these diverse constituencies.

Today, people with so-called "hidden disabilities" constitute one of the fastest-growing segments within our diverse university communities. However, unlike students with physical disabilities, such as mobility impairments, students with hidden disabilities are not visibly different from others. Similarly, the types of supports and strategies to enhance their academic success are also less apparent than, say, wheelchair ramps or guide dogs.

Students with hidden disabilities may fall into several categories. The most common are those with learning disabilities and/or attention deficits, cognitive impairment, or psychological conditions. Of these, students with learning disabilities (LD), who may comprise up to 10 percent of the Canadian university population (Hardy Cox & Klas, 1996), are probably the most likely to self-identify and seek out services (Stewart, Cornish, & Somers, 1995).

A learning disability is a neurobiological information-processing disorder (Fiedorowicz, Benezra, MacDonald, McElgunn, & Wilson, 1998), characterized by a significant discrepancy between an individual's overall intellectual ability (which must be at least average), and his or her academic functioning in one or more areas, such as reading comprehension or written expression (American Psychiatric Association, 1994). The diagnosis can only be made by a professional, such as a psychologist, after undergoing a thorough assessment using standardized measures of intellectual ability, information processing, and academic achievement. This information is then combined with historical data, clinical history, and other material to rule out other possible conditions and affirm the LD diagnosis (Stewart, 1994, 1995, 1998).

A learning disability is different than a motivation or skills deficit, language or speech problems, or intellectual deficiency. It is a disabling condition in which an individual's ability to encode or express learned material is not consistent with his or her intellectual ability. For example, a student with LD may be a brilliant abstract thinker, able to easily conceptualize and work with complex theoretical material, yet be unable to comprehend written text beyond a grade six level under timed conditions. Such a student is obviously bright enough to attend university and profit from it, but will clearly struggle with any tasks involving text comprehension. For this reason, *academic accommodations* are offered to students with diagnosed LD to compensate for their information-processing deficits (Scott, 1994). In the example above, the reading-disabled student may be offered taped textbooks to reduce the amount of reading required of him or her, and/or extended time on examinations to allow for a slower rate of reading. A range of other accommodations is available, including various forms of assistive technology (Day & Edwards, 1996), such as speech synthesis software, dependent on documented needs. Whatever their form or nature, all accommodations are offered as a way to "level the playing field" so that students with LD are evaluated on the basis of their abilities rather than their unaccommodated disabilities.

Some other types of hidden disabilities are related to LD, such as attention deficit hyperactivity disorder, which is characterized by significant difficulties in sustaining attention, controlling impulsivity, or both (APA, 1994), or cognitive disabilities, such as memory problems that may arise as a consequence of a head injury sustained in a car accident. Other types of hidden disabilities are related to psychological conditions, such as anxiety disorders or depression, which can interfere with academic functioning.

Psychological disorders are very common on university campuses, although because of the social stigma attached to these conditions (Canadian Mental Health Association, 2000; Weiner & Wiener, 1996), students are less likely to self-identify and seek out services. Anxiety is particularly pervasive, in part because a high-stress academic environment is likely to perpetuate anxiety disorders in those who are predisposed to the development of such conditions. Although exact numbers are difficult to ascertain, surveys of undergraduates using various measures have shown rates of clinically significant anxiety to be in the 20 percent range (Koverola, Proulx, Hanna, Battle, & Chohan, 1992; Proulx, Dyck, Quinonez, Chohan, & Koverola, 1991). When samples of students seeking counselling are examined, the rates go even higher, approaching 50 percent (Degen, Stewart, & Walker, 2000; Stewart, Johnson, Walker, & Degen, 2001). Not all students with high levels of anxiety require academic accommodations, such as a private testing space and extended time to allow for anxiety management practise, but it is clear that a subset of these students will be substantially disadvantaged without these resources (Stewart, 2001).

The practice of providing academic accommodations for students with hidden disabilities is controversial (Williams & Ceci, 1999). Although bona fide disabilities are recognized under federal and provincial human rights legislation as conditions requiring reasonable accommodation, universities struggle to deal with these matters in a balanced, equitable fashion that both respects the needs of the students, and maintains the academic integrity of the institution. For example, some professors may refuse to provide accommodations to students with diagnosed LD because they say it provides them with an unfair advantage over their classmates (Bourke, Strehorn, & Silver, 2000; Nelson, Dodd, & Smith, 1990). Research in this area, however, shows that students without LD profit minimally or not at all from the extended time, whereas students with LD profit substantially more (Alster, 1997; Runyan, 1990). This suggests that the extra time helps the students with LD to fully express what they have learned, but does not help the other students much because they have already expressed what they have learned. On this basis, it does not seem that offering extended time to students who qualify for it is offering them an unfair advantage; rather, it appears to be reducing the unfair disadvantage that an unaccommodated testing situation would pose for them.

Students with hidden disabilities can access services on their campuses through the office of disability services, the university counselling centre, or the student health centre. The first step, after establishing contact with one of these offices, is to arrange a thorough assessment to identify the student's needs and develop a plan to respond to them. Not all students who believe they have a hidden disability actually meet the diagnostic criteria to qualify for accommodations (Stewart, 1994, 1995, 1998), and some will be referred for other types of assistance, such as learning or study skills, or personal counselling.

When properly accommodated, students with hidden disabilities can function well at university and help to enrich the diversity of the campus. Promotion of an atmosphere of acceptance, understanding, and respect for this diversity will go a long way toward ensuring our institutions are accessible—in all respects, for all students.

Self-awareness

What do I know about my own community-building and networking capabilities? I've learned that my strengths in each of the following are:

Networking…

Team building…

Can I describe the capabilities I would like to develop?

Self-confidence

To increase my confidence in my ability to:

network more actively I will…

build teams more confidently I will…

Self-concept

Actions I can take to add to my networking abilities are…

Actions I can take to add to my team-building abilities are…

Chapter Summary

Having a supportive personal community is a great asset, in both your studies and your life. Successful students are integrated into the various social systems of an institution, as well as the local and global communities (Tinto, 1997). Your involvement in your community has a direct bearing on how successful you will be as a student (Astin, 1997). By enhancing your awareness of the value of community, understanding the unique value of various communities, and establishing linkages to these communities, you are able to expand your social identity. An important aspect of developing your community is to practise the skills of networking, team-building, and understanding others. This chapter describes strategies for expanding your awareness of various communities, eliminating barriers that interfere with involvement, and increasing engagement. As you increase your skills in establishing connections to your community, you enhance your sense of belonging and are better able to reach out to others so that they too feel welcome. Involvement and inclusion are fundamental to your motivation to learn, and add to your development personally, intellectually, and socially. By learning the strategies for connecting to your communities you are able to design support systems and socio-cultural environments that enhance your achievement.

Exercises

REFLECT–ACT

The following Reflect–Act exercises are designed to help you develop increased self-awareness of the communities that enhance your learning through the process of reflective thinking, analysis, and productive action. Self-reflection encourages you to consider information you learn and data you collect to increase your ability to know yourself and to manage yourself.

Reflect   Observe the actions and communication patterns of your study or discussion group. Identify one or two group-development strategies that the group could use to improve its functioning.

Act   Provide your group with this information and ask the group to consider this idea as a way to enhance progress and productivity.

Reflect   Of the various culture shock stages, identify the one that best describes where you are now.

Act   In order to deal successfully with culture shock, which stage(s) do you need to embrace? How will you go about this? Are there any individuals who you view as having achieved all the levels of culture shock who might be your mentor?

Reflect   Of the variety of different discriminatory responses toward students from diverse cultures, which ones best represent your experience as a student?

Act   In order to increase your inclusion in the learning environment, reflect on the various strategies that you can use to make your learning environment more pluralistic. If necessary, seek advice from your Equity Officer.

GROUP DISCUSSION

1.   Have the group come up with all the different types of negative phrases or words that stereotype students in the classroom. Discuss how best to deal with these as they come up during class. Describe the best approach for confronting the student who uses these words. Determine the best approach for confronting the professor who uses these words.

2.   As a group, have each person identify their current stage of culture shock. Find ways to help each other through the stages so that all may feel a sense of security in the learning environment.

3.   Compare the opportunities and supports available in the local community with those in the global community.

4.   Have each member of the group describe the rules and conditions in a discussion group that make it comfortable for everyone to participate. Evaluate whether or not these conditions are present in the classroom discussion groups.

APPLY TO LIFE

Now that you have developed an understanding of how to increase your efficiency in building community, developing networks, engaging in study groups, embracing cultural diversity, surviving cultural shock, and dealing with conflict, you can use this information to enhance your own learning environment. Use the following to more clearly discover your strengths and limitations as a networker and a group player. Choose an issue that you are currently dealing with as a student or see another student dealing with in class (e.g., discrimination, alienation, tokenism, etc.), and work your way through the following:

1.   Describe exactly the specific behaviours and attitudes of others that would define one of the forms of prejudices against you or the student in question.

2.   List the potential reasons that might account for this aversive behaviour or set of attitudes.

3. Engage others in discussion and problem solving by providing two to three friends with the information you have gathered in steps one and two and seek options.

4. Synthesize all the material from your discussion and identify the best solution(s).

5. Commit the solution to practice by making yourself accountable to your friends with a plan for acting on the solution.

6. Review with your friends your progress after 1–2 weeks. If your solution is successful, continue. If it requires changes, go through the process of identifying alternative solutions and implementing them.

Evaluating Learning Strategies 5

"There are no mistakes, no coincidences. All events are blessings given to us to learn from."

Elizabeth Kübler-Ross

Success on this educational journey is measured not only by the grades you earn, but also by the insights you gain and the wisdom you acquire as you develop the ability to learn from your experiences. Because learning is a process of experimentation and discovery that occurs through trials, errors, and victories, the better able you are to critically evaluate your performance, the more effective you become as a learner. While courses teach useful information, progress, accomplishments, and disappointments teach lessons about personal patterns that influence learning. The fifth secret, *Evaluating Learning Strategies,* provides an understanding of personal factors that influence achievement.

Learning propels you forward. Learning opens doors to future possibilities. By improving your learning capabilities and enhancing your efficiency, you are better able to achieve the consequences you desire. You can enhance your capabilities as a learner by becoming an objective and active spectator of your own actions. Through careful observations you can describe the repetitive patterns and processes that lead to success or failure. When you identify actions and attitudes that produce achievement, you are able to determine routines you can practise that will gain continued accomplishment. Equally important is to evaluate your failures and mistakes. "There are no mistakes, no coincidences. All events are blessings given to us to learn from." If you are willing to learn from them, failures and mistakes are simply opportunities for learning about yourself. They provide important feedback that allows you to adjust, adapt, and change. This feedback loop guides you, so that when necessary you can correct your course in order to continue along a personal success path.

The learning-style chapter provides you with various tools for evaluating your unique learning method. These tools are resources you can use to strengthen your natural capabilities as a learner. Some tools you will add easily to your learning repertoire, others will take more time. Your willingness to explore, experiment, evaluate, and evolve will allow you to design a personal learning system which maximizes personal accomplishment and academic achievement.

Using Personal Learning Styles for Academic Success

chapter 11

"Trust thyself." Ralph Waldo Emerson

Questions

How do I learn?

In which courses am I learning the most? How do I know?

How can I use my awareness of my own process of learning to improve my chances for success in university?

What adds to my confidence as a learner?

Are there strategies I can adopt that will make me a more efficient learner?

Objectives

- Increase my awareness of my personal learning style.

- Discover strategies for improving learning effectiveness and efficiency.

- Identify the factors that influence differences in learning approaches.

- Understand how to make myself more successful.

- Develop approaches for learning in different situations from professors with different approaches.

- Improve my confidence and competence as a self-directed learner.

Student Success Portrait

Improving My Learning Effectiveness

Steve Quigley
Memorial University

When I entered university in the Fall of 2001, I had no idea what types of challenges would be facing me throughout my first year. I honestly believed that I would fail everything and end up doing very poorly. Basically, university is a completely different learning environment and one in which I had to figure out different ways of learning and studying than I did in high school. The first challenge involved developing better study habits because in university the professors did not constantly remind any students about tests or assignments. Therefore I had to learn to take the initiative to study and keep track of all important due dates. For some of my friends this change in approach was very hard to get used to because they found the amount of independent study and work too much to handle. One helpful hint that worked for me was to buy a wall-sized calendar. I recommend using it on a regular basis, beginning at the start of the term by writing down all the important dates for tests and assignments. This way it is very difficult to forget about due dates. I also write down the dates on which I plan to start studying for a test, and try my best to follow this schedule.

This brings to mind the concepts of review and independent learning. In university it is not acceptable to start studying a day before an exam, or try to pull an "all nighter." All that is needed is regular review sessions, a few days before the exam, and you should be fine. This is what independent learning is all about, taking it upon yourself to review and complete all your work in an organized fashion. As well, it is about learning different ways to learn, and not confining yourself to the ways you learned in high school. I mean, let's face it, high school can be very easy for most students. However, once you enter university everything changes, and people who did extremely well in high school start to get lower scores on tests and exams. This is partly because they are not well adapted to having to do all of their work on their own. They rely on routine lazy habits and basically try to memorize a few definitions or paragraphs in a text the night before a test. Unfortunately, this does not work in university because professors are not concerned with how well you can memorize information. Instead professor's want to see how well you can apply what you have studied, and combine it with prior knowledge that you have, into an answer for a question. Therefore if you cannot develop a way of learning that enables you to cover these aspects, then you will probably find university very tough.

One way that I have learned to study is through hierarchies. Hierarchies are simply ways in which you can take chunks of complicated information and divide the information into something that is related, meaningful, and organized. Now, the hierarchy system may work for some and not work for others. But the idea behind it is that you are giving yourself something visual for each chunk and for the entire course. You will not have to waste your time memorizing lists and words; therefore you can spend more time actually understanding the material that you are studying. As I mentioned, this is not the only learning strategy; some people find it easier to write out notes and study from the notes and diagrams that they have constructed. This method is fine as long as it makes the material meaningful enough so that you have no problem retrieving and understanding it for an exam.

The last point I would like to talk about is directly first-year-related. Since many students are just out of high school it is easy to get caught up in the freedom that exists in university. The only thing I can tell you is don't let freedom interfere with success. I know how important it is to go to all classes despite the fact that the professor probably doesn't know whether or not students are there. Attending classes, studying regularly, and pacing learning are part of accepting personal responsibility for your own learning and success at university. They are essential for becoming an independent learner. That is what it is all about; it starts with you and the choices that you choose to make.

In the end, don't be afraid to tackle the challenge of becoming an independent learner. I think Michael Jordan said it best when he stated, "I've failed over and over in my life. And that is why I succeed." Basically, don't be afraid of the challenges ahead of you. Success happens when you are willing to work hard enough and try your best.

Learning… you have been doing it all your life. There have been moments when you learned easily, freely, almost effortlessly, and other times when learning was difficult and challenging. As you have settled into the routine of listening to lectures, conducting laboratory experiments, searching for library resources, preparing for examinations and writing papers, you have become increasingly aware of the learning demands of university. Some learning tasks are easy for you, while others can feel overwhelming. As you think about your university experience it becomes clear to you that there are a number of ways to approach learning that will allow you to reach your academic goals. You could focus on the course content, on the professor's style, or your own learning approaches. With further reflection it becomes clear that the area in which you have the greatest probability of success is in refining your own abilities as a learner.

The demands and experiences of university may cause you to reflect on the way in which you learn. As you cope with assignments with excessive time demands, required content areas that have always been difficult for you to master, and courses that seem so complex that you doubt your ability to master them, you want more than ever to know what you can do to be successful. Even as you have read the previous chapters of this text and learned about study strategies and personal management processes that produce success in university, you have discovered that knowing these strategies is not enough. Making them work for you is the real challenge. It is so much easier to do what you have always done. In fact, making even simple changes that you know would enhance your success and improve your learning can be difficult. As you figure out how to be the best learner you can be, you recognize that your success depends not just on how well you learn, but also on how you learn. To understand more about how you learn, you need to understand more fully the characteristics of your personal learning style.

You probably already know something about your learning style because of the courses you enjoy and those you do not. However, there is also a lot you do not know. Questions abound.

Why is it possible to easily learn some concepts while others are more difficult to grasp? Are there tips for improving learning efficiency? What are the factors that affect learning abilities? Is it possible to change or adapt learning styles? Are there abilities that affect learning capabilities in particular courses? How does your professor's teaching style affect your ability to learn? Answering these questions and others like them will provide you with an awareness of your own learning style and how to utilize it to your greatest personal advantage.

Factors Affecting Learning Style

Why do you learn the way you do? Your learning style is the result of both biological and environmental influences. Three important factors—culture, gender, and age—affect the development of learning preferences.

Culture is a particularly important influence on your learning style, as it provides the basis of one's identity, the nature of the expected relationships between student and professor, and the type of communication that is valued (Goldberger, 1996; Pai & Adler, 1997). Different cultures value different types of learning. Some cultures are less comfortable with the formal, factual information focus of the lecture-style format and learn more effectively through the interactive social exchange of interpersonal relationships (Pai & Adler, 1997). Others who value silence and respectful listening are not comfortable with the direct communication of ideas required in collaborative group learning (Goldberger, 1996). For large numbers of students, one of the challenges of university is learning how to adapt one's cultural learning preferences to fit the expectations and demands of the university learning environment. In developing an awareness of your cultural preferences you are better able to design study and learning strategies that facilitate your success in various courses.

Just as educators are becoming aware of the importance of culture to the learning styles of students, they are also learning more about the effect of gender on learning. Some of our initial understanding of gender differences relates to the developmental stages through which individuals progress as they develop understanding or ways of knowing. Men and women differ in the types of knowledge they prefer to learn and in the subjects they study. When men and women approach various subject areas they utilize different study strategies (Baxter Magdola, 1992; Severiens & ten Dam, 1994; Watkins & Hattie, 1981).

Perry (1970) has outlined four stages of cognitive development that describe the knowledge acquisition of male students. These include (1) dualistic (i.e., right and wrong), thinking with experts possessing the right answers, (2) multiplicity, where there is some uncertainty about information, (3) relativism, where knowledge is perceived within a contextual background and learners make their own judgments, and (4) commitment in relativism that facilitates the development of a personalized set of values. Further research has demonstrated that males prefer a learning approach that allows them to distance themselves from an idea, to challenge, to doubt, to analyze critically, to approach ideas objectively and to evaluate impersonally (Knight, Elfenbein, & Martin, 1997; Severiens & ten Dam, 1994). This has been described as **separate knowing** (Belenky, Clinchy, Goldberger, & Tarule, 1986; Knight et al., 1997). Males strive for mastery, use others' opinions as an opportunity to debate and challenge (Baxter Magdola, 1992), and are interested in courses as a source of qualification (Severiens & ten Dam, 1994).

In contrast to men's preference for separate knowing, women prefer **connected knowing**. This process follows five distinct stages that vary from those of male learners

(Belenky et al., 1986). These stages are: (1) silence, where the learner has no voice, (2) received knowing, where knowledge comes from an external source, (3) subjective knowing, that is intuitive rather than information-based, (4) procedural knowledge, where processes for understanding and evaluating information are developed, and (5) constructed knowledge, that recognizes that knowledge is contextual and the learner is part of that context. Belenky's findings are supplemented by the work of Baxter Magdola (1992), who observed that females are receptive learners who collect information about others' experiences through conversations, which they then use to productively formulate their own knowledge. They prefer a subjective approach to learning that involves striving to understand the ideas of others through careful listening, empathic concern, and perspective taking (Knight et al., 1997). They connect learning to people's experiences. Females enjoy learning for learning's sake and are more worried about their study success than are men (Severiens & ten Dam, 1994).

There are also age differences that are related to learning style. Non-traditional or older-than-average students tend to be more personally interested in learning than younger students (Severiens & ten Dam, 1997). Younger students appear to be ambivalent about their courses, lack self-regulation, and look to others to motivate them. Older students, on the other hand, have developed skills of self-regulation and are better able to develop learning models that allow them to process information at deeper, more abstract levels (Severiens & ten Dam, 1997).

Now that you understand that you may use different learning strategies depending on the interaction of your culture, age, and gender, you can use this information to enhance your learning effectiveness. This knowledge helps you adapt your style to the demands and expectations of university. Through figuring out how these different approaches to learning can work for you, you can add to your confidence as a learner.

Self-Confidence as a Self-Directed Learner

Each of the classes in which you are enrolled challenges you differently. As you have experimented with different note-taking, reading, test-taking, and presentation strategies, you have found that some of them work very well for you. Your success with these approaches adds not only to your efficiency and effectiveness but also to your sense of personal confidence. Each experience that helps you solve the mysteries of managing the workload, increases your ability to meet the challenges of the academic environment of university and adds to your capabilities as a self-directed learner.

It has been productive for you to recognize how to adjust your study approaches to the diverse learning demands of various courses. Applying the specific suggestions featured in Chapter 7 of this textbook has added to your ability to more efficiently learn course material. In adopting the attitudes of optimism, self-responsibility, and achievement orientation, along with a resolve to practise the self-regulation strategies of goal-setting and time management, you are reaping the benefits of the increased confidence that fuels your ability to perform well at university.

The insights you will learn in this chapter about the characteristics of your own unique learning style will add an important dimension to your confidence as a self-directed learner. Understanding your learning style and how it works provides you with the information you need to be successful in this new environment. When you use your learning style effectively you increase your ability as a self-directed learner. You understand the specific tactics that are effective for you. The success you achieve gives you the attitude of self-confidence that successful students have. It is an attitude that evolves from your systematic use of self-reflection and self-monitoring as a process to focus your efforts productively toward achieving your personal aspirations. It is an attitude that uses insights about personal differences to develop a personalized approach to learning effectiveness. You accept responsibility for your own work, use strategies to maintain your effort, motivate yourself with realistic goals, and focus your attention on the tasks that will promote success (Albaili, 1997). To commence this process of self-reflection, complete the following exercise.

Exercise 11.1 WHAT DO YOU DO WHEN YOU ARE LOST?

Think about a time when you visited a new place or lost your way while traveling. Describe the experience. Provide details about what you did and how you felt. How confident were you that you would find your way? What were the factors that added to, or detracted from your confidence?

How you reacted in this situation provides clues about how you learn. The following questions will help you begin to identify important characteristics that define your approach to learning.

Select the following description that most clearly describes you.

a. To solve this dilemma you visualize possible solutions and have a general idea of where you want to go. You trust your intuition and relate this situation to your own previous personal experience. It is useful for you to talk with others about possibilites and inquire about options.

b. This is a situation that you will solve on your own. You pause to think about possible steps you can take. You look around, notice details, and look for clues such as familiar landmarks that can guide you. You are confident that you will be able to figure out the steps that will get you to wherever you need to go.

Now, pick one of the following which most clearly describes you.

i. You remember a similar situation in your past, think about what you did then, and use the same approach now.

ii. You scan the environment for information that can help you. Then by systematically analyzing what you did to get to this point and weighing possible options, you select a solution that you believe will give you the greatest probability of success.

iii. You consider possible alternatives and pursue one of them immediately, figuring that if the first solution does not work out you will attempt another one.

iv. You choose a direction to pursue and follow it. You are comfortable taking risks, trust your abilities, and believe that it is okay to be lost because after you have tried all kinds of alternatives you will eventually find your way.

As you read this chapter you will learn more about the difference in learning approaches related to brain dominance. Right-brained dominance (a) is associated with intuitive, holistic learning, while left-brained learners (b) are analytical, linear learners. Later you will learn about Kolb's four types of learners: (i) divergers, (ii) assimilators, (iii) convergers, and (iv) accommodators.

Learning Styles

Thus far, you have learned a variety of strategies and skills that can assist you in becoming a more effective student. These skills and strategies are usually specific and focused. Learning styles, on the other hand, are generalized dimensions of how individuals learn how to learn. They are a set of personal characteristics resulting from biological and developmental factors that make one teaching approach effective for some and ineffective for others (Dunn, Beaudry, & Klavas, 1989).

Students differ in the ways in which they learn. Learning styles are influenced by environmental, physiological, emotional, and cognitive factors. Everyone has a learning style. It is as individual as your personal signature. It influences the differences that students experience when striving to concentrate in various environments, the patterns they use in order to effectively process information, and the senses through which they remember difficult information most easily. It encompasses cognitive styles, motivation, persistence, and the time of day when they are best able to concentrate.

As seen in the figure on page 263, individual learning styles are evidenced by different learning activities that students use during their learning process, by their views about the instruction, by their personal preferences, by the ways in which they process information, and by their approaches to studying. As you increase your awareness of your unique learning strengths, and match these abilities to course requirements, you improve your effectiveness and efficiency as a learner. Used appropriately, you can utilize your increased self-awareness to provide greater control over your learning. These various learning models present frameworks for improving your performance and managing the learning demands in various courses. With increased control comes greater self-confidence. With greater self-confidence, you are able to expand your study techniques, learning strategies, and classroom social supports. By continuing to add to your confidence and competence you evolve as a learner, resulting in attaining higher levels of academic and personal achievement.

As part of your initial assessment in Chapter 2 you answered questions that provide clues about some of your learning-style preferences. These results and the answers to additional questions included in this chapter are designed to help you reflect about personal learning needs and to learn more about the differences in learning approaches. They are informal measures that can assist you in developing initial impressions of your own learning tendencies. However, it is highly beneficial for you to get an accurate assessment of your learning style through the use of standardized learning style instruments, such as Kolb's *Learning Style Inventory* (Kolb, 1976, 1985), Myers-Briggs *Type Indicator* (Myers, 1985a, 1985b), or Entwistle's *Revised Approaches to Studying Inventory* (Entwistle & Tait, 1994). These tests are available from your university counselling service or academic learning centre. You will learn more about these approaches as you read this chapter.

The Classroom Environment

Your learning is influenced by the social environment of the classroom. Whether it is formal or informal, quiet or interactive, lecture-focused or discussion-focused, can either stimulate or inhibit your learning. Three social learning types have been identified: dependent learners, collaborative learners, and independent learners (Portis, Simpson, & Wiseman, 1993; Riechmann & Grasha, 1974). **Dependent learners** prefer instructor-directed, highly structured programmes with explicit assignments set and assessed. They

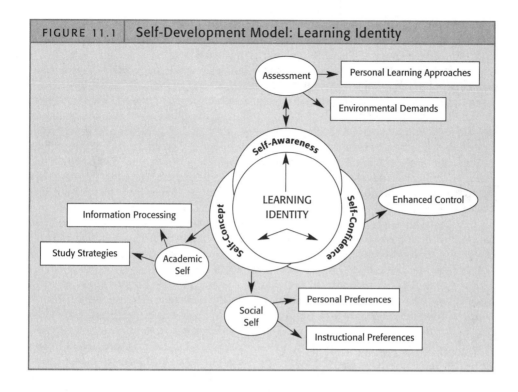

FIGURE 11.1 | Self-Development Model: Learning Identity

FIGURE 11.1 | Self-Development Model: Learning Identity

Assessment → Personal Learning Approaches

Environmental Demands

Self-Awareness

LEARNING IDENTITY

Self-Concept

Self-Confidence

Enhanced Control

Information Processing

Study Strategies

Academic Self

Social Self

Personal Preferences

Instructional Preferences

learn best through lectures and structured tutorials that provide specific guidance and direction. They prefer to be told what to learn. **Collaborative learners** favour discussion and group projects as a means of learning and are comfortable with role-playing, problem-solving groups, and business games. **Independent learners** want to have a role in decisions regarding the structure and content of their learning. They like to direct their own learning, and thus prefer learning situations in which they have the freedom to determine their own learning priorities and outcomes. Your comfort with particular learning environments and success in functioning in them depends on your own preferences for direction, social interaction, and cooperation. You can use these three learning approaches as a frame of reference for determining your own classroom preferences.

Brain Dominance

The differences in students' preferences for particular types of instruction is related to both biological and social factors. One of the significant variables is the way that the brain encodes and stores material. People vary in the way the brain processes information. These differences produce particular preferences for learning and mastering material (Dunn et al., 1989; Schmeck & Geisler-Brenstein, 1989).

Individuals described as **analytic learners** look first at details and then put them together. Those described as **holistic learners** form global impressions and see things as a whole. The university learning environment demands that students are able to effectively utilize both analytic and holistic approaches. Consequently, students' abilities to use their own dominant style effectively provides a source of confidence and capability that allows them to overcome those factors that may be adversely affecting their progress through the developmental stages of cognitive growth that lead to intellectual mastery. To recall these stages read about Bloom's taxonomy in Chapter 3.

Analytical learners process information in a linear, sequential, step-by-step, cause-and-effect approach. Analytic and inductive, their thinking processes are orderly, like a computer. For them, the best way to understand something is to break it down into components. They notice and remember details. As they develop critical thinking skills, as described in Bloom's taxonomy, they are most comfortable with analysis and application. They have difficulty understanding analogies, developing generalizations, seeing implications, and anticipating outcomes. Their thinking is focused as they make serial connections between one fact and another, or between one step and the next. Because they compartmentalize, memorizing facts is easy for them (Dunn et al., 1989; Schmeck & Geisler-Brenstein, 1989).

These students often relate to a professor impersonally, work independently, and are task oriented as they strive for personal recognition. Analytic learners prefer conventional, formal classrooms. They like structured presentations. They seek to understand how things operate and are interested in knowing the proper ways of doing things (Browne, 1986; Pask, 1988; Schmeck & Geisler-Brenstein, 1989).

Holistic learners process information holistically, visually, and deductively (Dunn & Dunn, 1988). Their approach is to build the big picture before they determine where the details fit. They quickly master the ability to synthesize, which is important in higher-level thinking (Bloom, 1956). Thus they anticipate, scan for information, and consider conclusions. They understand the connection between types of information that allows them to be adept at synthesizing information, perceiving similarities and differences, and considering conclusions (Schmeck, 1983). Because they are impulsive, they can miss some of the steps that would prevent them from overgeneralizing and misunderstanding. Rote memorization is not something they do easily; thus, to help them remember, they construct meaning through visual pictures, use metaphors, and relate concepts to their own personal situations. This results in a delay in answering when they are asked to respond because they do not use verbal labels to store their memories (Browne, 1986).

The social environment in the learning setting is very important to holistic learners. They avoid competition and seek a personal relationship with the professor. They are comfortable with change and prefer learning situations that provide variety, flexibility, and the opportunity for creative invention. Holistic learners prefer field trips, demonstrations, experiments, and role-playing as effective learning environments (Dunn et al., 1989; Dunn, Dunn, & Price, 1989; Dunn, Sklar, Beaudry, & Bruno, 1990).

Now that you are more aware of the relationship between the social environment of the classroom and your own learning efficiency, you can use this knowledge when deciding where you will study and what activities you will use. Another factor that is influential in determining the learning environments that best promote your learning is your personality.

Perceptual Preferences

Most students tend to favour one or more of their senses when learning. These include seeing-visual, reading-written, hearing-auditory, or doing-kinesthetic (Dunn, Griggs, Olson, & Beasly, 1995; Dunn & Stevenson, 1997). Successful students are known to use their learning preferences to adjust their style of studying and reading, thereby increasing their scholastic achievements (Dunn et al., 1995; Dunn & Stevenson, 1997; Nelson, 1993). For instance, if you are a visual learner, you learn effectively through mental pictures. Your most successful learning strategies include translating concepts into pictures, daydreaming concepts into reality, paying attention to pictures, concepts, graphs, charts, and creating mind maps and diagrams. If you learn best by reading, you get most details from a certain incident by reading a description of the event. Reading is an excellent learning strategy, especially when you highlight key words, read before the lecture, and take concise notes. If you are an auditory learner, you learn best from hearing information. Efficient learning strategies include reciting material out loud, audiotaping difficult lectures, and participating in study group discussions. Key for an auditory learner is to ensure that note-taking does not interfere with listening. In most cases, hearing the lecture first, followed by reading the chapter is a more effective strategy. If you are a kinesthetic or experiential learner, you tend to rely on physical activity to enhance your learning. This would include activities such as underlining, making note cards, diagrams, charts, role-playing, tutoring, participating in study groups, and enrolling in experiential learning courses that allow you to have some form of hands-on experiences.

Personality Preferences

Your learning style is critically shaped by your personality. In identifying your personality it is important to determine the stable characteristics that describe you. Personality affects the habits you have developed for processing information and making decisions. It influences how you react to various learning conditions. Knowing more about your personal preferences can help you find the strategies that make it easy for you to master material and maintain your interest. Your personality influences your selection of situations in which you learn best.

One model that clarifies the relationship of your personality to your ability to learn is the Myers-Briggs Type Indicator (MBTI). This instrument is based on a theory developed by Carl Jung (Jung, 1923) that identifies four core functions that influence the way individuals generally take in information, perceive the world, process information, and make decisions. Jung's model includes four pairs of adaptive orientations that are diametrically opposite to each other. These combinations describe where we get our energy (extrovert vs. introvert), how we gather information from the world around us (sensing vs. intuiting), how we prefer to process information (feeling vs. thinking), and preferences for making decisions (judging vs. perceiving). In general, individuals will have a tendency to prefer one of these orientations over the other (Lawrence, 1982, 1984; Myers, 1985a, 1985b).

The extroversion-introversion dimension describes the degree to which a student relies on activity as necessary for learning. **Extroverts** prefer active involvement, easily attempt new projects, and prefer a trial and error process that allows them to think while they are actively exploring ideas. Extroverts are social and get their energy from being around people. Thus they do their best thinking out loud and dialoguing with others, and perform best in classrooms that allow group discussions. Because they are less comfortable with the solitary activities of reading and writing, they frequently take active breaks from these activities. **Introverts** are oriented toward the inner world of ideas and feelings. Preferring thinking over activity, they need quiet time for concentration and study. They do their best through internal reflection and gain energy by creating private space even in large groups. They like lecture-based instruction. Because they are cautious, reflective, and think carefully before responding, they may perform poorly in question and answer sessions that require quick verbal responses. This dimension is particularly evident in classes in which there is group discussion. As a student, understanding your extroversion-introversion preferences can assist you in managing your participation levels. If you are an extrovert, you have no difficulty expressing yourself. In fact extroverts can easily dominate the discussion and may need to be encouraged to let others share their ideas. However, if you are an introvert you will need to develop a strategy to ensure that you are included in the discussion. Prepare and plan so that you can be ready to share your ideas and participate confidently (Lawrence, 1982, 1984; Myers, 1985a, 1985b).

The second core function, sensing-intuiting, includes preferences for taking information in from the world. *Sensors* prefer a concrete, logical approach in which they can analyze the facts and details of a situation. They are practical, focused, and uncomfortable with abstractions about the future. They like learning to be useful and realistic. Sensing students are most satisfied when they can put into use what they have learned. They like to learn a skill, perfect it, and practise it without much variation. *Intuitives,* on the other hand, are big picture, holistic learners who are imaginative and enjoy variety. They are focused on the future. They direct their energies to possibilities of what could be. Intuitives are stimulated by the challenge of mastering abstract concepts and complex theories. These two types of students prefer very different types of courses. Intuitives like courses in which they can explore diverse ideas, while sensing students like courses that provide them with useful, practical information (Lawrence, 1982, 1984; Myers, 1985a, 1985b).

The third core function, thinking-feeling, describes the process individuals use to make a decision or determine a conclusion. *Thinkers* solve problems through logic and rationality. They tend to perform best when given a clearly presented set of performance criteria. Orderly thinkers, they want to systematically understand concepts. They communicate directly and forcefully. Students whose favourite courses involve scientific reasoning and problem solving are probably classified as thinkers. Because these courses use a logical rather than subjective approach to mastering the material, thinkers prefer them. *Feelers* make decisions by focusing on the importance of human values and relationships. They perform best when their learning can be used to benefit others. To engage them productively in learning they need to form a personal connection to the material that they are learning. Because they value personal expressiveness, they prefer courses that allow them to express their opinions, demonstrate their values, and focus on relationships. Students who enjoy arts and humanities courses that emphasize human issues may have feeling preferences (Lawrence, 1982, 1984; Myers, 1985a, 1985b).

The fourth function, judging-perceiving, involves how individuals like to make decisions. *Judging* students like order. They make decisions to create order. *Perceiving* students like flexibility and prefer keeping options open. This dimension is useful in determining whether or not students prefer structured or unstructured learning environments. Because judging students value order, they seek closure and prefer structured learning situations in which goals and time frames are clearly established. They are organized and like working toward deadlines. When writing a paper or reading textbooks they appreciate an approach that allows them to complete components of these projects within detailed time plans. Those with perceiving preferences prefer being flexible and open-ended; thus, they see learning as a discovery process that is continuous and spontaneous. They like situations that provide them freedom to explore. When writing or reading, perceivers enjoy the process of uncovering ideas and gathering information. They perceive deadlines as limiting.

These descriptions are provided to assist you in understanding the patterns in your preferences for specific types of learning environments. Providing you with this information is not intended to create rigid labels for you. In fact, you may find that you fit the defining characteristics in several of the personality dimensions. Use the information to understand more fully the learning situations that seem to fit your personal preferences. The descriptions associated with these diverse personal dimensions can help guide you in designing the collection of learning strategies that can engage you.

Teaching Preferences

Just as your attitudes and personality influence your learning preferences, your professor's personality influences his or her teaching style. Those professors who encourage student participation, assign group projects, and stimulate student interest by continually changing the method of instruction are probably extroverts. Those professors who consistently follow the same format for all classes, usually lecture, and structure assignments so that they follow the textbook are probably introverts. Sensing professors emphasize factual material and ask concrete questions while intuitive professors focus on questions of conjecture, discuss theory, and allow students some choice in their assignments. Thinking types treat all members of the class the same and design their courses so that students are challenged intellectually and developmentally. This contrasts with those feeling-type professors who recognize individual differences among students and consequently plan assignments that are responsive to the individual needs of students. Judging professors are organized and predictable. Their course outlines have clear deadlines and schedules. Perceptive professors are more spontaneous and easily change the content of the class to reflect the changing priorities of students' interests. They use the course outline as a general frame of reference rather than a specific schedule.

Some professors are aware of individual differences in learning styles while others are not. In fact, many modify their teaching approaches in order to reach as many students as they can. However, instructors, like students, perform best when they are teaching according to their attitudinal and personality preferences. Thus, they will have a tendency to use their preferred approach most frequently. The language your professor uses and the types of questions frequently asked can give you insights into the teaching style of your professor. By figuring out how the professor's teaching style varies from your learning approach you can make adjustments in your study strategies that can complement the classroom environment. If you learn through the discussion of ideas and are best motivated when classroom content is personally relevant to you, but are enrolled in a class where your professor lectures about facts and maintains a formal decorum within the classroom, it would enhance your academic success if you participate in out-of-class group study sessions. Not only would this activity reinforce your learning preferences, but it would also help you maintain your motivational levels and integrate the material so that it is personally meaningful.

Now that you have figured out how you can improve your learning efficiency by creating learning surroundings that fit your personality and instructional preferences, you will feel more confident in your ability to learn in all types of learning situations. This is particularly important for you in those classes in which you previously felt uncomfortable or discouraged. Your awareness of these important social factors provides you with specific methods for adjusting your style and engaging in activities that advance your learning. As you learn about some of the strategies for learning information, retaining it, and studying effectively, you will develop even greater confidence.

Academic Self

You have discovered much about the factors that affect your learning effectiveness. But what about the courses? How can you improve your abilities in some of those courses that are particularly challenging? Through learning about the process by which you learn, you can maximize those strategies that work best for you. How you learn depends on the strategies, ideas, and rules you use to understand information. Your preferences for using particular strategies for perceiving and encoding new information influence the approaches you use to study and remember. You have already learned about the impact of differences in your brain dominance and your personality on the way you learn. Now you must develop an awareness about the way you take information in and retain it.

One helpful model, as displayed on this page, that can assist you in understanding more clearly how to maximize your learning effectiveness is the cycle of learning that has been delineated by Kolb (Kolb, 1976; Kolb, 1984). This educator observed that learning occurs through a four-stage process of experiential learning: feeling, watching, thinking, and doing. Effective learning involves using all of these processes. Kolb (1976) observed that learning is a cyclical, repetitive process. The first stage of the cycle—concrete experience—involves direct experiences related to the task or information you wish to learn. This produces either thoughts or feelings regarding your experience. In the second stage—reflective observation—you think about what you did and the resulting thoughts or feelings you have regarding the experience. The third stage—abstract conceptualization—involves attempting to understand your experience by forming rational conclusions or emotional insights. This information allows you to generalize your learning to other similar situations. This leads to the fourth phase—active experimentation—in which you

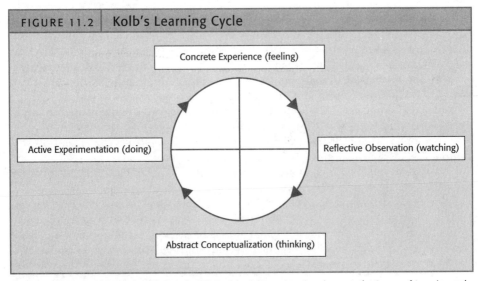

FIGURE 11.2 | Kolb's Learning Cycle

Concrete Experience (feeling)

Active Experimentation (doing)

Reflective Observation (watching)

Abstract Conceptualization (thinking)

Based on Kolb's Learning Cycle in Kolb, D.A. (1984). *Experiential Learning: Experience as the Source of Learning and Development.* Englewood Cliffs, NJ: Prentice Hall.

implement and test the principles you have learned from the experience. Through this process, you as a learner gain insights, test the implications of your new knowledge, refine ideas into your own belief systems, and attempt new experiences.

To assist you in understanding more clearly how Kolb's learning cycle facilitates learning, consider the stages you go through in learning how to write references for an academic term paper. During the concrete experience stage you write down the information that describes the title of an article and other identifying information. This is followed by the reflective observation of the next stage in which you stop what you are doing and evaluate whether your written description meets the conditions required for APA bibliographic entries. During the abstract conceptualization stage, you attempt to understand the principles underlying the order in the bibliographic entry so that you can generalize your understanding. In the final stage of active experimentation, you apply the principles you have learned in the previous stage to other situations so that you are able to proficiently and properly write a list of references for your paper.

Although effective learning involves all four processes, Kolb (1976) noted that most individuals operate with a particular preference toward a certain stage. That preference or learning orientation reflects whether they prefer concrete or abstract perceiving or whether they engage in active or reflective processing as a means of understanding. By combining these dimensions he was able to identify four types of learners: divergers, convergers, assimilators, and accommodators that describe how individuals take information in and retain it. Before we describe these four types of learning orientations, it is helpful to understand the two learning dimensions in Kolb's theory.

The first dimension describes the way in which people perceive and take in information. Kolb describes this continuum as either concrete or abstract processing. Individuals who tend to use an experiential approach of feeling their way through things as a way to learn are described as using **concrete experience.** They relate their personal experiences to the information they are learning. They are subjective learners who rely on their feelings and hunches as a means of solving problems. They like dealing with experiences in a social and personal way. At the opposite end of this continuum are individuals who analyze experiences and use reason as a means of conceptualizing. Described as using **abstract thinking,** these individuals are objective learners who prefer to analyze situations logically and impersonally.

The second dimension is the difference observed in how individuals process information. Kolb describes a process in which individuals gain understanding through either doing or observing. Those individuals who learn by doing and prefer practical, personal experience are described as using **active experimentation.** Those individuals who watch and observe are described as utilizing **reflective observation**. If you prefer active experimentation, you learn best when you can test the practicality of concepts or information. You prefer to solve problems through hands-on experience or in real-life situations rather than through impersonal analysis. On the other end of this continuum are individuals who use reflective observation as a means of comprehending new information. They learn by patiently, astutely, and thoughtfully observing and analyzing situations from various perspectives. They are insightful and learn by evaluating their own experience. Kolb believed that the combination of these two dimensions determines your unique learning style.

Kolb combines these learning processes into four learning types. As you review them, you may be able to select one that fits you better than the others. This provides you with increased understanding about which type of learner you are. It can provide you with some of the reasons why some classes are easier for you and others are more difficult. On page 261, when you considered what you typically do when you are lost, you identified one of four types of approaches that best fits you. These descriptions were examples of these four types of learning. Review your responses and use the following descriptions to gain a clearer understanding of your learning orientations.

Divergers

These learners perceive concretely and process information reflectively. In other words, they start with an experience, think about it, then generalize. They seek answers to "why" questions and use their personal experiences to understand new information. Divergers are imaginative and people-focused. They are adept at viewing situations from diverse perspectives; thus, they seek out multiple opinions and ideas. They learn best when they are personally engaged in discussion and when it is possible to make connections between course material and their own needs and values. They are similar to introverted feelers and connected knowers.

Assimilators

These abstract learners process information reflectively through detailed, sequential steps. They start with an idea and reflect on it. They appreciate theories, seek facts, and like to know what experts think. They are efficient at reasoning from particular observations and drawing conclusions. They are comfortable in the lecture format of traditional classrooms, like structure, and are effective in planning and organizing their assignments. Their rational approach compares to the style that is used by intuitive thinkers and separate knowers.

Convergers

These abstract learners process information actively and prefer pragmatic problem solving as a means of learning. They start with an idea and process it actively. They are efficient at solving problems, making decisions, and applying information practically. They like to use their common sense and are interested in experimentation. Their desire to apply what they learn, and to test for workability is similar to the learning approach of the extroverted thinker.

Accommodators

These concrete learners process information actively and need to be involved in risk-taking, experimentation, and testing experience. They start with what they experience and test it out. They are intuitive, learn by trial and error, and are adaptable to change. They excel in situations that require flexibility. They are action-oriented, task-focused problem-solvers who like getting things done. They look for relationships between learning and its application to the real world. Like extroverted sensors they learn through a personal process of information gathering.

The Kolb model provides a framework so you can assess your strengths and weaknesses as a learner. It is intended to assist you in gaining insights about the ways you learn and the approaches that work best for you. To obtain a valid assessment of your actual learning approaches and capabilities, it is useful to seek a formal assessment from your Counselling Centre.

Now that you have an understanding of the four types of learning processes and Kolb's learning cycle you are better able to clearly identify the ways in which you learn. One of the types may be more descriptive of you than others. Or you may have a combination of abilities. It is possible that you may notice that your performance in particular courses relates to your own abilities to use these processes. Perhaps now you can understand how a mismatch between your preferred approaches to learning and the learning methods required in the course can make that course more challenging and difficult for you. There are courses where your preferred style fits well, and others where it does not. Can you see any relationship between your preferred style and your favourite courses? Your favourite discipline? Your favourite instructor?

Effective learning involves all of the processes that Kolb has identified. As you evolve as a learner you will expand your abilities in order to be able to operate with equal facility in all four stages. Through the exercises in this chapter you have identified your strengths as a learner. Knowing these strengths helps you gain confidence in your ability to achieve in various courses and in your own ability to learn effectively. As you continue throughout your university education, you will learn to strengthen those capabilities you have identified as being weaker, and you will add important processes to make you a more effective learner.

As you have analyzed the different approaches to learning you have discovered that there are many ways to learn. You have probably also observed that many of these approaches complement the others. An important part of your discovery in your first year of university is identifying your strengths as a learner. Because you know that some courses require approaches that are not your strengths, you can master these courses by designing your study strategies to utilize your strengths. Your increasing awareness of your learning abilities and the demands of the learning environment provides you with an opportunity to develop yourself as a learner. Thus you may gradually develop learning approaches that complement your typical methods of learning. For example, if you have identified strengths in abstract thinking, you may complement your abilities in this area by learning to subjectively assess the material and trust your intuition.

Kolb challenges you to see that learning is an integrated process. It involves knowing how to be objective and subjective, to think abstractly and concretely, and to test implications and evaluate reflectively. Learning effectiveness is adversely affected when individuals get stuck in particular parts of this process or have not developed the competencies that allow them to skillfully move from analysis to synthesis, or from practical, personal, creative problem-solving to abstract, symbolic, rational, and theoretical thinking. As a first-year student, you succeed initially by recognizing and using those learning capacities that are natural for you. Then by attempting new approaches you can gradually add the dimensions that are missing.

Study Strategies: Surface and Deep Learning

How you learn and master information is not only affected by your learning style, it is also influenced by the approach you use to comprehend and retain information. Because much of what you must learn in university relates to reading and remembering, researchers have explored differences in the way that students study and learn information. What they have discovered is that students vary along a continuum of surface versus deep learning in their study approach. The approach you use relates to the outcome you expect and your motivations (Entwistle, 1988; Schmeck, 1983, 1988; Schmeck & Geisler-Brenstein, 1989, 1991). You can begin to understand the differences between surface and deep processing by answering the questions below.

Exercise 11.2 SURFACE AND DEEP LEARNING

The following questions will assist you in identifying the study strategy you prefer most. Select the responses that describe the approach you use most frequently.

1. The strategy I use the most in remembering information is:
   a) memorization.
   b) relating information to previous knowledge.
2. My responsibility as a student is:
   a) to learn the information the professor presents.
   b) to critically question the information that is presented in class.
3. My primary role as a student is:
   a) to gain skills and learn information so that I am prepared for a job.
   b) to develop an understanding of complex ideas and the meaning of life.

If you chose items (a), you prefer surface learning.
If you chose items (b), you prefer deep learning.

Surface processors (Entwistle, 1988) approach learning as a process of reproduction. They operate at the concrete operational level and perceive knowledge as information transmitted to them from others. Thus they take in information as it is found and strive to reproduce it exactly as it is presented. They accomplish this by using the professor's or author's own words. Rote learners, they memorize and work to remember as many things as possible in the order in which they were presented. Their goals are to accumulate more facts, gain skills, and complete the task requirements. Because information is accumulated unreflectively, they generally accept ideas without necessarily understanding them. They are motivated by extrinsic factors such as grades, the qualifications that particular courses provide, and a fear of failure. Surface learners look to others to focus their learning and have been described as passive learners (Gibbs, Morgan, & Taylor, 1984).

The surface-learning strategy can be effective in those courses in which large amounts of information must be retained for a short period of time. If you are required to know dates in a history course, terminology in a social science course, parts of the plant in a biology course, or formulas in a mathematics course, the surface-learning approach is useful. If the items on an examination require you to reproduce information, then surface learning strategies are appropriate.

Deep processors dig for meaning behind words and concepts. They analyze, hypothesize, make connections and draw conclusions. They look for the reasoning, justification, and logic behind ideas and attempt to comprehend the interpretations behind what an author is stating. These learners assiduously question, critically examine issues, and relate information to other parts of a course. They are actively involved in exploring ideas and learning information. Deep learners are motivated by an interest in the subject matter and in learning for learning's sake. Their goal is to understand. Learning assists them in making sense of complex situations, events or ideas. Deep learners try to abstract meaning or concepts from their learning experiences, to use these experiences to see the world differently, and to improve their own ability to learn. They seek integration and relate theoretical ideas to everyday experiences. Deep learning is associated with doing (Entwistle, 1988; Schmeck & Geisler-Brenstein, 1991).

The deep-processing study strategies are most useful in those courses that require integration and application of information. Because students who are able to motivate themselves generally use deep-processing study approaches, these strategies are associated with greater success in courses of independent study. Over time, deep-processing study strategies produce higher grade and achievement levels.

If you memorize, use mnemonic strategies, repeat information until you can reproduce it, and use rewards as a means of motivating yourself, you are using surface study strategies. If you seek understanding, attempt to master textbook material by restating concepts in your own words, and find personal relevance in the course, you are using deep, also known as meaningful, study strategies.

Like many first-year students it is quite possible that you rely extensively on surface learning strategies as your primary study approach. However, as you continue with your university study you will discover that increasingly greater numbers of your courses require you to use deep-learning strategies. As you learn to use both surface and deep strategies, you will find that the deep strategies allow you to productively appraise your own learning capabilities and deficits. The deep-learning strategies give you skills you can use so that you can make the improvements you want to make, in order to achieve your goal of being a self-directed learner.

To be a successful university student you must master the process of learning how to learn. This includes learning how to master the information and how to manage your self as a learner. To master the content of courses, you can learn how to flexibly adapt the strategies associated with various learning styles. You can apply the strategies that work best for you in those situations where the instructional approach is one that does not motivate you or works less effectively for you. By using learning approaches that engage you, you make the material personally relevant and the learning process becomes more meaningful. You can use the information provided below to identify those strategies you currently utilize and those you wish to develop.

Learning Strategies That Engage

Analytic	Break material down into meaningful components.
Wholistic	Draw a picture of the connections among ideas.
Introverted	Study in quiet places. Avoid interruptions.
Extroverted	Join out-of-class discussion groups.
Sensing	Design practical steps for learning material.
Intuitive	Imagine the future possibilities of what you are learning.
Thinking	Develop criteria for evaluating success.
Feeling	Relate course content to personally meaningful issues.
Judging	Keep a schedule of academic assignments. Note progress.
Perceiving	Schedule time for unstructured exploration.

Divergers	Collect data through interviews, observation, or field work to assess the relationship of ideas and experience.
Assimilators	Ask questions. Consider options. Think like a detective who must solve a mystery.
Convergers	Build a model to test ideas. Use computer simulations.
Accommodators	Experiment. Try role-playing or simulations.

Once aware of your capabilities as a learner, you are better able to add the additional competencies that will make you even more effective. Learning activities are opportunities for you to refine your current skills and develop others. Successful students cycle between holistic and analytical strategies, between conversation and reflection, and between abstract conceptualization and concrete experimentation. In order to ensure that you possess the cognitive strategies that produce success in university, it is important for you to develop an ability to use the holistic strategies of personal experience, visualization, analogy, and metaphor along with the analytic strategies of sequencing, causation, and analysis. It is to your benefit when you become adept at learning both collaboratively and independently. The more proficient you are in integrating reflective thinking with active experimentation, the easier it will be for you to adjust to the complex demands of university. By knowing when to employ the surface strategies of memorization and when to utilize the deep-study strategies of evaluation, you will find that learning becomes easier for you.

You can improve your ability in managing yourself as a learner through the process of self-analysis. As you have become increasing self-aware of learning style differences, the learning demands of university, your own abilities, motivations and preferences, and the options available, you have a new set of tools that you can use. Throughout this chapter you have developed an increased level of self-awareness about differences in learning style approaches and the complexities of the learning demands of university. This awareness provides you with strategies for adapting to the differences in classroom environments and professors' teaching styles so that you are best able to learn. In figuring out the descriptive nature of your own learning style, you have greater understanding of some of the factors that influence your comfort and discomfort, interest and disinterest, and difficulty and ease with particular courses. The exercise that follows on page 275 assists you in summarizing your personal insights about your own learning style.

The self-awareness you have gained provides you with information that can allow you to individualize your approach to learning. You can determine how to more effectively assess the factors in the learning environment that engage you and those that distance you. Through adjusting your own learning strategies you can improve your learning efficiency. Being aware of the stylistic differences between yourself and your professors or between yourself and other students allows you greater personal control. You can make more discriminating choices in seeking out professors or learning environments that fit you. Especially important is the understanding that differences in learning styles are value-free. In other words, learning one way is not better than or worse than learning another way. This means you are free to learn in a way that makes you successful. This may involve adjusting your outside-of-class study approaches, asking questions that force the professor to respond in a way that makes the information relevant to your learning style, or selecting courses that are taught in ways that meet your learning needs.

Exercise 11.3 MY LEARNING IDENTITY

This chapter has provided a number of models to assist you in developing greater self-awareness of the many dimensions of your learning style. By learning about these models, reflecting on your own experience, analyzing which characteristics and models fit you and which do not, and applying what you have learned about yourself to different courses, you will enhance your capabilities as a learner. Each model provides a framework for you to describe yourself, to highlight personal characteristics that uniquely describe you, to recognize aspects of the learning environment that engage you, and to compare this information with your current learning approaches. By reviewing the information you have learned and systematically pulling together the data you have collected about yourself in this chapter, you can develop plans and goals to perfect your strengths and add to your capabilities. Use the exercise that follows to summarize your insights.

Self-description	Personal Characteristics	Preferred Learning Environment	My Current Practices
Social self			
Instructional			
Analytic/Wholistic			
MBTI			
Academic self			
Kolb			
Surface-Deep			

Self-assessment

Briefly describe what you have learned about your learning style.

Describe how you can use this information to improve your learning.

What do you want to continue?

What do you want to change?

Equally important, your understanding of learning styles helps you figure out what motivates you and makes you learn. This awareness of your own strategies and motivations is critical to your personal success. When you understand the personal reasons for taking particular courses, and the factors that cause you to persevere in spite of difficulties, you possess important information that can add to or detract from the confidence you have as a learner.

By productively using the information that you have acquired about your learning style to develop more efficient ways of studying and mastering material, you enhance not only your ability to learn more effectively but also your feelings of confidence regarding your capabilities. These increased feelings of self-confidence provide the basis for you to overcome any feelings of doubt, anxiety, or fear that could adversely affect you. In using the personal learning strategies that work for you and recognizing your own developmental level, you can pace the evolution of additional learning skills that will add to your self-efficacy. Gradually, your ability to focus your learning skills will combine with increased feelings of self-confidence so that you develop enhanced feelings of control over your learning. This self-control adds to your confidence and the cycle repeats itself as seen in Kolb's Learning Cycle.

Be patient. Developing new learning strategies that will enhance your efficiency takes time. You will experience the greatest success when you accommodate or add new approaches in a course in which you already feel comfortable. The challenge will come in those courses where you do not feel comfortable. Set reasonable expectations. Ask for help. Make small adjustments that you can handle. Find resources that work for you. One way to expand your skills is to find role models you can imitate. This is best achieved by surrounding yourself with people who learn differently than you. Observe those role models. Emulate them. Remember that learning is a process of deliberate, extensive steps, so focus on the success you experience with each step. Remind yourself that challenging courses teach you much about yourself. It is especially useful to search for the positive lessons you wish to remember.

Becoming a successful learner takes time. It takes practice. It takes making mistakes and starting again. It takes believing in yourself. It takes focusing on your success while you eliminate inefficiencies. You are developing yourself as a learner and are figuring out what works for you. You are adding to your self-confidence so that you are better able to develop the strategies that work, to develop the insight about your personal motivations, to try out the strategies that make you more successful, and to reflect on the source of your own drive for becoming self-reliant. With time you may uncover your own answers for ensuring that the processes of self-awareness, self-confidence, and greater self-control produce feelings of self-sufficiency, personal resiliency, and a desire to be self-actualized.

Motivated by curiosity and a desire for mastery, you have discovered answers and developed abilities throughout your life that you now take for granted. Years from today you will be taking for granted the cognitive and social capabilities that you are striving to master now. Though some of the new ways of thinking and perceiving may initially be difficult to master, with practise and persistence you will succeed. Using the insights you have discovered about your personal learning style will assist you in maximizing your learning, regardless of the course or the way in which it is taught. You have the tools to take control of what you learn and how you learn it.

It's More Than Common Sense

Using Kolb's Learning Model to Improve Goal-Tending Skills

Adam Driedzic

An interesting application of using learning-style theory to improve performance is research that demonstrates its effectiveness in enhancing athletic performance. Adam Driedzic in his master's thesis investigated the usefulness of Kolb's theory in the coaching and training of roller hockey goaltenders.

Becoming a hockey goaltender requires both analytical thinking and reflexive actions. It is an individual position in a team sport. The diversity of the demands of the position entail using active, kinesthetic, social, cognitive, and solitary learning approaches. Yet individuals in the position generally do not have all of these learning preferences. Since a primary focus of effective coaching is to assist individual athletes enhance their playing capabilities, Driedzic hypothesized that one tool that could facilitate effective coaching is to develop training programs that use Kolb's learning model. He suggested that interventions that utilized players' dominant learning approaches and incorporated all phases of the Kolb learning cycle into the coaching plans would improve the athlete's performance.

Two athletes were selected to participate in a study incorporating Kolb's learning cycle into training plans to enhance their athletic abilities as roller hockey goaltenders. Initially, each athlete predicted their personal learning style: one athlete described himself as an assimilator, the other as an accommodator. Both athletes scored as assimilators on the Learning Style Inventory.

To ensure that all phases of Kolb's learning cycle were incorporated into training, the usual exercises were modified so that they reflected either thinking/watching activities that demanded both reflective observation and abstract conceptualization, or as doing/feeling activities that allowed active experimentation and concrete experience.

Thinking/watching activities included readings, video analysis, mental imaging, and visualization. Doing/feeling activities included scrimmages, shooting drills, skating drills, and fitness training. Each athlete identified two specific training goals. Each athlete's training programs utilized a combination of 20 thinking and doing activities related to their respective goals. Athletes evaluated the effectiveness of the doing and thinking activities as it affected their ability to achieve their goals.

The results of the athletes' evaluations demonstrated the value of using Kolb's learning styles to improve skill development. Both athletes achieved success in attaining their performance goals as observed by themselves, their coaches, and their fellow players. Both athletes reported that thinking activities were most beneficial to them in reaching their performance goals. They particularly enjoyed homework assignments in which they could watch professional goaltenders on television or observe their own performance on video. Their preferences for thinking activities were consistent with the needs of assimilators who are comfortable with reflective observation. Although both athletes acknowledged that thinking and doing activities are important for the overall development of an athlete, they reported they learned the most from those learning activities that fit their learning approach. Both described the value and importance of the learning-styles project for improving their mental and physical preparation for game situations.

This research was conducted by Adam Driedzic for his masters degree in College Student Personnel from Western Illinois University. Adam was born in Vancouver and received his Bachelor of Arts with a major in Anthropology from the University of Waterloo in Kitchener, Ontario. Most recently, he has served as the assistant director of housing at the Banff Conference Centre. Adam is currently pursuing additional leadership training at the Yamnuska Mountaineering School.

Success Strategies FOR DEVELOPING A PERSONAL LEARNING STYLE

Self-awareness
I have discovered that the learning style that best describes me is…
I recognize that I learn most effectively when I…

Self-confidence
I can increase my confidence in learning difficult material by…

Self-concept
I plan to implement the following learning strategies and study strategies…

Chapter Summary

Students can enhance their efficiency as learners by developing an awareness of diverse approaches to learning. This chapter delineates a number of theoretical approaches to learning styles and identifies culture, age, and gender preferences as influential factors producing important differences in learning approaches. The chapter provides students with information so that they can differentiate between analytic and holistic approaches to learning. It also contributes information about two learning models, Kolb and Myers-Briggs, which students can use to discover their learning preferences and expand their awareness of the relationship of social and academic factors to their learning efficiency. This chapter explains the importance of surface and deep learning in developing study strategies, which reinforce the retention of information. Throughout the chapter research findings are included to assist students in expanding their knowledge of the impact of numerous sociological, environmental and biological factors on learning styles. Students can apply the information included in this chapter to develop greater understanding of their own particular learning style and to determine steps to take in order to enhance their probability of becoming successful learners.

Exercises

REFLECT–ACT

Reflect   Identify your most favourite and least favourite courses. For each course use the models in this text to determine the learning orientation that is required in the course. Identify three specific learning strategies that you could use to reinforce your learning in your least preferred course.

Act   Select one or two of these strategies to use in the upcoming week. At the end of the week assess your progress. Use this information to plan continued strategies for improving your learning.

Reflect   Using the framework provided by the MBTI, select one of the dimensions that describes you. Identify three or four learning strategies that best fit these characteristics.

Act   In your next study session practise one of these learning strategies and note the ways in which it benefits your learning.

Reflect   Select one of your courses and describe some of the material you must learn in that course. Using Kolb's stage-learning cycle, develop four steps for learning this material.

Act   Use these four steps and evaluate your effectiveness.

Reflect   Select two of your courses that you believe demand different approaches to learning. Use Kolb's system to describe the learning strategies that are associated with each course. Explain how being aware of Kolb's cycle can benefit you.

Act   Identify complementary study strategies that utilize different aspects of Kolb's model. Try to use them to enhance your learning.

GROUP DISCUSSION

1. To master the information presented in different classes it is useful to know when to use surface-study strategies and when to use deep-study strategies. Bring examples of the information you must learn from each of your courses to class, and express the strategies you will use to master this material. As a group, identify those courses that require surface strategies and those that require deep strategies.

2. Brainstorm a list of typical learning problems of first-year students. Provide some examples of how students' awareness of learning styles can help them avoid some of these problems.

3. Compare courses in Science with those in Arts by using Kolb's model to identify the types of learning that is required in those courses.

4. Using some of the dimensions of the MBTI, have students who share similar preferences group together (e.g., extroverts in one group and introverts in another, sensors in one group and intuitives in another). Have the members of these groups describe their favourite course (and professor) by identifying the six to ten characteristics that depict these courses. Compare the lists that the diverse groups develop.

5. Your group has been asked to use Kolb's four-stage model of feeling, watching, thinking, and doing to develop the steps for learning one of the following tasks:

    a. The important skills for preparing for essay examinations.

    b. Strategies for critical review of material for an essay.

    c. The steps for developing an effective Power Point presentation.

APPLY TO LIFE

1. In preparation for an upcoming examination, your professor has provided you with two potential exam questions.

   a) Contrast the learning styles of extroverted and introverted students.

   b) Describe the teaching approach a professor should use to best respond to the learning needs of extroverted students. Using your knowledge of holistic and analytical thinking identify the types of thinking required to answer each of these questions. Which question would you find easier to answer? Describe how your awareness of the differences in global and analytic thinking can help you better prepare for potential essay examinations.

2. Your friend is having difficulty with an economics course in which he is enrolled. He describes the course as dry and detailed, and the professor as distant and detached. The professor's lectures emphasize abstract theories and statistical models. Occasionally she assigns homework that requires students to practically apply the concepts that have been learned in class. He was looking forward to gaining greater understanding of the relationship of people's experiences, belief systems, cultural and social backgrounds, lifestyle choices, and they ways they spend money. He is particularly frustrated because he is missing the opportunity to expand his ideas through discussion and he worries that the grades he is getting on multiple-choice exams do not demonstrate his ability level and interest in this area. Using Kolb's system, you can help your friend understand how his personal learning style differs from the teaching style of his professor. Identify the learning style of the student. Identify the teaching style of his professor. Describe the important sources of disconnection between the professor and the student. Given the nature of the student's learning style, suggest one or two ideas the student can use in this situation to facilitate his personal learning and improve his ability to demonstrate that he comprehends the material.

Solving Problems

"Success is to be measured not so much by the position that one has reached in life but by the obstacles he has overcome trying to succeed." Booker T. Washington

Your adventure will present you with challenges, hurdles, problems, and obstacles. Problems are a natural, inevitable, and important part of life. They are especially important for the lessons they teach you about yourself and about your own ability to learn from experience. "Success is to be measured not so much by the position that one has reached in life but by the obstacles he has overcome trying to succeed." The better able you are to improve your capabilities in *Solving Problems*, the more successful you become.

With the right tools and competencies, solving problems becomes easier. Different types of challenges require different strategies. Whether or not the problems you face are uniquely yours, or are common issues that other individuals experience, developing creative, methodical, flexible, and assorted strategies for solving them influences your success. By using the critical thinking and creative problem-solving strategies of the following chapter you can enhance your effectiveness and improve your capabilities to be victorious and to arrive successfully at your destination.

As you improve your critical-thinking capabilities, you add the ability to view problems impersonally, abstractly, and judiciously. Critical-thinking abilities allow you to explore problems in greater depth, understand the contextual factors producing particular difficulties, and define dilemmas from diverse perspectives. Critical-thinking competencies provide you with the basis for increasing your comprehension of the nature of the problem and expanding your options for solving problems.

Sometimes, solving problems requires shifting one's perspective in order to resolve issues or discover new options. By viewing issues from multiple perspectives, or conceptualizing them differently, you may be able to discover innovative solutions.

Learning how to think outside your usual frame of reference is an important part of creative problem solving. Striving to understand challenges from several vantage points allows you to devise numerous responses and develop alternatives for moving forward productively.

By refining your critical-thinking capabilities and practising numerous, creative problem-solving strategies, you can overcome impediments that block your progress. Learning to do things differently rather than repeating what you have always done lets you get results so that you progress toward the success you desire. Solving problems teaches you insight and understanding so that you are better able to productively use the obstacles life provides as opportunities for growth.

Thinking Critically and Solving Problems Creatively

chapter 12

"Making the simple complicated is commonplace; making the complicated simple, awesomely simple, that's creativity."

Charles Mingus

Questions

What skills do I have that help me distinguish truth from opinion?

How can I become a wiser consumer?

How can I best deal with life's challenges?

Objectives

- Learn how to think critically and to solve problems creatively.

- Identify intellectual tools in order to analyze information independently. With these tools, you can continue to educate yourself for the rest of your life.

- Know how to deal with different thinking styles required by different disciplines; learn across disciplines.

Student Success Portrait

Thinking Critically and Solving Problems Creatively

Robert Cegielski
The University of Manitoba

In university today, students are hit with more information, more obstacles, and more problems than ever encountered before. Being able to apply critical thinking is an encouraged technique that will help students attain their desired goals, and is also associated with problem-solving. Being able to diverge from habit and find new, innovative methods of attacking problems is an amazingly powerful skill that will prepare any student to face the challenges of university and overcome them.

Critical thinking is a cognitive skill that increased the desired outcome for many of my tests. At first, I was adapted to the high school methods of memorization, regurgitation, and learning the mechanical way of solving problems without putting in any real thought at all. Once I faced the challenges in university, I had to adapt myself quickly to this new environment, surpass my traditional ideas and patterns, and learn new, cutting-edge methods to approach these problems. Lucky for me, I had a very good professor, who happened to be a psychologist, in my first term of university. This teacher was particularly trained in the field of directing students to success and with his lecture notes and advice, I have been able to apply newly learned skills to my day-to-day academic challenges. However, I did not just develop good grades overnight. It required some major problem-solving skills. I imagined myself at my present state: a first-year student with dreams and ambitions. Then I imagined the state I wanted to be in, which was a position where all my goals were achieved and I was happy with my life. Problem-solving means making these two states as close to each other as possible and maneuvering around any obstacles between these two states. I have yet to master this technique; however, I take it one day at a time and have my goals in the back of my mind continuously. I constantly work on myself, being open to new ideas and suggestions, and I persistently try to meet new people of higher stature who may be able to give me good advice or offer me opportunities to give advice to others.

My advice to the students who take the time to read this is the same advice I had been given before I started university. I strongly recommend staying *on top of everything, and don't fall behind.* Once you fall behind, there's no way you will catch up and the skills you have developed will be useless for the vast amount of information needed to be learned in such a short period of time. Like my father once said: "The deeper you go into the jungle, the more trees you'll see." We are in the jungle here at university, and we have to fight to survive; so develop those skills necessary for survival, and you'll be the king or queen of the jungle.

Nothing is more basic to becoming educated than the ability to think. Yet what does it mean to think? As you have discovered, thinking is more than simply accumulating facts; it is the ability to evaluate those facts, to reason, to utilize information productively, to expand understanding, and to solve problems. Thinking does not occur automatically, nor is it something that everyone does instinctively. Thinking is a learned process. It involves developing a variety of cognitive capabilities and skills. Throughout the ages a fundamental goal of education has been to teach students to think. Long ago, the philosopher Descartes declared, "I think, therefore I am." In developing your ability to use a variety of reasoning skills to systematically think about issues, and solve problems, you are continuing a centuries-old tradition of being a critical thinker.

As seen on page 286, critical thinking and problem-solving are fundamental elements of a successful student's metacognitive identity. The metacognitive identity is made up of various aspects of critical thinking and creative problem-solving skills. In your quest for success as a student, you begin with self-awareness, by assessing your critical-thinking skills and creative problem-solving skills against those used by accomplished students. Your answers to the quiz in Chapter 2 provide you with basic information about your creative and critical-thinking capabilities. Self-confidence as a thinker is enhanced by attitudes of criticism, inquiry, reflection, and honesty. The development of thinking capabilities is influenced by both academic and social experiences. By developing procedural knowledge through pattern recognition, independent thinking, evaluating alternatives, perspective taking, likelihood calculations, scientific method or inquiry, decision making, logical reasoning, and problem solving, you enhance thinking skills that describe your academic self. Note that problem solving is an important part of procedural knowledge, as well as a critical component of the social self. By adding to the approaches you use to solve problems in living, you add to your adaptability and flexibility in your capability to handle dilemmas associated with your social self. Expanding the approaches you use to solve problems and think critically will add to your confidence about your ability to apply thinking skills to creatively solve a variety of personal and social problems. As you progress through this chapter, become aware of how successful students think and solve problems. By identifying the skills you have that overlap with them, celebrating these skills, and adopting those that you have not fully developed, you can strengthen your capabilities as a thinker.

Critical Thinking

Critical thinking is significant for the educated, especially those who will be responsible for dealing with complex issues in the future. As such, it is viewed as significant for life in a democratic society, given the freedom it holds for you as a citizen. Thus, the ability to think critically and to communicate effectively is central to life.

Critical thinking has received considerable research attention, yet defining it is somewhat challenging, given its complexity. As a purposeful act, critical thinking focuses on a goal of discovering the truth and the effort to achieve that goal. Throughout the search for truth, judgments used are constantly being assessed to ensure that personal biases are not influencing the thinking process. Critical thinking is viewed as a set of core mental processes (Bailin, Case, Coombs, & Daniels, 1999), that includes interpretation, analysis, evaluation, inference, explanation, and self-regulation (Facione, 1990). In order for consistency to occur throughout the critical thinking process, the explanation of truth depends on evidence, on how the concept is defined, on the method used to gather evidence, on the criteria used to judge its validity, and on the context from which the truth is derived. It is pervasive in that it attempts to get as much information as possible. It is self-rectifying in that the search for truth constantly replaces erroneous ideas with new, substantiated ones. As a complex mental process, critical thinking develops over time and through much effort. As an active process, critical thinking is evaluative. It assesses, judges, critically scrutinizes, searches for accuracy, consistency, and ultimately, the truth. In the search for truth and through reflective skepticism, it uncovers flaws in evidence.

Developmental Stages of Thinking

Becoming a critical thinker is a developmental process that is influenced by experience and education. Researchers Bloom, Perry and Clinchy have provided insight into the development of critical thinking capabilities. Interested in how students think, Bloom (1956) created a general cognitive taxonomy. As you will recall from Chapter 3, his view is a developmental process of critical thinking, beginning with the basic knowledge of a new idea and developing to the point of evaluation (Bloom, 1956). As seen in Table 3.2 on page 51, the student goes through six stages, progressively involving more effort and a

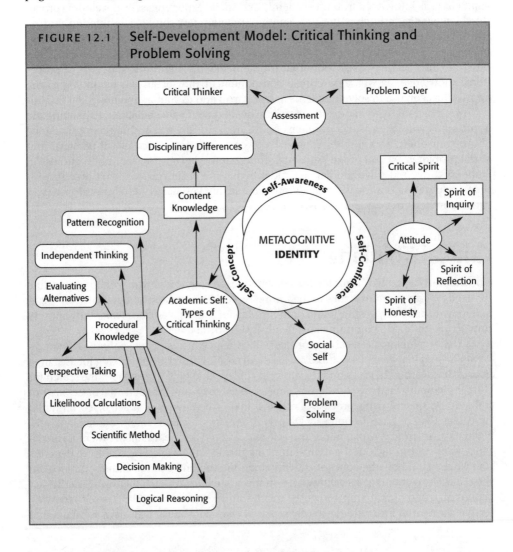

FIGURE 12.1 | Self-Development Model: Critical Thinking and Problem Solving

deeper level of thought: knowledge, comprehension, application, analysis, synthesis, and evaluation. Each successive stage is dependent on some form of mastery of the previous stage(s). For instance, in order for a student to successfully apply an idea, he/she will need to know, as well as comprehend, the idea. As described in Chapter 3, successful students are aware of these different cognitive levels, and are able to identify the levels expected in each of their various assignments, tests, and exams. Please review Bloom's taxonomy in Chapter 3 before proceeding.

Based on a four-year study of Harvard male undergraduates, Perry (1970) developed a scheme to trace the development of a student's view of the world of knowledge, truth, and value. Students begin as **dualistic** or absolute thinkers, assuming only one right answer to every question. For instance, euthanasia would be seen as wrong. The world is one of black and white, of right and wrong, and of true and false. Students at this stage depend on their professors as "the experts" to provide the "right" answers.

With increased exposure to university, students quickly realize that there are conflicting opinions among "the experts" (i.e., Critical Thinking Across the Disciplines section). Confronted by this non-dualist world-view, students' thinking is either threatened or it is challenged. Successful students tend to adopt a **multiplicity** view of the world by perceiving the world as having gray areas with few or even no absolute right answers. Truth is at best something personal and private. Everyone is entitled to his or her Truth and there are as many truths as there are people. In other words, each person's opinion can be valued as true, given that each person is the authority of his or her own truth. One point of view is as good as another. Although this way of thinking allows for the freedom of expressing opinions, the search for truth is no longer black and white, but at best an opinion, and challenges students to look further in their search for Truth. Looking at the issue of euthanasia, the student may discover that not everyone agrees with his/her view of it being wrong.

Desiring to find Truth and moving beyond simply accepting the opinion of others as equally valid, students mature to the **relativism subordinate** stage. Here they neither accept as Truth anything that "the experts" say, nor treat all opinions as equally valid. Rather, students adopt an analytical, critical approach, using the tools of their discipline to interpret and evaluate the ideas they are studying. In other words, Truth now becomes contextual, where the meaning of an idea is derived from its context and based upon the perspective from which it is evaluated. For instance, euthanasia is often viewed as a noble act by certain cultures. Thus, knowledge becomes Truth, relative to various contexts.

Realizing that there are multiple possibilities for deriving Truth, the student is challenged to take the final step—to make a strong, yet tentative **commitment** to some ideas. Students commit themselves to one of the many possibilities that define Truth and act upon that idea or set of ideas, fully realizing and embracing the possibility of an alternative explanation. Thus a student struggling with the issue of euthanasia at earlier stages of cognitive development, now approaches the issue, fully engages in a study of all its complexities and draws on a definitive answer, commits to that way of thinking by supporting that viewpoint through affirmative actions such as educating others on his/her viewpoint on euthanasia, defending the viewpoint in public debates, writing in support of the viewpoint, and even participating in the act.

In an attempt to provide an alternative explanation of critical thinking, Clinchy (1990) conducted her research on female students and discovered elements that parallel, as well as contradict Perry's theory. When students enter the university, they tend to adopt the role of **receiving knowledge** (Clinchy, 1990). Like Perry's dualistic thinkers, these students rely on "the experts" to provide them with knowledge, deriving their identity and their assigned roles from "the experts." Truth is external, something that only someone in authority can possess. Like processed food, the ideas of the students "come ready-made from the professors" (Clinchy, 1990).

Directly opposite to relying on authority for Truth, is the search for Truth from within or **subjectivism** (Clinchy, 1990). Truth comes from the heart, is personal, is intuitive, and comes from first-hand experiences. Comparable to Perry's "multiplicity" stage, students view that all have Truths: you have yours and I have mine. Based on intuition, an idea is true if it feels right. However, in order for students to learn, they are challenged to move beyond their personal Truths through systematic and deliberate procedures for creating, understanding, and evaluating new ideas (Clinchy, 1990). These systematic and deliberate procedures are the many ways of knowing that are important for expanding and refining students' thinking capabilities. Referred to as procedural knowledge, this stage is defined as either separate knowing or connected knowing.

Separate knowing is an objective, analytical procedure, as emphasized by critical thinking, scientific method, and textual analysis. Perry defined this as relativism subordinate. According to Clinchy (1990), the student detaches him/herself from the idea, and takes an impersonal stance while following certain rules to ensure that judgments made are not biased. Each discipline (e.g., psychology, literature, science), has a set of procedures and standards for students to follow for correctly analyzing and evaluating phenomena. Key to separate knowing is the art of doubting (Elbow, 1973), looking for opposing positions, and finding what is wrong with the phenomenon being investigated (Clinchy, 1990).

Connected knowing, on the other hand, focuses on believing, on finding why the idea makes sense, and discovering how it might be right (Clinchy, 1990). In an attempt to understand the idea, students immerse themselves in it—in an attempt to feel and think with the originator of the idea. Through "connected conversations," each student builds on the other's ideas. As a result of drawing out and entering into each other's ideas, and elaborating upon them, the combined efforts of the group far exceed the Truth constructed by any student alone (Clinchy, 1990). Hence, discussion and study groups are vital to your learning.

Each of these three theories provides a unique framework for how students develop critical thinking skills. They provide an awareness of the developmental process of thinking, of the differences in types of thinking, and of the interactive, social process that promotes cognitive development. Of importance to you is how you can further develop your critical thinking skills through procedures defining critical thinking.

Components of Critical Thinking

Educational researchers tend to delineate critical thinking into content knowledge, procedural knowledge, metacognition, and attitude (McKeachie, Pintrich, Lin, & Smith, 1986). Content knowledge requires a familiarity with the content within the discipline. Procedural knowledge involves the variety of procedures that can be employed in critical thinking. *Metacognition*, as defined in Chapter 7, involves the student's ability to be aware of and effectively employ thinking skills. Attitude requirements are inquisitiveness and honesty in the search for Truth. Each of these four approaches to critical thinking will be further explored below.

Content Knowledge

Background or content knowledge is a precondition for critical thinking to take place (Bailin et al., 1999). Before effective critical thinking can occur, it is necessary to understand the nature or background of the problem and its context, to help in determining what steps are appropriate in thinking. The context for most students would focus on the discipline knowledge. If you are investigating a psychological phenomenon, you would begin by focusing on content knowledge from a psychological viewpoint or disciplinary perspective. In other words, "critical thinking is an investigation with the purpose to explore a situation or phenomenon, question or problem solve to arrive at a hypothesis or conclusion that integrates all available information (in this case, from the domain of the psychology discipline), and that therefore can be convincingly justified" (Kurfiss, 1988, p. 12). In developing your content knowledge, you need to engage in the various practices conducted by academics.

For example, interested in how first-year students deal with text anxiety, academic scholars engage in four steps of developing content knowledge. First, they begin with an investigation that requires research through the collection of data or evidence. Data is collected through various means: literature review on the current research that focuses on students and test anxiety; experiments that provoke anxiety in students to determine how they will react in an exam situation; and a survey asking students what causes test anxiety, how they deal with it, and its impact on their learning. Second, a purpose or goal guides the investigation, such as discovering a strategy that reduces students' test anxiety. Third, there is an exploration of a situation or phenomenon, a question or a problem. For instance, academic scholars are exploring the various factors that cause test anxiety. Fourth, there is the integration of all available information into a convincing justification that provides the needed explanation. In the case-test anxiety, all the information collected through a literature review and extensive experimentation and survey would be compiled to come up with a conclusive outcome of what factors cause test anxiety and what steps can be taken to reduce its adverse affects on student learning. Based on these four critical steps, critical thinkers can come up with some form of Truth to explain the phenomenon at hand.

These four basic steps are performed on a daily basis at universities across the world. Scholars are conducting investigations of various kinds in their disciplines, such as the cures for cancer and AIDS, solutions to world peace and hunger, and new ways to use technology. These scholars have hypotheses that guide their data collection. Once ready, they disseminate their findings in convincingly justifiable manners that compel their research audiences. This is a vital aspect of the function of higher education. Once understood and applied, critical thinking can be effectively transferred to solve various life challenges, from simple daily survival issues, to the complexities of global issues. By thinking critically, you are able to challenge widely accepted, but erroneous beliefs. It aids you in becoming an active, astute judge of other people and their points of view, rather than a passive recipient of the latest intellectual fads and tyrannies.

Procedural Knowledge: Types of Critical-Thinking Strategies

Critical thinking also involves knowing the various principles that guide good thinking in each discipline (Bailin et al., 1999). Each discipline (esociology, biology, etc.), has a different set of strategies used to discern Truth. These thinking strategies can include any one of the following: pattern recognition, independent thinking, evaluating alternatives, perspective taking, likelihood calculations, scientific method or inquiry, decision making, logical reasoning, and problem solving. Each of these strategies generates ideas about many aspects of daily life and is useful in the search for Truth. Each is used for different reasons.

Pattern Recognition

Pattern recognition is defined as recognizing patterns in data. It is used most effectively in statistical situations. For instance, weather analyses, stock market analyses, trends in human behaviour, patterns in historical events, tendencies in political activities, and driving data from computers in cars are often based on statistical analyses of patterns of data. Important application areas are image analysis, character recognition, speech analysis, human and machine diagnostics, person identification, and industrial inspection. Adopting pattern recognition as part of your critical thinking involves identifying patterns in data. You can use this to your advantage as you look for patterns in your own life that provide you with greater understanding. For instance, throughout this textbook, we have encouraged you to reflect on the various skills that you use to learn effectively and to identify consistent, recurring behaviours or patterns. These patterns provide valuable information about how you learn.

Independent Thinking

Independent thinking requires you to derive an understanding of the world based on your own observations and experiences rather than just depending on others. You need to trust your own ability to make judgments, even when it contradicts the opinions of others. It is what Perry called "multiplicity" (Perry, 1970) or Clinchy called "subjectivism" (1990). In doing so, you may bring a new idea to fruition. Critical thinking helps you test your own ideas and may take you to new levels of thinking such as "relativism subordinate" (Perry, 1970) or "connected knowing" (Clinchy, 1990). Many, such as Einstein, Edison, and Ballard, have trusted their thinking and thereby discovered new Truths: atomic power, the light bulb, and hydrogen-powered vehicles. As you strive to find new ideas about how to learn most effectively, take the ideas of others as guides, yet focus on your own innovative learning methods. You may discover an alternative that is even more effective to enhancing your learning, and who knows, this new method may be used in future textbooks to help students learn.

Evaluating Alternatives

Evaluating alternatives is a strategy that provides the person with a variety of choices that are different from the usual or conventional (Merriam-Webster, 1986). These alternatives usually exist or function outside the established cultural, social, or economic system (Merriam-Webster, 1986). Similar to independent thinking, evaluating alternatives provides you with more than just the conventional conclusion about a given phenomenon. It encourages you to go beyond the norm, to develop alternative hypotheses for situations. In the research for the cure of diabetes, researchers were convinced that diabetes was controllable by certain diets. However, it was not until two Canadian researchers moved beyond the established research findings that they discovered the significance of insulin. As a student, allow your thinking to go beyond what is expected by the discipline, thereby enhancing your creative contributions to the search for Truth. As you discover the various challenges in learning successfully, take time to explore alternatives to what is suggested in this textbook or the lecture. For instance, you may discover alternatives to enhancing your learning, such as maintaining your sleep and nutrition, ideas not covered in detail in this textbook.

Perspective Taking

Perspective taking is defined as viewing things in their true relations or relative importance (Merriam-Webster, 1986). The best way to achieve this is to place yourself in the situation to better understand the phenomenon. A few medical experts subject themselves to the conditions they are studying. In an attempt to better understand hypothermia, Dr. Gordon G. Giesbrecht from the University of Manitoba has subjected his body to conditions that emulate this state. By taking on the perspective of the phenomenon, you are better able to compare and judge, thereby delineating the Truth. This also means taking on the perspective of the successful student, by trying to place yourself in their shoes and by adopting their strategies.

Calculating Likelihood

Calculating likelihood is defined as determining the chance that a given event will occur (Merriam-Webster, 1986). Part of this strategy involves likelihood ratios, which are a means of expressing the possibility of the phenomenon occurring. Likelihood ratios allow healthcare providers to estimate the odds of disease given the results of a person's history, physical exam, and lab tests; lifetime chances of going to prison by age, sex, race, and ethnic origin; the likelihood of having twins; weather speculation; and stock market calculations (e.g., futures market). This strategy is useful in future speculations. As a student, research shows that your high school grade point average (Clifton, 1997; Naumann, 1999), predicts your success as a student at the university, your relationship with professors, peers, and your involvement in study groups. The support that you get from your parents also predicts your future success as a student. If you were to continue your learning strategies from before, all these predictors would be adequate in calculating your likelihood of success. However, you can beat these likelihoods by actively applying all the strategies discussed in this book and joining the group of students who have moved beyond the control of these various predictors and have entered graduate school and completed their degrees.

Scientific Method or Inquiry

Scientific method or inquiry is defined as the "the collection of data through observation and experiment, and the formulation and testing of hypotheses" (Merriam-Webster, 1986). Most researchers use this method in exploring any and all aspects of the universe. It is as simple, yet as profound, as my three-year-old son and five-year-old daughter asking "Why?" For instance, you may be curious as to why test anxiety influences your performance as a student. Adopting the scientific method as part of your critical thinking involves the following five procedures highlighted on page 292. First, guided by your "why" question, you begin by observing the phenomenon of test anxiety and its impact on students' performance. Second, you create a tentative *hypothesis*, or description that is consistent with what you observe: high as compared to low levels of test anxiety reduce students' performance. Third, you make a prediction(s) based on the hypothesis: students with high test anxiety will have poorer achievement scores than students with low test anxiety. Fourth, you test the prediction(s) by further observations or experimentation, and change the hypothesis based on your results. You discover that first-year students' test anxiety scores at the beginning of the semester predict their final exam scores. Finally, you would repeat the last two steps until there are no differences between theory and observation and/or experiment. When you discover consistency between the hypothesis and the observations, the hypothesis becomes a *theory* and provides a coherent set of conditions that explain a class of phenomena. Through your observations and experimentation, you might discover that only students with extremely high test anxiety are most vulnerable to poor final exam scores. The theory, in turn, becomes the framework within which future observations are explained and predictions are made.

Decision-Making

Decision-making is defined as a determination arrived at after consideration (Merriam-Webster, 1986). Many professions use decision-making on a daily basis. For instance, medical experts use it to rule out a range of diseases to determine the exact prognosis, so that diagnosis is more successful (e.g., medications and/or operations). Engineers use it to discover the best material to use for certain applications. In doing so successfully, a tree diagram is often employed. The branches represent the various options or choices available with the associated risks, costs, consequences, or probabilities. As can be seen on page 293, a decision tree is a map of the reasoning process. It can be used to explain why a question is being asked. In real world problems, the intuition of a human expert, such as a medical doctor in medicine or an engineer in engineering, is necessary to determine the likely end node. Each end node would represent a situation with known effective and efficient outcomes. The figure on page 293 provides a helpful guide in dealing with test anxiety.

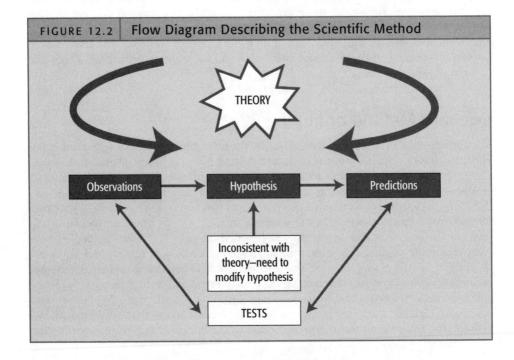

FIGURE 12.2 | **Flow Diagram Describing the Scientific Method**

THEORY

Observations → Hypothesis → Predictions

Inconsistent with theory—need to modify hypothesis

TESTS

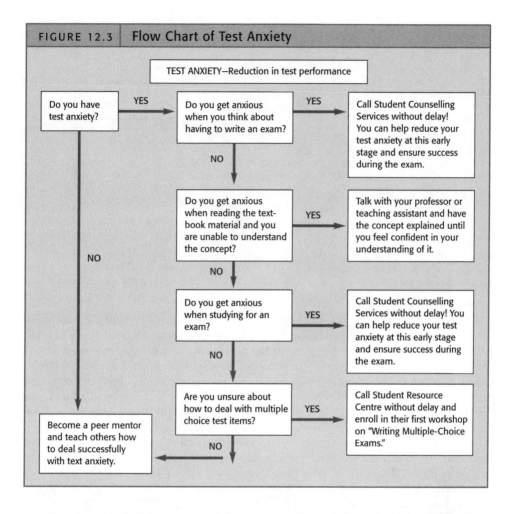

FIGURE 12.3 | Flow Chart of Test Anxiety

TEST ANXIETY—Reduction in test performance

Do you have test anxiety? — YES → Do you get anxious when you think about having to write an exam? — YES → Call Student Counselling Services without delay! You can help reduce your test anxiety at this early stage and ensure success during the exam.

NO

Do you get anxious when reading the text-book material and you are unable to understand the concept? — YES → Talk with your professor or teaching assistant and have the concept explained until you feel confident in your understanding of it.

NO

Do you get anxious when studying for an exam? — YES → Call Student Counselling Services without delay! You can help reduce your test anxiety at this early stage and ensure success during the exam.

NO

Are you unsure about how to deal with multiple choice test items? — YES → Call Student Resource Centre without delay and enroll in their first workshop on "Writing Multiple-Choice Exams."

NO

Become a peer mentor and teach others how to deal successfully with text anxiety.

One popular decision tree used by many students defines decision-making by a series of tasks (Bailin et al., 1999). Each of the six steps of the DECIDE model prescribes task descriptions for thinking to occur. This model outlines a problem-solving process of defining the problem clearly, evaluating potential solutions in light of consequences and choosing the most workable option. An important component of this and other problem-solving models is the evaluation of the effectiveness of the solution. Successful students tend to follow similar decision models to engage in effective decision-making. Compare your method of making decisions with the one on page 294. Add steps that you are missing to your thinking repertoire.

Logical Reasoning

What often characterizes critical thinking is the quality of logical reasoning (Bailin et al., 1999). *Logical reasoning* is defined as "the drawing of inferences or conclusions through the use of reason" (Merriam-Webster, 1986). Drawing or *formulating inferences* is further defined as "the act of passing from one proposition, statement, or judgment considered as true to another whose Truth is believed to follow from that of the former"

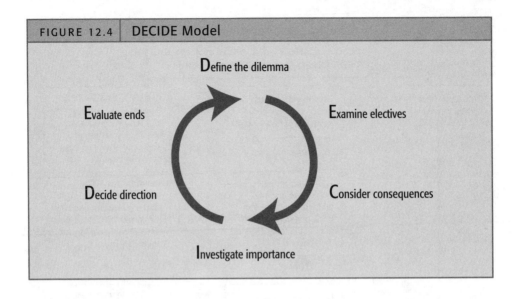

FIGURE 12.4 | **DECIDE Model**

Define the dilemma

Evaluate ends

Examine electives

Decide direction

Consider consequences

Investigate importance

(Merriam-Webster, 1986). Successful logical reasoning involves an argument (Copi & Cohen, 1990; Crossley & Wilson, 1979; Johnson & Blair, 1983). An **argument** is a set of two or more statements in which one of the statements has the special status of being the conclusion. A **conclusion** is a reasoned judgment; the necessary consequence of two or more propositions taken as premises (Merriam-Webster, 1986). The other statements, called premises, are intended to provide grounds for accepting the conclusion. In evaluating an argument, you ask two questions. First, are the premises true? This depends upon your knowledge of the subject matter. Second, supposing the premises were all true, would that circumstance provide a good reason for accepting the conclusion? In order to adequately use these two questions in evaluating an argument, you would engage in a process of either deductive or inductive logic (Copi & Cohen, 1990; Crossley & Wilson, 1979; Johnson & Blair, 1983).

Deductive logic or **validity** is the highest standard of logical strength in terms of providing support for a conclusion (Copi & Cohen, 1990; Crossley & Wilson, 1979; Johnson & Blair, 1983). It is often referred to as "all or nothing" or "black & white." An argument is said to be deductively valid if, and only if it would be impossible for the conclusion to be false in a world in which all the premises were true. Obviously, a deductively sound argument always has a true conclusion. For instance, the following argument is deductively valid, but not deductively sound:

Premise: Jane Smith is a student.

Premise: All students think that terrorism is evil.

Conclusion: Jane Smith thinks terrorism is evil.

A deductively valid argument cannot have all true premises and a false conclusion, but anything else is permissible:

1. true premises with a true conclusion:

   Premise: All cats are mammals. (true)

   Premise: All mammals breathe air. (true)

   Conclusion: All cats breathe air. (true)

2. one or more false premises with a false conclusion:

   Premise: All cats are mammals. (true)

   Premise: All mammals have wings. (false)

   Conclusion: All cats have wings. (false)

3. one or more false premises with a true conclusion:

   Premise: All birds are mammals. (false)

   Premise: All mammals have wings. (false)

   Conclusion: All birds have wings. (true)

Inductive logic or **inductive strength** is concerned with arguments that aim at achieving a less stringent standard (Copi & Cohen, 1990; Crossley & Wilson, 1979; Johnson & Blair, 1983). In other words, what is the minimum required to make the conclusion barely acceptable? An argument is inductively strong if and only if the premises would provide some reason for accepting the conclusion, supposing that they all were true. Inductive strength comes in degrees, unlike deductive validity. An argument is inductively sound if and only if it is inductively strong and its premises are all true. The following argument has a modest degree of inductive strength, yet may not be inductively sound:

   Premise: Jane Smith is a student.

   Premise: The great majority of students think that terrorism is evil.

   Conclusion: Jane Smith thinks terrorism is evil.

It would be possible for both premises to be true while the conclusion is false. That would be the case if Jane happened to belong to the minority of students who think that terrorism is noble.

Argumentative Analysis: Good Arguments and Their Fallacies

There are three basic requirements for a good argument (Copi & Cohen, 1990; Johnson & Blair, 1983). The premises must be:

1. relevant to the conclusion;

2. sufficient to warrant accepting the conclusion; and

3. acceptable in their own right.

The highest grade of logical sufficiency is attained in an argument that is deductively valid, for then the conclusion cannot possibly be false, provided the premises are true. Frequently, however, we must rely upon arguments that are not deductively valid, but have a reasonable degree of inductive strength. The highest grade of logical acceptability is to have premises known with certainty to be true. But it is reasonable to accept premises for which we have sufficient evidence to render them probable. A premise that is not acceptable, because of lack of evidence, may of course turn out to be true.

There are three families of fallacies that correspond to the three requirements above: irrelevant reason, hasty conclusion, and problematic premise (Copi & Cohen, 1990;

Johnson & Blair, 1983). Irrelevant reason occurs when the requirement of relevance is not met. For example, the federal Department of Health and Welfare had been cooperating with the Kellogg Company in the marketing of a cereal possessing little or no nutritional value (premises). As for the nutritional value of corn flakes, the milk you have with your flakes has great nutritional value (conclusion). Notice that the premises have no relevance to the conclusion.

A **hasty conclusion** is where the requirement of logical sufficiency is not met. Quote one or two good examples and then jump to the general conclusion you are after; most people will not notice the gap in your reasoning. A priceless example comes from a letter to Ann Landers. "My 16-year-old cousin sent for your booklet called 'Teenage Sex and Ten Ways to Cool It.' The booklet arrived; she read it right away. Well, Ann Landers, three months later she was pregnant and got married very fast! What I want to know is why do you recommend booklets if they don't do any good?"—Highly Disappointed!

When one or more premise fails to meet the requirement of logical acceptability, we have a **problematic premise**. For example, in the 1980s, many people argued: *Elvis Presley is alive. He will be performing again.* Their belief that Elvis was alive was based upon 'Elvis sightings' in various places throughout the United States, and maintained even though there was overwhelming evidence that Elvis was, in fact, dead.

When coming to a conclusion based on the temporal sequence of events, we may have a **false cause**. Here you would just point out that A was followed by B, and you can get people believing that A caused B. Nine months after a major power outage in Toronto, the maternity wards of the hospitals were scrambling for rooms. Power outages cause the conception of babies.

There are a number of common fallacies used on a daily basis in almost every area of life. These include *argumentum ad hominem, argumentum ad verecundiam, argumentum ad baculum, argumentum ad misericordiam*, and *argumentum ad ignorantiam* (Copi & Cohen, 1990).

Argumentum ad hominem is defined as arguing against the person. Avoid talking about what your opponent has said; just launch a personal attack. Two effective strategies have been used. The first is to point out some circumstance that will make your opponent lose face. For example, "The vice-president of Nauseous Pulp and Paper has produced some studies that conclude that the proposed new mill would not have any effect on the fish population in Forgotten Lake. Now just let me remind you that his company stands to make millions of dollars of profits from this mill, but would make a lot less if it were required to obey tougher emission standards." Second is to perform an outright character assassination. For instance, "Is that what you think! Well, what can we expect from a vice-president who regularly pollutes the environment with his second-hand smoke."

Argumentum ad verecundiam is defined as illegitimate appeal to authority. The strategy here is to back up your opinion by quoting some famous person that your audience admires, regardless of the fact that your authority figure is not an expert in this particular subject matter. Any well known Canadian Olympic stars, professional athletes, or Hollywood performers may be used as an authority on the merits of a given brand of beer, gasoline, over-the-counter medicine, or any other product you are attempting to market to young adult males.

Argumentum ad baculum is defined as the appeal to force, a powerful strategy used by many schoolyard bullies at any age and in any schoolyard. For example, "Let me remind you, Mr. Prime Minister, that our organization can swing 50 000 votes in marginal seats." The person can speak irrelevancies as long as he or she has power to force a decision.

Argumentum ad misericordiam is defined as the appeal to pity. By making people feel sympathetic to the cause you are promoting, it will make up for the fact that you do not have any good arguments: "I really need an A if I want to have any hope of getting into medical school."

Argumentum ad ignorantiam is defined as argument from ignorance, whereby you do not bother to argue for your opinion; just point out that it has not been proven to be false. "Sure it's safe to go snowboarding on Treacherous Hill. No one's been killed there yet."

Each of these fallacies occurs on a regular basis, in all forms of communication, both verbal and written. The key here is to be able to identify them when trying to discern the Truth. Accomplished students are fairly knowledgeable about these fallacies and use them to guard against accepting conclusions based on poorly constructed argumentation.

Critical Thinking Across the Disciplines

A significant part of university training is to promote freedom of thought. With freedom of thought comes a variety of ways to derive meaning from the same idea. This allows scholars from across the disciplines to expand a student's worldview. However exciting it is to have this exposure to the diversity of knowledge, the successful student is aware that differences in critical thinking do occur across the disciplines. In other words, ideas are discipline specific and formulated according to a set of theories and criteria that are discipline specific. For instance, if you are taking courses in biology, sociology, political sciences, philosophy, and economics, you need to be aware of the discipline differences in order to succeed. Different elements of critical thinking are seen as important, depending on the discipline. In economics, most writing projects are analytical and argue cases. Students present and defend contestable ideas; they analyze and evaluate the idea of others. Young analysts and economists are trained to use analysis, evaluation, and arguments (MacKinnon, 1993). For a historian, critical thinking involves comparing conflicting evidence and views from various sources, deriving a synthesis of the evidence, and disseminating this persuasively (Holt, 1990). For the scientist, critical thinking is demonstrated in the evidence that supports the writer's thesis.

By discovering the thinking criteria expected in a particular discipline you can begin to think accordingly. One of the reasons that you are encouraged to take a broad range of courses during your first year of university is so that you develop the flexibility to process information from a variety of disciplinary viewpoints. Each discipline encourages you to develop various methods of thinking. Your ability to utilize these diverse strategies and to ask questions allows you to expand your thinking capabilities. Develop an awareness of these disciplinary differences. Establish an overview of the field. Obtain additional reference material if necessary. Look for similarities between new subject matter and other academic fields that are familiar to you. Above all, be aware of overlap between disciplines that may distract you while studying similar issues from different perspectives.

Effective Use of Critical Thinking in Writing

In the academe, the development of new knowledge occurs as a result of employing various critical thinking strategies. Most common is the **dialectic process**, a process that involves "systematic reasoning, exposition, or arguments that juxtapose opposed or contradictory ideas and seeks to resolve their conflict" (Merriam-Webster, 1986). In other words, a logical debate is used to expose contradictory ideas and to find new answers. Many of your university assignments or exams, such as essay questions, are often used to demonstrate your understanding of a concept or idea. Typically there is no right answer. Rather it is your ability to critically think though identification, argumentation and debating the issue that counts. In writing critical thinking essays, Hegel's dialectic (philosopher, 1770–1831), can prove very rewarding. His method provides an opportunity to take any statement, break it apart and rebuild it again into a new and more powerful statement that has the potential of revealing more Truth. There are three simple steps involved in writing a critical thinking paper: the thesis, the antithesis, and the synthesis.

First, you need to explain the thesis of a given statement. Be aware that this thesis is different from your working thesis in writing a paper (see Chapter 10). The **thesis** requires an explanation of the statement. Consider the classic Nike statement: "Just do it." As part of the first step of the dialectic, you would provide an exegesis of what "Just do it" means. For instance, it might refer to the freedom of doing whatever you please. Or it could mean to enjoy life to the fullest. Note that there is no right answer. Key to excelling at this task is to provide the rationale that supports your thesis or your explanation. In other words, build the logic that would support your interpretation of this statement. Here you could refer to the fact that people should be given the chance to do as they please, for in doing so, life can be lived to the fullest. Or a person can realize his/her full potential only when given the opportunity to experience as much as possible. The more freedom to explore life's events, the more learning can occur. Evidence to support this would strengthen the thesis. For example, children who are given more opportunities to learn, tend also to excel academically.

Next, build the **antithesis**, a contradicting counterargument or alternative conclusion. Referring back to Nike's statement, a counter-argument might be "Don't do it." As part of the counterargument, you would explain and provide support for your statement. For example, "Don't do it" refers to the fact that one should not have the freedom to do whatever pleases the person. There are responsibilities that come with a person's actions that need to keep the freedom of doing it in check. Each action has some reaction or consequence. For instance, engaging in the freedom of sexual activity has the potential consequences of pregnancy and diseases.

The third step, **synthesis**, is, as Bloom (1956) defines it, the combination or the merging of the thesis and antithesis into a new idea, outcome, conclusion, and eventually a new Truth. Think of the thesis as white and the antithesis as black. However, do not transfer the moral indications of black as evil and white as good. Like a synthesizer in music, the synthesis mixes the thesis and the antithesis, the black and white, creating a new combination—grey. Many of the scientific discoveries, medical breakthroughs, and technological advances are a result of the synthesis of what has been always viewed as correct (white), in combination with a contradictory idea (black). In our Nike example, a synthesis of the thesis and antithesis might state that "Just do it" works in conjunction with "taking full responsibility for doing it." A person's freedom carries with it responsibilities and as long as these responsibilities are realized, than "Just do it" is possible.

Key to a successful dialectic is your ability to reason and to provide evidence to support each level; so there are no right answers. The best way to approach this type of task is to begin by creating a concept map with three major bubbles: thesis, antithesis, and synthesis. For each bubble, provide an exegesis of the original statement and follow it with supporting premises and/or evidence. Next, develop a paragraph for each of the components: thesis, antithesis, and synthesis. The introduction sentence for each paragraph should restate and define the thesis, antithesis, and synthesis. As with critical thinking, provide supporting evidence for the interpretation of the thesis, antithesis, and synthesis. Then complete each paragraph with a conclusion statement that integrates the interpretation with the evidence, in supporting the thesis, antithesis, and synthesis. The synthesis should provide a creative alternative that merges key ideas from both the thesis and antithesis and creatively comes up with a novel mix. This novel approach is defined, evidence is provided to support it and a conclusion is made that demonstrates the strength of the synthesis over the thesis and the antithesis. Before completing the task, create a catchy title that defines the dilemma of the thesis and antithesis.

Creative Problem Solving

Problems arising out of real life and academic life are abundant and pop up on a daily basis. What is the best route around this traffic congestion? How do I ask that person out for a date? What is the cure for AIDS? What makes students successful? Many of our daily problems are solved through trial and error. In Edison's laboratory, thousands of light bulb filaments were tested before stumbling onto the best one. For other problems, we might follow an algorithm—a procedure with various steps guaranteed to provide a solution—such as rebooting a computer system after it crashes. If we think for a moment, we might even be fortunate to have an insight, a sudden and novel realization of a solution, as did Geffory Ballard when he thought of fueling vehicles with hydrogen to produce water as an emission.

Whereas critical thinking focuses primarily on evaluating evidence and reasoning, creative problem solving focuses primarily on generating alternatives and finding answers to questions. Problem solving is a process that involves selecting and applying content knowledge, strategy knowledge, experiences and beliefs to deal with novel situations or new information, then to evaluate the outcomes of the action (Dewey, 1933; Miller, Cassie, & Drake, 1990; Wales, Nardi, & Stager, 1986). There are many problem-solving models available for you as a student. Most are based on Dewey's original model (Dewey, 1933). To provide you with the best, we have created a synthesis of the many current problem-solving models (Miller et al., 1990; Wales et al., 1986). As a progressive strategy, it involves defining the problem, listing the advantages and disadvantages of each alternative, finding the best solution/alternative, and then evaluating the effectiveness of the solution (Dewey, 1933; Miller et al., 1990; Wales et al., 1986).

Step 1: Stating the Problem

The first step involves stating the problem or the question to be answered (Dewey, 1933). This requires defining the situation by gathering as much information about the components of the problem (Wales et al., 1986), through the standard questioning process of *who, what, when, where, how,* and *why*. For example, a student concerned with lack of sleep begins by asking *Who*—Is it just me or are others in my dorm experiencing the same thing? *What*—A measure of the amount of sleep that I am getting per night and an assessment of amount that I need. I am only getting 4 to 5 hours sleep per night. *When*—Is this occurring during a particular time? Just during the term. At home I can sleep 8 to 12 hours per night. *Where*—Are there differences in sleep related to the places I sleep? Just in my room. At home or at my friend's place, I sleep fine. *How*—Are there patterns that I engage in that are related to sleep difficulties? I often lie restlessly before sleeping. *Why*—Do I have some hypotheses for factors that could be influencing this pattern? Some of my hypotheses include: room is too hot, types of activities I do before I go to bed. I study, eat, and watch TV in my bed, worries keep me awake, and the dorm is very noisy. Based on the answers to the above questions, you can begin to formulate a clear definition and description of the problem. This in turn, allows you to generate solutions that will truly solve the problem.

Another example is of a researcher concerned with identifying the roadblocks thwarting students' critical thinking. Notice that the same questions used by the student above are also utilized by the researcher to come up with identifying the problem. *Who*— all or just a particular group of first-year students. *What*—hypothesize about factors that are thwarting students from thinking creatively. Could it be lack of experience, fears, inability, misunderstanding, or lack of desire? *When*—certain type of classes, such as a philosophy class or certain content areas of classes, such as the application of new ideas in many social science classes. *Where*—at the university. *How*—through their writing assignments. *Why*—hypotheses include affective, behavioural, and cognitive barriers. This is a critical stage for the researcher and provides the framework that later produces a helpful guide, as can be seen in the table on page 302.

Step 2: Stating the Goal

With a clear definition of the problem, the student and the researcher list what they want to accomplish: for the student, a solution to sleep deprivation; for the academic, a list of barriers that thwart student critical thinking. Notice that key to problem solving is acknowledging that a problem exists and committing to solving it.

Step 3: Generating Ideas

Goal in hand, the student and researcher set out to generate as many ideas as they can to address the problem. Part of successfully identifying alternatives is the invitation of others in brainstorming novel solutions. In conversations with friends and family members, various alternatives may be suggested to the student: stop studying, eating, and watching TV while in bed, reduce the temperature in the room, move out of dorm, or use ear plugs. For the academic, a literature review; the input from a research team that may provide suggestions about various affective, behavioural, and cognitive barriers thwarting thinking; and suggestions from students themselves.

Step 4: Defining the New Situation

Armed with a number of potential suggestions, both the student and the researcher evaluate and compare alternatives. Where possible, new alternatives are generated through the synthesizing of existing alternatives (dialectic thinking). The student combines the suggestions and restricts the bed to sleeping. The academic synthesizes his list of affective, behavioural, and cognitive barriers to include perceptual, emotional, cultural, environmental, and intellectual. Prior to implementing the solutions, both the student and the academic test the alternatives in virtual reality. The student explores room options for studying, eating, and watching TV. The researcher strives to define each of the subcategories of barriers.

Step 5: Preparing a Plan

With the potential solution in hand, the steps required to administer it effectively and efficiently are devised. The student develops a reinforcement plan through the charting of sleeping in the bed, contracting with the roommate to ensure that only sleeping occurs while in bed, establishes an eating area and study area, while rewarding successful sleep behaviour with watching TV in the student lounge. The researcher writes a proposal for studying barriers of critical thinking, applies for grant money to offset research costs, hires a research assistant, and identifies all the resources in the literature needed to find the answers. Before acting on their plans, both the student and the researcher do a cost analysis to determine the advantages and disadvantages associated with their plans. Any potential risks are identified. For the student, the potential of peer pressure to do things other than sleep are noted. For the researcher, the potential of not getting funding is viewed as problematic and an alternative solution is put into place by applying for a Career Start grant to hire a research assistant.

Step 6: Taking Action

Now that both the student and researcher have a plan in place, each takes the effort to launch it. The student works at decreasing sleep deprivation and the researcher focuses on identifying the barriers to student thinking.

Step 7: Evaluating

Throughout the implementation of the plan, both the student and the researcher constantly monitor how well the planned action is working. Success indicators are being evaluated along the way. The student is monitoring sleep behaviour, while the researcher is evaluating the resourcefulness of information from the literature. Both are comparing their results with their initial goals. The student also asks friends and family members to evaluate and provide feedback on the success of the plan.

Step 8: Communicating the Findings

The final stage, which is missing in most of the current problem-solving models, is to communicate the findings (Dewey, 1933). An integral part of academia is to share with others how you solved a problem. For the student, it means sharing with others the successes of achieving the required sleep. For the researcher, it requires communicating the barriers thwarting students' critical thinking with others, as seen in the table on page 302 (Adams, 1979). When a new cure is found, when a new program is created, when a new solution is uncovered, the finding needs to be disseminated to the larger community through oral or written presentations. As a scholar, this act continues the progress of knowledge in your area, making the advancement of knowledge possible.

Creative problem solving can take on a variety of different strategies. Successful students use a variety of approaches to enhance their search for creating new ideas. Important to you is to find a strategy that fits your thinking style and complements your way of learning. Ideally, using each of these strategies in a group setting provides a larger wealth of information to draw from.

TABLE 12.1	Roadblocks to Critical Thinking	

Barriers	Definition	Characteristics
Perceptual Blocks	Occur especially when a problem is first perceived	• Stereotyping • Difficulty in isolating the problem • Delimiting the problem area too closely • Inability to see the problem from various viewpoints, interest, constituencies
Emotional Blocks	Colour and limit how we see, and think about a problem	• "I am the only one who feels this way" • Fear of taking a risk • Distaste for chaos • Judgment rather than generation of ideas • Inability to incubate • Fantasy and reflection are a waste of time: lazy
Cultural Blocks	Are acquired by exposure to a given set of cultural patterns	• Playfulness is for children only • Problem solving is a serious business • Reason, logic, practicality, utility = GOOD • Feelings, intuition, qualitative judgments, pleasure = BAD • Tradition is preferable to change • Any problem can be solved by scientific thinking and money
Environmental Blocks	Are imposed by our immediate social and physical environment values	• Taboos • Lack of trust and cooperation among colleagues • Autocratic boss who values only personal ideas • Distractions (phone, easy instructions) • Lack of support to bring Ideas into action
Intellectual and Expressive Blocks	Occur when information is incorrectly collected, formulated, or processed	• Habitual use of certain problem-solving strategies (verbal, mathematical, visual) • Lack of, or incorrect, information • Inadequate language skill to express and record ideas

Metacognition

Metacognition is central to critical thinking, whereby you learn how to evaluate your own inferences and thinking processes (Ennis, 1987; Facione, Giancarlo, Facione, & Gainen, 1995). It is the management of thinking through thinking about thinking, knowing what we know, how we know, and what we do not know (McKeachie et al., 1986). There are three basic metacognitive strategies (Blakey & Spence, 1990). First, the successful student connects new information to previously learned knowledge by organizing the new information with known information. Second, the successful student deliberately selects thinking strategies that are appropriate for the context. In a psychology class, he/she may refer to using the scientific method to determine truth. In a course on philosophy, the logical reasoning strategy would be used. Third, the successful student adopts "self-regulation" by planning, monitoring, and evaluating his or her thinking processes (Facione et al., 1995), by making thinking processes explicit. Successful students reflect on the effectiveness of their thinking strategies. Where they find problems, they seek advice on how to more successfully involve effective thinking strategies. Central to successful thinking is an increased awareness of the process of your own thinking in comparison to accomplished thinkers (Bonnett, 1995). Adopting metacognition as part of your critical thinking allows you to evaluate how you think and how you come up with conclusions. As part of your understanding of how you think critically, keep an active journal on your thought processes. Identify the types of thinking that you are most comfortable with. Engage in reflection by thinking about thinking. In doing so, you will advance in your thinking skills.

Attitudes that Support Critical Thinking

An attitude of openness to explore and explain is necessary in the development of critical thinking skills. Successful critical thinking requires a willingness to question, engage in inquiry, reflect, look beyond, and seek novel perspectives (Bailin et al., 1999). As such, successful students take on a critical spirit and the values that accompany this spirit (Ennis, 1987; Siegel, 1988). Active critical thinkers tend to be more skeptical about conclusions and explanations. They are critical readers, reading beyond the lines. They have an ability to inquire about causes and effects, and a refinement of curiosity about behaviour as expressed in raising issues, asking intelligent questions, and creatively solving problems.

Critical thinking thrives on a spirit of inquiry. As Albert Einstein said, "I have no special gift. I am only passionately curious." Out of the critically analyzed thought blooms a creative new idea that has the potential for moving people closer to Truth. As such it encourages creativity through the transformation of older ideas and their alternatives into new ideas and solutions.

Critical thinking requires reflection (i.e., metacognition), and a time for self-assessment and regulation, to see whether or not existing beliefs can be challenged and new beliefs adopted. By becoming more reflective, individuals can develop the experience and confidence to nurture open-mindedness while remaining distant enough so as not to accept everything. Reflection provides further direction and an answer to the hypothesis or conclusion at hand. Thus, critical thinking invites the student to believe and act on the newly synthesized idea. It is what Perry (1970) defines as "commitment." It is one thing to argue, defend, and debate an idea or conclusion; it is another to live it out, to apply it to daily life.

Finally, a critical thinker is guided by an honesty to discover Truth. The critical thinker is freed by intellectual independence to think beyond the norm, in control of the emotions associated with personal biases, and driven by a desire to know. As a result, a critical thinker becomes a more sophisticated student, a more knowledgeable consumer, and a more informed voter.

It's More Than Common Sense

Critical Thinking

Robert D. Renaud, Ph.D.
University of Manitoba

As a researcher with an educational psychology background, I am interested in finding out what helps students develop their critical thinking ability during the three to four years they spend in university. As we learn more about the factors that impact students' critical thinking, teachers (myself included), can use this information to help make courses more meaningful. One question I sometimes hear a student ask is "why do we have to learn this stuff?" In response to this question (and it is a fair question to ask), there are two reasons why I feel that emphasizing critical thinking is important. First, it can help students take a more active part in the learning process. Rather than simply receiving facts and enduring the monotonous task of memorizing the information for an exam, students are encouraged to think about concepts in novel ways. Second, engaging in activities designed to foster critical thinking can help show how the material could be applied in everyday situations which often involve the use of critical thinking to arrive at a desired conclusion or decision.

Most if not all educators would agree that the development of students' critical thinking skills is one of the more important outcomes that universities should strive for. One important question that has been explored in several studies is, "do students improve their critical thinking skills as a result of attending college or university?" Pascarella and Terenzini (1991) outline the following conclusions from their review of studies examining gains in critical thinking skills during university. Controlling for incoming ability and maturational effects, most studies found a significant gain in critical thinking going from first to fourth year. Furthermore, data obtained from alumni indicate that perceived gains in critical thinking exist long after graduation. Overall, going from first- to fourth-year results is an improvement of about 34 percentile points. These gains have been found after controlling for initial level of critical thinking, academic aptitude, maturation, socioeconomic status, or aspiration. In other words, among students who are similar in terms of many relevant aspects (e.g., intelligence, age, future goals), they have shown notable gains in their critical thinking skills over the four years they have studied in university.

Related to the first important question is another which asks, "If students do improve their critical thinking skills during the time they study in university, then what contributes or causes students to become better critical thinkers?" Unfortunately, although we know that students' critical thinking does improve as a result of attending university, we don't know very much about what occurs during the university experience that contributes to this improvement. One activity that ought to have an impact on the development of students' critical thinking skills is answering higher-order questions on assignments and tests. Briefly, higher-order questions represent those which could be classified into one of the four upper categories of Bloom's taxonomy of cognitive objectives (Application, Analysis, Synthesis, and Evaluation) (Bloom, 1956). According to these objectives, students could be asked to apply what they have learned in a new situation, or evaluate something in terms of its strengths and limitations. For example, in a statistics class, a student could be given an application-level question such as "Perform the appropriate analysis to determine the relation between level of caffeine intake and amount of time studying." In contrast, lower-order questions represent the two lower categories of Bloom's taxonomy (Knowledge and Comprehension). Lower-order questions typically require little more than a memorized response such as the answer to "In what year was helium discovered?" Basically, the difference between lower- and higher-order questions is that the former tend to ask students for a memorized response that answers "what," and the latter tend to ask students for a novel, more thought-out response (i.e., one that has not been taught in class or in the textbook) that answers "how" or "why."

Recently, four studies were conducted by Renaud (2002) to find out if university students showed larger gains in the development of their critical thinking skills when they answered higher-order questions on assignments and tests in coursework compared to students who were given lower-order questions. While it is difficult for a single study to avoid at least one serious methodological limitation, the four studies in the present research used different designs, samples, and instruments so that a potential limitation was likely dealt with in at least one of these studies. For example, one study related amount of higher-order questions on tests and assignments in actual classes to gains in critical thinking, while another study was a true experiment done in a controlled laboratory setting that compared the gains in critical thinking of students who were given either lower-order or higher-order review questions during the experiment. Overall, the findings of these studies clearly indicate that students are more likely to improve their critical thinking skills when they have answered higher-order questions in their coursework. This finding was encouraging for at least two reasons. First, having found the same conclusion using different methods and samples provides more convincing evidence of the effect of higher-order questions on gains in critical thinking skills. Second, these results are impressive when one considers the short time frame in which these studies were conducted. For example, in one study that focused on actual classrooms over the span of one semester, students in classes that assigned more higher-order questions tended to show bigger gains in critical thinking skills compared to students in classes that assigned fewer higher-order questions. Moreover, similar findings were obtained in the laboratory experiment that lasted under two hours.

While the results of this research clearly show that answering higher-order questions leads to further development in critical thinking skills, a couple of important qualifications are necessary. First, it must be emphasized that focusing on higher-order questions does not by any means give a complete picture of educational quality. As covered extensively in their review, Pascarella and Terenzini (1991) conclude that students learn and develop in many ways as a result of attending a post-secondary institution, and these outcomes are influenced by many factors that occur during this period. This research compared only one process (higher-order questions in course work), with one outcome (gains in critical thinking skills). Second, despite the findings of this research and the importance of critical thinking skills as an outcome variable, it would be a mistake to cast a negative light on a course that used few or no higher-order questions. Whether a course uses only a few or many higher-order questions obviously depends in part on the objectives of that course. For example, in an introductory course in a particular discipline such as biology, the objective may be to have students know a large number of terms to serve as a foundation for them to draw upon in subsequent courses.

Despite the narrow focus of this research, it does take an important step in helping us to understand exactly what contributes to certain types of student learning and development in universities. As we begin to identify, with supportive evidence, the factors that contribute to student outcomes, universities will be in a better position to provide a quality educational experience for its students.

Success Strategies FOR THINKING CRITICALLY AND CREATIVELY

Self-awareness
What do I know about my own critical thinking capabilities? I've learned that my strengths in each of the following are:

Critical Thinking…

Creative Problem Solving…

Can I describe the thinking capabilities I would like to develop?

Self-confidence
To increase my confidence in my ability to:

think critically more actively I will…

creatively solve problems more confidently I will…

Self-concept
Actions I can take to add to my critical thinking abilities are…

Actions I can take to gain greater control of my problem solving are….

Chapter Summary

Critical thinking is an integral part of your university experience and of becoming a wise consumer of thoughts and products. There are various strategies available to help you develop in order to succeed in your search for finding the Truth. Each one is useful for different types of phenomenon. The accomplished student is aware of each, and uses them appropriately as required by the discipline. However, in the process of adopting the various thinking strategies, be wary of losing your creativity to the mechanics of the process. As Pablo Picasso once said, *"Every child is an artist. The problem is how to remain an artist once he grows up."* The successful student is free enough to venture into creative problem solving to find new ways of looking at phenomenon. By complementing analytic thinking approaches with alternative strategies, the successful student develops the thinking skills that facilitate understanding, creative solutions, and proficiency as a critical thinker. As a successful critical thinker the student is characterized by inquisitiveness, being well-informed, honesty, meticulousness in making judgments, open-mindedness, being logical in deriving outcomes, forever looking for supporting information, being careful in the criteria used to make decisions, constantly searching, and persistence in his or her efforts to uncover Truth. A successful student employs one or more of these thinking strategies to uncover Truth. As you are faced with new challenges, use the most appropriate thinking strategy to help you find the answers you seek. Ideally, find ways to include others as you strive to find Truth. Dewey (1964) draws a parallel between a proficient thinker and an accomplished violinist. "It is a certain quality of practise, not mere practise, which produces the expert and artist" (p. 201).

Exercises

REFLECT–ACT

The following Reflect–Act exercises are designed to help you develop increased self-awareness of your critical thinking effectiveness through the process of reflective thinking, analysis, and productive action. Self-reflection encourages you to consider information you learn and data you collect to increase your ability to know yourself and to manage yourself.

Reflect   Of the various developmental stages, identify the one that best describes where you are now in terms of critical thinking.
Act   In order to increase critical thinking development, which stage do you need to embrace? How will you go about this? Are there any individuals who you view as having achieved the highest level of critical thinking development who might be your mentor in critical thinking?

Reflect   Note the various strategies of critical thinking. Which ones are most familiar to you? Where have you used each type of thinking successfully? Where has it been a challenge to use any one of these thinking strategies? What was the barrier that thwarted you from achieving success?
Act   In order to increase your use of each of the critical thinking strategies, identify the critical thinking approaches that would be most appropriate for each of your different classes. Next, determine which ones are problematic and discover ways to increase your expertise with each type.

GROUP DISCUSSION

1. Choose common commercials or advertisements that make generalizations. As a group, identify the thesis with supporting evidence, create an antithesis with supporting evidence, and develop a synthesis that combines the thesis and antithesis. Find an opportunity to share this with the larger class so that you can hear the perspectives of others in class.
2. Bring a copy of a news article to class that demonstrates one of the six fallacies of logical thinking.
3. As a group, classify courses that encourage dualistic thinking versus those that encourage multiplicity. Describe how this difference influences the assignments in these classes.

4. As a group, choose one of the following life challenges (Should I cheat on the mid-term? Is this the person I should marry? I have two great summer jobs; which should I take?), and work together to come up with a solution.

APPLY TO LIFE

Now that you have developed an understanding of how to increase your efficiency in critical thinking and creative problem solving, you can use this information to enhance your own performance. Use the following to more clearly discover your strengths and limitations as a thinker and problem solver. Choose an issue that you are currently deal-ing with as a student (e.g., money, relationship, grades, etc.), and work your way through the following.

1. Respond to each of the Decide Model steps as you explore the issue.

2. Engage in community help by inviting one of two close friends to help you work through your issue, providing them with the information you have gathered in steps one and two.

3. Synthesize all the material from you and your friends and identify the best solution(s).

4. Commit the solution to practice by making yourself accountable to your friends to act on the solution.

5. After a period of time, one or two weeks, sit down with your friends and provide an update on your progress. If your solution is successful, continue. If it requires changes, go through the process of identifying alternative solutions and implement them.

6. Once you have solved the problem, celebrate with your friends.

Seeking Personal and Professional Success

7

"The purpose of life is a life of purpose."

Traveling this journey of discovery lets you uncover many secrets that facilitate your success and promote your personal development. Continuing your search, your focus is directed toward finding the life path that will bring happiness and personal fulfillment. In *Seeking Professional and Personal Success* you discover activities that allow you to be true to yourself. By engaging in important, meaningful activities that matter to you, it is possible to be successful.

To experience professional and personal success requires more than simply finding a job or selecting an occupation that provides you with a lifestyle that you desire. To experience professional and personal success you need to do more than earn a living. You want to find a career that honors your unique ability to contribute to the world. And a career, which will be most personally satisfying, is one that describes your contributions around a meaningful purpose.

Although you may measure success differently than others, what you share in common with others is that each person finds success by discovering his or her unique purpose. "The purpose of life is a life of purpose." Purpose is defined by your description of meaningful accomplishment, which honours your values and expresses your talents. It provides a basis upon which you create work. The power of purpose provides you with goals, directs your dreams, and inspires you to continue in spite of setbacks. Finding personal answers for defining one's purpose focuses the career exploration process outlined in the following chapter.

This career exploration process will assist you in choosing appropriate career alternatives, clarifying your direction, and committing to plans for directing your career search. Because people become what they imagine themselves to be, understanding the dreams that motivate you is an important phase of discovering career possibilities. By identifying and committing to personal dreams you discover relevant and meaningful career options. Refining these options occurs when you evaluate who you are, what you like to do and where you can do the activities that are worthwhile to you. By knowing the career options that express your hopes, values, and capabilities, you can achieve the personal and professional success you desire. Through exploration and experimentation you can gradually discover your own purposeful life.

Designing Your Future

chapter 13

"Destiny is not a matter of chance; it is a matter of choice. It is not a thing to be waited for; it is a thing to be achieved."

William Jennings Bryant

Questions

How do I define success?

What career paths fit me?

How can I create career opportunities that will give me the fufillment I desire?

Where do I want to live and work?

What are the most important actions I can take to obtain my ideal job?

Objectives

- Discover answers and alternatives to the student quest for personal meaning.
- Increase my awareness of career self-identity.
- Identify the factors that influence and expand my own career possibilities.
- Develop strategies for gaining career-related experience.
- Improve my confidence and competence so that I can get the job I want.

Student Success Portrait

Exploring the Future

Adam Warren
Memorial University

When you look back on your university career, chances are that you won't remember your exact grade in a particular course, or a fraction of the information that you committed to memory when pulling an all-nighter. That's not to say that you shouldn't give 110 percent to your academics, but so much of a university education takes place outside the classroom.

I remember my first few days on campus. My entire high school was about the size of one of the buildings. How was I ever going to find my way around? And once I'd accomplished that much, what could I possibly do to make a difference on a campus this size? Someone found me stumbling around a hallway, looking for my class. After my face returned to its normal colour (because I had actually been right outside the door), he introduced himself, saying that he remembered what it felt like to be completely lost. He told me there was a clubs and societies fair that afternoon in the Student Centre. "You should check it out," he said. So I did. That's where it started... and it hasn't stopped since.

University life is about exploration, about testing the waters and trying new things. Pick something you've always wanted to do: theatre, nature hiking, film-making, wrestling... Maybe this is something that you didn't want to do alone. Maybe you just don't know where to start looking. In the sea of individuals that make up a campus, there is guaranteed to be *someone, somewhere* who feels exactly the way you do. There are ways to find them. Take advantage of student clubs and societies, attend multi-cultural nights, write for the student newspaper, run for council, join a team... Anything! And after all that, if there's still nothing that interests you, then start a club or society of your own. Take it upon yourself to bring all those people with interests like yours together.

There are other benefits to campus involvement as well, skills that you won't learn in many classrooms. Employers look at more than grades these days. A drama society in the hobbies/interests section of your résumé shows creative spirit and self-confidence. A seat on council means ambition and people skills. A team member is... well... a team member. Me, I'm a theatre guy, a regular on-campus jammer, and I'm president of a student-run centre for individuals with disabilities. Even in my first year, I sat on an awareness committee, or two. Besides enjoying these activities, I have developed skills and information that may be directly related to a future career.

That's what this is all about. It's about friendships, memory making, and skill development, sure. But it's also about having a voice. There is no better way to make sure that you don't become just another face on campus than to get involved! Academics have to come first, I can't stress that enough. Otherwise you can't stick around to enjoy all the other stuff that campus life has to offer. Social life runs a close second, though. These are the people and events that you'll remember long after you've left the campus behind. That's where you'll find something to hold onto when you think you're about to be crushed under a stack of books. The trick is to find that delicate academic/social balance. Once you have, jump in and hold on!

Discovering what you want to do with your life is much like the explorer seeking hidden treasures. As an explorer you must learn how to hunt, gather experiences, overcome hurdles, apply your expertise, and use insights in order to progress. Because explorers find excitement in the search, you are able to navigate unknown terrain and seek clues from various sources to guide you. You are on a path of discovery, a path that has many junctions, crossroads, and decision points; places where you must choose one direction and not another. Deciding on a career path is one of those choices. Choices are either easy or more complicated. Career choices can be in either category.

Each day you make hundreds of choices, some you consider seriously and thoughtfully, while others you make quickly. In spite of the ease or difficulty of the decision, each of your decisions has personal relevance for you. Each choice provides data for designing your future.

You may or may not have commenced university with a career path in mind. A few students have a definite idea about their career direction. But for the majority of first-year university students, clarifying one's career direction is part of the developmental process of the first year (Chickering & Reisser, 1993). Choosing the direction that best fits your competencies and fulfills your needs for security, esteem, belonging, love, and fulfillment (Maslow, 1970), gives you a focus for your academic courses. It provides a focal point for the learning in which you are engaged. In fact, it is quite typical for students to discover that those courses that are personally exciting, provocative, and engaging, may lead them into career paths previously not considered. Your grades in specific courses provide clues about your abilities and interests in various career fields. In designing your own future life of personal fulfillment, professional success, and purposeful activity, the career path you select can be the axis.

Do you choose a career path or does a career path choose you? How do you know which is the career path that best fits you? In the North American culture, you have the opportunity to choose your own career path. Within the limits of your abilities and opportunities, you can explore a variety of career options. For many students, the first year of university is a time of discovering career possibilities. This increased awareness can be exhilarating or intimidating. To manage this process, an outline of career-planning steps can assist you in focusing your questions and directing your energies.

Careers help define identity. Your career can give meaning to your life. A satisfying career will provide you with a source of challenge, a sense of control over your ability to create your future, a feeling of commitment to something greater than yourself, and a sense of accomplishment that provides your identity as a member in our society. Careers provide the basis for involvement in your community and define your contributions to the world. In other words, careers give you a sense of purpose.

Career Identity

Why is a career important? In today's society, work is the major focus of self-identity for a large proportion of individuals (Super, 1993). People define and describe themselves through their work. Personal success is measured by professional success. There are other ways to define yourself: hobbies, leisure activities, family responsibilities, or community involvement. However, for most university students, finding a personally meaningful and economically satisfying career is one of the most important reasons why they attend university, and it is an answer in their search for self-identity. It is the first step in creating one's life path. Finding a fulfilling career is more than simply picking a vocation. It involves encountering a series of developmental tasks and attempting to handle them in such a way as to become the kind of a person you want to become (Chickering & Reisser, 1993; Super, 1990).

How you develop your career identity has been explored by a number of researchers and theorists. Super (1990, 1992, 1993), has proposed that a major means of developing your career identity is by assuming various diverse roles within society. These roles vary depending on sociological factors such as age, developmental stage, family values, peer group influences, cultural characteristics, and economic background. They also depend upon personal characteristics such as your ability levels, interests, values, aptitudes, and achievements. Due to the synergistic interaction of sociological and personal factors, you will attempt some activities and avoid others. Since your career identity is formed through a process of experimentation and exploration with the roles and activities you assume, it is important that you widen your awareness of possible roles and avoid any limits that could occur as a result of sociological factors. Super (1993) observed that as you interact with the environment, expose yourself to new ideas, and uncover new information, you augment your career possibilities.

Because your life experiences are so influential in determining the career alternatives you pursue, it is critical that as a university student you take time to expand your knowledge of career possibilities and your knowledge of your career preferences. It has been demonstrated (Super, 1993) that the amount of satisfaction you gain in your work is directly proportional to the extent to which your career fits your self-concept. Thus, knowing your career identity provides the basis for personal fulfillment. According to Super (1990, 1992, 1993), the process of career development is one of developing and implementing an occupational self-concept. It is an ongoing learning process in which you experiment with roles, observe others, and learn from feedback so that you can synthesize your experiences and adjust your career aspirations. Several factors influence the evolution of your occupational self-concept and the occupational level you attain. Some of these factors you can control; others you cannot. Two factors that you can use to expand your occupational opportunities are education and exposure to learning opportunities. Both can assist you in overcoming limitations that may result from the other factors. Classes, volunteer activities, work opportunities, field placements, and role-playing activities provide useful vehicles to add to your awareness of your occupational self-concept.

Self-Efficacy

A critical factor influencing your career aspirations and career options is your self-confidence, or self-efficacy regarding your capability to do what you need to do in order to successfully make career decisions, gain relevant experience and obtain your ideal vocation (Bandura, 1977). This confidence is influenced by your beliefs, your self-talk, your activities, and your expected outcomes. Confidence inspires you to seek the life that you imagine for yourself. It allows you to overcome obstacles, tackle challenges and stay the course. Thus, adding to your confidence will add to your career success. In improving your **career self-efficacy** you feel more confident. You enhance your career self-efficacy by exposing yourself to situations that provide you the opportunity to master vocational skills and learn the strategies that are associated with career exploration. As you increase your career self-efficacy you expand your career possibilities.

Career self-efficacy is significantly related to vocational interests (Hackett & Betz, 1981; Luzzo, D. A. et al., 1999), selection and persistence in college majors (Pajares & Miller, 1995), and academic performance (Lent, Lopez, & Bieschke, 1993). Individuals with greater confidence levels regarding their ability to make career decisions are more likely to engage in the career preparation activities and job-seeking actions that lead to occupational opportunities, and enhance vocational awareness. They take greater control of their career search. Individuals with lower levels of confidence tend to be career indecisive and ineffective in their career exploration.

Students' self-efficacy beliefs influence the choices they make and the amount of effort they expend. Their beliefs affect their resilience to hardships, their persistence in face of adversity, and their ultimate success. When self-confidence is high, they are more likely to persist in occupationally relevant courses even when the material is challenging. For example, in courses such as mathematics, students' confidence in their mathematics capability influences not only their performance on mathematics tasks but also their career choices (Zeldin & Pajares, 2000). Those students with higher confidence levels will pursue additional education and seek mathematics-related jobs. Students with lower confidence levels avoid mathematical career paths as a result of this lowered confidence (Zeldin & Pajares, 2000).

Your career confidence is critically important to your success in discovering the career path that holds the greatest hidden treasures for you. It will help you overcome hurdles and allow you to use your expertise in order to progress. Your confidence, or attitude of knowing, is a tool that can help provide a sense of direction. Like a personal compass, it can point you where you need to go. Like most tools, you must learn how to use it. When you do, it can guide you effectively to make choices and decisions about career alternatives. It will provide a focus for deciding what you want in your life and clearly identifying what you are willing to exchange in order to have it.

Career as a Sense of Purpose

To commence a journey, you must decide on a destination. As you travel toward this destination you will experience fascinating sites along the way. There may be detours and alternative routes for which you had not planned. There will be times when you stop simply to enjoy the current vista. The destination is the life you envision, a life in which you are doing what fulfills you, in a place that fits you. To decide on the destination that belongs to you, you can begin by clearly identifying the activities that will give your life meaning and purpose.

Happiness comes from working hard for a purpose. Like most folks, your search for a career is the search for finding a job that gives personal fulfillment and one in which you feel that your energies and time matter. Purpose is the engine that powers life. Career paths are generally chosen because they provide a sense of purpose. That purpose may be to help others, advance science, contribute to society, become famous, use one's **talents**, write a book, or any one of a thousand other possibilities. Thus, a critical part of finding your career path is to identify a clear sense of your own purpose. This purpose relates to the interests in life about which you are passionate and includes the activities that you find personally meaningful. It also reflects your values and principles.

Finding your purpose, or mission in life, and fulfilling it is one of the most energizing and satisfying activities in which you can engage. Just as organizations have discovered the value of mission statements, people also benefit by developing personal mission statements that allow them to define a direction and purpose to their life. Developing your personal mission statement evolves from your values. It is uniquely descriptive of you and the life you desire for yourself. Simply stated and easily understood, it can be written in one sentence. Follow the guidelines on page 315 to develop your personal mission statement—it can be a critical tool for focusing your career search and inspiring you to become the person you truly want to be.

Exercise 13.1 CREATING A PERSONAL MISSION STATEMENT

Your personal mission statement is a one-sentence description of your unique life path. It is written simply, so that others can easily understand it. Yet it is personally descriptive of you, your values, and your passions. It provides a clear statement of the impact you wish to have in your life. It is action-focused and written in the present tense. It describes what you would like to do and the activities you find meaningful. Write in one sentence your personal mission.

The self-discovery process, with which you have become familiar, provides the course for assisting you in determining the career path that fits you. As seen on this page, you can use the self-discovery tools of reflection, monitoring, and assessment to more clearly understand your potential career paths, or career preferences, as well as the situational factors that will influence those preferences. Your answers to the questions in Chapter 2 are part of this initial assessment. By using the strategies that augment your self-confidence, you will be able to explore potential career options more fully, acquire career-related com-

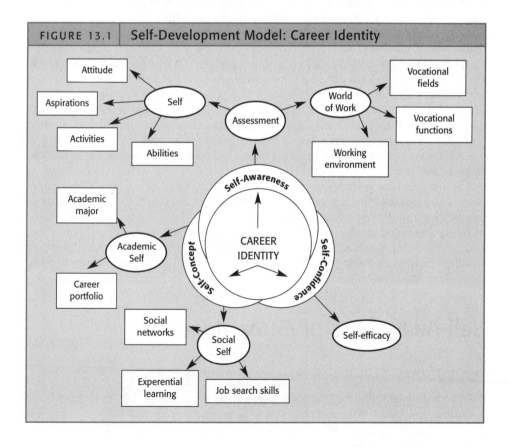

FIGURE 13.1 | Self-Development Model: Career Identity

petencies, and expand your social network. This process of exploration will allow you to uncover answers, which will provide the basis for determining your life direction.

The process of discovering your particular career identity includes becoming aware of your true self, as well as of the world of work. This discovery process is an active process in which you experiment, try options, discard some, add others, experience, reflect, take risks, analyze, explore, and imagine. It directs you to deliberately focus your efforts and activities. It is most beneficial when it occurs within a context that allows you to search for your sense of self in a supportive environment. Self-discovery requires both solitude and social connection. Much of your uncovering of your true self will occur through reflection and self-assessment.

In privately reflecting about your own purpose, dreams, needs, interests, values, abilities, and activities, you uncover your personal career path rather than the career path that others may have determined for you. Using the insights you gather about yourself, you are better able to connect to the resources that are available, and use the support systems within your educational community. Your discovery process leads to an increased awareness of the world of work. Through exploration, you gain a perspective about employer expectations, acquire insights about job futures, and enhance your understanding of career fields, and the functions expected in various occupational areas. This allows you to select an academic major that provides you with several career options. You can compliment your academic knowledge by getting involved in **experiential learning** activities, in which you gain important career-relevant experiences that form the basis of your portfolio of career competencies. Within the predictable developmental stages of your career identity discovery process, you will find the career path that fits you.

Your career identity reflects your authentic self. There are parts of your authentic self that are well known to you and to others, while other parts are hidden. The authentic self is like your fingerprint, unique to you. It is who you are and who you dream you can be. The self-discovery process will help you uncover how you will use your unique combination of characteristics and competencies to find your place and purpose in the world. There is much that you already know about yourself for you have been asking the question, "Who am I?" since the early days of your childhood. Now the focus of that question is directed toward the answers you seek regarding your career path.

Although your self-discovery process begins with where you are now, it is influenced by your past history and your future hopes. Your experience thus far benefits and restricts you as it affects your attitudes toward work, your networks, and your ideas about career possibilities. To avoid limiting yourself and to provide yourself with the greatest range of possibilities, use the opportunities provided by the self-discovery process to develop a more expansive and clearer vision of your future. Now is the time to dream, to augment your abilities and to expand your experiences. Like a quest, the search for your career identity involves discovering personal answers to perennial questions. Four guideposts, aspirations, attitudes, abilities, and activities, assist you in finding the answers you seek.

Self-Awareness of Career Identity

Aspirations

Take your dreams seriously. Dreams inspire you to reach and to risk. Remember those dreams of childhood? What did you want to be when you grew up? Those dreams held answers for you. If you look at them closely, they revealed needs that were important to you and may still be. Yesterday's dreams in combination with today's dreams provide glimpses of your ideal life, your future aspirations. Although your aspirations of what you want to do and who you want to be continue to evolve throughout your lifetime, your self-discovery process will help you connect to the core themes of those dreams. These themes are the values that define you, themes you can express through your career path.

Imagination is a powerful force in creating your future. To do something, you must first imagine it. Dreams reveal new opportunities and provide the impetus for exploring options that you had previously not considered. Reflecting about your dreams teaches you about the patterns that have influenced your personal view of your own possibilities. By using the insights you learn through your dreams, you increase your confidence to make your career dreams real. Do not limit your aspirations. Let yourself dream. Then take the insights you learn through this process to develop goals, intentions, and small steps for creating a career path that truly fits you.

Dream a future

In order to know more clearly your aspirations, it is important for you to create a picture of your ideal life. Take a moment to dream about your future. To do this you may want to tell a story, write a description, or create a picture collage. Some ideas will come from your own imagination. Others may be the result of identifying people you admire, describing what they do, and applying this to your own aspirations. Sometimes, it is helpful to relax and visualize yourself in a place that brings you joy and serenity. In designing this picture of your future life, include as many details as possible.

Select a time frame. The life you envision could be 10 years from today or 20 years from today. This time frame allows you to imagine yourself at a particular age and life stage.

Create the personal picture that is your life. Consider where you are and provide a description of the place and your working environment. Be as specific as you can. Where do you live? What does your place of work look like? How do you spend your day? When do you work? When do you play? Do weekends differ from weekdays; if so, how do they differ? What do you do? What skills are you using? Who is with you? What interests do you share? Use these questions to guide you in your writing or in creating the story you wish to share. Or if you wish, develop a visual picture of your future by creating a collage of images and pictures. Collect pictures from old magazines that symbolize your answers to these questions. Paste them together into a picture that you can use as a vivid reminder of the collection of experiences and hopes that you desire.

Now, describe how the vision of your future ideal life expresses your life mission.

Imagination is a powerful force in creating your future. When you are able to visualize a future that fits your core beliefs and passions, you are ready to begin the process for designing plans for creating your future. Specific images of your future aspirations serve as touchstones to motivate and inspire you.

Aspirations: Describe an image that inspires you.

Attitudes

The career path you decide to pursue will reflect your aspirations and also attitudinal factors, as revealed in your personality attributes, interests, and values. One of the best ways to find a fulfilling career is to ensure that it matches important personal characteristics. It suits the way you like to do things and exemplifies who you are. A satisfying career reflects your values and needs. Fortunately for you, there are any number of career possibilities that you could pursue. Finding the ones that fit you becomes easier when you match these possibilities to your personal qualities. By increasing your self-awareness and self-knowledge of your personal attitudinal factors you can find the career options that most clearly fit your personal style.

The best way to gain a systematic appraisal of your core personal traits is to use the resources of your university counselling or career centre. They will provide you with personality assessment tools such as the Myers-Briggs Type Indicator (1985), and the 16 PF Personal Career Development Profile (Walter, 1986; Russell & Karol, 1994), as well as vocational interests tests such as the Strong Interest Inventory (1994) or the Jackson Vocational Interest Survey (1990). These instruments are designed to guide you in matching your personal characteristics and interests to particular occupational categories.

You can use the insights you have learned about yourself through the process of self-discovery that has been part of this textbook, to guide your career exploration. Begin by reviewing your answers to the questions on career in Chapter 2. These answers give you an initial assessment of your career self-knowledge. Add to this the understanding that you have gained about yourself as a learner, and you have important basic information that can guide you in clarifying the preferences you may have for specific career paths. Remember those characteristics of extroversion and introversion, intuition and sensing, thinking and feeling, judging and perceiving, that have been identified by Myers-Briggs (Myers & McCaulley, 1985). Those characteristics, which assisted you in elucidating your personal learning style, can also be useful in directing your search for potential careers. Because your personality fits better with some careers than with others, your ability to clearly identify your personal characteristics can help you focus your natural strengths into career paths that will satisfy and stimulate you throughout your lifetime (Keirsey & Bates, 1978; Tieger & Barron-Tieger, 1995).

How do you spend your free time? What magazines do you read? Who are the people you would like to emulate? In reviewing past work experiences, what were your favourite activities? Your answers to these questions provide information about your vocational interests. Vocational interest inventories provide a more systematic assessment of your interests by matching your preferred activities, hobbies, and favourite pursuits with particular careers. Because people express their personality through their choice of a vocation, Holland (1966, 1985a, 1985b) created a classification system that matched people's personal interests to the personality of the job. He classified people and positions according to six general themes: realistic, investigative, artistic, social, enterprising, and conventional. Later, when you are evaluating which work environments fit you, you can use these six categories to ensure that the careers in which you are interested match your own interest areas.

One instrument that can assist you in identifying which of these six occupational interest categories are ones that apply to you is the Strong Interest Inventory (Strong, Hansen, & Campbell, 1994). With it you can explore 23 basic vocational interest scales and find the career paths that emphasize these interests. The usefulness of this instrument is that it allows you to direct your career search to areas that intrigue you, then expand your awareness of the variety of additional career paths that relate to your interests. It can be used in conjunction with the Skills Confidence Inventory (Betz, Borgen & Harmon, 1997), to evaluate both your career interests and your self-efficacy for those careers.

Another tool you could use to clarify your career interests is the Jackson Vocational Interest Survey (1990). This is a Canadian instrument, which measures career preferences in terms of vocational roles and work activities. With this instrument you can assess your interests in the vocational categories of arts, science and math, practical, outdoor activities, service activities, medicine and health, teaching and social welfare, business, law, and literary.

In addition to personality attributes and personal interests, a third attitudinal factor that is important in your career search is the needs or values that you seek to fulfill within your career. You may look to work as a source of personal satisfaction to meet any of the following needs: achievement, advancement, adventure, affiliation, approval, autonomy, belonging, companionship, community, compassion, competition, creativity, dependability, duty (doing what is expected), economic security, excitement, family, financial success, fun, health, independence, leadership, pleasure, power, prestige, privacy, prosperity, recognition, risk-taking, self-actualization, self-fulfillment, security, service, social interaction, spirituality, or status. Being clear about your values assists you in selecting the work environment you prefer, the occupation(s) you favour and the types of people with whom you are most comfortable.

The qualities that describe you, the interests that excite you, and the values that inspire you provide basic information necessary for choosing a career direction to pursue. These attitudinal factors assist you in focusing the vision of your future life into career interest areas that may relate to your academic major.

Exercise 13.2 ATTITUDINAL FACTORS—ATTRIBUTES, INTERESTS, VALUES

How would you describe yourself? How would others describe you? Select ten adjectives that most clearly describe you. Next, identify three hobbies, favorite pastimes, and interest areas that excite you, along with three primary values that you desire in a career. Now that you have this picture of important attitudinal factors that are unique to you, name two or three possible career paths in which you could express these factors.

Abilities

Creating the life you desire involves using the talents and abilities you possess. Because it is quite typical to take your abilities for granted, the self-discovery process is designed to remind you to recognize and affirm your talents. By knowing your unique abilities you are better able to pursue and prepare for what you want to do in life.

As a result of your life experience you have discovered certain abilities and talents. With additional experience you will discover more. Some of your abilities are reflected in the activities in which you participate and the courses in which you excel. Others are learned as you assume responsibilities in volunteer activities, hobbies, campus organizations, and work placements. There are various approaches for uncovering and develop-

Exercise 13.3 GETTING TO KNOW YOUR ABILITIES

Talents: Describe the natural abilities that you recognize in yourself or that others have noticed. When you find that you can easily do a particular activity, it is probably because you have talents in that area. (List between 5 and 10 talents).

Transferable Skills: Rate the following abilities as to your level of proficiency using a scale of 1 (low) to 7 (high or expert). Use a 0 if you do not have experience with that ability. Select 10 of these skills which you most enjoy.

Critical Thinking   **Rating**
- Access information
- Analyze situations
- Anticipate problems
- Assess data
- Evaluate various perspectives
- Identify root cause of problem
- Recognize the multidimensionality of problems
- Use facts to solve problems

Oral Communication
- Ask questions to understand
- Handle complaints
- Listen effectively
- Interview others
- Meet the public
- Present to large groups
- Promote
- Persuade others
- Share information using variety of technologies

Written Communication
- Correspond
- Edit
- Read and understand information presented in various forms (words, graphs, charts, and diagrams)
- Research information
- Synthesize evidence
- Write reports

Task Management
- Arrange functions
- Audit records
- Budget
- Buy products and services
- Calculate
- Check for accuracy

Task Management (*continued*)   **Rating**

    Coordinate activities

    Cope with deadlines

    Establish goals

    Follow directions

    Follow through

    Implement new initiatives

    Install new equipment

    Interpret data

    Locate information

    Plan and carry out projects from start to finish

    Monitor progress

    Raise money

    Select proper tools

Numeracy

    Budget

    Calculate numbers

    Decide factors for measurement

    Make estimates

    Project

    Record data accurately

Working with others

    Accept feedback

    Advise people

    Clarify objective

    Coach

    Collaborate

    Consult

    Delegate appropriately

    Direct others

    Discipline others

    Encourage

    Facilitate teamwork

    Handle complaints

    Interview others

    Lead

    Manage

    Mediate problems

    Meet people easily

    Mentor

    Motivate

    Perceive needs

    Respect diversity

    Resolve conflict

    Supervise

    Support others

    Teach

    Understand dynamics of group

Self-discipline	Rating
Assess personal strengths	
Be accountable for actions	
Be socially responsible	
Contribute to community	
Cope with uncertainty	
Establish goals and priorities: balance work and personal life	
Learn from feedback	
Learning goals	
Plan and manage time, money, and other resources to achieve goals	
Respond constructively to change	

ing your abilities. One approach is to expose yourself to a wide variety of different experiences, recognizing that through this process you will enhance your awareness and knowledge of your own broad range of abilities. As you add novel work experience or extracurricular activity you enlarge your repertoire of career competencies. Another option is to select a specific career or ability area and focus your efforts on developing and refining diverse competencies within that area.

The competencies you possess can be innate or learned abilities. Both your natural born abilities, or **talents**, and your learned competencies are expanded through education and experience. Some are specific to a particular field while others are general skills that can be used in many situations. These more general competencies are classified as **transferable skills**. Transferable skills are those competencies that you have developed in one setting, which can be applied in other vocational settings. The Conference Board of Canada (*www.conferenceboard.ca/nbec*) has identified a number of transferable skills that employers value. They include critical thinking, problem solving, communication skills, project management, numeracy, teamwork, adaptability, responsibility, positive attitudes, and self-discipline.

Knowing those abilities you currently possess and determining competencies you can gradually acquire provides you with useful information for developing your career identity. By adding this information to the knowledge you have already gleaned about your career aspirations and attitudes, you are piecing together the components of your personal map that can guide your career search.

Activities

Although you may not realize it, many of your current activities, summer jobs, and part-time employment positions have provided you with data that can be useful in designing your perfect career. In each of these positions, you have encountered activities you enjoyed and those you did not. If you are willing to reflect about these experiences, you can learn from them. By carefully considering what aspects of these experiences you enjoyed, and identifying those activities that provided you with a sense of personal satisfaction, you have important clues you can use for pinning down career interests.

Through your employment and extracurricular activities you have also developed competencies that you are now able to refine and expand. Some of these competencies are skills you will use in your career. Later in this chapter you will learn strategies for

Exercise 13.4 ACTIVITIES

By reviewing your previous job experience and the volunteer positions in which you have been involved, you can identify capabilities and activities that relate to your career plans. Begin by identifying two previous employment or extracurricular positions, which have provided you with experience and expertise.

The important next step is to analyze those positions, identify the activities you performed in these positions, relate them to specific occupational competencies and ascertain career options. For each position describe at least five activities you performed. Use action verbs to describe what you did. In reflecting about these activities, judge how interesting and satisfying these activities were to you personally. In considering how proficient you are in these activities, evaluate the match between these activities and your abilities and attitudes. Focus your reflection by rating personal satisfaction and personal proficiency regarding these activities from low to high. Determine the occupational competencies you have gained as a result of these activities that are related to this position and identify whether they are transferable skills or specific career-related skills. This process can be useful in clarifying career options, evaluating vocational opportunities, and preparing résumés.

Position 1:

Activities	Satisfaction	Proficiency	Occupational Competency
1.			
2.			
3.			
4.			
5.			

Position 2:

Activities	Satisfaction	Proficiency	Occupational Competency
1.			
2.			
3.			
4.			
5.			

Review your analysis of the activities and occupational competencies of these positions and describe two to four career options that may relate to these areas which you could explore.

Describe those academic interest areas that are related to the two career options you have identified.

If you were preparing a résumé to apply for your ideal career, how would you describe your previous volunteer or work positions in order to highlight your experience?

gaining important career-related experience that can ensure that you are well prepared for the career you desire. You can maximize the benefits of these experiences if you are able to highlight the proficiencies you have learned as a result of your work or volunteer activities, and focus your efforts into new activities to ensure that you learn those competencies that you have yet to acquire.

Through the process of personal reflection and self-discovery you have crystallized important information about your career identity. Each part of this self-discovery process has provided you with clues regarding your personal life and career direction. By collating and analyzing the information you have gathered you are better able to select potential career options. With this more detailed picture of your career interests you are better able to select your academic interest area. Your academic major is the subject area that most interests you. For those students enrolled in arts and science programs, your major will be a subject area such as history, psychology, biology, or chemistry. Once you have identified your academic interest area you will find there are a number of careers that you can pursue. Your academic major may also lead you into a particular professional school such as business, social work, education, or engineering.

While it is important to develop an understanding of your own career preferences through the self-identity process, clarifying your career options also requires that you understand more about the world of work, employers' expectations, and job futures, so that you can productively focus your career identity into realistic employment options. This means understanding the socioeconomic factors that affect employment, clarifying the functional characteristics of various positions, and developing effective social networks.

Awareness of the World of Work

In searching for the right career path for you, it is important to consider two perspectives related to the world of work: what the jobs are and where the jobs are. Jobs are complex and multidimensional, thus classification systems facilitate your understanding of the important dimensions of various jobs. These systems group jobs according to the different fields of interest and the distinct functions performed within these fields. Information about current employment and future employment in these occupational categories is announced regularly through government publications.

One of the most frequently used systems in Canada is the *National Occupation Classification* (NOC). This system describes jobs by occupational categories, sub-groupings of occupational interest areas, the functions in which workers are involved, and the training and education needed to enter the field. The NOC uses the following occupational fields: business, finance and administration, natural and applied science, health, art, culture, recreation and sport, sales and service, trades, transport and equipment operations, primary industry, processing, manufacturing, and utilities.

The NOC system assists you in expanding your awareness of the various types of jobs along with the responsibilities and duties that are associated with positions. If you want to work within a specific field of interest, you can learn about occupations in that field and discover related jobs you may not have previously considered. You can ascertain specific information about the responsibilities, duties, and activities associated with various occupations, as well as the education and training necessary to enter these positions. The NOC also assists you in understanding the similarities in positions across various fields of interest. By using the NOC you can develop greater understanding of what is actually done in particular occupations and you can become better educated about possibilities.

Exercise 13.5 CAREER PATH POSSIBILITIES

The self-discovery process of formulating your personal mission statement and identifying critical characteristics that define your unique career identity provides you with a framework for selecting possible career paths. Throughout the self-reflective process you have uncovered clues about occupations that would be fulfilling. The insights you have garnered about the interrelationships among your aspirations, attitudes, abilities, and activities allow you to focus your career search in specific directions.

Discovering career path possibilities involves synthesizing the information you have learned about yourself and matching that information to occupational interest areas. This process prepares you to select the academic interest area or majors that will lead you to satisfying employment, and allows you to focus your exploration of the world of work in specific areas. By completing the following sentences you are able to highlight significant insights and describe career areas that relate to those insights.

Insights I have learned:	Possible Career Paths

Aspirations that inspire me:

Attitudinal factors that influence me:

Abilities I have:

    Talents:

    Transferable skills:

Activities I find satisfying:

Personal Mission Statement:

Career Paths I want to consider:

Academic Interest areas:
(Possible academic major)

By using the descriptions included in the NOC classification system and matching the information you have learned about your career identity with these descriptions, you can find career fields that will be fulfilling. One tool that assists you in determining career fields that fit the dimensions of your career identity is Holland's classification system (1985a). Holland maintains that work environments have personalities that can be described by the functions of the workers in those areas. He devised a system of matching your own personality to that of the work environment. Holland has identified six types of occupations: realistic, investigative, artistic, social, enterprising, and conventional, and related these occupations to the classification codes.

Realistic occupations include technical, agricultural, mechanical, athletic, skilled trades, and military vocations. They are generally positions that involve working with equipment and tools. These positions appeal to people who like structure and deal with the environment in an objective, concrete, and physically manipulative way.

Investigative occupations include scientific, technical, mathematical, and medical science positions. People who enjoy theoretical tasks, scientific exploration, reading, collecting, foreign languages, and academic research find satisfaction in these positions. The work is focused on ideas and things.

Artistic occupations include artistic, musical, dramatic, and literary occupations. These positions fit people who appreciate subjectivity, enjoy introspection, desire creative expression, and are comfortable with ambiguity. Individuals who are comfortable using their intuition, emotional life, and personal knowledge to express themselves, solve problems, or produce material will find these positions gratifying.

Social occupations include education and social welfare. Their focus is to assist people. Individuals who are skilled in social skills, value nurturing others, desire community involvement, and are committed to service, find these positions fulfilling.

Enterprising occupations include managerial, political, public relations, and sales positions. These positions require an ability to direct or persuade others, plan activities, and take risks. People who are outgoing, self-confident, verbal, assertive, and adventure seeking are satisfied in these positions.

Conventional occupations include office practices and clerical positions, which demand that individuals are comfortable with the systematic, concrete, routine processing of verbal or mathematical information. Individuals who value established procedures, work efficiently within organizational structures, and are comfortable working with budgets are content in these positions.

By using what you have learned about your own attitudinal characteristics, aspirations, and academic interests you can use Holland's system to identify specific occupational interest areas that could provide you with meaningful career options. Your career options will reflect both your field of interests and the functions you like.

Besides identifying your field of interest, it is also important to determine the functions or activities you like to do. One important insight you discover as you learn more about various occupations is that similar activities occur across different fields of interest. If you enjoy managing, you could find yourself using your skills in the healthcare system, in business, in an educational organization, in an engineering experiment, or in an international development project. In other words, although the titles of positions may vary from field to field, there is similarity in activities, tasks, and responsibilities in various fields. By using your analytical thinking capabilities, you will begin to see the commonality across professional fields and thus be able to broaden your career possibilities.

There is more to a career than simply the activities of the job and the field of endeavor. Career paths vary along a number of dimensions that include work schedules,

Exercise 13.6 JOB CHARACTERISTICS

Fields: Identify two distinct career interest areas:

Functions: The following functions are activities associated with various positions. Survey the list and select the activities that you would find satisfying. Then review the list and identify the top ten activities that you would like to perform in your career.

Administrating	Facilitating	Preparing
Admitting	Financing	Programming
Analyzing	Handling	Proofreading
Appraising	Helping	Publishing
Assisting	Hiring	Qualifying
Budgeting	Illustrating	Rebuilding
Cataloging	Improvising	Recommending
Communicating	Influencing	Reforming
Contracting	Informing	Regulating
Coordinating	Inspecting	Repairing
Comparing	Instructing	Researching
Compiling	Interviewing	Selling
Computing	Manipulating	Serving
Convincing	Manufacturing	Setting up
Copying	Marketing	Speaking
Correcting	Mentoring	Studying
Counselling	Modeling	Supervising
Defending	Motivating	Synthesizing
Designing	Negotiating	Taking instructions
Diagnosing	Observing	Tending
Documenting	Organizing	Testing
Driving	Operating	Training
Editing	Persuading	Updating
Entertaining	Photographing	Writing
Examining	Predicting	

Where would you prefer to focus these activities? ____data, ____ people, or ____things?

Compare how you would use the top ten activities if you were employed in two different career fields.

If possible, use the NOC to compare descriptions of similar positions in two different occupational fields.

Exercise 13.7 LIFESTYLE PREFERENCES AND WORK ENVIRONMENT CONDITIONS

When making a career decision, it is useful to incorporate into your decision information about your lifestyle and work environment preferences. The following descriptive adjectives represent various working conditions and lifestyle needs that can add to, or detract from the career path you select. It is quite possible that some of these preferences may change as a result of experience and aging. The preferences are presented in a forced choice format. They are organized this way to focus you on making a choice, thus encouraging you to reflect honestly about your personal preferences.

Work Schedules

1. self-employed	or	working for others
2. extended work hours	or	standard eight-hour day
3. possible overtime	or	guaranteed regular hours
4. rigid schedule	or	flex time
5. fast pace, high pressure	or	slow pace, little pressure
6. similar duties daily	or	variety of duties

Working environment

7. creative environment	or	structured environment
8. no supervision	or	close supervision
9. security	or	challenge and risk
10. large organization	or	small organization
11. office	or	travel

Financial Remuneration

12. salary	or	incentives
13. benefits	or	bonuses

Geographical Location

14. urban	or	rural
15. small town	or	metropolitan area
16. close to family	or	new friends
17. explore new areas	or	remain in current place
18. quiet, relaxed	or	bustling, varied lifestyle
19. cultural events	or	outdoor recreation
20. live close to work	or	commute to work
21. sense of belonging	or	sense of anonymity

Characteristics of Colleagues

22. innovative	or	traditional
23. competitive	or	cooperative
24. predictable	or	spontaneous
25. private	or	social

Write down the five conditions that are essential for you.

amount of independence and creativity, risk, financial remuneration, and geographical location. Job descriptions may or may not include specific information about these dimensions. However, evaluating the importance of these work dimensions and matching them to descriptions of career options and labour market information can provide you with important data for evaluating potential career paths. Students often consider these factors indirectly. However, by ensuring that you explicitly identify those work and lifestyle elements that are critically important for you, you gain a more comprehensive portrayal of your career needs. You are also better able to judge the suitability of specific career options for you. The rating scale of environmental factors on page 328 can assist you in assessing the lifestyle and work environments that suit you.

Once you have fully explored the diverse types of jobs that are of interest to you, and selected vocations that can meet the lifestyle and work environment needs that are important for you, you are ready to learn about the future demand for these positions. Due to varying economic, social, technological, and demographic factors, the availability of careers within various geographical areas varies. Yesterday's hot jobs may be tomorrow's duds, and vice versa. In planning your career you want to know the possibility of being hired in a career that interests you. Therefore, a factor you need to consider in planning your career is the employment market.

To assist you in learning about future prospects of various careers, there are publications available featuring occupational trends, employment possibilities, and labour market statistics that are regularly produced by governments and educational organizations. These reports are designed to give you current local and national occupational statistics and projections of future trends. This information is published regularly in formal government publications, books, newsletters, or CD-ROMs. It is generally available from career counselling offices or libraries.

Information is also available on the Internet. A number of sites are available on the Internet to assist you in learning more about careers and employment. These include several sites developed by the Canadian government that allow you to increase your awareness of jobs within diverse interest areas and employment possibilities within different career categories. These sites are also useful for evaluating growth for particular occupational areas due to demographic trends, technological advancements, and cyclical occupational patterns. The resources available on the Internet grow every day. Thus, using the Internet can be fascinating and fruitful as well as confusing and frustrating. Some sites are free; others charge a fee. Some contain accurate information; others do not. It is useful to think of the Internet as a large library, which can be best utilized when you have a focus to your search and use tools that can guide you.

Internet sites

Due to the changing nature of the Internet, locations of various sites may change and be relocated to other addresses. Some may even have disappeared by the time you read this. These sites provide a place for you to begin, but it is important to use other resources to complement your search (these sites are provided for information only and are not necessarily recommended by the authors).

Job Futures:

www.jobfutures.ca: Canadian occupational outlook by field
www.jobsetc.ca/career_e.html: Canadian government jobs

www.waytogonetwork.com: 100 top careers in Canada
www.bls.gov/oco: US Occupational Outlook Handbook
www.acinet.org/acinet/default.htm: Wage trends in geographical areas
www.jobbank.gc.ca/: Jobs in various provinces
www.workopolis.com: Job listings according to sector
www.campusworklink.com: Jobs for university graduates
www.jobbus.com: Connections to companies
www.workdestinations.ca: Provincial employment information

Career Search:

www.jobhuntersbible.com: Dick Bolles Job Search site
www.jobtrak.com: The Riley Guide
www.monster.com: The Monster Board
www.careerexperience.com: Personalized career profiles
www1.umn.edu/ohr/ecep/résumé/: Résumé tutor
www.canadiancareers.com: Résumé help and job hunting
www.conferenceboard.ca/nbec: Job Skills

There is no better time than the first year of university to explore potential career options. The self-awareness exercises you have just completed start you on this exploration. Putting together the information you have learned about your aspirations, attitudes, abilities, activities, fields of interest, occupational functions, and employment trends, you have a roadmap for pursuing a career direction that fits you. This map guides you in making choices related to your academic major, in selecting appropriate training or experiential learning opportunities, and in perfecting competencies that lead to employability.

As you journey confidently toward the career that you desire, the roles you assume teach you about career. By experimenting with various roles, you learn about yourself. You add experience, expand your expertise, and evaluate options. An important benefit of these experiences is that they also provide you with people who can assist you: mentors, guides, and role models. Expanding your social networks and refining career competencies will add to your ability to create the career of your dreams.

Social Networks

It is quite probable that you will find your ideal job as a result of the connections you make. There is a great amount of evidence that indicates that the majority of career positions are gained through the hidden job market. Many positions are not posted or advertised. Some are internal to an organization, thus only those within the organization are considered. Others are offered to individuals because people know they have the experience and ability to do the job. You learn about these positions through conversations and social connections. Therefore, one of the most important priorities of the first-year university student is to begin to expand their social networks. You can do this through a deliberate process of interviewing individuals and adding them to your network, and by meeting people through a variety of work, volunteer, and educational experiences (see Chapter 10 for more details).

A critical part of expanding your social network and searching for a job is the interview. There are two types of interviews: **information interviews** and **employment interviews**.

Information interviews allow you to explore potential fields of interest and expand your social network. The goal for you is to meet different people within particular vocations and to ask questions so that you have greater knowledge about specific occupational areas. You can inquire about the nature of the work, the satisfaction associated with the occupation, the competencies required to perform the job well, and possible avenues you could follow to become employed in a similar position. In addition to broadening your knowledge of particular positions, these interviews provide a process for enlarging your social network. Information interviews teach you how to contact others for information and to expand interviewing skills. Used appropriately they build your self-confidence and assist you in expanding your social network. Some universities have **career mentor programs** that provide a structured process for assisting you to expand your career awareness of particular occupational fields and develop these important interviewing skills.

While information interviews assist you in career exploration, employment interviews assist you in getting hired. Employment interviews are the interviews with human resource professionals, potential supervisors, or possible employers in which you use your knowledge of a particular vocation and your knowledge of yourself to demonstrate your suitability for a particular position. There are two types of employment interviews: screening interviews and selection interviews. Screening interviews allow the employer to narrow the field of applicants. Since the focus is on qualifications and consistencies within your **résumé**, these interviews usually call for more concise answers. Your goal is to be one of the final applicants. Selection interviews are designed to determine if you are the best person for the position. These interviews require more open-ended responses, an awareness of the company, specific assessments of your personal capabilities, and job-related qualifications. The insights and experience you gained during your information interviews can be helpful in this process.

Academically Relevant Work Experience

You cannot learn anything about experiences you have never had. Therefore you must reach out of your everyday sphere of influence and add to your experience base. Offered throughout the university are a number of experiential learning opportunities that complement your academic learning and provide employment-related experience. Experiential learning placements provide you with practical, career-related employment experience. The goal of experiential learning is to place you in positions in which you can apply the concepts and skills you have learned in the classroom to relevant, real-life situations. These positions allow you to develop those employability skills that are valued in the career path of your choice. They also broaden your social networks. They can be paid or unpaid. Examples of experiential learning include internships, service learning, and Co-op programs. Many students also gain career-relevant experience by volunteering and through on-campus employment.

Internships are designed to provide students with a chance to work in pre-professional positions. Many have academic credit associated with them and are offered as part of the educational program. Depending on the academic area they may also be classified as field work or practicum placements. Students gain skills related to academic areas and professional programs. The time frame may vary from an academic term to a year.

A recent development in experiential learning is offering students the opportunity to participate in community service projects that relate to their academic courses. This is called service learning. Service learning provides a unique opportunity for students to meet public needs, expand their awareness of societal issues, volunteer, and gain grassroots experience in community development. Service learning provides liberal arts students with public service work experience.

Co-op programs are academic programs that offer paid, professional, and progressively responsible off-campus work experience as an integrated component of the educational program. Work experience is an essential component of the program. Students are evaluated on their progress during the work terms and this information is included as part of their academic record. Depending on the program, the work terms may or may not count as academic credit.

To make the most of career-related employment experiences it is useful to identify the competencies you have learned and the benefits of the experience. One of the ways to keep track of your progress as you develop your employability skills is to maintain a **career skills portfolio**. A career skills portfolio is a compilation of career skills you have developed through various experiences that provides examples of these skills. It may include summaries of your responsibilities, supervisor feedback, letters of commendation, and awards that you have received. It reveals your development and presents a portrayal of your successes and skills. You may wish to organize your career portfolio according to the Conference Board of Canada Employability Skills format. (For further information check their web site: *www.conferenceboard.ca/nbec.*) The portfolio can be used to update and supplement your résumé.

Your résumé is a two-page summary which you will use as part of the process of applying for a position. It includes contact information, your career objective, and facts about your education, skills and abilities, work experience, interests, and hobbies. It also includes a list of references who can share specific knowledge about you related to particular positions. Résumés vary in format. Some are chronological, summarizing your job experience in reverse order. Others are functional, and focus on your skills and abilities. Several Internet sites (see pages 329–30), as well as word processing software (e.g., Microsoft Word and WordPerfect) offer you templates to use in developing your résumé. In applying for a position, you should always send both a résumé and a letter of application. The letter of application is designed to demonstrate your reason for applying, offer evidence as to your unique suitability for the position, and to ask for an interview.

Included as part of your résumé is a listing of **referees** who can provide prospective employers with information about your experience and expertise. Referees can be supervisors, employers, professors, or managers who have an awareness of your competencies, work experience, and occupational aspirations. As you add to your occupational experience you also add to your network of potential referees. Before including an individual on your résumé as a referee it is customary to ask their permission and to provide them with information about the position for which you are applying.

You can maximize your chances of getting the occupational positions you desire by developing a diverse composite of competencies and capabilities. This is best achieved by planning your experiential learning opportunities and occasional employment positions to provide you with the environments in which you can develop the expertise and experience that are valued in the career path you seek. The more deliberate you are in planning your career experience, the better able you are to build a strong résumé. Because your résumé provides a snapshot of where you are now, it can be useful in assisting you in planning where you want to go. The occupation you seek today will lead to additional career possibilities tomorrow.

As a youngster, the roles you assumed as you played, the ideas you imagined, and the books you read provided you with visions of your future life. You are now creating that future life. Discovering your career path is part of that creative process. Along the way, the words of Dr. Seuss in *Oh, the Places You'll Go!* give you a reminder that can guide you.

You're off to Great Places!

You're off and away!

Your journey of discovery has only just begun. As is true in many journeys, taking the first steps can sometimes be the most difficult and challenging part. But you have done so. You have ventured forth. You have explored options. You have sought answers to the career question each of us must answer—how to find the career that uses your talents, nourishes your spirit, inspires your commitment, and ensures you live your life happily and meaningfully. You have discovered some answers; you will discover more. Finding the answers helps you choose the paths you most want to travel. Day by day you are making your way. With each step you take, you are directing your destiny.

It's More Than Common Sense

Constructing a Life: A Developing Project

Richard A. Young, Ph.D.
University of British Columbia

A primary challenge the authors of this book present to you is "How does one construct a life?" As this chapter points out, *career* is one of the important concepts that people use to construct their lives. But what exactly is a career? A range of definitions identify *career* as an occupation, an occupational goal, an occupational route that a person is committed to, and all the occupational activities that people are involved in throughout their lives. These descriptions of what a career is, while useful, have been criticized—they are bound too closely to occupations and don't allow us to consider other aspects of our lives as integral to our careers. Some have criticized *career* as a term that refers to a few "elitist" occupations. Others see it as too hierarchical, as in working one's way up the occupational ladder in an organization. It has also been seen as too linear a concept, presuming life is a straight line without alternative paths, forks in the road, retracing one's steps, and new beginnings.

The world, including the world of work, is changing too quickly to think in static concepts. At the same time, there is evidence that in this new world, careers as we have known them present some inherent challenges. For example, the sociologist Richard Sennett (1995) raises the question of whether a career path is possible in the current economy. He is concerned that without careers, the possibility of developing our lives is substantially lessened. Given the change in today's working world, the challenge is how to construct our own identity, and thus, the question that began this essay, "How does one construct a life?" is relevant.

Over a number of years my colleagues and I have endeavoured to develop a solution to these dilemmas and to offer a theory, that at its core addresses this basic question. Our approach is based on the premise that as human beings, most of our behaviour is goal-directed and intentional. Crossing the street, taking the bus, and browsing the Internet are not random acts. They are intentional and goal-directed, even though it is not completely clear to us why we are doing them. But, as we know, there is more to human action than outward behaviour. Human action involves both internal cognitions (thoughts and feelings) and the meaning that we and others attribute to it. Our thoughts and feelings regulate and steer our actions while we use feedback and feed-forward processes to make meaning of our actions.

When we consider our actions, we readily find that they are not independent of each other. Rather, we recognize that they are related in a variety of ways. Consider, for example, a parent who encourages her daughter to become an engineer. The action may repeat itself over time and be manifest in several ways: providing a comfortable place for her daughter to study, seeking tutorial assistance in math, supporting her financially to the extent possible while in university, and being a "listening post" during tough times in her studies. All of these are goal-directed actions. But they are also linked by the mother's goal, which is to encourage her daughter to consider engineering and become an engineer. We can call these linked actions across time a *project*. In this scenario the daughter joins her mother in the project either actively or reluctantly. Thus a project, in our definition, is a series of actions over a period of time that are linked in terms of the meaning they provide.

Considering a career as a project is a particularly useful idea. Rather than trying to think of something that will virtually define your whole life, at least occupationally, why not consider something of shorter duration that is more focused. "Project" has some particular advantages. As a noun, "project" means a plan or proposal, and an undertaking requiring effort. As a verb, it denotes to thrust outward or forward. We see from these dictionary meanings how the word "project" is quite strong—implying action, direction, intentionality, and purpose in time and space. Another asset of the word "project" is that it is in common use—it resonates with our experience as human beings. While we may be unsure or unclear about our careers, we can all think of projects in which we are engaged: getting a university degree, enhancing relationships, tutoring children in ESL, or practising a slap shot. What characterizes these projects is that they are intentional, constructed, and provide a perspective from which to view life and meaning. All of them involve others in some way or another, so we consider them joint projects.

In the occupational field, project has been used to refer to new forms of contract and short-term work (Littleton, Arthur, & Rousseau, 2000). For example, Jones (1996) used the film industry to illustrate how work is organized into projects, in which whole teams are assembled in reference to the production of a film, and then disbanded when the film is complete. This usage is important not only because it reflects actual practice in the world of work, but it also demonstrates the need for a connection between the micro-level and the macro-construct career. The hi-tech industry is another example in which "project" rather than "career" is used extensively.

We know that projects are to some extent intended, or planned in advance, but at the same time, there is an unplanned part that arises from, or within, the project itself. Everything isn't determined in advance. We often recognize projects as we engage in them and find new goals emerging from them. The psychologist Linell (1998) wrote: "The projection involves the opening of horizons for future actions and contributions. It embodies ideas guiding personal direction" (p. 218). Phrases like "opening of horizons" and "guiding personal direction" indicate how projects contribute to the task of constructing a life. Another important characteristic of projects is that they are ways of making sense of our past experiences (retrospective) and anticipating our future experiences (prospective).

In the contextualist action theory of career theory that my colleagues and I have elaborated, four important constructs are related: action, joint action, project, and career (Young & Valach, 1996, 2000; Young, Valach, & Collin, 1996). Each of these constructs assists people in organizing and making sense of their own and others' behaviour. Each is more complex and longer-term than the preceding one and involves a denser social network. The focus of our attention is at the project level because we think that it represents a level that engages most of us as we live our daily lives.

At the same time that we are constructing our own lives through projects, we are building up and being built up by the groups, societies, and cultures in which we live. We do not stand alone as much as we think we do; we are connected to others through our joint actions, projects, and careers.

We suggest that *project* is a particularly functional construct for people generally, but particularly for university students, to use to view their lives. Ask yourself: What projects am I engaged in? How do they help me organize and make sense of my experience? What bigger picture do they contribute to? Putting the pieces together allows you to reflect on how you are constructing your life.

Success Strategies FOR CAREER DEVELOPMENT

Self-awareness
I have discovered that the career path(s) that could fulfill me are…

Self-confidence
I can add to my confidence to be able to do activities that my ideal career demands by…

Self-concept
To get more relevant career experience I plan to…

Chapter Summary

Choosing a career path is perhaps one of the most important life choices facing the university student. By revisiting and further developing ideas from previous chapters, such as self-efficacy and goal-setting, this chapter assists students in linking their university studies to a future career. The chapter provides students with a process of discovering personal attributes and abilities which are associated with various career options. The focus is not only the self-identification of personal values, needs, skills, and talents, but also includes practical information about employment trends, occupational categories, and personal networking. Students are presented with strategies for gaining important career-relevant experience, which can be particularly useful in assisting them in getting their foot in the door, so that they can get started on their dream career.

Exercises

REFLECT–ACT

The following Reflect–Act exercises are designed to assist you in developing increased self-awareness of your career identity through the process of reflective thinking, analysis, and productive action. These exercises encourage you to use the insights you have developed as you have explored your own career possibilities to engage in concrete activities that can help you gain career relevant experience.

Reflect   Identify two or three jobs that you could do that would allow you to fulfill your personal mission.
Act   Interview someone who currently has this job and discover more about the responsibilities of this position.

Reflect   Using the information you have learned previously about goal-setting, develop a goal that can be one step toward achieving your aspirations.
Act   Engage in activities this week that will allow you to succeed with this goal. Evaluate your success.

Reflect   Imagine that you are a referee writing a letter describing your personal abilities. Describe the three most important points you would state in the letter.
Act   Show this letter to someone who knows you well and gather feedback regarding its accuracy.

Reflect   Design a résumé and letter of application for your dream job. Include in your résumé information you have learned about yourself through the self-awareness exercises in this chapter.
Act   Compare this résumé with the NOC description of this position.

Reflect   Develop a list of the "top ten tips" for getting your perfect job.
Act   Pick one of those tips and practise it. Note your success.

GROUP DISCUSSION

1. Join with others who are interested in the same subject area as you are. Brainstorm all the different jobs you might do in this area.
2. Consider information you have learned about demographic trends, current events, scientific breakthroughs, and international developments. Use this information to develop a list of the hot jobs of the future.
3. Decide which factor is more important in developing a well-developed career identity: passion or purpose. Provide evidence to support your decision.

4. Identify the factors you believe produce career indecision and confusion for first-year students. Brainstorm possible solutions to help reduce this indecision.

5. Develop a list of ten creative alternatives for developing the transferable skills that employers value.

APPLY TO LIFE

Technological advancements, the global economy, and demographic factors all influence the career search of students today. You have been asked to write a magazine article featuring ideas students can utilize to ensure they are adequately prepared to meet these challenges. Include in your article information about the influence of these factors on students' career search process, as well as specific strategies students can use to enhance their employability.

Using the ideas you have presented in this article, develop your own personal plan of goals and objectives for gaining the expertise and experience that will ensure that you are ready to meet the career challenges of the twenty-first century.

I can be...me

Creating the life I love is possible you see.

When I answer life questions to uniquely fit me...
    Finding something to do which defines me.
        something to learn which refines me.
        something to anticipate which inspires me.
        something to love which affirms me.
        something to give which outlasts me.

I can be all I'd like to be, if I simply use the power within me.

I will be all I dream I can be, when I remind myself to believe in me.

I can be the best I can be for I'll practise those 10 magic words that help me succeed.

If it is to be.... It is up to ME.

— lilly

Glossary of Key Terms

Abstract thinkers—individuals who are objective learners who prefer to analyze situations logically and impersonally.

Academic procrastination—the last-minute preparation of term papers, or cramming for examinations.

Academic self—a description of one's abilities to handle the cognitive complexity and informational demands of courses.

Academic stress—apprehension, worry, and physical symptoms associated with those situations when students experience difficulties in managing academic tasks such as taking tests, writing papers, or reading assignments.

Academic writing—writing that builds on the work of others, integrates the student's thinking with the work of others, and demonstrates logical reasoning. It presents a well-evidenced, personal position as opposed to a personal opinion.

Academicians—referred to as scholars, they are the members of an academy that promotes the discovery and dissemination of Truth.

Accommodators—individuals who are concrete learners and process information actively; they start with experience and test it out.

Achievement orientation—is defined by the need for achievement, expected value of a task, the student's sense of confidence or self-efficacy in completing the task, the hope, the attributional style chosen for similar tasks completed, and the goals set in order to achieve the task.

Acquiring—the ability to transfer new information from working memory into long-term memory. This involves making sense of what the new material means and linking it with previously learned material.

Active experimentation—a process of learning by doing and using practical, personal experience to develop understanding and mastery.

Active listening—an active process of attending to others, acknowledging their concerns, validating their importance by trying to empathetically understand what the other is trying to say. It is an activity that considers another's needs and experiences, it affirms others, it restates feelings, and it empowers self-understanding.

Adviser—a person who can provide guidance in answering questions related to academic success.

Analysis—involves being able to identify the elements, relationships, and organizational principles of a situation.

Analytic learners—individuals who look first at details and then put them together.

Antithesis—a contradicting counterargument or alternative conclusion.

Application—using the content information from your textbooks and classes in order to solve a problem.

Argument—a set of two or more statements in which one of the statements has the special status of being the conclusion.

Assimilators—individuals who are abstract learners and process information reflectively through detailed, sequential steps; they start with an idea and reflect about it.

At-home phase—the fourth stage of culture shock; the visitor embraces the customs of the new culture, the "at-home" phase has been reached.

Attending—the ability to select the important or key information by flagging material that has been presented in assigned readings and lectures.

Attributional style—the reason you give for explaining your successful or unsuccessful outcome.

Bloom's taxonomy—refers to the cognitive development continuum, beginning with the acquisition of new information or knowledge, and ending with the evaluation of complex thought.

Career mentor programs—provide a structured process for assisting individuals to expand their career awareness of particular occupational fields and develop important interviewing skills by providing the opportunity to meet professionals in various career fields.

Career self-efficacy—confidence in one's capability to do what is needed in order to make career decisions, gain relevant experience and obtain one's ideal vocation.

Career skills portfolio—a compilation of career skills individuals have developed through various experiences and samples of these skills.

Chunking—involves the grouping of words or ideas into categories that reflect some common and meaningful elements.

Climate facilitator—a person who monitors and evaluates the concerns, needs and frustrations of group members to ensure effective group functioning.

Collaborative learners—individuals who learn best by sharing information. They favour discussion, role-playing, problem-solving sessions and business games as means of learning.

Commitment—to act upon that idea or set of ideas, fully realizing and embracing the possibility of an alternative explanation.

Communication—a process by which information is exchanged between individuals through a common system of symbols, signs, or behaviours. It is an active reciprocal process of sending and receiving messages.

Community—a unified body of individuals where people with common interests live in a particular area, or an interacting population of various kinds of individuals in a common location.

Competitive conversationalist—a person who launches into a conversation, totally ready to share a story before acknowledging what the other is saying—jockeying for a chance to be heard.

Comprehension—involves the skills of transposing, translating, interpreting, and extrapolating from a certain body of knowledge.

Compulsive procrastination—wavering in decision-making so that an individual attempts to follow one course of action, then changes his/her mind and attempts another.

Conclusion—a reasoned judgment; the necessary consequence of two or more propositions taken as premises.

Concrete learners—individuals who relate their personal experience to information they are learning; subjective learners who rely on feelings and hunches to solve problems.

Connected knowing—a learning approach that involves subjective learning, striving to understand the ideas of others through careful listening, empathic concern, perspective taking and connecting learning to peoples' experiences.

Control—implies that you can actually adapt a personal characteristic to improve your learning.

Convergers—students who are abstract learners and prefer pragmatic problem solving to learn; they start with an idea and process it actively.

Counter-dependency—the second stage of group development; defined by disagreement and conflict among members about group goals and procedures. Also called fight phase.

Course goals—the specific goals that ensure one masters both the content of the courses and the learning processes that will increase effectiveness in handling continuing courses.

Cramming—involves studying hastily for an imminent exam.

Critical thinking—a set of core mental processes that include interpretation, analysis, evaluation, inference, explanation, and self-regulation.

Decisional procrastination—the inability to make timely decisions in a variety of social, academic, and personal situations.

Deductive logic—the highest standard of logical strength in terms of providing support for a conclusion, often referred to as "all-or-nothing" or "black & white."

Deep processors—learners who dig for meaning behind words and concepts; they analyze, hypothesize, make connections and draw conclusions.

Defining hierarchies—used to organize material into a few broad topics and further subdivide them into more refined ideas and concepts; aid in reconstructing the memory of the material during examination.

Dependency—the first stage of group development and is illustrated by significant dependency on the designated leader, concerns about safety, and inclusion issues. Also called inclusion phase.

Dependent learners—students who prefer instructor-directed, highly structured programmes with explicit assignments set and assessed; they learn best through lectures and structured tutorials that provide specific guidance and direction.

Dialectic process—a process that involves systematic reasoning, exposition or argument that juxtaposes opposed or contradictory ideas and seeks to resolve their conflict.

Discrimination—the systematic, intended or unintended, denial of recognition, power, privilege, and opportunity to certain people based on the groups to which they belong.

Distributed practice—involves spacing studying time over several shorter time periods rather than one long period.

Divergers—individuals who perceive concretely and process information reflectively; they start with experience, think about it, then generalize.

Drafting—the process of creating the written document. Drafting is a process that includes developing and refining a writing plan, including a thesis statement; and writing in accordance with the plan, filling in gaps as needed, and presenting information so that it achieves the objectives of the plan.

Dualistic thinkers—assume only one right answer to every question.

Editing—a stage in the writing process that focuses on the small details of writing: spelling, punctuation, sentence structure, grammar, and proper use of a particular presentation style such as MLA or APA.

Employment interviews—interviews with human resource professionals, potential supervisors or possible employers in which individuals use their knowledge of a particular vocation and their knowledge of themselves to demonstrate suitability for a particular position.

Energizing source—when test anxiety provides the student with motivation to try harder to find ways to solve the problem.

Evaluation—includes skills for making critical judgments and assessing the value or worth of information in your discipline, based on internal and external criteria.

Experiential learning—educational placements that provide students with practical, career-related employment experience that complement their academic interests.

Expressiveness—a teaching behaviour that enhances students' attention to material, involving eye contact, hand gestures, voice intonation, content-appropriate humour, and movement.

Extracurricular activities—activities outside of academic classes.

Extroverts—individuals who prefer active involvement, are social and get their energy from being around people. They do their best thinking out loud and in group discussions.

Fallacy—a plausible argument using false inferences.

False cause—coming to a conclusion based on the temporal sequence of events.

Financial stress—worry and concern associated with the pressures that students experience related to financing their education.

Goal—a purpose to which a person is unalterably committed.

Goals—provide the institutions with an end to which effort can be directed.

Hasty conclusion—where the requirement of logical sufficiency is not met.

Hierarchies—an organizational strategy that involves organizing material into a few broad topics and further subdividing the topics into more refined ideas and concepts.

Holistic learners—individuals who form global impressions and see things as a whole.

"I" language—allows communicators to take responsibility by specifically stating needs, asking for clarification, or using accurate descriptors that present a personal viewpoint or reaction.

"I" messages—responses to others that begin with "I" and are usually strategic methods of communicating when potential conflict may exist between two or more individuals. It often reduces the defensive response by the other.

Independent learners—students who want to have a role in decisions regarding the structure and content of their learning; they like to direct their own learning and prefer learning situations in which they have the freedom to determine their own learning priorities and outcomes.

Inductive logic—concerned with arguments that aim at achieving the less stringent standard.

Informal writing—writing forms such as letter and journal writing. This kind of writing may be personal and expressive. It does not rely on documentation and standard forms of presentation.

Information interviews—allow individuals to explore potential fields of interest and expand their social network. They provide an opportunity to meet people in different vocations and ask questions in order to gain greater knowledge about particular occupational areas.

Integrating—expanding or adding personal experiences and information to the new material that help to strengthen the learning of it.

Interference model—the attention reduction and distraction as a result of being anxious, and excessive rumination about failure and vulnerability.

Interpersonal communication—involves communication between or among people.

Introverts—learners, as described by Myers-Briggs, who prefer to think about issues, consider perspectives, and reflect about their own experience. They prefer quiet study environments.

Knowledge—involves the basic facts about a discipline.

Life routine procrastination—the difficulty some individuals have in scheduling the timing of normal, recurring chores.

Mastery goals—focus on the acquisition of new skills, improving competencies, or gaining knowledge. They are also called learning goals or task orientation.

Medium—the channel in which the message is conveyed such as oration, interpretive dance, or drama.

Mentor—a trusted guide, tutor, or coach who provides guidance during a student's academic development.

Message—a set of key ideas that the speaker desires the audience to appreciate, understand, and apply. It can be informational—providing important novel facts; creative—inviting the audience to help develop new ideas; or motivational—challenging change.

Metacognition—an ability to observe, analyze, and think about your thinking processes.

Metacognitive strategies—include planning strategies such as setting learning goals, skimming, and generating questions; monitoring strategies such as self-testing, attention-focus, and test-taking strategies; and regulating strategies such as adjusting reading rate, re-reading, and reviewing.

Mission statements—define the specific tasks that are to be carried out in a university or college.

Mnemonics—effective organizational strategies that includes both acoustic and visual codes such as acronyms, taking the first letter of each word in a list and creating a new word or jingle.

Multiplicity—perceiving the world as having grey areas with few or even no absolute right answers.

Networking—a process of expanding social connections through the exchange of information or services among individuals, groups, or institutions.

Neurotic procrastination—the tendency to postpone major life decisions such as choice of a career path or academic major.

Nonverbal language—includes body posture, facial cues, eye contact, and gestures that communicate the message without the use of verbal utterances.

Optimism—an emotional predisposition, a predictor of successful adaptation to stressful encounters. As a belief that good prevails over evil, optimism is the tendency to take the most positive or hopeful view of circumstances in most situations.

Organizing—the ability to make connections among ideas in working memory through such devices as concept maps or coherent and organized outlines.

Paraphrase—a detailed interpretation of a specific section of the work of another person described in your own words, to better explain the original work to a particular audience.

Performance goals—a type of goal that focuses on outcome, and measures success by comparing one's achievements to the achievements of others. They are also called ego orientation, and they view learning as a means to an end.

Philosophy statement—clarifies what a university stands for, provides rationale for its existence, guides its operation, and organizes the evaluation of teaching.

Plagiarism—a process in which a writer uses the work of another person without giving proper credit. This can include original ideas, strategies, research, tables and graphics, and written words. Most universities have guidelines assisting students so that they can avoid this problem and thus avoid being accused of academic dishonesty.

Pluralistic university community—a community where all worldviews are treated equally and equity of all members is rewarded.

Presentation—a commitment by the presenter to help the audience do or learn something.

Pre-writing—a stage in the writing process that allows the writer to develop a clear understanding of the task, gather information, read and take notes, and organize and make connections between different pieces of information. With this information the writer is able to outline a plan for the task.

Problematic premise—when one or more premises fail to meet requirement of logical acceptability.

Procedural knowledge—various principles that guide good thinking in each discipline such as pattern recognition, independent thinking, evaluating alternatives, perspective taking, likelihood calculations, scientific method or inquiry, decision making, logical reasoning, and problem solving.

Procrastination—the act of postponing and delaying needlessly.

Professor expressiveness—includes physical movement and voice intonation, eye contact, and humour. These behaviours help to engage tudents.

Professor organization—includes the course syllabi and lecture outlines, and the use of headings that can help you to increase your learning substantially.

Purpose goals—a set of goals aimed at achieving overall outcomes that provide a sense of personal fulfillment.

Receiving knowledge—to rely on "the experts" to provide them with knowledge, deriving their identity and their assigned roles from "the experts."

Recorder—the role of a group member who keeps a written account of what happens during the meetings

Referee—an individual who is willing to testify as to the character and experience of an applicant for employment.

Reflective observation—an approach to learning, described by Kolb, in which individuals master information through observation and analysis. Understanding occurs by evaluating one's own experience.

Refueling—the process of using supportive audience members to regain one's confidence during a presentation. Their smiling and approving faces will re-energize the speaker to continue.

Relativism subordinate—to neither accept as truth anything that "the experts" say nor treat all opinions as equally valid. Rather, adopt an analytical, critical approach, using the tools of the discipline to interpret and evaluate the ideas.

Résumé—a two-page summary of one's career objectives and relevant experience that is used as part of the process of applying for a position.

Revising—a phase of writing in which the writer critically evaluates the draft. It entails a critical analysis of the content, organization, and evidence presented in the document. It also includes a careful assessment of the technical aspects of writing such as punctuation, grammar, and spelling.

Selecting main ideas—involves identifying the key aspects of the text in a given chapter and trying to make connections between primary and supporting ideas.

Self-awareness—the process of increasing self-knowledge. It includes being able to be introspective, to reflect, and to exam oneself within the context of situational demands and social expectations.

Self-concept—an assessment of one's competencies in comparison to those of others; it includes an objective description of roles, traits, experiences, and abilities.

Self-confidence—an attitude toward, and assessment of, one's adequacy and worth; it is influenced by one's capabilities to reliably meet various challenges in life, to set realistic goals, and to motivate oneself.

Self-efficacy—a belief in one's own capabilities to succeed.

Self-monitoring—observing one's self through systematic recording, planning, and analysis to provide information about the real self, as well as any academic or personal areas that are problematic.

Self-reflection—engaging in an honest self-appraisal of your attitudes, patterns of time use, problem areas, and procrastination tendencies.

Self-regulation—an ability to control and direct actions so that a specific goal can be achieved.

Self-talk—an interpretation of experiences and an inner dialogue within yourself; this affects both self-confidence and self-efficacy.

Separate knowing—an objective, analytical procedure, as emphasized by critical thinking, scientific method, and textual analysis.

Sex-role socialization—a factor that influences how men and women communicate differently.

Social self—an assessment of one's ability to establish and maintain relationships. It is influenced by one's social confidence in different situations, the ability to understand and get along with others, popularity, leadership capabilities, and engagement with others.

Social stress—stress related to dealing with peers, family, or faculty.

Stereotyping—the behaviour that influences the expectations of certain individuals.

Students' Code of Responsibilities—include a commitment of all its members to the advancement of learning, the dissemination of knowledge, and the well-being of all its members. A set of equally important values defines how the commitments are to be carried out by all members, including students.

Studying—the active processing of information that involves attending, acquiring, organizing, and integrating it into memory.

Subjectivism—the search for truth from within, from the heart It is personal, intuitive, and comes from first-hand experiences.

Success identity—a belief in one's own abilities to adapt effectively to changing life circumstances, to overcome threatening situations, to manage difficulties, to progress, and to accomplish goals.

Summary—a concise statement of the main idea expressed in a section of text, described in the author's own words.

Support groups—a network of people who share a common interest, provide advice, answer questions, or boosts personal confidence.

Synthesis—involves the skills to produce unique communication (whether written or oral) in the form of a plan, a proposed set of operations, a derivation of a set of abstract relations, or a prediction of probable consequences of a belief or course of action; the combination or the merging of the thesis and antithesis into a new idea, outcome, conclusion, and eventually a new truth.

Talents—natural-born abilities.

Target goals—the methods used to achieve an objective.

Task facilitator—the role of a group member who keeps the group on task and moving toward the shared goal by checking on the progress of group members.

Test anxiety—results in feelings of apprehension and nervousness, worried thoughts and physical symptoms such as an upset stomach and headaches. It is a pattern of intense and substantial reactions that results in one of the most pervasive problems of university students.

Thesis—an explanation of the statement.

Time limits—specific, allotted times or dates for accomplishing goals.

Transferable skills—skills and competencies that have been developed in one setting that can be applied in other vocational settings.

Trust—the third stage of group development in which group members' communication becomes more open and task-oriented. Also called structure phase.

Two-for-one rule—guideline that states that you should study a minimum of two hours for every hour you spend in class.

University—a society or a community. Together, its members are in the pursuit of knowledge to have a better attitude toward and understanding of life.

It's More Than Common Sense
References

Chapter 1

Aylesworth, L.S., & Bloom, B. L. (1976, May). College experiences and problems of rural and small-town students. *Journal of College Student Personnel*, 236–242.

Baker, R. W., & Siryk, B. (1989). *Student adaptation to college questionnaire.* Los Angeles: Western Psychological Services.

Beil, C., Reisen, C. A., Zea, M. C., & Caplan, R. C. (1999). A longitudinal study of the effects of academic and social integration and commitment on retention. *NASPA Journal*, 37(1), 376–385.

Birnie-Lefcovitch, S. (2000). *Transition from high school to university: rural/urban differences.* Paper presented at the annual conference of the Canadian Association of College and University Student Services, York University, Toronto.

Bray, N. J., Braxton, J. M., & Sullivan, A. S. (1999). The influence of stress-related strategies on college student departure decisions. *Journal of College Student Development*, 40(6), 645–657.

Goudie, A. (1996). Adjusting to university in St. John's and its academic implications. *Focus on the Student Occasional Paper Series, 2*(2). St. John's, NF: Memorial University, Centre for Institutional Analysis and Planning.

Jackman, A. M. (1994). Involvement and intent to return of freshman students from rural resource dependent communities and of natural resource students. *Dissertation Abstracts International, 55* (11), 3470A. (University Microfilms No. DA9507689)

Levitz, R., & Noel, L. (1989). Connecting students to institutions: Keys to retention and success. In M. L. Upcraft & J. N. Gardner (Eds.), *The Freshman Experience: Helping Students Survive and Succeed in College.* San Francisco: Jossey-Bass.

MacGregor, J. (1988). Design and implementation of four learning community models. In Washington Centre for the Improvement of Quality in Higher Education, *Final Report to the Ford Foundation.* Washington, DC: Washington Centre for Improving the Quality of Undergraduate Education.

Pascarella, E.T., & Terenzini, P. T. (1991). *How college affects students.* San Francisco: Jossey-Bass.

Stoecker, J., Pascarella, E. & Wolfle, L. (1988). Persistence in higher education: A nine-year test of a theoretical model. *Journal of College Student Development, 29*, 196–209.

Tinto, V. (1993). *Leaving College: Rethinking the Causes and Cures of Student Attrition.* (2nd ed.). Chicago: University of Chicago Press.

Tokuno, K. A. (1993). Long-term and recent outcomes of the Freshman Interest Group Program. *Journal of the Freshman Year Experience, 5*(2), 7–28.

Tokuno, K. A., & Campbell, F. L. (1992). Freshman Interest Groups at the University of Washington: Effects on retention and scholarship. *Journal of the Freshman Year Experience, 4*(1), 7–22.

Chapter 2

Anonymous (1998). CIOs on the lookout for soft skills. *CIO Canada*, 6(10), 7.

Conference Board of Canada (1997). *Employability Skills Profile.*

Frank, T. (1997, May). What do employers want? *University Affairs.*

Grayson, J. P. (1999a). Using surveys to measure value added in skills in four faculties. *The Canadian Journal of Higher Education.* 29(11), 111–142.

Grayson, J. P. (1999b). The impact of university experiences on self-assessed skills. *Journal of College Student Development*, 40(6), 687–700.

Grayson, J. P. (2001). *Factors Affecting the Quality of University Graduates' Jobs*. York University: Center for Research in Work and Society.

Jones, E. et al. (1994). *Essential Skills in Writing, Speech and Listening, and Critical Thinking for College Graduates*. Pennsylvania State University: National Center on Postsecondary Teaching, Learning, and Assessment.

Chapter 3

Clifton, R. A. (1996, October). Improving education for teachers in Manitoba. *Policy Options, 17*, 54–56.

Clifton, R. A. (1999). The education of university students: A social capital perspective. *College Teaching, 47*(3), 114–118.

Clifton, Rodney A. (2000, March). Student evaluation. *University Affairs*, 5.

Clifton, R. A., Etcheverry, E., Hasinoff, S., & Roberts, L. W.. (1996). Measuring the cognitive domain of the quality of life of university students. *Social Indicators Research, 38*, 29–52.

Clifton, R. A., Mandzuk, D., & Roberts, L.W., (1994). The alienation of undergraduate education students: A case study of a Canadian university. *Journal of Education for Teaching, 20*, 179–192.

Clifton, R. A. & Roberts, L. W. (1993). *Authority in classrooms*. Scarborough, ON: Prentice-Hall.

Clifton, R. A., & Rubenstein, H.. (1998, June). Improving university teaching: A performance-based approach. *Policy Options, 18*, 36–39.

Cohen, E. H., Clifton, R. A., & Roberts, L. W. (2000). The cognitive domain of the quality of life of university students: A re-analysis of an instrument. *Social Indicators Research, 53*, 63–77.

Chapter 4

Försterling, F. (1985). Attributional retraining: A review. *Psychological Bulletin, 98*(3), 495–512.

Hyllegard, R., Radlo, S. J., & Early, D. (2001). Attribution of athletic expertise by college coaches. *Perceptual and Motor Skills, 92*(1), 193–207.

Mizuno, S. (1998). The relationship of causal attribution, guilt, and shame to the academic adjustment of Japanese students in the United States. *Japanese Journal of Counseling Science, 31*(3), 259–269.

Perry, R. P. (1991). Perceived control in college students: Implications for instruction in higher education. In J. Smart (Ed.), *Higher education: Handbook of theory and research: Vol 7*. (pp. 1–56). New York: Agathon Press.

Perry, R. P. (1997a). Perceived control in college students: Implications for instruction in higher education. In R. P. Perry & J. Smart (Eds.), *Effective teaching in higher education* (pp. 11–60). New York, Agathon Press.

Perry, R. P. (1997b). Teaching effectively: Which students? What methods? In R. P. Perry & J. Smart (Eds.), *Effective teaching in higher education* (pp. 154–168). New York, Agathon Press.

Perry, R. P., Hechter, F. J., Menec, V. H., & Weinberg, L. (1993). Enhancing achievement motivation and performance in college students: An attributional retraining perspective. *Research in Higher Education, 34*, 687–723.

Robertson, J. S. (2000). Is attribution training a worthwhile classroom intervention for K–12 students with learning difficulties? *Educational Psychology Review, 12*(1), 111–134.

Schönwetter, D. J., Perry, R. P., & Struthers, C. W. (1993). Students' perceptions of control and success in the college classroom: Affects and achievement in different instructional conditions. *Journal of Experimental Education, 61*, 227–246.

Schönwetter, D. J., Walker, L. J., Hladkyj, S., Perry, R. P., Kobylak, J., & Hall, N. (2001, April 13). *Facilitating the academic development of high-risk first year students through a deliberate teaching strategy*. Paper presented at the American Educational Research Association, Seattle, Washington.

Schönwetter, D. J., Walker, L. J., Taylor, K. L., & Cameron, B. (2001, June). *First-year seminar: Strategies for success*. Paper presented at the Society for Teaching and Learning in Higher Education, St. John's, NF: Memorial University.

Stojanowska, E. (1999). Self-descriptions, expectations and causal attribution of success and failure formulated privately and in the self-presentation situation by people with different ego strength: A natural experiment. *Polish-Psychological-Bulletin, 29*(3), 199–216.

Van Overwalle, F. (1989). Structure of freshmen's causal attribution for exam performance. *Journal of Educational Psychology, 81*, 400–407.

Van Overwalle, F., Segebarth, K., & Goldchstein, M. (1989). Improving performance of freshmen through attributional testimonies from fellow students. *British Journal of Educational Psychology, 59*, 75–85.

Weiner, B. (1986). *An attributional theory of motivation and emotion.* New York, Springer-Verlag.

Weiner, B. (1989). *Human motivation.* Hillsdale, NJ: Lawrence Erlbaum Associates.

Weiner, B., Frieze, I., Kukla, A., Reed, L., Rest, S., & Rosenbaum, R. M. (1971). Perceiving the causes of success and failure. In E. E. Jones et al (Eds.), *Attribution: Perceiving the causes of behavior.* Morristown, NJ: General Learning Press.

Weiner, B., & Litman-Adizes, T. (1980). An attributional expectancy-value analysis of learned helplessness and depression. In J. Garber & M. E. P. Seligman (Eds.), *Human control* (pp. 35–57). New York, Academic Press.

Weiner, B., Russell, D., & Lerman, D. (1979). The cognitive-emotion process in achievement-related contexts. *Journal of Personality and Social Psychology, 37*, 1211–1220.

Wong, P. T. P., & Weiner, B. (1981). When people ask "why" questions and the heuristics of attributional search. *Journal of Personality and Social Psychology, 40*, 650–663.

Chapter 5

Bandura, A., & Schunk, D. H. (1981). Cultivating competence, self-efficacy, and intrinsic interest through proximal self-motivation. *Journal of Personality and Social Psychology, 41*, 586–598.

Latham, G. P., & Seijts, G. H. (1999). The effects of proximal and distal goals on performance on a moderately complex task. *Journal of Organizational Behavior, 20*, 421–429.

Locke, E. A., & Latham, G. P. (1990). *A theory of goal setting and task performance.* Englewood Cliffs, NJ: Prentice-Hall.

Pinder, C. (1998). *Work motivation in organizational behavior.* Upper Saddle River, NJ: Prentice-Hall.

Seijts, G. H. (2001). Setting goals: When performance doesn't matter. *Ivey Business Journal, 65*(3), 40–44.

Seijts, G. H., & Latham, G. P. (2000). The effects of goal setting and group size on performance in a social dilemma. *Canadian Journal of Behavioural Science, 32*, 104–116.

Seijts, G. H., & Latham, G. P. (2001). The effect of distal learning, outcome, and proximal goals on a moderately complex task. *Journal of Organizational Behavior, 22*, 291–302.

Seijts, G. H., Meertens, R. M., & Kok, G. (1997). The effects of task importance and publicness on the relation between goal difficulty and performance. *Canadian Journal of Behavioural Science, 29*, 54–62.

Seijts, G. H., Taylor, L., & Latham, G. P. (1998). Enhancing teaching performance through goal setting, implementation and seeking feedback. *International Journal of Academic Development, 3*, 156–168.

Chapter 6

Flett, G. L., Hewitt, P. L., & Martin, T. R. (1995). Dimensions of perfectionism and procrastination. In J. R. Ferrari, J. Johnson & W. G. McCown (Eds.), *Procrastination and task avoidance.* New York: Plenum Press.

Gollwitzer, P. M., & Brandstatter, V. (1997). Implementation intentions and effective goal pursuit. *Journal of Personality and Social Psychology, 73*, 186–199.

Lay, C. (1987). A modal profile analysis of procrastinators: A search for types. *Personality and Individual Differences, 8*, 705–714.

Lay, C. (1988). The relationship of procrastination and optimism to judgments of time to complete an essay and anticipation of setbacks. *Journal of Social Behavior and Personality, 3*, 201–214.

Lay, C. (1997). Explaining lower-order traits through higher-order factors: The case of trait procrastination, conscientiousness, and the specificity dilemma. *European Journal of Personality, 11*, 267–278.

Lay, C., & Schouwenburg, H. C. (1993). Trait procrastination, time management, and academic behavior. *Journal of Social Behavior and Personality, 8,* 647–662.

McGregor, I. (1998). *An identity consolidation view of social phenomena: Theory and research.* Unpublished doctoral dissertation, University of Waterloo, Waterloo, Canada.

Taylor, S. E., Pham, L. B., Rivkin, I. D., & Armor, D. A. (1998). Harnessing the imagination: Mental simulation, self-regulation, and coping. *American Psychologist, 53,* 429–439.

Chapter 7

Brown, J. I., Fishco, V. V., & Hanna, G. (1993). *Nelson-Denny reading test.* Chicago: Riverside Publishing Company.

Doyle, M., & Garland, J. (1999, June). *UCC2020: Applied cognitive and affective learning strategies. Evaluation results: Fall 1997 to Winter 1999.* Paper presented at the annual conference of the Canadian Association of College and University Student Services, University of Victoria, BC.

Doyle, M., & Garland J. (2001). A course to teach cognitive and affective learning strategies to university students. *Guidance & Counselling, 16*(3), 86–91.

Flavell, J. H. (1979). Metacognition and cognitive monitoring: A new area of cognitive-developmental inquiry. *American Psychologist, 34*(10), 906–911.

Garland, J., & Doyle, M. (2001). *UCC2020: Applied cognitive and affective learning strategies (Learning-to-Learn). Course workbook and manual.* St. John's, NF: Memorial University of Newfoundland.

Kolb, D. A. (1981). Disciplinary inquiry norms and student learning styles: Diverse pathways for growth. In A. Chickering, (Ed.), *The modern American college.* San Francisco: Jossey-Bass.

McCrindle, A. R., & Christensen, C.A. (1995). The impact of learning journals on metacognitive and cognitive processes and learning performance. *Learning and Instruction, 5,* 167–185.

Nist, S., & Holschuh, J. L. (2000). Comprehension strategies at the college level. In R. F. Flippo & D. C. Caverly, *Handbook of college reading and study strategy research.* Mahwah, NJ: Lawrence Erlbaum.

Sarason, I. G. (1956). Effect of anxiety, motivational instructions and failure on serial learning. *Journal of Experimental Psychology, 51,* 253–260.

Schmeck, R. R., Ribich, F. D., & Ramanaiah, N. (1977). Development of a self-report inventory for assessing individual differences in learning. *Applied Psychological Measurement, 1*(3), 412–431.

Chapter 8

American Library Association. Presidential Committee on Information Literacy. January 10, 1989, Washington, D.C. *http://www.ala.org/acrl/nili/ilit1st.html.*

Chiste, K. B., Glover, A., & Westwood, G. (2000). Perspectives on . . . infiltration and entrenchment: Capturing and securing information literacy territory in academe. *Journal of Academic Librarianship, 26*(3), 2–9.

Council of Prairie and Pacific University Libraries (2001). Doing research from a distance: A guide for western Canadian students *http://www.royalroads.ca/coppul/default.htm.*

Harris, R. (1997). Evaluating Internet Research Sources. *Virtual Salt. http://www.virtualsalt.com/evalu8it.htm.*

Troutman, L. (2000). User education. *Notes, 56*(3), 620–628.

Chapter 9

Coleman, H. L. K., & Freedman, A. M. (1996). Effects of a structured group intervention on the achievement of academically at-risk undergraduates. *Journal of College Student Development, 37,* 631–636.

Cornish, P. A., & Benton, D. (2001). Getting started in healthier relationships: Brief integrated dynamic group counseling in a university counseling setting. *Journal of Specialists in Group Work, 26,* 129–143.

Newby-Fraser, E., & Schlebusch, L. (1997). Social support, self-efficacy and assertiveness as mediators of student stress. *Psychology: A Journal of Human Behavior, 34,* 61–69.

Santiago-Rivera, A. L., Gard, T., & Bernstein, B. (1999). The importance of achievement, intimacy, autonomy, and life events among first year college students. *Journal of College Student Psychotherapy, 13,* 57–73.

Watton, S. (2001). *The first year experience of new students at Memorial University.* St. John's, NF: Memorial University.

Yalom, I. D. (1995). *The theory and practice of group psychotherapy* (4th ed.). New York: Basic Books.

Chapter 10

Alster, E. H. (1997). The effects of extended time on algebra test scores for college students with and without learning disabilities. *Journal of Learning Disabilities, 30,* 222–227.

American Psychiatric Association (1994). *Diagnostic and statistical manual of mental disorders* (4th ed.). Washington: Author.

Bourke, A. B., Strehorn, K. C., & Silver, P. (2000). Faculty members' provision of instructional accommodations to students with LD. *Journal of Learning Disabilities, 33,* 26–32.

Canadian Mental Health Association. (2000). *Higher education for people with mental illness: Best practice accommodation strategies.* Toronto: Author.

Day, S. L., & Edwards, B. J. (1996). Assistive technology for postsecondary students with learning disabilities. *Journal of Learning Disabilities, 29,* 486–492, 503.

Degen, G., Stewart, D., & Walker, J. (2000, June). *Social phobia: Prevalence, impact, treatment.* Presented at the Annual Conference of the Canadian Association of College and University Student Services, Toronto.

Fiedorowicz, C., Benezra, E., MacDonald, W., McElgunn, B., & Wilson, A. (1998). *Neurobiological basis of learning disabilities.* Ottawa: Learning Disabilities Association of Canada.

Hardy Cox, D., & Klas, L. D. (1996). Students with learning disabilities in Canadian colleges and universities: A primer for service provision. *Journal of Learning Disabilities, 29,* 93–97.

Koverola, C., Proulx, J., Hanna, C., Battle, P., & Chohan, M. (1992, June). *Identifying mediators of adjustment in sexual abuse survivors: A scientist-practitioner approach.* Symposium presented at the Annual Convention of the Canadian Psychological Association, Quebec City, QC.

Nelson, J. R., Dodd, J. M., & Smith, D. J. (1990). Faculty willingness to accommodate students with learning disabilities: A comparison among academic divisions. *Journal of Learning Disabilities, 23,* 185–189.

Proulx, J., Dyck, K., Quinonez, R., Chohan, M., & Koverola, C. (1991, June). Attributional dimension and clinical symptomatology in child sexual abuse survivors. In C. Koverola (Chair), *Integrating empirical investigations of attributions and psychological functioning in psychotherapy with sexual abuse survivors.* Symposium conducted at the Annual Convention of the Canadian Psychological Association, Calgary, AB.

Runyan, M. K. (1990). The effect of extra time on reading comprehension scores for university students with and without learning disabilities. *Journal of Learning Disabilities, 24,* 104–108.

Scott, S. S. (1994). Determining reasonable academic adjustments for college students with learning disabilities. *Journal of Learning Disabilities, 27,* 403–412.

Stewart, D. (1994). Distinguishing "yearning disabilities" from learning disabilities in postsecondary settings. *Guidance & Counselling, 9*(5), 11–13.

Stewart, D. (1995). Counselling strategies for postsecondary students with yearning disabilities: A case study. *Guidance & Counselling, 10*(2), 31–33.

Stewart, D. (1998). Self-deception and entitlement in postsecondary students with false learning disabilities. *Guidance & Counselling, 13*(4), 25–27.

Stewart, D. (2001, June). *A dialogue about accommodations for test anxiety.* Presented at the Annual Conference of the Canadian Association of College and University Student Services, Montreal, QC.

Stewart, D., Cornish, P., & Somers, K. (1995). Empowering students with learning disabilities in the Canadian postsecondary educational system. *Canadian Journal of Counselling, 29,* 70–79.

Stewart, D., Johnson, E., Walker, J., & Degen, G. (2001, June). *Prevalence of social phobia and its relationship with psychopathology and egocentrism in a university setting.* Presented at the Annual Convention of the Canadian Psychological Association, Quebec City, QC.

Weiner, E., & Wiener, J. (1996). Concerns and needs of university students with psychiatric disabilities. *Journal of Postsecondary Education and Disability, 12*, 2–9.

Williams, W. M., & Ceci, S. J. (1999). Accommodating learning disabilities can bestow unfair advantages. *The Chronicle of Higher Education, August 6th*, B4–5.

Chapter 12

Bloom, B. S. (Ed.). (1956). *Taxonomy of educational objectives: Cognitive domain.* New York: McKay.

Pascarella, E. T., & Terenzini, P. T. (1991). *How college affects students.* San Francisco: Jossey-Bass.

Renaud, R. D. (2002). *College performance indicators: A review of their relationship with student outcomes.* Unpublished manuscript.

Chapter 13

Jones, C. (1996). Careers in project networks: The case of the film industry. In M. B. Arthur & D. M. Rousseau (Eds.), *The boundaryless career: A new employment principle for a new organizational era* (pp. 58–75). New York: Oxford University Press.

Linell, P. (1998). *Approaching dialogue: Talk, interaction and contexts in dialogical perspectives.* Amsterdam: John Benjamins.

Littleton, S. M., Arthur, M. B., & Rousseau, D. M. (2000). The future of the boundaryless career. In A. Collin & R. A. Young (Eds.), *The future of career* (pp. 101–114). Cambridge, Eng.: Cambridge University Press.

Sennett, R. (1998). *The corrosion of character.* New York: Norton.

Young, R. A., & Valach, L. (1996). Interpretation and action in career counseling. In M. L. Savickas & W. B. Walsh (Eds.), *Handbook of career counseling theory and practice* (pp. 361–376). Palo Alto, CA: Davies-Black.

Young, R. A., & Valach, L. (2000). Reconceptualising career theory and research: An action-theoretical perspective. In A. Collin & R. A. Young (Eds.), *The future of career* (pp. 181–196). Cambridge, Eng.: Cambridge University Press.

Young, R. A., Valach, L., & Collin, A. (1996). A contextual approach to career. In D. Brown, L. Brooks, & Associates, *Career choice and development* (3rd ed.) (pp. 477–512). San Francisco: Jossey-Bass.

Chapter References

Chapter 1

Affairs, S. (1999). First-year student survey. *Student Affairs Research Report: Housing and Student Life, 10*(3), 1–2.

Astin, A. W. (1993). *What matters in college: Four critical years revisited.* San Francisco: Jossey Bass.

Astin, A. W. (1996). Involvement in learning revisited: Lessons we have learned. *Journal of College Student Development, 37* (2), 123–134.

Astin, A. W. (1997). *What matters in college: Four critical years revisited.* San Francisco: Jossey-Bass.

Bandura, A. (1977). *Social learning theory.* Engelwood Cliffs, NJ: Prentice-Hall.

Bandura, A. (1986). *Social Foundations of Thought and Action.* Englewood Cliffs, NJ: Prentice-Hall.

Bandura, A. (1989). *Conclusion: Reflection of thought and action: A social cognitive theory.* Engelwood Cliffs, NJ: Prentice Hall.

Baxter, M. M. (1992). Cocurricular influences on college students' intellectual development. *Journal of College Student Development, 33,* 203–213.

Belenky, M., Clinchy, B., Goldberger, N., & Tarule, J. (1986). *Women ways of knowing.* New York: Basic Books.

Chickering, A. W., & Reisser, L. (1993). *Education and Identity* (2nd ed.). San Francisco: Jossey-Bass.

Ellis, A. (1995). Rational emotive behavior therapy. In R. J. Corsini & D. Wedding (Eds.), *Current psychotherapies* (5th ed.). Itasca, IL: Peacock.

Försterling, F. (1985). Attributional retraining: A review. *Psychological Bulletin, 98,* 495–512.

Garner, R. (1987). Strategies for reading and studying expository text. *Educational Psychologist, 22,* 313–332.

Kuh, G. D. (1993). In their own words: What students learn outside the classroom. *American Educational Research Journal, 30,* 277–304.

Luft, J. (1969). *Of human interaction.* Palo Alto, CA: National Press Books.

Maslow, A. H. (1970). *Motivation and personality.* New York: HarperCollins.

Meichenbaum, D. H. (1977). *Cognitive-behavior modification: An integrative approach.* New York: Plenum Press.

Mruk, C. J. (1995). *Self-esteem research, theory and practice.* New York: Springer.

Noel, J. G., Forsyth, D. R., & Kelley, K. N. (1987). Improving the performance of failing students by overcoming their self-serving attributional biases. *Basic and Applied Social Psychology, 8,* 151–162.

Pascarella, E., & Terenzini, P. (1991). *How college affects students: Findings and insights from twenty years of research.* San Francisco: Jossey-Bass.

Pekrun, R. (1992). The impact of emotions on learning and achievement: Towards a theory of cognitive/motivational mediators. *Applied Psychology: An International Review, 41,* 359–376.

Perry, R. P. (1991). Perceived control in college students: Implications for instruction in higher education. In J. Smart (Ed.), *Higher education: Handbook of theory and research, Vol. 7.* (pp. 1–56). New York: Agathon Press.

Perry, R. P., & Penner, K. S. (1990). Enhancing academic achievement in college students through attributional retraining and instruction. *Journal of Educational Psychology, 82,* 262–271.

Perry, W. G. Jr. (1970). *Forms of intellectual and ethical development in the college years: A scheme.* New York: Holt, Rinehart & Winston.

Peterson, C., & Barrett, L. C. (1987). Explanatory style and academic performance among university freshmen. *Journal of Personality and Social Psychology, 53,* 603–607.

Schönwetter, D. J. (1996). *Effective instruction and student differences in the college classroom.* Unpublished doctoral thesis, University of Manitoba, Winnipeg, MN.

Schönwetter, D. J., Perry, R. P., & Struthers, C. W. (1993). Students' perceptions of control and success in the college classroom: Affects and achievement in different instructional conditions. *Journal of Experimental Education, 61*(3), 227–246.

Solberg, V. S., Gusavac, N, Hamann, T., Felch, J., Johnson, J., Lamborn, S. & Torres, J. (1998). The adaptive success identity plan (ASIP): A career intervention for college students. *Career Development Quarterly, 47*(1), 48–95.

Springer, L., Terenzini, P., Pascarella, E., & Nora, A. (1995). Influences on college students' orientations toward learning for self-understanding. *Journal of College Student Development, 36*, 5–18.

Walker, J. L. (1998). *Survey of first-year university students: Summary of major findings.* Winnipeg, MN: The Canadian Undergraduate Survey Consortium.

Weiner, B. (1986). *An attributional theory of motivation and emotion.* New York: Springer-Verlag.

Chapter 2

Astin, H. S., & Kent, L. (1983). Gender roles in transition: Research and policy implications for higher education. *Journal of Higher Education, 54*, 309–324.

Belenky, M., Clinchy, B., Goldberger, N., & Tarule, J. (1986). *Women ways of knowing.* New York: Basic Books.

Bidwell, C. E. (1989). The meaning of educational attainment. *Research of Education and Socialization, 8*, 117–138.

Chickering, A. W., & Reisser, L. (1993). *Education and Identity* (2nd ed.). San Francisco: Jossey-Bass.

Clifton, R. A. (1997). The effects of social psychological variables and gender on the grade point averages and educational expectations of university students: A case study. *The Canadian Journal of Higher Education, 27*, 67–90.

Kuh, G. D. (1993). In their own words: What students learn outside the classroom. *American Educational Research Journal, 30*, 277–304.

Maslow, A. H. (1970). *Motivation and personality* (2nd ed.). New York: Harper & Row.

Pascarella, E., & Terenzini, P. (1991). *How college affects students: Findings and insights from twenty years of research.* San Francisco: Jossey-Bass.

Pascarella, E. T., Ethington, C. A., & Smart, J. C. (1988). The influence of college on humanitarian/civic involvement values. *Journal of Higher Education, 59*, 412–437.

Perry, W. J., Jr. (1970). *Forms of Intellectual and ethical development in the college years: A scheme.* New York: Holt, Rinehart, & Winston.

Chapter 3

Astin, A. W. (1993). What matters in college. *Liberal Education, 79*, 4–15.

Astin, A. W. (1997). *What matters in college: Four critical years revisited.* San Francisco: Jossey-Bass.

Bloom, B. S. (1956). *Taxonomy of educational objectives.* New York: David McKay.

Briggs, J. (1999). *Teaching for quality at the university.* Buckingham, England: Society for Research into Higher Education.

Encyclopædia Britannica. (2001). *Nalanda.* Available: *http://www.britannica.com.*

Dalhousie University. (2001, January 24). *History of Dalhousie University.* Available: *http://www.dal.ca/campus/history/index.html.*

Duggan, S. (1948). *A student's textbook in the history of education.* (3rd ed.). New York: Appleton-Century-Crofts, Inc.

Evers, F. T., & Gilbert, S. N. (1991). Outcomes assessment: How much value does university education add? *The Canadian Journal of Higher Education, 21*, 53–76.

Grayson, J. P. (1994). First year science in a commuter university: Where to intervene. *Canadian Journal of Higher Education, 24.*

Kuh, G. D. (1993). In their own words: What students learn outside the classroom. *American Educational Research Journal, 30*, 277–304.

Marsh, J. H. (Ed.). (2000). *The Canadian Encyclopedia.* Toronto, ON: McClelland & Stewart.

Memorial University of Newfoundland. (2001). *Calendar.* St. Johns', NF: Memorial University.

Merriam-Webster, A. (1986). *Webster's Ninth New Collegiate Dictionary.* Markham, ON: Thomas Allen and Son.

Office of the Registrar. (2001). *Code of Student Conduct and Disciplinary Procedures in Non-Academic Matters.* Brock University, St. Catharines, ON. Available: *http:// www.brocku.ca/registrar/graduate/ code_of_conduct.html#preamble* [May 1, 2001].

Pascarella, E. T., & Terenzini, P. (1991). *How college affects students: Findings and insights from twenty years of research.* San Francisco: Jossey-Bass.

Seeley, R. S. K. (1948). *The function of the university.* London: Oxford University Press.

Sheehan, N. M. (1985). History of higher education in Canada. *The Canadian Journal of Higher Education, 15,* 25–38.

University of Calgary. (2001). *Calendar.* Calgary, AB: University of Calgary.

University of Manitoba. (2002). *Undergraduate calendar.* Winnipeg, MN: University of Manitoba.

Tinto, V. (1993). *Leaving college: Rethinking the causes and cures of student attrition.* Chicago: University of Chicago Press.

Chapter 4

Abry, D. A. (1999). A structural model of self-regulatory behavior and college student achievement. *Dissertation Abstracts International Section A: Humanities and Social Sciences, 59,* 2338.

Astin, A. W. (1997). *What matters in college: Four critical years revisited.* San Francisco: Jossey-Bass.

Atkinson, J. W. (1964). *An introduction to motivation.* Princeton, NJ: Van Nostrand.

Bandura, A. (1982). Self-efficacy mechanisms in human agency. *American Psychologist, 37,* 122–147.

Bandura, A. (1986). *Social Foundations of Thought and Action.* Englewood Cliffs, NJ: Prentice-Hall.

Beck, A. T., & Emery, G. (1985). *Anxiety disorders and phobias: A cognitive perspective.* New York: Basic Books.

Blankenstein, K. R., Flett, G. L., & Batten, I. (1989). Test anxiety and problem-solving self-appraisals of college students. *Journal of Social Behavior and Personality, 4,* 531–540.

Civikly, J. M. (1986). Humor and the enjoyment of college teaching. Communicating in the college classroom. *New Directions for Teaching and Learning, 26,* 61–70.

Dansereau, D. F. (1985). Learning strategy research. In J. Segal, S. Chipman & R. Glaser (Eds.), *Thinking and learning skills: Relating instruction to research.* Hillsdale, NJ: Lawrence Erlbaum Associates.

Darke, S. (1988). Anxiety and working memory capacity. *Cognition and Emotion, 2,* 145–154.

Deece, J., & Deece, E. K. (1979). *How to study.* New York: McGraw-Hill.

Domino, G. (1975). Let the punishment fit the crime: Teacher-student interactions. *The Journal of Educational Research, 69,* 8–11.

Feldman, K. A. (1984). Class size and college students' evaluations of teachers and courses: A closer look. *Research in Higher Education, 21,* 45–116.

Feldman, K. A., & Paulsen, M. B. (Eds.) (1998). *Teaching and learning in the college classroom* (2nd ed.). Needham Heights, MA: Simon and Schuster.

Försterling, F. (1988). *Attribution theory in clinical psychology.* New York: Wiley.

Frank, B. M., Garlinger, D. K., & Kiewra, K. A. (1989). Use of embedded headings and intact outline with videotaped instruction. *Journal of Educational Research, 82,* 277–281.

Geen, R. G., Beatty, W. W., & Arkin, R. M. (1984). *Human motivation.* Boston: Allyn and Bacon.

Gentilhomme, Y. (1992). Humor: A didactic adjuvant. *International Journal of Humor Research, 5,* 69–89.

Grimes, S. K. (1997). Underprepared community college students: Characteristics, persistence, and academic success. *Community College Journal of Research and Practice, 21,* 47–56.

Hembree, R. (1988). Correlates, causes, effects, and treatment of test anxiety. *Review of Educational Research, 58,* 47–77.

Johnson, H. A. (1990). Humor as an innovative method for teaching sensitive topics. *Educational Gerontology, 16,* 547–559.

Lyons, K. J., Young, B. E., Haas, P. S., Hojat, M., & Bross, T. M. (1997, May 18–21). *A study of cognitive and noncognitive predictors of academic success in nursing, allied health and medical students.* Paper presented at the Association for Institutional Research, Orlando, FL.

Mayo, M. W., & Christenfeld, N. (1999). Gender, race, and performance expectations of college students. *Journal of Multicultural Counseling and Development, 27*, 93–104.

McClelland, D. C., Atkinson, J. W., Clark, R. W., & Lowell, E. L. (1953). *The achievement motive.* New York: Appleton-Century-Crofts.

McKeachie, W. J. (1980). Class size, large classes, and multiple sections. *Academe, 66*, 24–27.

McKeachie, W. J., Pintrich, P. R., Lin, Y.-G., & Smith, D. A. F. (1986). *Teaching and learning in the classroom: A review of the literature.* Ann Arbor, MI: University of Michigan.

McKeachie, W. J., Pollie, D., & Spiesman, J. (1985). Relieving anxiety in classroom examinations. *Journal of Personality and Social Psychology, 50*, 93–98.

Murray, H. G. (1938). *Explorations in personality.* New York: Oxford University Press.

Myers, L. B., & Steed, L. (1999). The relationship between optimism, dispositional pessimism, repressive coping and trait anxiety. *Personality and Individual Differences, 27*, 1261–1272.

Palmer, S., & Cochran, L. R. (1988). Parents as agents of career development. *Journal of Counseling Psychology, 35*(1), 71–76.

Pekrun, R. (1992). The impact of emotions on learning and achievement: Towards a theory of cognitive/motivational mediators. *Applied Psychology: An International Review, 41*, 359–376.

Perry, R. P. (1991). Perceived control in college students: Implications for instruction in higher education. In J. Smart (Ed.), *Higher education: Handbook of theory and research, Vol. 7.* (pp. 1–56). New York: Agathon Press.

Perry, R. P., Hechter, F. J., Menec, V. H., & Weinberg, L. (1993). Enhancing achievement motivation and performance in college students: An attributional retraining perspective. *Research in Higher Education, 34*, 687–723.

Pintrich, P. R., Cross, D. R., Kozma, R. B., & McKeachie, W. J. (1986). Instructional psychology. *Annual Review of Psychology, 37*, 611–651.

Plutchik, R. (1980). *Emotion: A psychoevolutionary synthesis.* New York: Harper and Row.

Rothblum, E. D., Solomon, L. J., & Murakami, J. (1986). Affective, cognitive, and behavioral differences between high and low procrastinators. *Journal of Counseling Psychology, 33*, 387–394.

Safford, F. (1991). Humor as an aid in gerontological education. *Gerontology and Geriatrics Education, 11*(3), 27–37.

Scheier, M. F., & Carver, C. S. (1987). Dispositional optimism and physical well-being: The influence of generalized outcome expectancies on health. *Journal of Personality, 55*, 169–210.

Schönwetter, D. J. (1993). Effective college lecturing: A review of the literature. *Canadian Journal of Higher Education, 23*, 1–18.

Schönwetter, D. J. (1996). *Effective instruction and student differences in the college classroom.* Unpublished doctoral thesis, University of Manitoba, Winnipeg, MN

Schwarzer, R. (1981). *Stress, angst und hilflosigkeit.* Stuttgart, Germany: Kohlhammer.

Schwarzer, R., Jerusalem, M., & Stiksrud, A. (1984). The developmental relationship between test anxiety and helplessness. In H. M. Van Der Ploeg, R. Scharzer & C. D. Spielberger (Eds.), *Advances in test anxiety research, Vol. 3.* (pp. 73–79). Hillsdale, NJ: Lawrence Erlbaum Associates.

Sherwood, J. V. (1987). Facilitative effects of gaze upon learning. *Perceptual and Motor Skills, 64*, 1275–1278.

Spielberger, C. D., Gonzalez, H. P., & Fletcher, T. (1979). Test anxiety reduction, learning strategies, and academic performance. In H. F. O'Neil & C. D. Spielberger (Eds.), *Cognitive and affective learning strategies, Vol. 1.* (pp. 111–131). New York: Academic.

Sternberg, R. J. (1985). *Beyond IQ: A triarchic theory of human intelligence.* Cambridge, Eng.: Cambridge University Press.

Swanson, S., & Howell, C. (1996). Test anxiety in adolescents with learning disabilities and behavior disorders. *Exceptional Children, 62*, 389–397.

Terenzini, P. T., Pascarella, E. T., & Blimling, G. S. (1999). Students' out-of-class experiences and their influences on learning and cognitive development: A literature review. *Journal of College Student Development, 40*(5), 610–623.

Tobias, S. (1985). Test anxiety: Interference, defective skills, and cognitive capacity. *Educational Psychologist, 20*, 135–142.

Tobias, S. (1986). Anxiety and cognitive processing of instruction. In R. Schwarzer (Ed.), *Self-related cognitions in anxiety and motivation* (pp. 135–142). Hillsdale, NJ: Lawrence Erlbaum Associates.

Upcraft, M. L., & Gardner, J. N. (1989). A comprehensive approach to enhancing freshman success. In M. L. Upcraft & J. N. Gardner & Associates (Eds.), *The freshman year experience: Helping students survive and succeed in college.* San Francisco: Jossey-Bass.

Van Overwalle, F., & Metsenaere, M. (1990). The effect of attribution-based intervention and study strategy training on academic achievement in college freshmen. *British Journal of Educational Psychology, 60*, 299–311.

Webb, N. M. (1982). Student interaction and learning in small groups. *Review of Educational Research, 52*(3), 421–445.

Weiner, B. (1986). *An attributional theory of motivation and emotion.* New York: Springer-Verlag.

Weiner, B. (1988). Attribution theory and attribution theory: Some theoretical observations and suggestions. *British Journal of Clinical Psychology, 27*, 93–104.

Weiner, B. (1989). *Human motivation.* Hillsdale, NJ: Erlbaum.

Ziv, A. (1988). Teaching and learning with humor: Experiment and replication. *Journal of Experimental Education, 57*, 5–15.

Chapter 5

Albaili, M. A. (1998). Goal orientations, cognitive strategies and academic achievement among United Arab emirates college students. *Educational Psychology, 18*(2), 195–203.

Allgood, P. W., Alvarez, M. C., & Fairbanks, M. M. (2000). Factors that influence study. In R. F. Flippo & D. C. Caverly (Eds.), *Handbook of college reading and study strategy research.* Mahwah, NJ: Lawrence Erlbaum Associates.

Ames, C., & Archer, J. (1988). Achievement goals in the classroom: Students' learning strategies and motivation processes. *Journal of Educational Psychology, 80*(3), 260–267.

Bandura, A. (1977). Self-efficacy: Toward a unifying theory of behavioural change. *Psychological Review, 84*, 191–215.

Bandura, A. (1986). *Social foundations of thought and action.* Englewood Cliffs, NJ: Prentice-Hall.

Bergin, D. (1995). Effects of a mastery versus competitive motivation situation on learning. *The Journal of Experimental Education, 63*(4), 303–314.

Birnie-Lefcovitch, S. (2000). Student perceptions of the transition from high school to university: Implications for preventative programming. *Journal of the First-Year Experience, 12*(2), 61–68.

Braxton, J. M., Brier, E. M., & Hossler, D. (1988). The influence of student problems on student withdrawal decisions: An autopsy on "Autopsy" studies. *Research in Higher Education, 28*(3), 241–253.

Chickering, A. W., & Reisser, L. (1993). *Education and identity* (2nd ed.). San Francisco: Jossey-Bass.

Cochran, L. R. (1978). Issues in the development of academic support courses. In B. M. Schoenberg (Ed.), *A handbook and guide for the college and university counseling center.* Westport, CT: Greenwood.

Crabb, L., & Allender, D. (1984). *Encouragement: The key to caring.* San Francisco: Zondervan Publishing House.

Craik, F. I. M., & Lockhart, R. S. (1972). Levels of processing: A framework for memory research. *Journal of Verbal Learning and Verbal Behavior, 11*, 671–676.

Crozier, S., Dobbs, J., Douglas, K., & Hung, J. (1999). *Career counselling position paper.* McMaster University, Hamilton, ON: Canadian University and College Counselling Association.

Doyle, M., & Garland, J. (2001). A course to teach cognitive and affective learning strategies to university students. *Guidance & Counselling, 16*(3), 86–92.

Dweck, C. S., & Leggett, E. L. (1988). A social-cognitive approach to motivation and achievement. *Journal of Personality and Social Psychology, 54*, 5–12.

Entwistle, N. (1988). Motivational factors in students' approaches to learning. In R. R. Schmeck (Ed.), *Learning strategies and learning styles.* New York: Plenum.

Frewin, C. (1977). *The relationship of educational goal setting behavior to the conceptual level model.* Paper presented at the Adult Education Research Conference, Minneapolis, MN.

Garland, J. C., & Doyle, M. (2000). *UCC 2020: Applied cognitive and affective learning strategies.* Course manual and workbook. St. John's, NF: Memorial University of Newfoundland.

Greene, B. A., & Miller, R. B. (1996). Influences on achievement: Goals, perceived ability, and cognitive engagement. *Contemporary Educational Psychology, 21*, 181–192.

Harackiewicz, J. M., Barron, K. E., & Elliot, A. J. (1998). Rethinking achievement goals: When are they adaptive for college students and why? *Educational Psychologist, 33*(1), 1–21.

Kaufman, M. A., & Creamer, C. G. (1991). Influences of student goals for college on freshman-year quality of effort and growth. *Journal of College Student Development, 32*, 197–206.

Lan, W. Y. (1996). The effects of self-monitoring on students' course performance, use of learning strategies, attitude, self-judgement ability, and knowledge representation. *The Journal of Experimental Education, 64*(2), 101–115.

Locke, E. A., Frederick, E., Buckner, E., & Bobko, P. (1984). Effect of previously assigned goals on self-set goals and performance. *Journal of Applied Psychology, 69*(4), 694–699.

Locke, E. A., Shaw, G. P., Saari, L. M., & Latham, G. P. (1981). Goal setting and task performance: 1969–1980. *Psychological Bulletin, 90*, 125–152.

Marton, F., & Saljo, R. (1997). Approaches to learning. In F. Marton & D. Hounsell & N. Entwistle (Eds.), *The experience of learning: Implications for teaching and studying in higher education* (Vol. 2). Edinburgh, Great Britain: Scottish Academic Press.

Maslow, A. H. (1970). *Motivation and personality* (2nd ed.). New York: Harper and Row.

Paul, K. (1996). *Study smarter, not harder.* Bellington, WA: Self-Counsel Press.

Pike, G. R. (1991). The effects of background, coursework, and involvement on students' grades and satisfaction. *Research in Higher Education, 32*(1), 15–31.

Schmeck, R. R., Ribich, F. D., & Ramanaiah, N. (1977). Development of a self-report inventory for assessing individual differences in learning. *Applied Psychological Measurement, 1*(3), 412–431.

Schraw, G., Horn, C., Thorndike-Christ, T., & Bruning, R. (1995). Academic goal orientation and students' classroom achievement. *Contemporary Educational Psychology, 20*, 359–368.

Shen, J. (1997). Structure of the theoretical concept of educational goals: A test of factorial validity. *The Journal of Experimental Education, 65*(4), 342–352.

Stark, J. W., Shaw, K. M., & Lowther, M. A. (1989). *Student goals for college and courses: A missing link in assessing and improving academic achievement.* ASHE-ERIC Higher Education Report 6. Washington, DC: George Washington University.

Tinto, V. (1993). *Leaving college: Rethinking the causes and cures of student attrition* (2nd ed.). Chicago: University of Chicago Press.

Tinto, V. (1997). Classrooms as communities: Exploring the educational character of student persistence. *Journal of Higher Education, 68*(6), 600–623.

Tuckman, B. W. (1996). The relative effectiveness of incentive motivation and prescribed learning strategy in improving college students' course performance. *The Journal of Experimental Education, 64*(3), 197–210.

Vermetten, Y. J., Lodewijks, H. G., & Vermunt, J. D. (2001). The role of personality traits and goal orientations in strategy use. *Contemporary Educational Psychology, 26*, 149–170.

Chapter 6

Baumeister, R. F. (1997). Esteem threat, self-regulatory breakdown and emotional distress as factors in self-defeating behavior. *Review of General Psychology, 1*(2), 145–174.

Blaxter, L., Dodd, K., & Tight, M. (1996). Mature students markets: An institutional case study. *Higher Education, 31*(2), 187–203.

Blunt, A. K., & Pychyl, T. A. (2000). Task aversiveness and procrastination: a multidimensional approach to task aversiveness across stages of personal projects. *Personality and Individual Differences, 28*, 153–167.

Britton, B. K., & Tesser, A. (1991). Effects of time management practices on college grades. *Journal of Educational Psychology, 83*(3), 405–410.

Chickering, A. W., & Reisser, L. (1993). *Education and Identity* (2nd ed.). San Francisco: Jossey-Bass.

Cope, R. G., & Hannah, W. (1975). *Revolving College Doors: The causes and consequences of dropping out, stopping out and transferring.* New York: Interscience.

Covington, M. V. (1993). A motivational analysis of academic life in college. In J. R. Ferrari & J. L. Johnson & W. G. McCown (Eds.), *Procrastination and task avoidance: Theory, research and treatment* (pp. 80–83). New York: Plenum Press.

Day, V., Mensink, D., & O'Sullivan, M. (2000). Patterns of academic procrastination. *Journal of College Reading and Learning, 30*(2), 121–134.

DeMeuse, K. P. (1985). The life events stress-performance linkage: An exploratory study. *Journal of Human Stress*, 35–40.

Eison, J., & Holtschlag, D. (1989). Time management difficulties: A self-assessment and problem-solving activity. *Journal of the Freshman Year Experience, 1*(1) 99–110.

Effert, R., & Ferrari, J. R. (1989). Decisional procrastination: Examining personality correlates. *Journal of Social Behavior and Personality, 4*, 151–156.

Ellis, A., & Knaus, J. K. (1977). *Overcoming procrastination.* New York: Institute for Rational Living.

Feather, N. T., & Bond, M. D. (1983). Time structure and purposeful activity among employed and unemployed university graduates. *Journal of Occupational Psychology, 56*, 241–254.

Flett, G. L., Blankenstein, K. R., Hewitt, P. L., & Koledin, S. (1992). Components of perfectionism and procrastination in college students. *Social Behavior and Personality, 20*, 85–94.

Gallagher, R. P. (1992). Student needs surveys have multiple benefits. *Journal of College Student Development, 33*, 281–282.

Hill, M. B., Hill, D. A.,Chabot, A. E., & Barrall, J. F., (1978). A survey of college faculty and student procrastination. *College Student Personnel Journal, 12*, 256–262.

Iwasaki, Y. (2001). Contributions of leisure to coping with daily hassles in university students' lives. *Canadian Journal of Behavioural Science, 33*(2), 128–141.

Kuh, G. D. (1993). In their own words: What students learn outside the classroom. *American Educational Research Journal, 30*, 277–304.

Lay, C. (1987). A modal profile analysis of procrastinators: A search for types. *Personality and Individual Differences, 8*, 705–714.

Lay, C. (1997). Explaining lower-order traits through higher-order factors: The case of trait procrastination, conscientiousness, and the specificity dilemma. *European Journal of Personality, 11*, 267–278.

Lazarus, R. S., & Folkman, S. (1984). *Stress, Appraisal and Coping.* New York: Springer Publishing.

Macan, T. H., Shahani, C., Dipboye, R. L., & Phillips, A. P. (1990). College students' time management: Correlations with academic performance and stress. *Journal of Educational Psychology, 82*(4), 760–768.

McCown, W., Johnson, J., & Pretzel, T. (1989). Personality and chronic procrastination by university students during an academic evaluation period. *Personality and Individual Differences, 12*, 413–415.

Melichar, B. E. (1994). Instructors' attitudes toward nontraditional students positive: Study shows. *Adult Learning, 6*(1), 27–29.

Metzner, B. S., & Bean, J. P. (1987). The estimation of a conceptual model of nontraditional undergraduate student attrition. *Research in Higher Education, 27*, 15–38.

Milgram, N., Mey-Tal, G., & Levison, Y. (1998). Procrastination, generalized or specific, in college students and their parents. *Personality and Individual Differences, 25*, 297–316.

Milgram, N., Sroloff, B., & Rosenbaum, M. (1988). The procrastination of everyday life. *Journal of Research in Personality, 22*, 197–212.

Myers, I. B. (1980). *Gifts differing.* Palo Alto, CA: Consulting Psychologists Press.

Nonis, S. A., Hudson, G. I., Logan, L. B., & Ford, C. W. (1998). Influence of perceived control over time on college students' stress and stress-related outcomes. *Research in Higher Education, 39*(5), 587–605.

Provost, J., & Anchors, S. (Eds.). (1987). *Applications of the Myers-Briggs Type indicator in higher education.* Palo Alto, CA: Consulting Psychologists Press.

Pychyl, T. A., Lee, J. M., Thibodeau, R., & Blunt, A. (1999). Five days of emotion: An experience sampling of undergraduate student procrastination, *Journal of Social Behavior and Personality, 14,* 1–16.

Rawson, H. E., Bloomer, K., & Kendall, A. (1994). Stress, anxiety, depression and physical illness in college students. *The Journal of Genetic Psychology, 155*(3), 321–330.

Rocha-Singh, I. A. (1994). Perceived stress among graduate students: Development and validation of the graduate stress inventory. *Educational and Psychological Measurement, 54*(3), 714–727.

Rothblum, E. D., Solomon, L. J., & Murakami, J. (1986). Affective, cognitive, and behavioral differences between high and low procrastinators. *Journal of Counseling Psychology, 33,* 387–394.

Ryan, N. E., Solberg, V. S., & Brown, S. D. (1996). Family dysfunction, parental attachment, and career search self-efficacy among community college students. *Journal of Counseling Psychology, 43,* 84–89.

Schouwenburg, H. C., & Lay, C. H. (1995). Trait procrastination and the big five factors of personality. *Personality and Individual Differences, 18,* 481–490.

Senecal, C., Koestner, R., & Vallerand, R. J. (1995). Self-regulation and academic procrastination. T*he Journal of Social Psychology, 135*(5), 607–619.

Silver, M., & Sabini, J. (1981). Procrastinating. *Journal for the Theory of Social Behaviour, 11,* 207–221.

Solberg, V. S., Gusavac, N., Hamann, T., Felch, J., Johnson, J., Lamborn, S., & Torres, J. (1998). The adaptive success identity plan (ASIP): A career intervention for college students. *Career Development Quarterly, 47*(1), 48–95.

Solberg, V. S., Hale, B., Villarreal, P., & Kavanagh, J. (1993). Development of the College Stress Inventory for use with Hispanic populations: A confirmatory analytic approach. *Hispanic Journal of Behavioral Sciences, 15,* 490–497.

Solomon, L. J., & Rothblum, E. D. (1984). Academic procrastination: Frequency and cognitive-behavioral correlates. *Journal of Counseling Psychology, 31,* 503–509.

Trueman, M., & Hartley, J. (1996). A comparison between the time-management skills and academic performance of mature and traditional entry students. *Higher Education, 32*(2), 199–215.

Walker, L. J. S. (1988). Procrastination: Fantasies and fears. *Manitoba Journal of Counseling, 25*(11), 23–25.

Walker, L. J. S., & Stewart, D. (2000). Overcoming the powerlessness of procrastination. *Guidance & Counselling, 16*(1), 39–42.

Welsley, J. C. (1994). Effects of ability, high school achievement and procrastinory behavior on college performance. *Educational and Psychological Measurement, 54,* 404–408.

Chapter 7

Bandura, A. (1986). *Social Foundations of Thought and Action.* Englewood Cliffs, NJ: Prentice-Hall.

Barr, R. B., & Tagg, J. (1995). From teaching to learning—A paradigm for undergraduate education. *Change, 27,* 12–25.

Brown, A. L., Bransford, J. D., Ferrara, R. A., & Campione, J. C. (1983). Learning, remembering, and understanding. In P. H. Mussen (Ed.), *Handbook of child psychology* (pp. 77–166). New York: John Wiley & Sons.

Corno, L., & Mandinach, E. (1983). The role of cognitive engagement in classroom learning and motivation. *Educational Psychologist, 18,* 88–100.

Craik, F. I. M., & Lockhart, R. S. (1972). Levels of processing: A framework for memory research. *Journal of Verbal Learning and Verbal Behavior, 11,* 671–676.

Cross, K. P. (1990). Teaching to improve learning. *Journal on Excellence in College Teaching, 1,* 9–22.

Dansereau, D. F. (1985). Learning strategy research. In J. Segal & S. Chipman & R. Glaser (Eds.), *Thinking and learning skills: Relating instruction to research.* Hillsdale, NJ: Lawrence Erlbaum Associates, Inc.

Erwin, T. D. (1991). *Assessing student learning and development.* San Francisco: Jossey-Bass.

Feldman, K. A. (1997). Identifying exemplary teachers and teaching: Evidence from student ratings. In R. P. Perry & J. C. Smart (Eds.), *Effective teaching in higher education: Research and practice* (pp. 368–395). New York: Agathon Press.

Gardner, J., & Jewler, A. (1997). *Your college experience: Strategies for success.* Belmont: Wadsworth Publishing Company.

Hult, R. E., Cohn, S., & Potter, D. (1984). An analysis of student note-taking effectiveness and learning outcome in the college lecture setting. *Journal of Instructional Psychology, 11*(4), 175–181.

Kiewra, K. A. (1983). The relationship between notetaking over an extended period and actual course-related achievement. *College Student Journal, 17,* 381–385.

Kiewra, K. A. (1989). A review of note-taking: The encoding storage paradigm and beyond. *Educational Psychology Review, 1*(2), 147–172.

Kiewra, K. A., Mayer, R. E., Christensen, M., Kim, S., & Riskh, N. (1991). Effects of repetition on recall and note-taking: Strategies for learning from lectures. *Journal of Educational Psychology, 83*(1), 120–123.

McKeachie, W. J., Pintrich, P. R., Lin, Y. G., & Smith, D. A. F. (1986). *Teaching and learning in the classroom: A review of the literature.* Ann Arbor, MI: University of Michigan Press.

McMillan, J. H. (1988). Assessing students' learning. *New Directions for Teaching and Learning, Vol. 34.* San Francisco: Jossey-Bass.

Merriam-Webster, A. (1986). *Webster's Ninth New Collegiate Dictionary.* Markham, ON. Thomas Allen and Son.

Myers, D. G. (2001). *Psychology* (6th ed.). Holland, MI: Worth.

Naumann, W. C. (1999). Predicting first-semester grade point average using self-regulated learning variables. *Dissertation Abstracts International: Section B: The Sciences and Engineering, 59,* 4503.

Pascarella, E. T., & Terenzini, P. (1991). *How college affects students: Findings and insights from twenty years of research.* San Francisco: Jossey-Bass.

Pauk, W. (1968). *Reading for success in college.* Oshkosh, WI: Academia Press.

Pressley, M. (1986). The relevance of the good strategy user model to the teaching of mathematics. *Educational Psychologist, 21,* 139–161.

Robinson, F. P. (1946). *Effective study.* New York: Harper & Row.

Thorndike, R. L., & Hagen, E. P. (1995). *Measurement and evaluation in psychology and education* (4th ed.). Toronto, ON: John Wiley & Sons.

Waldrop, M. M. (1987). The workings of memory. *Science, 237,* 1564–1567.

Walvoord, B. E., & Anderson, V. J. (1998). *Effective grading.* San Francisco: Jossey-Bass.

Weinstein, C., & Meyer, D. (1991). Cognitive learning strategies and college teaching. In R. Menges & M. Svinicki (Eds.), *College teaching: From theory to practice.* New Directions for Teaching and Learning, Vol. 45 (pp. 15–26). San Francisco: Jossey-Bass.

Weinstein, C. E., & Mayer, R. E. (1986). The teaching of learning strategies. In M. Wittrock (Ed.), *Handbook of research on teaching* (pp. 315–327). New York: McMillan.

Chapter 8

Association of College and Research Libraries. (2001). Objectives for information literacy instruction. *College and Research Libraries News, 61,* 416–428.

Boice, R. (1990). *Professors as writers: A self-help guide to productive writing.* Stillwater, OK: New Forums Press.

Buckley, J. (1995). *Fit to print: The Canadian student's guide to essay writing.* Toronto, ON: Harcourt Brace.

Click, B. A. L. (1996). Educating students to write effectively. *New Directions for Higher Education,* No. 96 (pp. 31–44). San Francisco: Jossey-Bass.

Conference Board of Canada. (2000). Employability Skills 2000+. Retrieved March 20, 2001, *from www.conference board.ca/ nbec*

Duffin, K. (1998). Overview of the academic essay. Retrieved December 20, 2001, from *www.fas.harvard.edu/%7Ewricntr/ documents/Overvu.html*

Elder, L., & Paul, R. (no date). Universal intellectual standards. Retrieved December 21, 2001, from *www.criticalthinking.org/ university/unistan.html*

Emig, J. (1981). Non-magical thinking: Presenting writing developmentally in schools. In C. H. Frederiksen & J. F. Dominic (Eds.), *Writing: The nature, development and teaching of written communication* (pp. 21–30). Hillsdale, NJ: Erlbaum.

Flower, L., & Hayes, J. H. (1981). Plans that guide the composing process. In C. H. Frederiksen & J. F. Dominic (Eds.), *Writing: The nature, development and teaching of written communication* (pp. 39–58). Hillsdale, NJ: Erlbaum.

Frederiksen, C. H., & Dominic, J. F. (1981) Introduction: Perspectives on the activity of writing. In C. H. Frederiksen & J. F. Dominic (Eds.), *Writing: The nature, development and teaching of written communication* (pp. 1–20). Hillsdale, NJ: Erlbaum.

Gardner, J. N., Jewler, A. J., & Robb, A. (1995). *Your first-year experience: Success strategies for Canadian students*. Toronto, ON: Nelson.

Gibson, J. B., & Killingsworth, M. J. (1991). *Academic writing: An introductory guide*. Dubuque, IA: Kendall-Hunt.

Green, G. M., & Morgan, J. L. (1981). Writing ability as a function of the appreciation of differences between oral and written communication. In C. H. Frederiksen & J. F. Dominic (Eds.), *Writing: The nature, development and teaching of written communication* (pp. 177–188). Hillsdale, NJ: Erlbaum.

Harris, R. A. (2001). *The plagiarism handbook: Strategies for preventing, detecting and dealing with plagiarism*. Los Angeles: Pyrczak Publishing.

Hilgers, T. L., Hussey, E. L., & Stitt-Bergh, M. (1999). "As you are writing, you have these epiphanies": What college students say about writing and learning in their majors. *Written Communication, 16*, 317– 354.

Hunter-Carsch, C. M. (1990). Improving students' essay writing. *Reading, 24*, 76–91.

Kellogg, R. T. (1990). Effectiveness of pre-writing strategies as a function of task demands. *American Journal of Psychology, 103*, 327–342.

Kennedy M. L., Kennedy, W. J., & Smith, H. M. (2000). *Writing in the disciplines: A reader for writers*. Upper Saddle River, NJ: Prentice Hall.

Kennedy, M. L., & Smith, H. M. (1994). *Reading and writing in the academic community*. Englewood Cliffs, NJ: Prentice-Hall.

Lloyd-Jones, R. (1981). Rhetorical choices in writing. In C. H. Frederiksen & J. F. Dominic (Eds.), Writing: *The nature, development and teaching of written communication* (pp. 169–176). Hillsdale, NJ: Erlbaum.

Nold, E. W. (1981). Revising. In C. H. Frederiksen & J. F. Dominic (Eds.), *Writing: The nature, development and teaching of written communication* (pp. 67–80). Hillsdale, NJ: Erlbaum.

Perkins, D., & Salomon, G. (1989). Are cognitive skills context-bound? *Educational Researcher, 18* (1), 16–25.

Petraglia, J. (1995). Writing as an unnatural act. In J. Petraglia (Ed.), *Reconceiving writing, rethinking writing instruction* (pp. 79–100). Hillsdale, NJ: Erlbaum.

Procter, M. (2001). Taking notes from research reading. Retrieved December 20, 2001, from *http://www.utoronto.ca/writing/notes.html*

Reynolds, R. C. (1982–83). Understanding the purpose of the essay. *The English Quarterly, 15* (4), 28–41.

Risemberg, R, (1996). Reading to write: Self-regulated learning strategies when writing essays from sources. *Reading Research and Instruction, 35*, 365–383.

Simon, L. (1991), Decoding writing assignments. *History Teacher, 24*,149–155.

Slattery, P. F. (1994). Teaching for various literacies. *Journal of Teaching Writing, 13* (1–2), 15–31,

Spatt, B. (1983). *Writing from Sources*. New York: St. Martin's Press.

Strode, C. B. (1991). Writing as a tool for learning. *Issues and inquiry in college learning and teaching, 15* (2), 46–59.

Topping, G. (1995). Why can't a woman be more like a man? *Oxford Today, 8* (1), 1–4.

Torrance, M., Thomas, G. V., & Robinson, E. J. (1994) The writing strategies of graduate research students in the social sciences. *Higher Education, 27*, 379–392.

Ward, D. (2001). The future of information literacy: Transforming the world. *College and Research Libraries News, 61*, 922– 925.

Chapter 9

Augsburger, D. (1982). *Caring Enough to Hear and Be Heard*. Scottsdale: Herald.

Ayres, J. (1986). Perceptions of speaking ability: An explanation of stage fright. *Communication Education, 35*, 275–287.

Ayres, J. (1992). An examination of the impact of anticipated communication and communication apprehension on negative thinking, task relevant thinking, and recall. *Communication Research Reports, 9*, 3–11.

Beatty, M. J. (1988). Situational and predispositional correlates of public speaking anxiety. *Communication Education, 37*, 28–39.

Beatty, M. J., Balfantz, G. L., & Kuwabara, A. Y. (1989). Trait-like qualities of selected variables assumed to be transient causes of performance state anxiety. *Communication Education, 39*, 142–147.

Book, C. L. (1985). Providing feedback: The research on effective oral and written feedback strategies. *Central States Speech Journal, 36*, 14–23.

Booth-Butterfield, M., & Booth-Butterfield, S. (1986). Effects of evaluation, task-structure, trait-CA, and reticence on stated-CA and behavioral disruption in dyadic settings. *Communication Monographs, 53*, 144–159.

Bowers, J. W. (1986). Classroom communication apprehension: A survey. *Communication Education, 35*, 372–378.

Brizee, R. (1993). *The gift of listening.* St. Louis, MS: Chalice Press.

Connell, S. H., & Borden, G. A. (1987). Incorporating treatment for communication apprehension into oral communication courses. *Communication Education, 36*, 56–61.

Davidson, C. I., & Ambrose, S. A. (1992). Presenting talks on research results. In C. I. Davidson & S. A. Ambrose (Eds.), *The new professor's handbook: A guide to teaching and research in engineering and science* (pp. 159–169). Bolton, MA: Anker Publishing Company.

Drakeford, J. W. (1967). *The Awesome Power of the Listening Ear.* Waco, TE: Word Books.

Dunn, J. (1983). How to become a good listener. *Discipleship Journal, 17*, 19–20.

Edwards, R. (1990). Sensitivity to feedback and the development of the self. *Communication Quarterly, 38*, 101–111.

Elgin, S. H. (1996). *The gentle art of communicating with kids: Toddlers to teens.* New York: John Wiley & Sons, Inc.

Feingold, A. (1992). Good-looking people are not what we think. *Psychological Bulletin, 111*, 304–341.

Florence, I. (1983). *Perceptive listening.* New York: Holt, Rinehart, & Wilson.

Glass, L. (1992). *He says, she says: Closing the communication gap between the sexes.* New York: Putnam.

Hamilton, C., & Parker, C. (1993). *Communicating for results: A guide for business and professionals* (4th ed.). Belmont, CA: Wadsworth.

Hoff, R. (1992). *I can see you naked.* Kansas City, KA: Andrews and McMeel.

Huggett, J. (1988). *Listening to others.* Illinois: Intervarsity Press.

Kolb, J. A. (1994, December). Adapting corporate presentation skills training practices for use in the university classroom. *The Bulletin*, 1–8.

Locke, L. F., Spirduso, W. W., & Silverman, S. J. (1998). The oral presentation. In L. F. Locke & W. W. Spirduso & S. J. Silverman (Eds.), *Proposals that work: A guide for planning dissertations and grant proposals* (3rd ed., pp. 130–144). Newbury Park: Sage.

Maletzke, G. (1963). *Psychologie der Massenkommunikation.* Hamburg, Germany: Verlag Hans Bredow-Institut.

Nichols, M. P. (1995). *The lost art of listening.:* New York: Guilford Press.

Renfrow, D., & Impara, J. C. (1989). Making academic presentations–effectively! *Educational Researcher, 18*, 20-21.

Riediger, M. (1992). The art of listening to hurting people. *Directions, 21*, 64-72.

Schönwetter, D. J. (1993). Attributes of effective lecturing in the college classroom. *Canadian Journal of Higher Education, 23*, 1–18.

Tannen, D. (1990). *You just don't understand: Women and men in conversation.* New York: William Morrow.

Taylor, K. L., & Toews, S., M. (1999). Effective presentations: How can we learn from the experts? *Medical Teacher, 21*(4), 409–414.

Tournier, P. (1984). *A listening ear.* Minneapolis, MN: Augsburg Publishing House.

Wolfgang, A. (1984). *Nonverbal behavior.* Toronto, ON: Hogrefe Inc.

Chapter 10

Arthur, N. (2001). Using critical incidents to investigate cross-cultural transitions. *International Journal of Intercultural Relations, 25*(1), 41–53.

Astin, A. W. (1997). *What matters in college: Four critical years revisited.* San Francisco: Jossey-Bass.

Brookfield, S. D., & Preskill, S. (1999). *Discussion as a way of teaching: Tools and techniques for democrative classrooms.* San Francisco: Jossey-Bass.

Chapman, J. G., & Morley, R. (1999). Collegiate service-learning: Motives underlying volunteerism and satisfaction with volunteer service. *Journal of Prevention and Intervention in the Community, 18*(1–2), 19–33.

Chickering, A. W. (1974). *Commuting versus resident students: Overcoming educational inequalities of living off-campus.* San Francisco: Jossey-Bass.

Chickering, A. W., & Reisser, L. (1993). *Education and Identity* (2nd ed.). San Francisco: Jossey-Bass.

Collett, J., & Serrano, B. (1992). Stirring it up: The inclusive classroom. In L. Border & N. V. N. Chism (Eds.), *Teaching for diversity: New Directions for Teaching and Learning, Vol. 49* (pp. 35–48). San Francisco: Jossey-Bass.

Collins, L. H. (1998). Competition and contact: The dynamics behind resistance to affirmative action in academe. In L. H. Collins (Ed.), *Career strategies for women in academe: Arming Athena* (pp. 45–79). Thousand Oaks, CA: Sage Publications Inc.

Crawford, M., & MacLeod, M. (1990). Gender in the college classroom: An assessment of the "chilly climate" for women. *Sex Roles, 23*(3–4), 101–122.

Grosset, J. (1997). *Beating the odds: Reasons for at-risk student success at Community College of Philadelphia* (Institutional Research Report 93). Philadelphia: Community College of Philadelphia.

Gurung, R. A. R., Sarason, B. R., Keeker, K. D., & Sarason, I. G. (1992). *Family environments, specific relationships, and general perceptions of adjustment.* Paper presented at the American Psychological Association, Washington, D.C.

Hertel, J. B. (1997). First-generation and second-generation college students: Similarities, differences, and differential factors in their adjustment to college. *Dissertation Abstracts International Section A: Humanities and Social Sciences, 58*(6–A), 2070.

Inman, P., & Pascarella, E. (1998). The impact of college residence on the development of critical thinking skills in college freshmen. *Journal of College Student Development, 39*(6), 557–568.

Jacoby, B. (1999). Partnerships for service learning. *New Directions for Student Services, Vol. 87.* (pp. 19–27). San Francisco: Jossey Bass.

Kanar, C. C. (2001). *The Confident Student.* Boston: Houghton Mifflin Company.

Karenga, M. (1995). Afrocentricity and multicultural education: Concept, challenge, and contribution. In B. P. Bowser & T. Jones & G. A. Young (Eds.), *Toward the multiculural university* (pp. 41–64). Westport, CT: Praeger.

Kieffer, C. C. (2001). Phases of group development: A view from self psychology. *Group, 25*(1–2), 91–105.

Kuh, G. D. (1993). In their own words: What students learn outside the classroom. *American Educational Research Journal, 30,* 277–304.

Lindeman, E. C. (1987). Democratic discussion and the people's voice. In S. D. Brookfield (Ed.), *Learning democracy: Eduard Lindeman on adult education and social change.* London, England: Croom Helm.

MacKinnon, M. M. (1999). CORE elements of student motivation in problem-based learning (78th ed., Vol. 78, pp. 49–58). San Francisco: Jossey-Bass.

Maslow, A. H. (1970). *Motivation and personality* (2nd ed.). New York: Harper & Row.

Merriam-Webster, A. (1986). *Webster's Ninth New Collegiate Dictionary.* Markham, ON: Thomas Allen and Son.

Pascarella, E. T., Whitt, E. J., Edison, M. I., & Nora, A. (1997). Women's perceptions of a "chilly climate" and their cognitive outcomes during the first year of college. *Journal of College Student Development, 38*(2), 109–124.

Pedersen, P. (1995). *The five stages of culture shock: Critical incidents around the world.* Westport, CT: Greenwood Press/Greenwood Publishing Group.

Sadker, M., & Sadker, D. (1992). Ensuring equitable participation in college classes. In N. V. N. Chism & L. Border (Eds.), *Teaching for diversity, Vol. 49* (pp. 49–56). San Francisco: Jossey-Bass.

Schoenhals, M., Tienda, M., & Schneider, B. (1998). The educational and personal consequences of adolescent employment. *Social Forces, 77*(2), 723–762.

Tinto, V. (1997). Classrooms as communities: Exploring the educational character of student persistence. *Journal of Higher Education, 68*(6), 600–623.

Wheelan, S., & Tilin, F. (1999). The relationship between faculty group effectiveness and school productivity. *Small Group Research, 30*(1), 59–81.

Whitt, E. J., Edison, M. I., Pascarella, E. T., Nora, A., & Terenzini, P. T. (1999). Women's perceptions of a "chilly climate" and cognitive outcomes in college: Additional evidence. *Journal of College Student Development, 40*(2), 163–177.

Chapter 11

Albaili, M. A. (1997). Differences among low, average and high-achieving colleges students on learning and study strategies. *Educational Psychology, 17*, 171–177.

Baxter Magdola, M. B. (1992). *Knowing and reasoning in college: Gender-related patterns in students' intellectual development.* San Francisco: Jossey-Bass.

Belenky, M., Clinchy, B., Goldberger, N., & Tarule, J. (1986). *Women ways of knowing: The development of self, voice and mind.* New York: Basic Books.

Bloom, B. S. (1956). *Taxonomy of educational objectives.* New York: David McKay.

Browne, D. (1986). Learning styles & native Americans. *ERIC Document Reproduction Service #ED297906.*

Dunn, R., Beaudry, J. S., & Klavas, A. (1989). Survey of research on learning styles. *Educational Leadership, 46*(6), 50–57.

Dunn, R., & Dunn, K. (1988). Presenting forewards backwards. *Teaching K-8, 19*, 71–73.

Dunn, R., Dunn, K., & Price, G. E. (1989). *Learning styles inventory.* Lawrence, KS: Price Systems.

Dunn, R., Griggs, S. A., Olson, J., & Beasly, M. (1995). A meta-analytic validation of the Dunn and Dunn model of learning style preferences. *Journal of Educational Research, 88*(6), 353–362.

Dunn, R., Sklar, R. I., Beaudry, J. S., & Bruno, J. (1990). Effects of matching and mismatching minority developmental colleges students' hemispheric preferences on mathematics scores. *Journal of Educational Research, 83*(5), 283–288.

Dunn, R., & Stevenson, J. M. (1997). Teaching diverse college students to study with a learning-styles prescription. *College Student Journal, 31*(3), 333–339.

Entwistle, N. J. (1988). *Styles of Learning and Teaching.* London: David Fulton.

Entwistle, N. J., & Tait, H. (1994). *The Revised Approaches to Studying Inventory.* Edinburgh: Scotland: University of Edinburgh, Centre for Research into Learning and Instruction.

Goldberger, N. R. (1996). Cultural imperatives and diversity in ways of knowing. In N. R. Goldberger & J. M. Tarule & B. M. Clinchy & M. F. Belenky (Eds.), *Knowledge, difference and power.* New York: Basic Books.

Jung, C. (1923). *Psychological types.* London: Routledge & Kegan Paul.

Knight, K. H., Elfenbein, M. H., & Martin, M. B. (1997). Relationship of connected and separate knowing to the learning styles of Kolb, formal reasoning and intelligence. *Sex Roles, 37*, 401–414.

Kolb, D. A. (1976). *Learning Style Inventory: Technical manual.* Boston: McBer.

Kolb, D. A. (1984). *Experimental learning: Experience as the sources of learning and development.* Englewood Cliffs, NJ, USA: Prentice-Hall.

Kolb, D. A. (1985). *Learning Style Inventory.* Boston: McBer.

Lawrence, G. (1982). *People types and tiger stripes: A practical guide to learning styles.* Gainsville, FL: Centre for Applications of Psychological Type.

Lawrence, G. (1984). A synthesis of learning style research involving the MBTI. *Journal of Psychological Type, 8*, 2–15.

Myers, I. B., & Meyers, P.M. (1985a). *Gifts differing.* Palo Alto, CA: Consulting Psychologists Press.

Myers, I. B., & Briggs, C. K. (1985b). *Myers-Briggs type indicator.* Palo Alto, CA: Consulting Psychologists Press.

Nelson, B. (1993). Effects of learning style intervention on college students' retention and achievement. *Journal of College Student Development, 34*(5), 364–369.

Pai, Y., & Adler, S. A. (1997). *Cultural foundations of education* (2nd ed.). Upper Saddle River, NJ: Prentice Hall.

Pask, G. (1988). Learning strategies, teaching strategies and conceptual or learning style. In R. R. Schmeck (Ed.), *Learning styles and learning strategies* (pp. 83–100). New York: Plenum Press.

Perry, W. J., Jr. (1970). *Forms of Intellectual and ethical development in the college years: A scheme.* New York: Holt, Rinehart, & Winston.

Portis, S. C., Simpson, F. M., & Wiseman, R. A. (1993). Convergence or divergences? Perspective as experience and cognitive styles of prospective teachers. *ERIC Document Reproduction Service #354236.*

Riechmann, S. W., & Grasha, A. F. (1974). A rational approach to developing and assessing the construct validity of a student learning styles scale instruments. *Journal of Psychology, 87,* 213–223.

Schmeck, R. R. (1983). Learning styles of college students in individual differences in cognition. In R. Dillon & R. R. Schmeck (Eds.) (Vol. 233–279). New York: Academic Press.

Schmeck, R. R. (1988). *Strategies & styles of learning.* New York: Plenum Press.

Schmeck, R. R., & Geisler-Brenstein, E. (1989). Individual differences that affect the way students approach learning. *Learning and Individual Differences, 1,* 85–124.

Schmeck, R. R., & Geisler-Brenstein, E. (1991). Self-concept & learning: The revised inventory of learning processes. *Educational Psychology, 11,* 343–361.

Severiens, S., & ten Dam, G. (1997). Gender and gender identity differences in learning styles. *Educational Psychology, 17,* 79–93.

Severiens, S., & ten Dam, G. T. N. (1994). Gender differences in learning styles: A narrative review and a quantitative meta-analysis. *Higher Education, 27,* 487–501.

Watkins, D., & Hattie, J. (1981). The learning processes of Australian university students: investigations of contextual and personological factors. *British Journal of Educational Psychology, 51,* 384–393.

Chapter 12

Adams, J. L. (1979). *Conceptual blockbusting: A guide to better ideas* (2nd ed.). New York: Norton.

Bailin, S., Case, R., Coombs, J. R., & Daniels, L. B. (1999). Common misconceptions of critical thinking. *Journal of Curriculum Studies, 31*(3), 269–283.

Blakey, E., & Spence, S. (1990). Developing metacognition. *ERIC Digest, ED327218.*

Bloom, B. S. (1956). *Taxonomy of educational objectives.* New York: David McKay.

Bonnett, M. (1995). Teaching thinking and sanctity of content. *Journal of Philosophy of Education, 29*(3), 296–301.

Clifton, R. A. (1997). The effects of social psychological variables and gender on the grade point averages and educational expectations of university students: A case study. *Canadian Journal of Higher Education, 27,* 67–90.

Clinchy, B. M. (1990). Issus of gender in teaching and learning. *Journal of Excellence in College Teaching, 1,* 52–67.

Copi, I. M., & Cohen, C. (1990). *Introduction to logic* (8th ed.). New York: Macmillan.

Crossley, D. J., & Wilson, P. A. (1979). *How to argue: An introduction to logical thinking.* New York: Random House.

Dewey, J. (1933). *How we think.* Boston: D. E. Heath.

Dewey, J. (1964). What psychology can do for the teacher. In R. D. Archambault (Ed.), *John Dewey on education: Selected writings* (pp. 195–211). Chicago: University of Chicago Press.

Elbow, P. (1973). *Writing without teachers.* London: Oxford University Press.

Ennis, R. H. (1987). A taxonomy of critical thinking dispositions and abilities. In J. B. Baron & R. J. Sternberg (Eds.), *Teaching thinking skills: Theory and practice* (pp. 9–26). New York: Freeman.

Facione, P., Giancarlo, C., Facione, N., & Gainen, J. (1995). The disposition toward critical thinking. *Journal of General Education, 44*(1).

Facione, P. A. (1990). *Critical thinking: A statement of expert consensus for purposes of educational assessment and instruction: Research findings and recommendations (The Delphi Report).* Committee on Pre-College Philosophy of the American Philosophical Association.

Holt, T. (1990). *Thinking historically: Narrative, imaginative, and understanding.* New York: The College Entrance Examination Board.

Johnson, R. H., & Blair, J. A. (1983). *Logical self-defence* (2nd ed.). Toronto, ON: McGraw-Hill Ryerson.

Kurfiss, J. G. (1988). *Critical thinking: Theory, research, practice, and possibilities* (ED304041). Washington, DC: Association for the Study of Higher Education.; ERIC Clearinghouse on Higher Education.

MacKinnon, J. (1993). Becoming a rhetor: Developing writing ability in a mature, writing-intensive organization. In R. Spilka (Ed.), *Writing in the workplace: New research perspectives* (pp. 41–55). Carbodale, IL: Southern Illinois University Press.

McKeachie, W. J., Pintrich, P. R., Lin, Y. G., & Smith, D. A. F. (1986). *Teaching and learning in the classroom: A review of the literature.* Ann Arbor, MI: University of Michigan.

Merriam-Webster, A. (1986). *Webster's Ninth New Collegiate Dictionary.* Markham, ON: Thomas Allen and Son.

Miller, J. P., Cassie, J. R. B., & Drake, S. M. (1990). *Holistic thinking: A teacher's guide to integrated studies.* Toronto, ON: Ontario Institute for Studies in Education.

Naumann, W. C. (1999). Predicting first-semester grade point average using self-regulated learning variables. *Dissertation Abstracts International: Section B: The Sciences and Engineering, 59,* 4503.

Perry, W. J., Jr. (1970). *Forms of Intellectual and ethical development in the college years: A scheme.* New York: Holt, Rinehart, & Winston.

Siegel, H. (1988). *Educating reason: Rationality, critical thinking, and education.* New York: Routledge.

Wales, C. E., Nardi, A. H., & Stager, R. A. (1986). *Professional decision-making.* Morgantown, WV: University of West Virginia, Centre for Guided Design.

Chapter 13

Betz, , N. E., Borgen, F. H., & Harmon, L. W. (1997). *Skills Confidence Inventory.* Palo Alto, CA: Consulting Psychologists Press.

Chickering, A. W., & Reisser, L. (1993). *Education and Identity* (2nd ed.). San Francisco: Jossey Bass.

Hackett, G., & Betz, N. E. (1981). A self-efficacy approach to the career development of women. *Journal of Vocational Behavior, 18,* 326–336.

Holland, J. L. (1966). *The psychology of vocational choice.* Waltheim, MA: Blaisdell.

Holland, J. L. (1985a). *Making vocational choices: A theory of vocational personalities and work environments* (2nd ed.). Englewood Cliffs, NJ: Prentice Hall

Holland, J. L. (1985b). *Manual-Self-directed Search.* Odessa, FL: Psychological Assessment Resources.

Jackson, D. N. (1990). *Jackson Vocational Interest Survey.* Jackson Sigman Assessment Systems.

Keirsey, D., & Bates, M. (1978). *Please Understand Me.* Del Mar, CA: Prometheus Nemesis.

Lent, R. W., Lopez, F. G., & Bieschke, K. J. (1993). Predicting mathematics-related choice and success behaviors: Test of an expanded social cognitive model. *Journal of Vocational Behavior, 42,* 223–236.

Luzzo, D. A., Hasper, P., Albert, K. A., Bibby, M. A., & Martinellli, E. A. (1999). Effects of self-efficacy-enhancing interventions on the math/sciences self-efficacy and career interests, goals, and actions of career undecided college students. *Journal of Counseling Psychology, 46*(2), 233–243.

Maslow, A. H. (1970). *Motivation and Personality* (2nd ed). New York: Harper Row.

Myers, I. B., & McCaulley, M. H. (1985). *Manual: A guide to the development and use of the Myers-Briggs Type Indicator.* Palo Alto, CA: Consulting Psychologists Press.

Pajares, F., & Miller, D. (1995). Mathematics self-efficacy and mathematics performances: The need for specificity of assessment. *Journal of Counseling Psychology, 42,* 190–198.

Russell, N. J., & Karol, D. L. (1994). *The 16 PF Fifth Edition Administration Manual.* Institute for Personality and Ability Testing.

Strong, E. K., Hansen, J., & Campbell, D. P. (1994). *Strong Interest Inventory (SII).* Stanford, CA: Consulting Psychologists Press.

Super, D. E. (1990). A life-span, life-space approach to career development. In D. Brown & I. Brook (Eds.) *Career choice and development: Applying contemporary theories to practice* (pp. 197–261). San Francisco: Jossey-Bass.

Super, D. E. (1992). Toward a comprehensive theory of career development. In D. Montrose & C. Shinkman (Eds.), *Career development theory and practice* (pp. 35–64). Springfield IL: Charles C. Thomas.

Super, D. E. (1993). The two faces of counseling: Or is it three? *The Career Development Quarterly, 42*(2), 132–136.

Tieger, P. D., & Barron-Tieger, B. (1995). *Do what you are: Discover the perfect career for you through the secrets of personality type.* Boston: Little, Brown & Co.

Walter, V. (1986). *Sixteen PF Personal Career Development Profile (PCDP).* Institute for Personality and Ability Testing.

Zeldin, A. I., & Pajares, F. (2000). Against the odds: Self-efficacy beliefs of women in mathematical, scientific and technological careers. *American Educational Research Journal, 37*(1), 215–246.

Index

Mastery goals, 98
  vs. performance goals, 99
Mature student, 232–33
McKay, Krista, L., 94
Meaning orientation, 98
Mentoring, 47, 53
  in Honour's Program, 54
  as sharing with others, 59
Mentors, 50, 239–40
  career, 331
  peer, 53
  spiritual, 55
Metacognition, 11, 166–68, 288, 302–303
Metacognitive strategies, 83
Mission statements, 48
  personal, 315–16
Mnemonics, 157
Modern Language Association (MLA) style, 186
Mood, and self-talk, 86
Motivation, 80
  extrinsic vs. intrinsic, 86
  and goals, 95, 98–99
  progress charts, 86
Multiple-choice tests, 52, 161
Myers-Briggs Type Indicator (MBTI), 265–66, 318

National Occupation Classification (NOC), 324
Needs, Maslow's hierarchy of, 6
Networking, 241
Neurotic procrastination, 122
Nonverbal language, 206–207, 210
Notes, taking, 154, 155

O'Brien Leggott, Trina, 195
Occupations, types of, 324–26, 329
Office hours, 53
Online courses, 56
Online resources, 187
Optimism, 71–73
  and text anxiety, 76
Organization
  and note taking, 155
  professors, 74
  study environment, 84–85
  and time management, 68, 84
Orientation, 100
Out-of-class activities, 58. See also Extracurricular activities
  learning from, 77

Pacing workload, 119–20
Passive-aggressive procrastination, 125
Peak time, 135
Peer educators, 53

Peers
  in the classroom, 54
  engaging with, 77
  informal network, 239
  learning from 58
Perceptual preferences, and learning, 264–65
Perfectionist, 117
Performance goals, 98, 99
Persistence
  and goals, 95, 98–99
and involvement, 58
  and study success, 85
Personal community, 235–36
  influence of, 235
  productive involvement in, 235–36
Personal development resources, 53–55
  cognitive, 53–54
  financial, 55
  physical, 54
  psychological, 54
  social, 55
  spiritual, 54–55
Personality types, 265–67
  extrovert, 265
  feeler, 266
  introvert, 265–66
  intuitive, 266
  judging, 266
  perceiving, 266
  sensor, 266
  thinking, 266
Pessimism, 72
Philosophy statements, 48
Physical activities, goals for, 101
Physical movement, professors, 74
Physical resources for personal development, 54
Plagiarism, 185
Planning work, 119, 130–33, 158
  academic success plan, 130–33
  term plan, 130–31
  to do lists, 133, 134
  weekly timetable, 131–33
Politician, 118
Postponer, 118
Powell, Colin, 94
Practical intelligence, 86
Presentations, 211–22
  audience, 213
  criteria, 212–13
  elements of, 212
  environment, preparing, 215
  evaluating, 219–22
  follow up, 218–22
  giving, 216–18
  handouts, 214, 215

  organizing, 213
  preparing for, 212–15
  rehearsal, 214
  script, 213–14
  self-awareness, 211
  sequence, 217–18
  supplementary material, 214
  time duration, 213
  visuals, 214
Presenter
  appearance, 216
  eye contact, 217
  nervousness, 216–17
  stance/gait, 216
Priorities, establishing for work, 120
Problem solving, 120–21, 133, 135–36
  action, taking, 301
  creative, 299–301
  evaluating, 301
  findings, communicating, 301
  goal, stating, 300
  ideas, generating, 300
  new situation, defining, 300–301
  plan, preparing, 301
  problem, stating, 299–300
Problems, common in time management, 121
Procrastination, 122–25, 136–38
  causes, 123
  coping strategies, 124
  styles, 123–25
  tasks, 123
Professional development resources, 55–56
  administration, 56
  career, 55
  communication, 55
  computer technology, 56
  creative, 84
Professor-student relationship, 236
Professors. See also Teachers; Teaching
  decoding, 74
  effective, characteristics of, 61, 75
  expressiveness, 74
  getting information about, 74–75
  organization of, 74
  respect for, 78
  teaching styles, 267–68
  test clues from, 156
Progress charts, 86
Psychological resources for personal development, 54
Punisher, 118